MIDNIGHT AND NOONDAY

MIDNIGHT
AND NOONDAY

or

THE INCIDENTAL HISTORY OF
SOUTHERN KANSAS AND THE
INDIAN TERRITORY, 1871-1890

By

G. D. FREEMAN

Edited, with an Introduction and Notes, by
RICHARD L. LANE

UNIVERSITY OF OKLAHOMA PRESS : NORMAN

Library of Congress Cataloging in Publication Data

Freeman, G. D. (George Doud), 1842-1913.
  Midnight and noonday, or, The incidental history of southern Kansas and the Indian territory, 1871-1890.

  Originally published: 1890.
  Bibliography: p. 287.
  Includes index.
  1. Freeman, G. D. (George Doud), 1842-1913. 2. Sumner County (Kan.)—Biography. 3. Caldwell Region (Kan.)—Biography. 4. Peace officers—Kansas—Caldwell—Biography. 5. Sumner County (Kan.)—History. 6. Caldwell Region (Kan.)—History. 7. Crime and criminals—Kansas—Sumner County—Biography. I. Lane, Richard L. (Richard Lee), 1927-   . II. Title. III. Title: Midnight and noonday. IV. Title: Incidental history of southern Kansas and the Indian territory, 1871-1890.
F687.S9F73   1984   978.1'87   83-40330
ISBN 0-8061-1875-X (alk. paper)

The paper in this book meets the guidelines for permanence and durability of the Committee on Production Guidelines for Book Longevity of the Council on Library Resources, Inc.

CONTENTS

Editor's Preface   xiii

Editor's Introduction   3

Chronology   15

Author's preface   21

CHAPTER 1

Trip to Caldwell   23

CHAPTER 2

View of Caldwell   31

CHAPTER 3

The Return to Caldwell   36

CHAPTER 4

Adventure with a Mountain Lion   42

CHAPTER 5

A Brief History of Caldwell   44

CHAPTER 6

Organization of the County   49

CHAPTER 7

The Killing of Wm. Manning   56

CHAPTER 8

The Buffalo Hunt   60

CHAPTER 9

A Buffalo Hunt—The Homeward March   66

CHAPTER 10

The Murder of Dave Fielder   72

CHAPTER 11

The Killing of Anderson   76

CHAPTER 12

The Shooting of McCarty   81

CHAPTER 13

Busey Nicholson Arrested   89

CHAPTER 14

Cowboys' Carousal   93

CHAPTER 15

The Killing of Oliver's Herder   96

CHAPTER 16

Stealing of My Team and Wagon   100

CHAPTER 17

In Pursuit of the Thieves   104

CHAPTER 18

Arrest of Tom Smith   110

CHAPTER 19
The Hanging of Tom Smith   117
CHAPTER 20
Charlie Smith's Threat   125
CHAPTER 21
The Drought of 1874   130
CHAPTER 22
Indian Raid on Kiowa   135
CHAPTER 23
In Pursuit of the Indians   139
CHAPTER 24
The Colonel and Mrs. Leonard Shoot a Buffalo   143
CHAPTER 25
Indians on the War Path   147
CHAPTER 26
The Stage Stock Is Stolen   158
CHAPTER 27
A Vigilance Committee   170
CHAPTER 28
L. L. Oliver Shoots a Shoemaker of Caldwell   176
CHAPTER 29
Description of the First Election at Caldwell   179
CHAPTER 30
Cowboys Attempt to Take the Town   185
CHAPTER 31
Caldwell Becomes a Railroad Town   192
CHAPTER 32
Frank Hunt Slain   201
CHAPTER 33
George Brown Appointed Marshal of Caldwell   206
CHAPTER 34
Must the Officers Be Hunted Down?   210
CHAPTER 35
The Marshals of Caldwell Attempt to Rob the Medicine Valley Bank   216
CHAPTER 36
The Robbers Taken to Medicine Lodge   223
CHAPTER 37
A Man Borrows a Shot Gun and Leaves the Country   229
CHAPTER 38
The Indian's Custom When Traveling Among White Settlers   232
CHAPTER 39
Court in Session Before a Justice in Caldwell   237

CHAPTER 40
Escape of a Horse Thief from the Sheriff of Cowley County, Kansas 245
CHAPTER 41
Jim Talbot and His Gang of Desperadoes Arrive in Caldwell 250
CHAPTER 42
Jim Talbot and Party Reach the Canyons Near Deer Creek 261
CHAPTER 43
The Citizens Are Struck with Horror At a Hanging 268
CHAPTER 44
Murder of Bob Sharp 274
CHAPTER 45
Sketch of the Lives of the Remaining '71'ers 280
Bibliography 287
Index 291

ILLUSTRATIONS

G. D. Freeman   20

W. B. King   27

Freeman's Residence in Caldwell, 1881   132

W. E. Malaley   154

A. M. Colson   159

Captors of the Medicine Lodge Bank Robbers   221

The Bank Robbers of Medicine Lodge   224

J. A. Ryland   284

MAPS

Central Kansas and Indian Territory   22

Sumner County, Kansas   50

Caldwell in the 1870s and 1880s   195

EDITOR'S PREFACE

As a compulsive reader of prefaces, I have always admired those writers most who can claim a purely altruistic purpose in producing the work at hand. I wish I could make that claim for myself. To be sure, G. D. Freeman's *Midnight and Noonday,* because it is a unique and valuable frontier memoir, deserves to be available to a broader audience than the collectors of rare books. But in all candor, that reason was not in the forefront of my mind when I undertook this edition.

I first encountered *Midnight and Noonday* in the course of researching the life of Joseph M. Thralls, a frontier lawman. Thralls appears in several episodes of this book, and so Freeman's accounts were of more than casual interest to me. Almost from the outset, I knew I was in trouble.

Only those who have tried to use *Midnight and Noonday* for purposes of research can appreciate fully the problems the original presents. These range in nature from obscurities within the text to the untested reliability of the author. I have discussed these problems in some detail in the Editor's Introduction and will not repeat them here. The point is, I desperately needed to use this book, but I could not use it as it stood. In short, I edited *Midnight and Noonday* because I could not work around it.

I hope the resulting version is useful to other students of the Old West and that what I have contributed enhances the accessibility of a work I have come very much to admire.

Writing and research are solitary occupations, but nobody completes such work by himself. There are many who deserve public acknowledgment and thanks for the help they provided me.

Acknowledgment is herewith accorded for a passage, in note 2 of Chapter 1, reprinted by permission of the publishers, the Arthur H. Clark Company, from *The Cowman's Southwest* by Angie Debo.

Special acknowledgment is due the University Research Committee, University of Nebraska at Omaha, for a summer research fellowship, travel funds, and a grant-in-aid.

The English Department, UN-O, provided a travel grant as well as other important support, not the least of which was the encouragement of my departmental colleagues to undertake this project outside my teaching discipline. Two chairmen, Robert Detisch and Gordon Mundell, have been particularly supportive, as have Judy Boss, John McKenna, and Susan Rosowski.

I wish to thank Joseph W. Snell, director of the Kansas State Historical Society, for sharing various materials, particularly the Stephen E. Smith marginal notes to *Midnight and Noonday.* KSHS staff members who have been especially gracious, patient, and helpful are Mary Lou Anderson, Marian Bond, Mary Beth Dunhaupt, Susan Forbes, Bobbie Pray, and Margo Swovelan.

In the earliest stages of this work I was fortunate to receive the kind and generous assistance of Violet Fein of the Sumner County Historical Society and the Chisholm Trail Museum, Wellington, Kansas; Tom Schwinn and Catherine Knowles of Wellington and Eugene Neal of Caldwell were also gracious and helpful at particularly crucial times.

I am indebted to Patricia Martinson for her efficient, accurate preparation of the final draft of the manuscript; Marvin J. Barton for his painstaking cartography; Herb Hyde for his editorial contributions; and Dorothy Dick for picking up after me.

Grant T. and Mickey Anderson of Portland, Oregon, provided hospitality and resource materials, the latter as invaluable as the former was warm. Grant (J. M. Thralls's grandson) also performed yeoman service in proofreading. Roger O'Connor of Mostly Books, Omaha, Nebraska, has been generous in lending me his rare books, sharing his expertise, and reading my manuscript. Joseph G. Rosa contributed suggestions, leads, and timely encouragement as well as a model of excellence to shoot for.

Finally, there are those whose help, encouragement, and affection have sustained me in this and many endeavors—my friends, Richard M. and Dorothy Devereux Dustin; my children, Elizabeth Crain and John; and my wife, Carolyn Stanley Lane.

RICHARD L. LANE

Omaha, Nebraska

MIDNIGHT AND NOONDAY

EDITOR'S INTRODUCTION

G. D. Freeman was a blacksmith who decided to write a book. He had never heard the axiom that it takes as much effort to write a bad book as a good one, and it never occurred to him that a blacksmith might more than likely write a bad one. He just rolled up his sleeves and pitched in—one sentence after another, one chapter after another, never looking back, never blotting a line, dipping his pen and forging on—until at last he had it finished. He called it *Midnight and Noonday or the Incidental History of Southern Kansas and the Indian Territory.*

For all the geographical scope promised in the subtitle, the book is mainly about Caldwell, Kansas, both before and during her heyday as a wild and woolly cattle town. It was a subject Freeman was qualified to write about, for he had witnessed nearly all of it: He was one of the earliest settlers in the Caldwell vicinity, and except for a six-year hiatus from 1873 to 1879, he saw at first hand her development from tough border settlement to wide-open railhead. For a time he was a local lawman and, as such, figured principally in some of the episodes. He knew what he was talking about.

In some ways, *Midnight and Noonday* is a book such as a blacksmith *would* write: rough-hewn and gap-toothed and gawky. In all of the important ways, however, it is a good book—certainly one of the best memoirs to come out of the cow-town frontier. In fact, *Midnight and Noonday* is the most nearly complete extant record of Caldwell's turbulent youth, and most of what has since been written about that time and place derives from this one book. It is a valuable and unique historical document. And that represents no mean achievement for an obscure village blacksmith.

George Doud Freeman was born in Richland, Ohio, on 15 June 1842. Nothing is known of his childhood or his education, but the latter appears to have been limited to a few years of grammar school. By 1861 he was living in Michigan, where at the age of 19 he married Laura A. Pool at Charlotte in Eaton County.[1]

On 26 February 1864, Freeman enlisted in the Twenty-seventh Regiment, Michigan Volunteer Infantry, and was assigned to the First Independent Company of Sharpshooters. At the time of his enlistment he was described as six feet, one-half inch tall, with hazel eyes, brown hair, and fair complexion. He was 22 years old; and Laura was pregnant with their first child, Rhoda, who would be born on May 4.

Freeman's military career was not distinguished, at least by achievements

---

[1] Biographical data, unless otherwise specified, are taken from Freeman's pension records in the National Archives.

3

on the battlefield: he spent most of his period of enlistment in the hospital. On the first day of his first combat engagement, the Battle of the Wilderness, he was taken prisoner. The next day, 6 May 1864, he was paroled, evidently because of illness, for he was immediately assigned to the hospital. The nature of his malady is unrecorded, but it kept him incapacitated until September 19, when he returned to his unit. By November 28, he was back in the hospital, this time with jaundice. During this confinement, he fell and dislocated his hip, an injury which would be the basis for a disability claim later. He remained hospitalized until his discharge from the service on 8 July 1865. During the brief period between confinements—from September 19 until November 28, 1864—he may have participated in the Action at Blue Springs, 10 October 1864, and the Knoxville Campaign, which began on 17 November 1864 and lasted through December 5.[2] The only reference in *Midnight and Noonday* which might reflect his military experience appears in chapter 17, where he compares his sleeping comrades to bodies of the dead collected for interment after a battle.

At some time after his discharge, Freeman moved to Kansas. He was there by 1867, for his pension records show that his son Elihu was born in Kansas on January 4 of that year. The specific town or county is unrecorded, but presumably it was in Butler County, near Augusta; at least that was Freeman's home, as he reports in his book, before he moved to Caldwell.

From 1871 to about 1885, Freeman's life is sketchily outlined in *Midnight and Noonday.* After taking a claim just west of Caldwell in 1871, Freeman farmed and also worked as a blacksmith, with a side appointment as a Caldwell Township constable. In the fall of 1873, he returned to Butler County, where he again took up farming.

Laura Freeman died on 17 September 1874, leaving George with four small children: Rhoda and Elihu, along with Oscar, born 11 August 1867, and Susan, an infant less than a year old. Freeman remarried early in December, barely six weeks after Laura's death.

His second marriage, to Emmaline Covert of Butler County, lasted until his death. Little more is known of Emmaline than of Laura. She, too, had come to Kansas from Michigan, so possibly Freeman had known her there. She was born in Indiana, but the date is not known. Census records show her variously as one to four years younger than George, but her claim for a widow's pension after Freeman's death indicates she may have been two years older than he. They had one child, John W., born on 13 February 1879.

Shortly after the birth of John, the Freemans returned to Caldwell. George had abandoned farming by this time and was attempting to earn his living

---

[2] Actions in which the Twenty-seventh Michigan participated are recorded in Frederick H. Dyer, *A Compendium of the War of the Rebellion*, III, 1292-93.

as an itinerant photographer, having purchased a "daguerreo car," which he describes in Chapter 21.[3]

Freeman engaged in the photography business in Caldwell for about seven months, first in partnership with a man named Brodie, possibly the Brodie from Augusta (Butler County) mentioned in Chapter 25. Another partner named Page, apparently Brodie's successor, is mentioned in the *Caldwell Post* of 17 July 1879, when it was announced that the partners planned to erect a building to house their gallery.[4]

By December of 1879, Freeman had turned to blacksmithing in partnership with one Riswell (*Caldwell Post,* 18 December 1879). He appears to have continued at this line of work, with or without partners, until 1890.

Some time after his return to Caldwell, Freeman was appointed to fill a vacancy as township constable. He was elected to the post in February of 1880. Of this later constabulary service, Freeman recounts little. In Chapter 37 he tells of arresting a man who had stolen a shotgun, but he makes no mention of a more interesting arrest reported in the *Caldwell Post* of 9 September 1880:

> G. D. Freeman has recovered his horse which was stolen from him on Tuesday evening, of last week. Mr. Freeman had a suspicion who the thief was, and started promptly in pursuit. The first clue he received was from a person he met on the hill, just south of the city, and following down the trail about 95 miles, he caught his man with the horse, at Kingfisher ranch. The thief, whose name is Brown, is the same whom Freeman arrested about two months ago, on Polecat creek, for stealing a horse 18 miles north of Caldwell. He was lodged in jail at Wellington, but succeeded in escaping, and arriving here, stole Freeman's horse to expedite matters.

Freeman's 1880 term as constable appears to have been his last service as a lawman. After 1880, he is mentioned rarely in the Caldwell newspapers. At about the same time he also ceased to advertise his blacksmith shop in those papers, which may or may not account for the lack of interest shown him in the chatty "locals" columns, which could balloon even a citizen's new hat into a few lines of copy.

Indeed, one is struck by Freeman's general failure thereafter to make the newspapers. He appears to have been one of those ill-starred individuals who are always forgotten or overlooked when the minutes are written up. Even

---

[3] Examples that can be identified as Freeman's photographic work are not known to have survived, but presumably some of the photographic illustrations in *Midnight and Noonday* were taken from his files. Of those reproduced for this edition, the portraits of W. B. King and A. M. Colson and the view of the author's home appear to be the most likely representatives of Freeman's work.

[4] One of their second-floor tenants was George Brown, who operated an oyster bar there for a short time (*Caldwell Post,* 30 October 1879). Brown was later killed in the line of duty as city marshal, an event Freeman recounts in his book.

in the various retrospective pieces dealing with Freeman's pursuit and capture of "Tom Smith," either Freeman is not mentioned or the credit for the capture is given to someone else. And on the one occasion that his wife made the newspapers, she is not identified with him.[5] Perhaps it was this almost studied lack of recognition which prompted Freeman to write his book.

Freeman did receive some publicity during 1885, but even that was negative. It appears that Freeman was among the citizens of Caldwell who became interested in the Oklahoma Boomer movement following the election of Grover Cleveland as president, when it seemed likely that settlement of the Territory would be approved by the new federal administration. Parties were organized at Caldwell in February of 1885 to go to Arkansas City and wait at the border for the presidential approval, which was thought to be imminent. Freeman was placed in charge of a group of twenty-five. Tell Walton, editor of the *Caldwell Journal,* was no lover of Boomers, but his mock-heroic references to Freeman in this connection seem gratuitously acerbic:

> Col. George Freeman's colony [of twenty-five men] reached Arkansas City on Sunday morning and are camped at that point waiting for the roses to come. The Colonel came home Monday night and arranged his garden so that his family will not suffer while he "goes to the wah." He reports his colony in splendid health and able to eat three times a day and sleep sixteen hours of the twenty-four [*Journal,* 12 March 1885].
>
> George Washington Freeman spent last week at home visiting his family. He is still booming it at Arkansas City [*Journal,* 23 April 1885].

When the Boomers' expectations were dashed, they moved their headquarters to Caldwell, and Freeman presumably returned home for good. His name is not mentioned by the *Journal* in connection with the Boomers again; he does not even appear in the pages of the *Oklahoma War Chief,* the movement's newspaper, except as an advertiser (27 May 1886).

When he commenced work on *Midnight and Noonday* is uncertain, but by April of 1890 he had completed it, as the following news story reports:

> George Freeman returned from Chicago where he has been making arrangements for the publication of his book on life on the border. He brought back with him proofs of the first few pages which are now on the press and says that the book will be printed and on sale in a very few weeks. George is one of the oldest settlers here and has been an eye witness to about all the killings and devilment perpetrated in this "neck of the woods." He is very

---

[5] Both the *Post* and the *Commercial* of 14 October 1880 report that Mrs. A. C. Jones had two hundred dollars stolen from under her pillow one night during her husband's absence. Apprehensive about staying alone, Mrs. Jones had persuaded a neighbor lady to stay overnight with her. During the night, the Jones family and the neighbor apparently were chloroformed and the money was stolen. The neighbor was identified in the papers only as "Mrs. Freeman" (actually, the *Post* committed a naughty typographical error and reported that "Mr. Freeman" had spent the night with Mrs. Jones).

enthusiastic over the book and predicts a fortune out of its sale [*Journal*, 17 April 1890.][6]

I have found no record of how Freeman's fellow Caldwellites received the work at the time of its appearance. The *Caldwell News* of 8 December 1891 reprinted a review which had appeared in the *Sedan* (Kansas) *Republican:*

> George D. Freeman of Caldwell paid us a visit on last Saturday. Mr. Freeman has written a book entitled Midnight and Noonday, or Dark Deeds Unraveled. [This subtitle does not appear on the book's title page. It is the running title, found inside the book at the top of each right-hand page of text.] The book is a history of Caldwell and life on the border from 1871 to 1890. It cannot fail to interest all those who have lived on the border since the early days. . . . The book sells for one dollar. From a literary standpoint many criticisms might be urged against the book but as a faithful narration of interesting events on the frontier, we believe it to be deserving of an ample sale.

A second printing, struck from the same plates, was issued in 1892, to which was added a testimonial, provided by prominent citizens, to the book's accuracy.[7] (A reissue of the 1892 version was published by the Sumner County Historical Society in 1976. Called the Bicentennial Edition, it is now out of print.)

Despite the second printing, it is unlikely that *Midnight and Noonday* earned Freeman the fortune he had hoped for. That hope may have prompted him to sell his blacksmith shop in June of 1890 (*Caldwell Journal*, 12 June 1890), but it is more likely that, at 58 years of age, he was reaching the end of his ability to do the work: that same year he filed a disability claim for his Civil War service, stating that he suffered from paralysis of his left side because of the dislocation of his hip, which occurred at the military hospital in 1865. He also reported that he suffered from deafness and a crippled left hand.

Freeman died on 29 October 1913 of angina pectoris. His newspaper

---

[6] It seems clear that Freeman paid to have the book printed and bound; no publisher is identified in the original volume, and Caldwell is listed as the place of publication. It appears that Freeman was also the principal retailer of the book.

[7] "We, the undersigned pioneers of Caldwell, Kansas, and vicinity have read "MIDNIGHT AND NOONDAY" by G. D. Freeman, and pronounce the facts recorded therein to be correct, as near as present research can make them. The reader therefore can safely conclude that when reading the book, he is reading correct history.

"Names of pioneers: J. A. Ryland, A. M. Colson, Representative at large, Oklahoma, W. J. Lingenfelter, C. B. Dixon, J. T. Richmond, H. J. Devore, J. M. Thomas, J. P.

"I desire to state that I am acquainted with the above-named signers, and know them to be men of truth and veracity.

R. T. Simons,
Editor *Caldwell News.*"

obituary was brief and not particularly eulogistic, but it did contain these lines:

> Mr. Freeman came to Caldwell in the spring of 1871 and soon became one of the leading spirits in the suppression of outlawry, which was rampant at that time. He was the author of "Midnight and Noonday," historical sketches of people and incidents in Caldwell and surrounding territory. The book was widely circulated over the southwest, sold directly by the author [*Wellington* (Kansas) *News*, 31 October 1913].

"One of the leading spirits in the suppression of outlawry." It probably would have pleased him, but it was a role he had never claimed for himself, at least not in his book.

Midnight and Noonday is not the kind of frontier memoir calculated to cover its author with glory. Freeman never advanced himself as an intimate of the famous or the infamous. He does not represent himself to be a hard case or even a tamer of hard cases. Whatever ulterior motive he may have had for writing the book, it was clearly not to brag about George D. Freeman. That is what gives *Midnight and Noonday* its fundamental credibility.

This is not to say he was above stretching the truth now and then. One is inclined to raise an eyebrow, for example, when Freeman reports that he and a few companions were seriously thinking of "surrounding" the large band of Indians which earlier in the day had raided the settlement at Kiowa, Kansas (chapter 22).[8] Or, again, when he relates an encounter he had with his nemesis, "Charlie Smith" (chapter 20): At the beginning of the episode, Freeman asserts that he had drawn his pistol and was holding it at his side; later, he has clearly forgotten the pistol, for he alludes to a dirk in his belt and says that "if Smith had shot and missed me I certainly would have used the knife to the best of my ability." In short, Freeman's fabrications, in the instances when he essays them, are artless and transparent. He was not a man of great subtlety.

This is reflected in many ways within the pages of his book but perhaps most fundamentally in his organizational plan, the incidental or episodic history. His interpretations of incidents, when he troubles to interpret them at all, are temperance-tract platitudes as a rule: whiskey is the cause of all

---

[8] Perhaps this and the following incident are what one old-timer, George Fletcher, had in mind when he said, "Freeman's book is a pretty good and true story; but he tried to make himself out a brave man, but he was the biggest coward in town" (quoted by John F. Ryland in an interview, *Caldwell Messenger*, 8 May 1961). Weighing the entire book, however, I believe no serious case can be made that Freeman overstates his own bravery. Indeed, he recounts incidents which make the reader wonder at Freeman's timidity. On the other hand, as noted earlier, Freeman pursued a horse thief ninety-five miles into the lawless Territory—hardly the act of a coward—and did not see fit to mention the event in his book.

human orneriness and grief. He sees no larger picture, no subtle cause and effect. For example, he sees no evident connection between the Talbot raid on Caldwell and the wanton killing of Marshal George Brown some months later; indeed, his order of presentation only blurs any sense of causation or climax the reader might otherwise infer.

His anecdotal approach also diffuses or distorts his occasional effort to deal with basic issues central to Caldwell's development. Perhaps he is at his best when he is dealing with the difficult days of Caldwell's early settlement, when legitimate settlers were trying to establish themselves alongside the rough and untamed types who had taken more or less permanent claims near Stone's store, the first legal liquor outlet north of Indian Territory. Freeman gives us a pointed picture of the settler's vulnerability to outlaws and desperados who could break the law and quickly disappear into the vast expanse of the Territory. Highly organized bands of rustlers could, and systematically did, strip the sodbusters of the livestock vital to their survival.

That the settlers' eventual response was lynch law is a truism, but it is a truism given flesh-and-blood imperative in this work. We are reminded, if we have forgotten our Thomas Josiah Dimsdale, that revenge-frenzied lynch mobs are a cinematic stereotype, that more often than not lynchings were carried out with cool deliberation—even military precision—by commonplace people whose sole alternative to retaliatory action was to resign themselves to being victims. In a time when few, if any, lawmen were expected to face down outlaws alone, when the ordinary citizen was expected to take up arms and assist in making arrests, lynch law might have been seen as the logical extension of *posse comitatus.*

To say these things is not to subvert the rule of law and due process; it is the recognition of historical truth. Nor must we forget that the ordinary citizen, even while participating, was never altogether comfortable with lynch law, an attitude which also comes through in Freeman's book. Indeed, before he is finished, Freeman presents the unredeemable side of lynch law as well. The people who hanged Frank Noyes in 1885 (chapter 43) were obviously not poor homesteaders struggling to protect their little all. And the murder of George Flatt, probably by Caldwell city officials, speaks to the cowardly legacy of a practice once chosen out of desperation.

Where Freeman is weakest is in conveying the internal difficulties Caldwell faced during the boom years, principally the classic cow-town problem of self-definition.[9] Catering to the cattle trade required a certain permissiveness toward liquor, gambling, prostitution, and high-spirited hell raising. The farmers, and a faction of the merchants with whom they did business, had a

---

[9] Robert R. Dykstra's *The Cattle Towns* includes a treatment of Caldwell's social, political, and economic development during the years Freeman describes.

different plan for Caldwell's future: churches, schools, law and order. Many were prohibitionists (Freeman, it appears, among them), who saw liquor as the root cause of everything undesirable, from the firing off of pistols in the public streets to the abuse and abandonment of children. Thus the important struggle was not the locals against the Texas transients, but the townspeople against each other. All this came to a head in 1885, the lynching of Frank Noyes being merely its most external symptom.

It is the external and sensational that characterize Freeman's treatment of the cow-town years, and even here he is selective. He omits reference to the near lynching of J. S. Danford, whose bank swindle generated more Caldwell newspaper copy than did the celebrated Talbot raid that same month and year. Freeman gives us no sense of Caldwell's uneasy political relationship with the Cherokee Strip Live Stock Association. He makes no mention of the Boomer movement, which bitterly divided a town anxious about its economic future. He gives us mostly the lurid side of things—shootings and knifings and gore —as though he supposed his readership was wholly conditioned by dime-novel action and the fictionalized history of the subscription books.

Yet it is precisely here, in the blood-and-thunder arena, that Freeman makes his own curious contribution to the history of the Old West. Ironically, for all the sensational subject matter, his is a book remarkably devoid of sensationalism. In comparison with the contemporary newspapers' versions of the George Flatt shootout in the Occidental saloon, for example, Freeman's account (chapter 30) is restrained and matter of fact. Moreover, it appears to lack even the little imaginative embroideries that the passage of a decade normally attaches to human recollection.

Freeman says in his preface that he intended to present the particulars which would separate the "straight veracity from the fiction" surrounding Caldwell's notoriety. In the main, he was true to his aim. Modern retellers have not improved upon his "straight veracity." If anything, they have found him too tame and have pumped up his plain recollections with hyperbolic war paint and crusty cowboy lingo. Not that Freeman himself was innocent of overwriting; he wasn't. But he didn't write the way a cowboy talked (or at least the way moderns seem to believe a cowboy talked). His purple prose is that of the last century's sentimentalism and schoolroom oratory. At times he writes as though his pen were dipped in tears. At other time his prose is reminiscent of a circus poster: all rhetorical curliques and gold-leaf screamers. The saving grace is that behind Freeman's occasional gingerbread lies true reportage.

From time to time he gives us the observed detail that rings like crystal. For example, he shows us Bat Carr, Caldwell's first gunfighter cum marshal, decked out in a brass-buttoned uniform, more Keystone Kop than Matt Dillon. And his description of George Flatt's adrenaline-charged agitation after the

Occidental saloon shootout probably cuts closer to the human truth about gunfighters than does any cool-hand shootist the cinema ever conceived. In brief, what he gives us are some insights into a way of life that Hollywood has so stylized and distorted that we no longer know quite how to separate the fiction from the truth.

For that reason alone, *Midnight and Noonday* would be an irreplaceable primary source for students of the Old West. But its contribution goes beyond the much-studied mayhem of the Kansas cow town. A large portion of this book deals with the years 1871 and 1872, a time when Caldwell was no more than a ragtag settlement alongside the Chisholm Trail and a far cry from the bustling Queen of the Border she would become in the 1880's. It happens to be a period in Caldwell's history when little else by way of historical records has survived. A few scattered issues of county newspapers remain, some county records are extant, but the rest is silence—except for Freeman. The student of the cow town in its infancy will find nothing that I know of, not even Joseph G. McCoy's depiction of early Abilene, that gives a better sense of a frontier community planting its fragile roots in a sea of grass.

It is probably no accident that Freeman devoted so much of his book to those days. They represent the time when he was most active as a lawman, the time of his mature vigor and probably his highest hopes. Much of the prairie was still unplowed and the primitive still abounded: a catamount might enter a man's dugout of a night; or the Indians might suddenly come raiding, as they did Dutch Fred a few miles down the creek. For G. D. Freeman, the really exciting time—the Golden Age—had nothing to do with Caldwell's cow town heyday. There may be a lesson in that.

The problems connected with editing Freeman's text are manifold. It is fair to surmise that Freeman never revised a line of his first-draft manuscript or proofed a word of copy. While great portions of the book hold up well in spite of that, some sections bear the obvious marks of haste or fatigue or both: ambiguities, perplexing constructions, and other difficulties are rife; typographical errors abound.

My intention has been to present a version which has improved clarity without doing violence to the content or to the flavor of the original. Thus I have silently emended punctuation where clarity seemed to dictate, but I have suppressed my pedantic impulse to make everything conform to modern usage; where nineteenth-century conventions (or Freeman's own erratic practice) do not seriously interfere with sense, I have left the original punctuation alone. In the same spirit, I have not corrected Freeman's grammar unless a given construction was misleading. Otherwise, I have mostly followed conventional practice of marking emendations with brackets, but exceptions do exist. For example, I have silently corrected all obvious typographical errors. Where the text shows variant spellings for proper names (as in *Drum/Drumm*), I have made all conform. Where Freeman consistently misspells a name (as in *Peas* for *Peay*), I have bracketed the corrected spelling at the point of first occurrence only, silently correcting subsequent entries in order to avoid distracting clutter. References to the more significant emendations are included in the notes.

Some of the text's difficult readings yielded to minor adjustment in punctuation or word order, once the intended meaning was recognized. Others could not be clarified by any amount of editorial tinkering; they simply made no sense. Most of these would appear in this edition in all their enigmatic glory had not luck—or the ghost of G. D. Freeman—led me to some external sources from which Freeman plagiarized. These include a couple of newspaper articles as well as Albert A. Richards' "History of Sumner County" in John P. Edwards' *Historical Atlas of Sumner County, Kansas.* In these I found statements or paragraphs which Freeman had lifted out of context and awkwardly placed in his own work. The plagiarized passages, *mirabile dictu,* were frequently those which, in Freeman's context, had made no sense. The originals have helped me shed light on Freeman's intended meaning in several instances. I have indicated these in the notes.

A few puzzling passages remain for which I have found neither the source nor the key. Here I have offered, in the notes, a paraphrase representing my educated guess about meaning. Fortunately, the incidence of these is not high.

The plagiarism itself deserves some comment, both as to nature and extent. As nearly as I have been able to determine, Freeman's chief larceny occurs in chapters 35 and 36, where he draws heavily, both in language and facts, from the *Caldwell Standard* Sunday extra of 4 May 1884 for the account of Henry Newton Brown's fiasco at Medicine Lodge. Otherwise, he lifts an occasional sentence or paragraph verbatim from the sources described above, principally for background color or detail.[10]

Over against this, one must place most of the book, where contemporary

---

[10] An exception might occur in chapter 45. On the basis of style, I suspect that J. A. Ryland wrote his own biographical sketch, and one or two other people profiled there may have done the same thing. Ryland may have written more. His son, John F. Ryland, in an interview published in the *Caldwell Messenger* of 8 May 1961, asserted that Freeman merely related the episodes to the elder Ryland, who wrote the text of the entire book. I suspect that over the years the younger Ryland's memory probably magnified the extent of his father's contribution. For one thing, Ryland was an educated man, one who would hardly be responsible for—or wish to claim—a work which, even in 1891, was acknowledged to be of dubious literary merit. Further, a man of Ryland's achievements and ability would scarcely plagiarize material such as I have identified. If J. A. Ryland wrote more of this book than his own biographical sketch, I suspect his contribution is virtually limited to chapter 1, which shows a grace of style not evident in later chapters.

sources, in revealing Freeman's inaccuracies in such things as dates and names, confirm that in fact he worked mostly from memory. The weight of the evidence also indicates that Freeman, unlike many frontier types whose reminiscences have seen print, fabricated no events, incidents, or encounters. Wherever verification has been possible I have found Freeman's version to be as accurate as one can reasonably expect of an old-timer's memory. Sometimes he even exceeds that expectation. He tried, within his human limits, to give the "straight veracity," and we have his contemporaries' testimony (see note 7) to back him up in his achievement. The Old West might have produced more polished memoirs than *Midnight and Noonday* but none more fundamentally honest, particularly in its presentation of events which the author participated in or witnessed.

The limitations of even a witness-participant are universally recognized and need no elaboration here. There are, after all, no completely unimpeachable sources. Errors can and do appear in official records. The *Caldwell Journal* will not agree in every "factual" detail with the *Caldwell Post*. In the face of all this, one can measure the veracity or reliability of a given source only with a mixture of erudition, perspicacity, and Kentucky windage. Then one makes up his mind.

Throughout the notes I am forthcoming with my opinion, when I have one, about the most reliable version of an incident, but I hold with the philosophy that all who read may run—and ought to. Therefore, I have tried at least to summarize other contemporary versions of an event where space did not allow full quotation. These annotations should not be taken as a sign that I am trying to challenge Freeman at every turn. Rather, they are included to help the reader make up his own mind.

One last word about the annotations. I have included the kind of background detail that I myself had wanted when I first read Freeman's book, details which would clarify and add context to the narrative. This includes identifying, to some extent at least, the host of obscure people Freeman mentions in his text. I could not identify them all, but I have managed to learn something about most of them. I hope the reader will find it as interesting as I do that the lawmen of Caldwell included a gunsmith, a grocer, and a violin-playing paperhanger, among others. I hope the reader will in some measure agree with me that all of these obscure people—all of them—deserve to be remembered, because the history of the Old West is finally not the history of the brothers Younger but the history of Reuben Riggs and S. Harvey Horner, and Wilder B. King, the small-time lawyers and druggists and Civil War veterans who came west and made a go of it.

Eight of the sixteen illustrations from the 1892 printing have been reproduced for this edition. Those omitted were deemed to be wholly unrelated to the text or inaccurate in what they purport to portray. The maps were prepared for this edition and have no counterparts in any previous imprint. *Midnight and Noonday* is indeed an "incidental history"; Freeman eschews chronology in favor of the unstructured and anecdotal. For the reader who would like to put all these incidents in their proper sequence, I have provided the chronology that follows, keyed to chapters wherever appropriate.

CHRONOLOGY

1870	October 14	John E. Reid settles near future Caldwell (chapter 2)
	Winter, 1870-71	Freeman's two companions lost on buffalo hunt (chapters 8, 9)
1871	February 7	Governor Harvey establishes Sumner County (chapter 6)
	March 1	Caldwell established (chapter 5)
	15	First building erected in Caldwell by C. H. Stone (chapter 2)
	May 22-25	Freeman's first trip to Caldwell (chapter 1)
	June 6	Freeman returns to Caldwell with his family (chapter 3)
	15	Indians attack Dutch Fred Crats on Bluff Creek (chapter 3)
		First meeting of the temporary county commissioners (chapter 6)
	Summer (?)	Freeman's adventure with a mountain lion (chapter 4)
	July 3	George Peay killed (chapter 5)
	17	Town of Meridian organized (chapter 6)
	September 26	First county election—the special election (chapter 6)
	November 7	Second county election—the first regular election and the first held in Caldwell (chapter 29)
1872	February	William Manning killed (chapter 7)
	April	Second election of township officers in Caldwell (chapter 29); Freeman elected constable (chapter 10)
		Dan Fielder killed by McCarty (chapter 10)
		Doc Anderson killed by McCarty (chapter 11)
		McCarty lynched (chapter 12)
		Curly Marshall sells the Last Chance (chapter 12)
		Freeman arrests Busey Nicholson (chapter 13)

	June	Reciprocal killing of two cowboys (chapter 14)
	(?)	City Hotel employee dunked in swill barrel (chapter 29)
	5	Freeman serves papers on the cattleman Oliver (chapter 15)
		"Tom Smith" and Dalton steal Freeman's team (chapter 16)
	6-10	Freeman and posse pursue "Smith" and Dalton (chapters 16, 17)
	10	"Smith" and Dalton captured (chapter 18)
	11-13	Posse returns to Caldwell (chapters 18, 19)
	13	"Tom Smith" lynched (chapter 19)
	14	Freeman reports to sheriff at Wellington (chapter 19)
	July	Freeman and Bent Ross capture a horse thief (chapter 40)
	29	Freeman and party set out to hunt buffalo and horse thieves (chapter 22)
	30	Indians attack settlement at Kiowa (chapter 22)
	31	Freeman and party resume buffalo hunt (chapter 23)
1872	August 2 (?)	Buffalo hunt along Medicine Lodge River (chapters 23, 24)
	August (?)	Freeman's first confrontation with "Charlie Smith" (chapter 20)
	September 10	Freeman is bailiff at trial, *King* v. *Turner* (chapter 39)
	19	Freeman goes to West Wichita after horse thieves (chapter 24)
	20	Horse thieves captured in West Wichita (chapter 24)
	October (?)	Freeman's second encounter with "Charlie Smith" (chapter 20)
1873	Summer	Busey Nicholson gives Freeman a cow (chapter 13)
		A. C. McLean sues Freeman (chapter 39)
	Fall	Freeman moves back to Butler County (chapter 20)

1874	Spring	Freeman rents his father's farm in Butler County (chapter 21)
	July 4	Pat Hennessey killed (chapter 25)
	6	Indian scare in Sumner County begins (chapter 25)
	16–26	Sumner County posse pursues horse thieves (chapter 26)
	28	Sheriff Davis arrests horse-thief suspects in and around Caldwell (chapter 27)
	30	Brooks, Hasbrouck, and "Smith" lynched (chapter 27)
	August 1	Grasshopper invasion (chapter 21)
	5	A. C. McLean tried as a horse thief (chapter 27)
	19	F. Ricer killed; L. L. Oliver lynched (chapter 28)
	September 17	Laura Pool Freeman dies (chapter 21)
	December 8	Freeman marries Emmaline Covert (chapter 21)
1875-1878		Freeman in Butler County
1878	Fall (?)	Freeman becomes a traveling photographer (chapter 21)
1879	April	Freeman returns to Caldwell (chapter 21)
	May, June (?)	Freeman appointed constable (chapter 21)
	July 7	George Flatt and John Wilson kill George Wood and Jack Adams (chapter 30)
		Caldwell incorporated as a city of the third class (chapter 31)
	August 7	City election in Caldwell; George Flatt appointed city marshal (chapter 31)
1880	April	The Red Light dance house moves to Caldwell (chapter 31)
	June 19	George Flatt killed (chapter 31)
	25	Mayor and officers of Caldwell arrested for conspiring to murder George Flatt (chapter 31)
	Summer	Railroad reaches Caldwell (chapter 31)
	(?)	Freeman arrests a shotgun thief (chapter 37)

	October 8	Frank Hunt killed (chapter 32)
1881	August 18	Charley Davis kills George Woods (chapter 32)
	December 17	Jim Talbot shoots up Caldwell (chapter 41)
	18	Talbot's gang escapes the posse (chapter 42)
1882	April 10	George S. Brown appointed marshal (chapter 33)
	June 22	George S. Brown killed (chapter 33)
	(?)	Red Light dance house closed permanently (chapter 32)
	27	Bat Carr appointed marshal (chapter 34)
	December 2	Henry N. Brown appointed marshal (chapter 34)
1883	May 14	Spotted Horse killed by Brown (chapter 38)
1884	March 26	Henry N. Brown marries Alice Maude Levagood (chapter 34)
	April 30	Brown, Wheeler, Smith, and Wesley attempt to rob the bank at Medicine Lodge (chapters 35, 36)
	May 1	Brown, Wheeler, Smith, and Wesley lynched (chapter 36)
1885	August 31	Enos Blair's house burned by arsonist (chapter 43)
	December 7	Frank Noyes lynched (chapter 43)
1886-1887	No entries	
1888	October 28	Douglass Riggs kills Robert Sharp (chapter 44)
1890	May (?)	First printing of *Midnight and Noonday*

MIDNIGHT AND NOONDAY

G. D. Freeman

THE AUTHOR'S PREFACE

From time immemorial it has been the custom of the writers of books to give to the reading public the reasons for so doing. In accordance with this old time custom I will say to the reader that the notoriety obtained by Caldwell, "Queen of the Border," not only at home, but far away in Eastern States, is such that the public, seeing in newspapers deeds of daring and bloodshed, are led to wonder if such things are merely fiction and "nothing more."

The inquisitive mind will naturally want to learn the particulars, thinking thereby to discover the true from the false, or the straight veracity from the fictitious. Many of the events herein chronicled have been done so for the first time, while several have been imperfectly published in the newspapers of the land. It has been my utmost endeavor in this book to ascertain the real facts and particulars of events before publishing the same. Realizing the fact that "truth is stranger than fiction," and that the historical student is after only that kind of history, the title of my book, "Midnight and Noonday," is in itself suggestive of a conclusion. There is presumed to be no darker time than midnight or no brighter time than noonday. The early history of all countries seems to be fraught with peril, daring, and bloodshed. And especially is this true of border towns. The desperado is social in his nature, courts danger, and strives to conquer. The town affords him an opportunity to gratify all of his attributes; the saloon in which to be social, the drunken brawl in which he finds danger, and the civil law and her officers to conquer.

I give the reader deeds of crime and dark deeds of horror as "Midnight," and the beautiful country of the plains and the grand "Queen of the Border," as they are seen to-day, as "Noonday."

Respectfully,

G. D. FREEMAN, Caldwell, Kan.

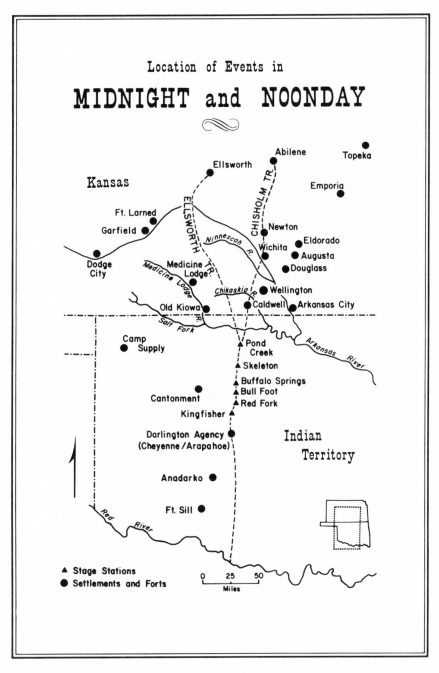

Location of Events in

MIDNIGHT and NOONDAY

Topeka

Abilene

Ellsworth

Kansas

Emporia

Ft. Larned

ELLSWORTH TR.

CHISHOLM TR.

Garfield

Newton

Ninnescah R.

Eldorado

Wichita

Dodge
City

Medicine
Lodge.

Medicine Lodge

Augusta

Douglass

ELLSWORTH TR.

Chikaskia R.

Wellington

Old Kiowa

Caldwell

Arkansas City

Salt Fork

Camp
Supply

Pond
Creek

Arkansas River

Skeleton

Buffalo Springs

Bull Foot

Cantonment

Red Fork

Kingfisher

Darlington Agency
(Cheyenne/Arapahoe)

Indian

Territory

Anadarko

Ft. Sill

Red River

▲ Stage Stations
● Settlements and Forts

0   25   50
Miles

Central Kansas and Indian Territory

CHAPTER 1

Trip to Caldwell—Geographical Description of the Country—
Attempted Horse Race on the Ninnescah—Our Fellow
Travelers—a Race with a Horse Thief—
Arrival at Caldwell.

In the early part of the spring of 1871, I conceived the idea of profiting by the advice of a wise statesman, "Go West young man and grow up with the Country." Having lived in a civilized portion of Kansas for a number of years, I considered myself able and competent to battle with the roughs and privations of an early pioneer settler. But little did I dream of the insurmountable hardships of a frontier settlement. Neither did I, in my most wandering imagination, conceive to what extent ruffianism, theft, murder and crimes of various sorts are carried when beyond the pale of civil law.

In this book, I shall attempt to narrate truthfully, incidents as they occurred under my own observation or near at hand, without being ornamented by fiction or embellished by romance. And as I necessarily shall be compelled to refer to my personal experiences I hope the reader will not criticize me as an egotist.

In the late winter and early spring of the year above referred to, it was currently reported that Sumner County was the one offering the greatest inducements of any frontier county to the immigrant seeking a home. This county is located on the South line of Kansas, bordering on the Indian Territory, and about the center of the state, East and West. Many towns were rapidly springing up in the county, each striving for a supremacy. Some were vying with each other as to which of them should be the county seat; while others were content to rely on local and transient trade for support, and look to natural advantages, fine climate, and future greatness, etc. Among the latter class and the most noted of them was Caldwell, located on the southern border of the county, and about two and one-half miles from the Indian Territory and at a point where the great thoroughfare, known as the Chisholm Cattle Trail, enters the state. This trail was laid out and cattle driven over it first in 1868, by a Texas cattle man by the name of Chisholm, and hence the name.[1] The State of Texas in its early history was a vast unfenced scope of pasture land. In time, cattle men, owners of ranches and large herds of cattle,

---

[1] Freeman repeats the popular but incorrect attribution to cattleman John Chisum. The trail was named for trader Jesse Chisholm, who is credited with establishing a major portion of the trail in 1865. Accounts of the establishment of the trail and Jesse Chisholm's contribution can be found in, among others, A. T. Andreas, *History of the State of Kansas,* p. 1385 (cited hereafter as Andreas); Wayne Gard, *The Chisholm Trail,* pp. 70-75; and Sam P. Ridings, *The Chisholm Trail,* pp. 15-28.

began to seek a market for their herds. Markets were far distant. The nearest shipping point by railroad for Western Texas cattle was Abiline, a town on the Kansas Pacific, about 100 miles north of the south line of Kansas. The Texas cattle were originally from the old spanish stock, introduced into Old Mexico and Southern Texas by the Spaniards, in a very early day. They are of lean and lank build and well able to travel thousands of miles to a shipping point or to a market if necessary. During the summer of 1868 the trail reaching from Central Texas to Abilene, Kansas, was started and quite a number of herds were driven over the trail to the shipping point that season. During the summer season of 1869, the number of cattle driven over the trail was increased by many thousands, and for several succeeding years, the drive showed a still greater increase.

I have thus given the reader a partial geographical description of the country and the location of Caldwell, that he may more fully understand the thrilling events which I am about to record in these pages. After receiving many flattering reports of the country around Caldwell, and of the probability of that town being the great metropolis of the new Southwest, I reasoned after this fashion: I, at that time, had a wife and three children; we all stood greatly in need of a home to call our own; Uncle Sam, at that time, had plenty of land around Caldwell, out of which to make homes for the homeless; I thought that the transient trade, afforded by the travel over the trail by Texas men with herds from Texas, could not fail to make a red hot town. Yes indeed a red hot town it did become; for many a time did the wild and wooly cowboy "paint the town red."

On a bright, balmy, and breezy morning on the twenty-second of May 1871, I concluded to go and visit Caldwell and vicinity, that I might see for myself if newspaper reports were fully verified by actual facts. So, I hitched my team to the wagon and in company with W. B. King, afterwards known as Buffalo King,[2] to use western slang we "lit out" for the famous border town. After leaving Augusta [Butler County, Kansas], we traveled all day without incident worthy of mention, and at night arrived at Wichita and camped there for the night. The next morning, leaving Wichita at our backs, and looking to the right and to the left, in front as far as the eye could reach, there was presented to view a grand panorama of nothingness. Save an occasional herd of cattle, there was nothing to be seen that bore the slightest impress of civilization. Whether or not the grand march of American Civili-

---

[2]Wilder B. King was forty-six years old in 1871. He was a Civil War pensioner, having suffered a gunshot wound in the hip (*Caldwell Journal,* 7 February 1884). Freeman gives more particulars on King in chap. 45. For Oliver Nelson's reminiscence of King's days as a freighter from Caldwell to Indian agencies in the Territory, see Angie Debo, *The Cowman's Southwest,* pp. 34, 159-60. Nelson remembered King as "about six feet tall, weighed 305 pounds, and his yell would nearly knock your hat off."

zation would ever reach and beautify this immense expanse of apparently waste land, once known as "The Great American Desert," time alone could tell. For hundreds of years, the Indian and the Buffalo had held full dominion and had truthfully been "monarchs of all they surveyed." But now, the signs of the times point to a change. The great struggle for the Union has long since passed away. The smoke of battle, where first it raised its curling head, is now settled in slumber. Peace and good will now reign supreme in Kansas, where was the first battle ground of the great struggle. The Star of Empire points Westward. Millions of American people are without homes of their own and it only remained to be seen whether or not this immense tract of prairie land could be so utilized as to make profitable homes for the poverty stricken homeless.

After traveling till nearly night, we reached Cowskin Creek. This creek, after winding itself like a serpent through the prairie for about fifty miles, enters the Arkansas River. On the bank of this stream, where the trail crossed and, as we were traveling on the trail, where we also crossed the creek, there was a trader's ranch.[3] Now, for the benefit of the eastern reader, I will say that this word *Ranch* is borrowed from the Mexican word *Ranchero,* and has a double meaning, as used in the southwest. A trader's ranch is a house of some description in which is kept for sale, such articles as the traveler or drover usually needs. These ranches in those days were never considered as having a complete stock unless they kept a barrel or two of the poorest kind of whiskey. The cattle drover himself is usually a man of temperate habits. But his employees, or cow-boys as they are called, are many times addicted to the use of strong drink. The second use of the word *Ranch,* as used in the southwest, is in connection with the raising and keeping of live stock. The stock ranch is the general headquarters for the men who are in charge of the stock. Here they meet to take their meals and at night to take their rest. The herders are sometimes supplied by the owner of the herd with a cheaply provised cabin, but more frequently they have to be content with a

[3] The obvious route from Wichita to the budding Caldwell was the Chisholm Trail, which was well worn even by 1871. The trail also accounts for the number of so-called traders' ranches that Freeman encountered at nearly every major stream and river crossing where the trail outfits might be induced to stop for groceries or liquor. In 1871 the ranch on the Cowskin was operated by Babcock and Wemple, according to Andreas, p. 1388, and by Babcock and Parmelee, according to Charles Goodyear in D. B. Emmert's "History of Sedgwick County," which prefaces John P. Edwards' *Historical Atlas of Sedgwick County, Kansas,* p. 10 (Emmert is obviously the principal author of the Sedgwick County portion of Andreas; the *Atlas* and Andreas differ in wording only occasionally; I suspect that the inconsistency here is a printer's error in Andreas). The Cowskin Creek trail crossing, in Waco Township, Sedgwick County, would have been no more than nine miles south of Wichita, so Freeman and King must have got an extremely late start that day if they reached the Cowskin "after travelling till nearly night."

tent or a common dugout, as a place to call their home. (As I digress so frequently from my description of my trip to Caldwell, I hope the reader will bear with me, if I should fail at any time to gracefully "ketch on" where I left off.)

We passed the ranch that night about a mile and went into camp. After supper was over, as the shades of night began to chase the shadows away, I began to feel the loneliness of the situation. My partner, sitting by the embers of the smouldering camp-fire, was soon fast asleep. And, by the way, my partner was a most noted sleeper. If the thunder roared and the lightning flashed, he was sure to be asleep. If he was set to making a fire and getting dinner, he would go to sleep before it was done. If he were placed on guard to keep thieves from stealing our horses, he was sure to go to sleep. Or if his meal was cooked, and coffee boiled and his tin cup filled for him, he was liable to go to sleep and spill his coffee while the tin was being carried to his mouth. Yes, indeed he was a number one on the sleep. I sometimes used to think he would take a nap while riding a fast horse on a race course. Well, I guess I had not better go back on my partner in this way; I will just say the cause of his being so sleepy was said to be a disease called Somnia.[4]

As I said, I began to feel lonesome. My partner asleep, I felt as much alone as if I had been a thousand miles from anybody. On different sides around me, I could hear the night herder's lullaby to his cattle. This however, only added to my far away off and lonesome feeling. For every man we had seen that day seemed to me as if he bore marked resemblance to the noted Claude Duval, or some other fictitious outlaw. I presume that most of the men we had seen that day were cattle drovers and cow-boys, and that they were not near as bad looking as they seemed to me. In that day it seemed to be a part of the cow-boys business to carry two heavy revolvers and sometimes a large knife, in his belt. I was what in the West has been styled a "tenderfoot," and such moving arsenals did not exactly meet my notions of propriety. But I soon learned by future experience that a tenderfoot, in the West, was quite sure to have his feet hardened so that he would soon pass as an old frontiersman.

The night was spent with very little sleep for me. I was the owner of the team we were driving,[5] and a very good one it was, too, and I thought if anybody's team would be worth stealing it would certainly be mine. These reflections, together with the appearance of the men seen the day before, led

---

[4] Apparently some form of hypersomnia, narcolepsy perhaps, characterized by the kind of sleep disorder Freeman describes. One form of hypersomnia is associated with obesity, a condition from which King evidently suffered (William R. Shapiro, "Sleep and Its Disorders," *Cecil Textbook of Medicine*, pp. 651-55).

[5] Freeman and King were riding in a buckboard or a buggy. My impression is that this, rather than the saddle horse, was the more usual mode of transportation in that time and place, colorful stereotypes notwithstanding, even over open country.

W. B. King

me to conclude that I had better keep an eye on my horses, lest they should be stolen. I slept at short intervals during the night and in the morning found my horses all right and my partner, as usual, asleep. After we had got up and had our breakfast we again started on our way to the city (town it was then) on the border. The cattle herds were growing thicker as we go southward. They got so thick on the trail that there was but little room for us to use as a highway. But as we met the herds we drove around and by them the best we could, but made very slow progress on our journey. In the forenoon we passed a stream called the Ninnescah. This stream after running about a hundred miles in a southeasterly course empties its waters into the Arkansas.

On the north bank of the Ninnescah was a trader's ranch with a few little shanties around it, giving a slight evidence of a town in embryo.[6] It was plainly evident that the ranchman here did not fail to keep the one thing needful to the cow-boys' happiness—a little of the ardent. A couple of them undertook to run a horse-race, but neither of them could ride, as business had been most too good for the ranchman on that day in that special line of goods.

After leaving the Ninnescah we again began traversing a gently rolling prairie quite similar to the one we had recently passed over, but a little more rolling. After going a short distance we stopped to rest and graze our horses and get some dinner. The great number of cattle that had been grazed along the trail for the past month made picking rather short for our horses, so we remained in camp until 2:30 o'clock when I hitched up my team, awoke my partner, and we rolled on. At about 4 o'clock in the afternoon we arrived at a small stream called Slate Creek. This stream, like the others we had crossed, was ornamented by a trader's ranch.[7] As the day was only partly gone we concluded to make a short drive on our road before camping for the night.

[6] The Ninnescah crossing (Ninnescah Township, Sedgwick County) was about ten miles from the Cowskin crossing. In 1871 the trader's ranch referred to was operated by McLean and Russell and remembered as "the rendezvous for all the desperadoes along the border." McLean was A. C. McLean, later operator of the Last Chance ranch, south of Caldwell, and a prominent figure in subsequent episodes of this book. The Ninnescah ranch had been owned by "Charlie Smith," who was to become Freeman's nemesis within the next year (Andreas, p. 1387).

[7] The Slate Creek crossing (Sumner Township, Sumner County) was about eleven miles from the Ninnescah crossing and approximately eight miles northwest of the site of Wellington. In 1871 the ranch was operated by Charles Russell and Frank Holcroft, who had taken claims nearby (Andreas, p. 1494; *Sumner County Press Chronology,* 1 January 1880. In the 1 January 1880 issue of the *Sumner County Press,* published in Wellington, Kansas, there appeared a chronological listing of major—and some minor—events in the history of Sumner County from 1870 through 1876. It was worked up by A. A. Richards, who wrote, in addition to several retrospective pieces for the newspaper, "History of Sumner County" in John P. Edwards' *Historical Atlas of Sumner County, Kansas,* as well as the Sumner County section of Andreas. The *Sumner County Press* and the chronology are cited hereafter as *SCP* and *SCP Chronology,* respectively).

After we had crossed the creek and while we were looking for wood to camp with, two men on horseback came riding across the creek. In conversation with them I learned that they, also, were on their way to Caldwell. They proposed to ride along with us till camping time and to camp with us, if we did not object. My partner by this time being engaged in taking a nap, I was expected to make the reply. First looking at one, then the other, and as one of them wore a palm-leaf hat and neither of them either by clothes or appearance showed any signs that they were either ruffians or thieves, after hesitating a moment, I said, "all right."

The names of these two men were A. M. Colson and J. A. Ryland.[8] Some of the readers of these pages, I have no doubt, know them, as they both became old settlers near Caldwell. During this trip my greatest fears were that some one would steal my horses, and thus I would be left a long ways from home with a wagon to ride in but no team to pull it. And another and stronger reason for not wanting my team taken was, that not being sumptuously supplied with this world's goods, I was not able to lose my horses.

We soon secured wood enough for the night's camping, and then with our new found fellow travelers we rolled out. After traveling five or six miles we reached the head-waters of Prairie Creek and camped for the night.[9] It was one of those calm, still nights that make one think of an earthly heaven. The air seemed to come to the nostrils of the weary traveler heavy laden with purity; after supper, the moon in all her resplendent loveliness raised her head above the Eastern horizon; as she sailed forth in the heavens, she shed her radiant light over hill and dale, making it almost as light as day. Although the night was uncommonly bright, I thought it might be safer to bring my team up to the wagon under which I slept. The country furnished such a grand chance for stealing horses, I feared my team might tempt some thief more than he was able to bear. The prairies at that time furnished plenty of grass for stock, so that a thief with a stolen horse and a handful of "grub" could travel to the southwest for hundreds of miles without being seen by anyone. That horse-thieves were abroad in the land no one could doubt, judging by the numerous horses that had "strayed off" from their owners and could never be found.

That night we slept well, but before retiring, I cautioned our new friends not to go near any of our horses during the night, as I should sleep with my Winchester by my side, and, if I should see any one near the horses I might think it a thief and treat them as such. This caution however, was entirely unnecessary, as they, second only to my partner, were excellent sleepers, for

[8]Both Colson and Ryland are subjects of sketches in chap. 45, and Colson figures prominently in several episodes in this book.

[9]The trail crossed the west branch of Prairie Creek in Downs Township, Sumner County, about ten miles south of the Slate Creek crossing.

the next morning when they awoke the sun was shining in their faces. Soon as we had cooked and eaten our morning meal we again hitched up and pursued our journey. After we had gone perhaps a mile or so there passed us on the trail a man riding a very fine horse. From his general appearance, the quality and speed of the horse he rode, we concluded that he probably was a horse thief and that the horse was stolen property. We noticed that as we drove faster he would also increase his speed, and to put the matter to still further test we selected two of the fastest horses in our outfit and Colson and I pursued him, leaving the remaining two boys to bring the wagon. We had not pursued the chase a very great distance before we were quite well satisfied that he had the fastest horse. He gained on us so rapidly that before we had followed him more than five or six miles he had left us entirely out of sight. Who he was or where he went we never knew, but probably he was a member of a gang of thieves and cut-throats that at that time infested the southwest. The horse was quite likely a race horse stolen from some border settlement.

At about 10 o'clock we crossed the Chikaskia River. On the north bank of this stream there was a ranch kept by Frank [H.] Barrington and Dr. [T. D.] Hahn.[10] These were the first ranchmen whom we had seen on our trip that looked as if they had ever lived "back east." After a drive of about eight miles over as fine appearing country as nature ever brought into existence, we arrived at Caldwell about 1:30 o'clock on the 25th of May 1871.

[10] The Chikaskia River crossing was about two miles beyond the crossing of Prairie Creek. Frank Barrington, along with Colson, figures in the great horse-thief chase of 1874, as described in chap. 26. Both Hahn and Barrington had moved to Chautauqua County by 1891 (*Caldwell News*, 8 December 1891).

CHAPTER 2

View of Caldwell—Talk with Thomas—Claim Takers—Claim Jumpers—
Meeting with Reid—A Bit of Reid's Bitter Experience—
Trading for His Claim—Arrival Home.

As it was afternoon and we had not yet had our dinner, we concluded to drive a short distance southeast of town, and camp on the banks of a creek known by the name of Fall Creek. This creek flows to the southeast and surrounds the town on two sides, its course being from the northwest to southeast. The town is located where the creek makes a bend in its course.

Here we found a good supply of wood to use as fuel. After we had eaten our dinner, we turned our horses loose to graze, and leaving my partner as watchman, also to keep the horses from straying far from camp, we started for the town.

We had not proceeded far when I turned and, looking in the direction of camp, saw my partner leaning against the wagon wheel enjoying a good sleep. We did not intend to be gone but a short time and thought the horses would not go very far from camp, so we decided to go on.

Upon arriving at the town, we found two log cabins used as store-rooms. The first building was erected by C. H. Stone, on March 15th, 1871, and used as a grocery store, with liquid groceries predominating.[1]

---

[1] C. H. Stone, one of the original town company of Caldwell, was a prominent, if mostly absentee, figure in Caldwell's early history, successfully speculating in city real estate as well as cattle. A biographical sketch can be found in Andreas, p. 1504. See also chap. 5, n. 2.

Texas cattleman William B. Slaughter recalled Stone's store and Stone himself: "[At] Sewell Branch Supply Station . . . we secured enough supplies to carry us to Bluff Creek, where Capt. Stone had a large store. All of the old trail men knew Capt. Stone, who in later years was one of the great buyers of our Texas cattle, when they reached Kansas" (J. Marvin Hunter, ed., *Trail Drivers of Texas*, 2:869). Slaughter, however, places Stone on Bluff Creek in 1870.

E. R. Rachal (*Trail Drivers of Texas*, 2:806) remembered seeing "the first house of Caldwell . . . being put up" when he passed through sometime after 20 March 1871. According to the *Caldwell Messenger* of 3 September 1953, Stone's building, 18 by 36½ feet, of cottonwood and hackberry logs, was a store jointly owned by Stone and J. H. Dagnar, another member of the original town company. (I am indebted to Robert R. Dykstra, *The Cattle Towns*, for this newspaper source. As Dykstra points out, its excellent information is obviously drawn from material now lost.) On 25 September 1872, a correspondent of the *Wellington Banner* refers to the proprietors as the "Stone Bros., grocers, . . . energetic young men." I find no other authority for a brother of Stone involved in the operation. It is possible that Dagnar was confused for a brother.

Whatever Freeman independently remembered of Stone's stock in trade, he lifted his language from the *Caldwell Journal* of 1 January 1885: "The first founder . . . started a grocery store, with liquid groceries preponderating." One suspects that some allowance

Time passed on, when Cox & Epperson, inspired by the greed for gold, settled down by him and also sold wet and dry groceries.[2] J. M. Thomas was under their employ as clerk in the establishment.[3]

There was also a building about fourteen by sixteen feet in dimensions, with a roof in shape like a car roof. This building was used as a saloon, and in it was kept some of the cheapest grades of whiskey. The proprietor was a man by the name of John Dickie.[4]

After looking around awhile, we fell in conversation with J. M. Thomas. He gave us considerable information in regard to the country, and in conclusion told us where in all probability, we might secure two good claims near the town.

We returned to camp, waked up our partner who had put in a couple

---

must be made for editorial flamboyance. A. A. Richards says Stone used the log house for "a dwelling and a storehouse" ("History of Sumner County," *Historical Atlas*, p. 8).

According to the *Caldwell Messenger* (3 September 1953), Stone's first sale, for $711, was made to Colonel James Oakes, in charge of a U. S. Cavalry unit en route from Texas to Fort Riley. The Federal Writers' Project, however, cites the $711 as the total proceeds from Stone's first day of business (*Kansas: A Guide to the Sunflower State*, pp. 462-63). Neither source offers documentation. Whatever the case, Stone's business judgment had been quickly vindicated.

[2]Freeman's sequence here is confusing. The second log cabin did not house Cox & Epperson but rather the saloon described in his next paragraph. In alluding to the "greed for gold" and "wet and dry groceries," Freeman again cribs from the *Caldwell Journal*, 1 January 1885.

In chap. 45, Freeman identifies Cox & Epperson as a Kansas City firm which leased a log structure from J. M. Thomas during the summer of 1871. Of the firm, at least Cox appears to have been present at the Caldwell store as late as August of that year, for H. C. St. Clair reported meeting him at Caldwell (*Belle Plaine Herald*, 19 August 1871). Cox was possibly Morgan Cox, unsuccessful candidate for county commissioner from the Third District in the special election of 26 September 1871.

[3]In his Andreas biography (p. 1504, where he is erroneously listed as J. W. Thomas), Thomas states that he opened a general supply store in Caldwell in 1871, making no reference to Cox & Epperson. Thomas served with the Seventh Ohio Cavalry during the Civil War. He married Fannie Devore, daughter of early Harper County settler H. J. Devore, who figures in this narrative later. (See also chap. 26, n. 5.) Freeman gives a biographical profile of Thomas in chap. 45.

[4]I have found no other reference to Dickie as the proprietor of the saloon, nor can I identify him in any other way. He may have been an employee of Milam Fitzgerald. E. R. Rachal (p. 807), who noted Stone's store going up in 1871, visited Fitzgerald on the same occasion: "Here [at Bluff Creek] we found an old friend, Milam Fitzgerald, with a tent full of trail supplies."

The log building is described as 16 by 16 feet in the *Caldwell Messenger,* 3 September 1953, and is reported to have been occupied by Fitzgerald, "Jones and Heitrich, J. L. Jones, D. P. Terrell and Hank Zuber." Of these, Dave Terrill and J. L. "Deacon" Jones appear later in this book. One of the Joneses is mentioned as a "dealer in 'red hot' and Kansas 'tangle leg' whiskey" in the *Wellington Banner* (9 September 1872) and at the time appears to have been the only one of the above group associated with the saloon.

of hours sleeping, hunted our horses, which we experienced no difficulty in finding, and started to look over the country and to try and secure the claims spoken of by our new found friend.

To say we were pleased with the country would be putting it too mild. We were perfectly delighted with the beautiful and ever changing panorama, which excited our highest admiration. Looking to the North, South, and East, we were enabled to scan the country as far as the eye could reach, presenting to us a picture of living verdure.

As we journeyed to the West, after leaving our home in Augusta, we began penetrating the Indian Country, leaving civilization behind us; we no longer enjoyed the sights of forests, for the only trees to be seen were scattered along the banks of the streams.

Upon examining the soil, we found it to be a deep black loam, resting on a lighter colored sub-soil, consisting of a loam, gravel, and clay, both soil and sub-soil being so porous that surface water rapidly passes through them.[5]

We came back to town and to our noon camp along near sundown. We had traveled quite a distance up Fall Creek and over to another stream about a mile away called Bluff Creek. It was not difficult to find plenty of excellent claims, but it seemed that all of them that were very desirable had been taken sometime previous to our arrival there. I learned afterwards that many times a half-dozen or more claims were taken by one individual under different names. The taking of a claim simply consisted of placing on said claim, in the form of a log house foundation, four logs, and in sticking in the ground a board, upon which was the taker's name. It will readily be seen that the one who sailed under the most aliases could take the most claims.

The few parties at that time up and down the creeks were single men and generally lived in a dug-out and "batched it." By taking several claims each, they would be prepared to sell a claim to anyone who came into the country and wanted to secure a home for himself and family. I had come to the country in search of a home and expected to get one at "Uncle Sam's" price under the exemption laws. Here I found, that for the sake of gain, roving plainsmen had taken and marked all of the choicest claims. Of course a person desiring a claim could have "jumped" one of those already taken, but the character of the ones holding them would lead one to conclude that it might be a little dangerous. To shoot a man in those days was not considered a very grave offense unless the person doing it should be caught, and the chance to get away was so good, a "claim jumper" might be left dead to

[5]The skeptical reader may well question whether Freeman and his companions made so deep and thorough an examination of the soil. Freeman lifted the description verbatim from the *Caldwell Post* of 8 January 1880, from the words "a deep black loam" through the end of the paragraph. The *Post* attributes the soil analysis to "a letter written by the editor of the American Agriculturist."

hold the claim, while the murderer had gone to (for him) a more healthful clime.

As I said, we arrived at camp where we had stopped for dinner, a little before sundown. Soon after our arrival, and after we had unhitched our team, we began to consider what we had best do. After thinking and talking over the claim matter for a short time, we noticed, at about a hundred yards distant on the banks of the creek, was what seemed to be a clay bank or knoll. Soon we saw a man coming up the bank near where the knoll was and start in the direction of our camp; when he arrived, he said that *that* was his claim, and what we had thought to be a clay bank, was his dug-out.

From him we learned that his name was Reed [Reid], and that he was the oldest settler in this vicinity, having located his claim in 1871 [1870].[6] The many privations, he and his family had endured, words will ever fail to express. A few things however in reference to his life, here may be of interest to the reader.

Reid was a Scotchman by birth, and came to America when in his minority. His father rented and farmed land in Illinois for a good many years. Finally young Reid became of age and married a young lady in Illinois. He also engaged in his father's avocation, that of the farmer. After living in Illinois for several years he moved to Missouri; he remained there two years; when the tide of immigration began to flow into Kansas, he with his family—a wife and five children—fell in line in the Westward march.

He, like most immigrants into a new country, would like to be exactly suited with a claim before taking it. He kept going until he reached the place where we found him. When leaving Missouri, he had a team to haul his effects, and also enough money, with what he could earn teaming, to keep him, until he could get a start on his farm. But how often it is, the brightest hopes are not realized, and grief and sorrow take their places. In this case it was fully verified. He arrived at his destination in the fall of 1871 [1870]; soon after his arrival his horses took sick and died, thus leaving him without any means of support except his two hands and what little money he had. Labor was quite scarce, except freighting, and as he had no team he could not freight.[7] He had not lived in his new home very long before his family were all sick with chills and fever; as cold weather came on they gradually

---

[6] John E. Reid was the first settler in the Caldwell vicinity, arriving in October of 1870 (Andreas, p. 1495). Freeman consistently spells the name Reed.

[7] Freighting was, for some time, an important cash source for settlers in Sumner County, who would haul government supplies from the nearest railhead to the Indian agencies or military posts in the Territory. As late as 1881, when the railhead was Caldwell itself, farmers had driven freighting prices down so much that regular freighters were unable to compete. As a result, when the farmers turned to their spring plowing, a minor crisis occurred as Indian Territory supplies began to stack up at the Caldwell depot (*SCP*, 1 January 1880; *Caldwell Commercial,* 14 April, 21 April 1881).

recovered, all except his wife, who lingered for sometime and finally died. Now he drinks his griefs to the dregs. With five children, some of them small, his wife dead, and provisions fifty miles away, while he had but little money to buy with and no team to go after them! let us draw a curtain over the scene until we tell you that dire necessity drove him to the extremity of carrying his provisions fifty miles on his back to keep his family alive.

Well, Mr. Reid had become dissatisfied with the country, and wanted to sell his claim and leave. After some bartering, I bought his claim, agreeing to give him the horse I was driving and fifty dollars upon my return from a trip after my family. This piece of land afterward became very valuable, it being a part of the town, and the Rock Island and Santa Fe Depots were built upon it.[8]

The next morning, my partner and I awoke early, got our breakfast, hitched up our team, and started to Butler County after our families, leaving our friends Colson and Ryland at Caldwell. We arrived safely at our homes and found all anxiously awaiting our return.

[8]The depot, built in 1880, was on Cheyenne Street, due south of the western edge of original Caldwell and west of Big Casino Creek (*Historical Atlas of Sumner County,* p. 75).

CHAPTER 3

The Return to Caldwell—Reid Backs out of His Bargain—
Takes a Claim—A Fright Caused by Indians—The
Shooting of Fred Crats—Building the
"Dug-Out"—A Shot at Gray
Wolves.

On the 6th day of June we arrived in Caldwell and immediately drove to our claim. We were surprised to find that Reid had regretted his trade with me and had concluded to back out. He did not think he was receiving enough for it, therefore would not trade that way. He finally told me, however, that if I would give him another horse, one that I was driving, he would call it a trade. I told him I would not trade that way, as I, like himself, was getting sick of my bargain, for the place was not a desirable one on which to take my family, as the cattle trail run through the place, upon which thousands of cattle were driven. Besides this objection I had another reason for not wanting it. My wife had been living in a good neighborhood with many friends with which to associate, and I realized this fact, that if I lived here she would, more or less, see a rougher class of people than she was accustomed to seeing, and it would naturally have a tendency to make her discontented with her surroundings. She was a very timid woman and of a nervous temperament and it would have been far wiser to have never brought her on the western frontier.[1]

And now here I was with my family and with no place to call my home. I left my family at Reid's while King and myself went to see if we could find us a claim.

We had no trouble in getting each of us a good one. Mine was located one and a half miles West of town, King's claim joining mine on the North. King was not satisfied there, but continued to live there until fall, when he took another claim about six miles farther west. This time he got a choice piece of land on the Bluff Creek bottoms. He continued to live on his farm until a couple of years ago, when he sold it and went to Washington Territory, where he is still living.

When we had found our claims we returned to Reid's after our families, and moved to our new home. We camped under a large cottonwood tree, whose shade made it very pleasant during the day. Near by was a spring which afforded good drinking water; also plenty for cooking purposes.

My partner concluded to camp with us until we could build each of us a

---

[1]Laura A. Pool married Freeman on 13 February 1861 in Eaton County, Michigan (Pension Records, National Archives).

house, as the women would get very lonely in our absence from camp.[2] We were very comfortably settled and enjoyed ourselves nicely. The weather had been delightful during our trip from Augusta. The nights had been equally as beautiful as the days, and the moon was now full and shone so brightly, making it almost as light as day.

Nothing happened to mar our happiness and contentment until the next day about 10 o'clock, when J. M. Thomas, the man I have referred to before as the clerk of Cox & Epperson, came riding up to our camp at full speed, saying the Indians were making trouble in our locality and that they had probably killed a man by the name of Fred Crats.[3] While he was telling us about it, C. H. Stone came up and said he did not think there was any danger of the Indians molesting us, as they were going up Bluff Creek! This creek was about two miles south of our camp.

Upon hearing this startling news my wife became badly frightened and it was some time before we could quiet her fears. I was well aware that when people were frightened they were liable to misrepresent circumstances and make things appear as bad as they possibly can.

I will tell the actual facts relating the shooting of Crats by the Indians, as he afterwards told it.

It seems Crats had a claim on Bluff Creek some five or six miles from Caldwell. At the time the shooting occurred he had been to town and was on his return home. He was riding on a fine, large mule and was about a mile and a half from town when he was overtaken by two Indians. The Indians were riding ponies and one was armed with a gun while the other had a bow and a quiver of arrows.

As they came up to him he saluted them with the usual way of saluting the Indian, by saying, "How." Their responding salutation consisted of low grunts. His fears were aroused by their manner of addressing him, as they commonly address a man with, "How, John."

As they rode up to his side one of them threw up his coat tail, as he supposed, to see if he was armed. In those days if a man had no gun with him he was almost sure to have on a belt containing a couple of revolvers and many times a knife.

Crats had neither a gun, revolver, or knife (excepting a small pocket knife), which they soon found out by raising his coat. Crats said it was the only time he had ever left home without taking his revolvers.

[2]Freeman's children at the time were Rhoda (b. 4 May 1864), Elihu (b. 4 January 1867), and Oscar C. (b. 11 August 1867). King had four children, ranging in age from fifteen years to two years, and his wife was pregnant with a fifth (Pension Records; 1875 Census Records, Caldwell Township, Kansas State Historical Society Archives [cited hereafter as KSHS]).

[3]The *SCP Chronology* (1 January 1880) gives the date of the attack on Dutch Fred as 15 June 1871. Freeman's narration makes it appear that the incident occurred on June 7.

The Indians appeared very brave after they saw they had the advantage of him, and Crats knowing that fact became submissive at once. He was a German and a powerfully built man, and could have whipped them both in a fist-fight, but that was not their mode of fighting just then.

One of the Indians rode in front, took hold of the mule's bridle, while the other pretended to drive it. By their gestures and broken English they told Crats they wanted him to go on a buffalo hunt, which Crats knew meant death for him. He thought they wanted his mule, and to get it they would take him away from the settlement and kill him.

They traveled until they were within a hundred yards or more from a bend in the creek. Then, seeing a chance for life, he quickly jumped from his mule and started on a run for the brush and bluffs.

When he had got a short distance the one with the gun fired at him, but the bullet had nearly spent its force before reaching him. About this time the gun was a new weapon to the Indians, and consequently they were not very well versed in the manner of loading them; many times they would load too heavy and often they would load their guns only putting in powder and paper.

The bullet from the Indian's gun did not have force enough to kill him, for when it struck his back-bone it glanced off and did not enter his body.

The other Indian shot at him with his bow, this shot taking effect. The arrow struck him in the arm, glanced upward, tearing his arm in a frightful manner up to his shoulder.

When they saw he was not yet their game they let the mule loose and started and ran after him. He dodged them and succeeded in crossing the creek. They saw him after he had crossed and started to find a place they could cross with their ponies. Here the creek has bluffs on both sides and it is very difficult to cross [except] at the fords, which are sometimes many miles apart. Perhaps it would be well enough to say Bluff Creek derived its name from its banks, which are very high and bluffy.

The Indians went down the creek for the purpose of finding a crossing, thinking Crats would hide in the grass and they could easily find him. But instead of going south he again crossed the creek and hid himself in a pile of driftwood, which would merely conceal him from their view should they come that way.

The idea did not strike them that he would return to the north bank, so after searching among the bluffs and looking through the tall grass without finding him, they rode on up the creek. They also failed to catch the mule again after turning it loose when they were in pursuit of Crats.

Crats lay for several hours in the drift and was bleeding profusely, weakening him very much. He managed to reach Reid's dug-out where a physician was called to attend him.[4]

His escapade nearly cost him his life, and as it was he was left considerably defective in a physical point of view. It is said Crats presented a claim to the government against the Osage Indian fund for five thousand dollars. Whether his claim was allowed or not I never learned. But I am quite sure his claim for damages was entirely too low, as he, in all probability, will be an invalid and a partial cripple for life; for the bullet entering his back affected the spine, causing a lameness of the back, and the arrow entering his arm [made] a cut which caused a partial paralysis.[5]

When we had recovered from our Indian scare sufficiently to change the theme of conversation, I told Mr. Thomas we were about to commence building a dug-out to live in. He said he would get some help for us, and went back to town. Soon after several men came, bringing spades, shovels, and axes with them. We were soon at work plowing, digging, and shoveling dirt.

My dug-out was to be fourteen by twenty-eight feet in dimensions. To make it required three logs twenty-eight feet long; also poles enough to cover the top closely. First we plowed what we could, then took spades and shovels and began spading the earth out in the shape required. After digging perhaps six or seven feet in the ground, we made a door at the opening, put on a ridge pole in the center, then laid on the poles we had hauled for that purpose and covered it with dirt, after first covering the poles with straw, dried grass or hay. The dirt is thrown on top until the dug-out resembles an ordinary mound of earth some four or five feet in height.

[4]The physician was probably Dr. B. W. Fox (Andreas, p. 1503), who will appear again in this narrative.

The attack on Crats apparently was witnessed by Texas cowboys. W. F. Cude (*Trail Drivers of Texas,* I, 218): "Next morning just about sunup, I heard a gunshot down at [Bluff] creek and in a few minutes we saw two Indians running two mules as fast as they could go. They had shot a white man with a gun and arrows. He came dragging up to our camp with one arrow still sticking in him and one of the boys pulled it out and we carried him to a tent not far away." Though Cude dates the incident 1872, it appears to be the same episode Freeman describes.

The incident was reported in the *Oxford Times,* 22 June 1871, with the intelligence that Dutch Fred was reported to be "in the habit of selling liquor to the Indians, and some trouble had occurred between him and the tribe," which the *Times* identifies as Osage. The *Times* also reports Crats as having "four arrows in him and two wounds from pistol shots." Oxford is about thirty miles northeast of Caldwell. The reader with a mathematical bent can calculate the exact percentage per mile by which a piece of news could become exaggerated in 1871.

[5]I have been unable to find a record of a claim for damages—which is, of course, not the same thing as saying no claim was ever filed. Anyone who has tried to trace early claims for Indian depredations will understand the inherent difficulties. This particular search is further handicapped by the fact that Freeman, not always reliable with names, is the only known source for Dutch Fred's last name.

We worked far into the night and about 9 o'clock the finishing strokes were done and we began unloading the wagons. Our household furniture was very limited. When we spoke of the cupboard, in reality we meant a cracker-box with a partition in the center of it, the box being fastened against the wall. And often when we spoke of a chair, in reality we would mean a box which we used in the place of that article. Our beds many times were made of poles and corded with a rope, which we used in preference to making slats of cottonwood poles.

The next in order would be something to eat, which the women soon prepared. Our friends and co-laborers ate supper with us and several remained over night at our dug-out.

The men, or cow-boys, as they were called, worked manfully. They were very energetic and a nice class of young men. The reader must not picture the cow-boy as a desperado, for many times they are kindhearted and sympathetic. I have known a number of very fine, cultured young men, who hungered for notoriety, who satisfied this appetite by becoming cow-boys. The majority of the cow-boys are a drinking, carousing set of young men, and are rough when under the influence of liquor, but take them when they are sober and you will not find any one that will help you in time of trouble more than this class of young men.

The cow-boy endures many hardships while attending to his duty; rain or shine, hot or cold, he is always to be found at his post. The more severe the weather the more his services are needed; their life is indeed a hard one to live; quite often they use their saddle for a pillow, the saddle blanket for a coverlet, and mother earth as their bed.

They are generally a healthy class of boys when they first begin to "herd," but, a continuation of sleeping on the ground, night herding in the rain or snow storm, and the habit of frequently indulging in a social glass of whiskey, soon break them down in constitution and before they have lived to that age in which manhood is supposed to reach its prime, they find themselves to be old men and a wreck, physically speaking.

We were now comfortably fixed and settled down to housekeeping; my wife busied herself with her duties and household cares, while I set myself to work fixing up our new home. Sometimes I would take my gun and dogs, and go hunting. Game was very plentiful, and it was not difficult to go out a short distance from the dug-out and shoot either a plover, prairie chicken, or jack rabbit.

Wolves too, abounded here; the few chickens which were brought from the East fared very hard; at night they were shut up in a close coop, to keep the wolves from getting them.

One beautiful moonlight night I heard my dog howling, and seemingly, coming in the direction of the dugout;[6] every yelp he gave I thought would be his last; I got my gun, a trusty Winchester rifle, and went to the door; I had no sooner opened it, when the dog leaped into the room and seemed to be very much frightened.

I looked out to see what had caused his terrible fright, and saw four big, gray wolves, within thirty yards of the dug-out.

I shot at them but did not kill any. The next morning I was out in that direction and saw where I had shot my plow; it had been left there on the prairie, where we had been plowing.

We were well pleased, this far, with our late move. The women were lonesome, but they enjoyed themselves in roaming up and down the banks of the little stream near our claims.[7]

The weather continued to be delightful, the air pure and fragrant, the climate entrancingly mild, the sky clear and blue, and we thought we had, indeed, found a paradise.

I began plowing and planting corn; I broke the prairie, then planted the corn on the sod; I also planted some late garden seeds, and in a short time we reaped a benefit from both, for the season proved to be a favorable one for us.

---

[6] Apparently Freeman was no longer living in the dugout when this particular incident occurred. The same thing may be said of the mountain-lion episode in the next chapter. The reader is reminded that Freeman was careless of transitions and chronological sequence.

[7] Probably Little Casino Creek, which empties into Fall Creek south of Freeman's claim.

CHAPTER 4

Adventure with a Mountain Lion—The Mountain Lion Seeks
Refuge in the Dug-Out Window—A Fight in Which Both
Dogs Are Whipped—The Lion Makes J. M.
Thomas Leave the Road—Finally
Killed by O. G. Wells.

Soon after my arrival in Caldwell in 1871, and while I was living on my claim one and a half miles west of town, I had an adventure with a mountain lion.

One beautiful moonlight night, after we had retired for the night, I had about entered the land of dreams, when I was aroused from my slumbers by the barking of my dog; I hastily left my bed, without taking the necessary time to arrange my toilet, and I just got to the door in time to see an animal jump into the dug-out window with my dog in pursuit, not very far distant, barking furiously.

I concluded to take in the chase, and ran out the door and up to the window and looked in to see where and what it was.

I saw what I supposed to be a dog, and thinking to start the chase again, I would kick it and thereby cause it to jump out of the window. In this I was mistaken, for, instead of retreating, it manifested a desire to hold the fort; so you may imagine who did the retreating.

By this time my wife appeared on the scene, and asked "what is it?" I made the reply, "we'll soon see what it is," and went out and untied a large dog, which I kept as a watch dog.

I knew the fighting qualities of that dog was hard to beat, as he was sure to be the champion in a dog fight, and I thought he would come out victorious now.

As soon as he knew he was loose, he started for the animal, and I suppose, he "smelt the battle afar," and knew it was better to run like a man than be whipped like a coward. For, notwithstanding my many words of encouragement, and with a promise to help him win the day, he stood as still as a monument.

I finally told my wife to keep the dogs with her and I would reconnoiter a little. I soon had my gun, and entered the dug-out for the purpose of shooting the animal.

In the dug-out I had a portion partitioned off in which I kept my horses at night. To get in a suitable position for shooting, I had to pass between my horses; when I had arrived at a place in which I could use my gun to an advantage, the animal, like the dog, had "scented the battle afar," and I have no doubt, concluded the reception would be too warm for it.

As it leaped from the window, both dogs were soon upon the animal, I ran out to see the fight, thinking the dogs would surely kill it. I soon saw, to my surprise, that the dogs were getting the worst of the fight, as they would give an occasional yelp, which convinced me that they were being badly dealt with.

I could not shoot to advantage for fear of hitting one of the dogs, and I soon saw it was not a dog they were fighting, but a large mountain lion.

These lions are very ferocious when attacked by man. They resemble the African lion in most respects, only in size, the mountain lion being the smaller of the two. Had I known what it was, I certainly should have hesitated before kicking at it.

After fighting the dogs awhile, it started on the run; before I could get ready to shoot, it had bounded away in the darkness.

The next morning J. M. Thomas had an encounter with the lion, near my house. He had been to the ranch of Cox & Epperson and was on his return home. He said he was riding along peacefully, enjoying the morning air, when suddenly his horse shied, and on looking before him saw a mountain lion in the road.

He rode on, thinking every moment to see it bound away and hunt a place of refuge. But to his astonishment, he found it had no idea of leaving just then.

He concluded that "discretion is the better part of valor" and pulled his horses rein to guide him safely by.

A short time after this happened, O. G. Wells shot and killed a mountain lion.[1] Upon measuring it, it was found to be nine foot two inches long.

The lions are often seen near the cattle ranches, and many times show a disposition to fight when they are attacked by man. They are frequently to be seen devouring a cow which they have killed and many are the calves which give up their lives to satisfy their appetites.

---

[1] Orman G. Wells is listed in the roster of Upton Post, Grand Army of the Republic, as having been a private in the First Iowa Battery (*Caldwell Journal,* 27 March 1881). He was married to one of the daughters of H. J. Devore (see chap. 2, n. 3, and chap. 26, n. 5). Wells became proprietor of the Skeleton Creek Stage Ranch, Indian Territory, in 1885. Wells and his wife were remembered as excellent hosts at Skeleton Creek during the days of the Cherokee Strip Live Stock Association (*Caldwell Journal,* 5 November 1885; George D. Rainey, *The Cherokee Strip,* p. 193).

Freeman says Wells shot a lion "shortly after" the wounding of Fred Crats. Either Freeman has telescoped time or Wells was the premier lion killer of southern Kansas, for in 1879 he is credited with leading the attack against a catamount treed on I. N. Cooper's place, just south and west of town. The hide of the slain beast was delivered for display at the Mammoth Cave Drug Store (*Caldwell Post,* 11 September 1879).

CHAPTER 5

A Brief History of Caldwell—The Killing of George Peay—The Friends
of Peay Act as Watchers—Arrival of the Winfield
Sheriff—O'Bannan Skips the Country.

After giving the reader a description of Caldwell as she appeared in her infancy, I will endeavor to give a history of facts and incidents that have actually occurred within her borders.

Every name given in this book [is] real, not fictitious, and many of the people, whom I shall mention before this work is completed, are residents of Caldwell or are earning their living by honest toil, living on their farms in this vicinity.

On March 1st, 1871, the town of Caldwell was located, and named in honor of United States Senator Caldwell, of Leavenworth, Kansas, by a company consisting of C. H. Stone, J. H. Dagner, and G. A. Smith.[1]

The great Chisholm trail, entering the State near this town, gave it the name of a "cattle town." Consequently it had in and about it a class of people who have caused much disorder and bloodshed.

From its location, it was always the favorite resort of the desperadoes and thieves, as it was only a short distance from the Indian Territory, which place afforded them a hiding place after they had indulged in some shooting affray or had been on a thieving expedition. It was also the home of the "cowboy" upon entering the state, after a long, dusty twelve hundred mile ride. Need we wonder why, in its early day, it was a fast and dangerous town.

The "cow-boy" was not considered a resident, for his was only transient trade. Upon entering the state they would visit the supply stores, lay in a supply of coffee, flour, bacon, and gather in the entire stock of liquids.

As the tide of civilization crowded west, and men of integrity, ability, and of a determined character immigrated to the western towns and became enterprising citizens, the rougher element could not prevail, hence they too must immigrate west to the frontier towns. It has been said that on these conditions, the crowded cities of Emporia, Newton, and Wichita gave up their most reckless citizens to make up a band of rustlers, horse thieves, and bad characters to populate Caldwell.

---

[1] The town company consisted of Charles Gilbert, president; G. A. Smith, secretary; C. H. Stone, treasurer; and J. H. Dagnar, according to A. A. Richards (Andreas, pp. 1501-1502, and "History of Sumner County," *Historical Atlas,* p. 8). The *Caldwell Messenger* (3 September 1953) adds George Vantilberg and Chris Pierce, identifying all six men as residents of Wichita.

The succeeding six paragraphs contain sentences randomly plagiarized from Richards in the *Historical Atlas* and from the *Caldwell Journal* of 1 January 1885.

It is said by many that Caldwell was started with a population of two, and both of them non-residents.[2]

The railroad terminus was about one hundred and fifty miles distant; consequently all supplies had to be hauled on wagons. Emporia furnished the base of supplies for the groceries and saloon.[3] Articles in the line of provisions were very limited. The grocers stock consisted of flour, bacon, salt, soda, coffee, tobacco, and whiskey. Often the "cow-boy" would buy all his groceries; he would then buy another invoice very much like the first, excepting that it was not so large and of a poorer quality.[4]

I will now chronicle the killing of George Peas [Peay], which occurred on the second [third] day of July, 1871.[5] He was the first victim to fall at the hands of his adversary. In those days strength was not the criterion by which we read the character of the man, relative to his bravery. Strength only consisted in the man who stood the firmest behind the six-shooter, and the six-shooter cut quite a figure in the early part of the history of Caldwell.

This man Peay was a claim taker and was looked upon by the people as a man that would use "stray stock" to his own advantage and for the good of his pocket-book.

He was a large, well built man, some six feet in height, and probably weighing two hundred pounds. He was a very quarrelsome man when under the influence of whiskey, always boasting of his physical strength. He was rarely engaged in a fight because his arrogant boasts would intimidate his comrades.

He was living on a claim five or six miles East of Caldwell, near Bluff Creek, and on adjoining claims lived four or five friends of his. They were "batching" and spent the greater part of their time in town.

The man who killed him, O'Bannan by name,[6] was a very different man

[2] According to the *Caldwell Journal* (1 January 1885), referring to C. H. Stone and Mr. Cox. Stone, despite his Andreas biography, was associated with Wichita and Coffeyville as late as 1883 (*Caldwell Journal*, 10 May 1883).

[3] Freeman garbles his source at this point. The nearest railhead in 1871 was Abilene, some 180 miles from Caldwell; in 1872, Wichita, 80 miles distant. Emporia, over 200 miles away, may have been a supply source, but Freeman has fused two sentences from the *Caldwell Journal* (1 January 1885), one dealing with supplies from the railhead and the other dealing with Emporia as a principal source of Caldwell's early roughneck population.

[4] This confusing statement results from Freeman's garbling his source again. The original reads: "He [the grocer] settled down, started a grocery store, with liquid groceries preponderating, and after awhile the cowboys . . . dropped down on him, gathered in his bacon, coffee and beans and entire stock of liquids. He bought another invoice just like the first, except that it was larger and of a poor quality" (*Caldwell Journal*, 1 January 1885; see also chap. 2, n. 1, for a previous use of this same passage).

[5] 3 July 1871 is the date given by Andreas, p. 1495, and the *SCP Chronology* (1 January 1880). Freeman consistently spells the name *Peas*.

[6] O. Bannon is the name given in Andreas and the *SCP Chronology*. To my knowledge Freeman is the only extant source with full descriptions of the participants.

in disposition and character. O'Bannan was a Canadian by birth, a man small of stature, but very different in character. He bore a favorable reputation, was courageous in movements of peril, was not hasty in disposition, and controlled his temper at his bidding.

He, in company with George Mack and H. H. Davidson,[7] was living in a "dug-out" west from Caldwell, about five miles. They were also keeping cattle on the same range together, and the three men "batched" together.

On the day the shooting occurred, Peay with his friends were in Caldwell, having a fine time, so to speak. Peay was considerably under the influence of whiskey, and his friends thought he was liable to have trouble and took his revolver from him. O'Bannan happened to be in town the same day, and to all appearances was attending to his own business affairs.

Peay came up to O'Bannan and wanted to fight. O'Bannan knew Peay would be the best man in a fight, and not wanting to have anything to do with him, told him he did not care to fight and left Peay. He turned and went into the store, followed by Peay who soon began to talk in an insulting manner and all the while trying to get O'Bannan to fight with him. O'Bannan finally told him to let him alone, and if he did not he would certainly wish he had, and went out of the store.

Soon he was followed by Peay, who by this time was determined to pick a quarrel; he walked up to O'Bannan as though he intended to take hold of him. At this O'Bannan pulled his revolver intending to shoot at him. The revolver was [of] the cap and ball style and would not go off. He then told Peay to let him alone, saying "my revolver failed to fire that time, but perhaps it won't next time."

O'Bannan borrowed a revolver from a friend of his; this one proved to be a good one, as the friends of Peay found out after he had been its target. As soon as Peay saw O'Bannan again, he became abusive as before. By this time, "forbearance had ceased to be a virtue" with O'Bannan, and he was determined he would not be imposed upon by Peay.

As Peay came to him he took his revolver from his belt and taking deliberate aim, seemingly as cool as though he was going to shoot a beef, pulled the trigger and Peay staggered backward and fell, saying as he did so, "God, boys, I'm shot."

O'Bannan seemed wholly unconcerned, but was satisfied. His aim had been true and his bullet had accomplished its errand. There on the sidewalk in front of him lay Peay breathing his last breath. As soon as the report and the smoke of the revolver had died away, O'Bannan turned on his heel, half-way round, and facing the friends of Peay, said, "gentlemen, I have killed

---

[7] George Mack was elected justice of the peace for the Fourth Precinct in the special election of 26 September 1871. H. H. Davidson became a prominent Shorthorn cattle breeder in Sumner County, settling in Wellington in 1873 (Andreas, p. 1498).

Peay, now if there is any one here that wants to take it up, they have the privilege of doing so, for I am in good shooting order."

The friends of Peay had nothing to say and O'Bannan got on his horse and left town.

It was then late in the afternoon and the friends of Peay took his body to an old vacant building, which I think had been used as a saloon. They intended to act as "watchers" over the dead body of their friend. They were still drinking freely of the vile stuff known as whiskey.

After they had removed Peay's body, they took turns in drinking and watching. They would get on their horses, ride up and down the street yelling like demons and firing off their revolvers. Then they would return to the house, talk to their dead friend, and beg of him to get up and take a drink. This barbarous treatment was kept up during the night, and when the sun rose above the horizon it looked upon a scene which would arouse the sympathy in any kind heart, and put a blush of shame upon the cheek of the drunkard.

O'Bannan went to King's camp (which was located on my claim in front of my dug-out) after leaving town, and on his way shot and killed a steer belonging to Cox & Epperson. I heard of it and told them about it. O'Bannan found out I had reported to Cox & Epperson concerning it, and threatened my life. I did not know but what he would come to my place and make trouble. But if he had any idea of carrying out his threat, he certainly thought it best not to try it, for when we got up next morning we found he had left King's camp.

In the meantime the officers at Winfield had been informed of the shooting affray at Caldwell, and Deputy Sheriff T. H. B. Ross[8] came over to arrest O'Bannan. O'Bannan had said no live man could arrest him, as he considered he had only defended himself. Ross remained in Caldwell several days thinking O'Bannan would come to town. O'Bannan's friends sent him word that the Deputy Sheriff was in town for him, and after remaining in his dug-out for a few days he left the country.

[8] Why the deputy sheriff of Cowley County would have jurisdiction is a question I cannot answer. Possibly he also held a deputy U. S. marshal's commission, a circumstance which seems to have been common for local law officers at that time. Thomas Hart Benton Ross figures in this narrative again, identified as Bent. He was the son of early Cowley County settler T. B. Ross (Andreas, p. 1596). Bent Ross served in the Civil War as a private in Company K, Eighty-ninth Illinois Infantry (*Caldwell Journal,* 27 March 1884). He left Winfield and settled in Caldwell by 1873, where he died in January, 1885. Ross practiced law in Caldwell and was involved in almost every civic project the city undertook. His activities ranged from functioning as school board secretary (over nine years) to managing the Opera House Skating Rink. At the time of his death he was city police judge and justice of the peace for Caldwell Township (*Caldwell Post,* 5 October 1882; *Caldwell Commercial,* 8 February, 5 April 1883; *Caldwell Journal,* 29 January 1885; see also chap. 39, n. 7).

From Caldwell, he went to Abilene, Kansas, and I heard he said "while he believed he was justified in killing Peay, he did not care to stand trial."

Thus the chapter closes, chronicling the first murder committed in Caldwell.[9]

---

[9]In 1874, inquiries about Peay's killing were made in Sumner County on behalf of Peay's family and heirs in Cherokee County. It seems that one of Peay's friends had attempted to negotiate a note for $900, property of the deceased. Whether Freeman was asked to testify is unknown. The newspaper account of this inquiry includes a version of the affray which differs in many particulars from Freeman's: "George Peay was not quarrelsome, but his blood was warmed by drink, when a thoughtless word, half in jest, brought the answering taunt which provoked a keen retort—met halfway by the pistol's dash, and the remains of George Peay were laid away from mortal sight." O'Bannan is not named; the murderer is said to be one of the "army of reckless cowboys" that plagued Caldwell in those days (*SCP*, 15 October 1874). The foregoing reads as though it were written for Cherokee County consumption. Freeman seems more credible.

CHAPTER 6.

Organization of the County—Officers Elected—Towns Con-
tending for the County Seat—Governor Harvey Makes
Appointments—Wellington Comes Out Victorious.
Arrests Made by the Officers—Prisoners Cut
Their Way out of the "Cooler"—The
Bondsmen Pay the Bond.

Up to this time the county was yet unorganized.[1] The people began to awaken to the fact that county officers were badly needed. For the past two years, the rougher element had full control of the county, but now the people were determined that lawlessness should not prevail at all hazards. The people had organized themselves into committees by different names, the most conspicuous assuming the name of the Vigilants. The majority of the law-abiding citizens became members of this committee and concluded to take the law into their hands, for murder, thefts, and lawlessness of various kinds must be subdued either by civil law or justice meted out at the end of a rope which was tied to the limb of a cotton-wood tree.[2]

The people were becoming aroused by the numerous outrages committed, and deemed it necessary to act immediately upon some measure to quell all disturbances, and have peace and good-will reign supreme.

This county was named in honor of Hon. Charles Sumner, of Massachusetts. Many of the Senator's admirers opposed the proposition of giving the name of Sumner to this treeless and trackless portion of "The Great American Desert," contending it would be an insult to his greatness.[3]

---

[1] Freeman appears to mean by "the county was yet unorganized" that officials had not yet been elected—that is, if one takes the term "up to this time" to mean up to July, 1871, when the events of the preceding chapter occurred. In point of fact, as Freeman notes later, the county was officially organized by the proclamation of Governor James M. Harvey on 7 February 1871.

The appointed, temporary county commissioners having done nothing toward holding an election of county officers, a settlers' meeting was called on 15 July 1871 by certain citizens in order to force the issue.

[2] Vigilante committees figure prominently in this history, but this is the principal occasion on which Freeman gives a credible account of the makeup of such groups. When he gets down to specific vigilante activities, Freeman becomes coy or evasive about participants, which is only to be expected when one's neighbors and possibly oneself have been involved. As to the morality of frontier vigilante groups, I leave the final decision to the reader, noting only that Freeman's history itself dramatizes that the settlers in this border community were sorely and repeatedly provoked.

[3] A paragraph loosely paraphrased from Richards, "History of Sumner County," *Historical Atlas,* p. 7.

It is difficult to imagine that as late as 1871 people in southeastern Kansas could still

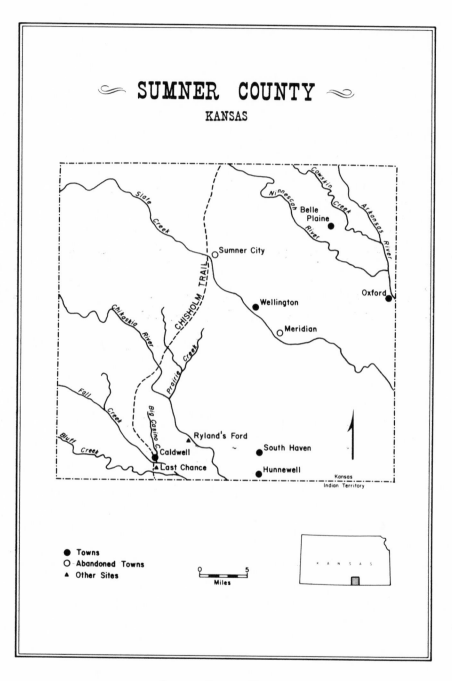

Sumner County, Kansas

50

Sumner County is thirty-three miles wide, North and South, and thirty-six miles wide, East and West, the Indian Territory bordering it on the South its entire length. It contains 760,320 acres of land.

The county was formally organized by the governor's proclamation on February 7th, 1871, and the first county seat election, and election of permanent county officers, was held on September 26th, 1871. The county was divided into three commissioner's districts, and into four voting precincts.[4] The election of the first precinct was held at Belle Plaine; the election of the second precinct was held at the house of Henry Brown, in Greene Township; the third precinct held their election at Wellington; the fourth voting precinct included the southwest quarter of the county; the election was held at Colson and Ryland's Ranch.[5] This territory has since been divided,[6] and now includes the following named townships: Morris, Chikaskia, Downs, Jackson, South Haven, Falls, Caldwell, and Bluff.

The first county officers elected were the following named individuals:[7] County Commissioner, First District, David Richards;[8] Second District, A. D. Rosencrans; Third District, Reuben Riggs;[9] County Clerk, C. S. Broadbent;[10]

---

believe that the country west of the Arkansas River was indeed a desert. Yet, as John H. Folks explains, the belief was fed by the fact that immediately east of the Arkansas, the country was "disfigured by huge boulders and piles on piles of rocks and stones." He recounts the wonder with which he viewed the fertile prairie of Sumner County on an exploratory trip in the spring of 1871 (*SCP,* 1 January 1880).

[4] Andreas (p. 1495) mistakenly asserts that the county was divided into only three "Commissioners Precincts," omitting Wellington as a polling place. Freeman's description is correct (per "Special Election Proclamation" in the *Oxford Times,* 24 August 1871).

[5] A. M. Colson and J. A. Ryland have, since we encountered them in chap. 1, established a claim on the Chikaskia River about five miles north and east of Caldwell. Their brief partnership is described in chap. 45.

[6] By "this territory" Freeman means the Fourth Voting Precinct.

[7] The special election of 26 September 1871 was occasioned by pressure from the settlers on the temporary county commissioners. However, since a regular election was due to be held in November, most of those elected in September did not bother to qualify for the offices by posting the requisite bond; and, of those who did, few appear to have performed any official duties (J. G. Campbell in *Wellington Monitor-Press,* 24 August 1921). It was just as well. The November election produced a new clutch of officers, the only survivors being C. S. Brodbent, G. M. Miller, C. D. Brande, W. A. Thompson, and Reuben Riggs, though Riggs was now county attorney instead of Third District Commissioner (Andreas, pp. 1495-96).

[8] David Richards operated the county's first ferry, across the Arkansas River opposite Belle Plaine (Andreas, p. 1495). Richards was also one of the temporary county commissioners, being appointed on 15 June 1871 to replace J. J. Abeel.

[9] Reuben Riggs deserves enshrinement somewhere. He was a frontier settler of the first water, moving west each time community became oppressive. He was the first county attorney elected in Marion County, Kansas (7 August 1865), and shortly thereafter he was elected senator from that county (November, 1865). He was the first probate judge elected

County Treasurer, R. Freeman;[11] Probate Judge, G. M. Miller; Register of Deeds, J. Romine;[12] Sheriff, J. J. Ferguson;[13] Coroner, Charles D. Brande;[14]

---

in Sedgwick County, Kansas (April, 1870). His election as the first Third District commissioner in Sumner County must give him the world's record for firsts (Andreas, pp. 1255, 156, 1385). As Albert A. Richards said, Riggs was indeed one of these who "made the settlement and organization of new counties a lifetime profession." Richards went on to say that Riggs "was a man of more than three score years and yet he had never seen an apple hanging on a tree, so constantly had he been on the frontier, having assisted in the organization of eleven counties in Illinois, Missouri, Iowa, Nebraska, and Kansas, and eventually he died, January 7, 1873, from the effects of a severe freezing which he underwent while on a trip west to help organize Barber county" ("History of Sumner County," *Historical Atlas*, p. 8). H. C. St. Clair reported that Riggs moved from Tennessee when a boy; "in his lifetime he has improved seventeen farms" (*Belle Plaine Herald*, 19 August 1871, repr. *SCP*, 28 September 1882).

[10] C. S. Brodbent was one of the pioneer settlers of Sumner County, arriving in November of 1870 (Letter to *SCP*, 22 January 1880) and settling on Slate Creek southeast of Wellington. Brodbent was elected to the office of county clerk at three consecutive elections. He was appointed by Governor Thomas A. Osborn to the first Board of Commissioners on Public Institutions in 1873 (Andreas, pp. 1495-96, 281). He resigned his offices in 1875 and left for Texas, bitter over mudslinging against him, which had begun in his 1873 campaign for county clerk and had increased in the period following (*SCP*, 9 October 1873; Correspondence Received, Papers of Governor T. A. Osborn, KSHS). Brodbent had poor luck as a Texas cattleman (*Trail Drivers of Texas*, 2:592-94) and eventually settled in San Antonio, where he became an active and prominent citizen (*Wellington Monitor-Press*, 24 August 1921). Though he never returned to Kansas as a resident, Brodbent was a frequent correspondent to Sumner County newspapers throughout the years, and his reminiscences in those periodicals remain valuable sources of frontier history.

[11] R. Freeman was one of the earliest settlers of Sumner County and a member of the company which organized the short-lived town of Nennescah (Andreas, p. 1495). He was not related to the author as nearly as I can determine.

[12] Romine settled in Sumner County near Oxford in the fall of 1870. He was a disabled Civil War veteran, having lost his right arm in battle. The *Oxford Times* endorsed Romine for the office of register of deeds on the grounds that "It is our duty to place such heroes in positions they can acceptably fill, thereby paying off a debt of gratitude we owe every one of them" (9 September 1871). While Romine carried the day in the special election, he lost to William Nixon in the regular November election. The *Time*'s appeal to gratitude was countered by the *Belle Plaine Sumner County Herald*, which asked, "Are we duty bound to place the affairs of our county in the hands of inexperienced and incompetent individuals because of their bodily ailments?" It went on to assert that "it is a fact established beyond a doubt that all bodily ailments effect the mind and destroy in a degree, its effectual workings and vigor." The *Herald*, in the same issue, contained the announcement of William Nixon as a candidate for the office of register of deeds. Nixon was editor of the *Herald* (*Oxford Times*, 14 October 1871; Andreas, p. 1505). Sometime after 1875, Nixon fled to Texas. A. A. Richards later observed, "His absence was an honor to the county." Nixon, it seems, had debauched a Wellington girl (*SCP*, 18 March 1880, 2 June 1881).

[13] J. J. Ferguson was from Belle Plaine (*SCP*, 18 March 1880).

[14] Brande served as coroner until 8 November 1874, when he moved from the state (Richards, "History of Sumner County," *Historical Atlas*, p. 10).

County Attorney, George N. Godfrey;[15] Clerk of the District Court, W. A. Thompson;[16] Superintendent of Public Instruction, A. M. Colson;[17] County Surveyor, W. A. Ramsey.

As this book relates largely to the southern part of the county, I will only name the officers elected to office in the Fourth Precinct: C. E. Sullivan,[18] Trustee; M. H. Lester and George Mack, Justices of the Peace;[19] Frank Barrington,[20] Clerk; G. W. Peters, Treasurer; C. P. Epps[21] and John J. Youell, Constables; T. S. Anderson and Noble Jewitt, Road Overseers. The total number of votes polled in the county was 805.

During this time a great race was being made to determine where the county seat should be located. The towns contesting for the county seat were Wellington, Sumner City, Meridian, and Belle Plaine.[22] Gov. Harvey issued

[15] George N. Godfrey of Oxford was elected at the settlers' meeting of 16 July 1871 to a committee to press the temporary commissioners for an election of county officers (*Oxford Times*, 20 July 1871).

[16] W. A. Thompson, as clerk of the district court, was the victim of a zealous partisan in the county-seat contest. On 9 April 1872, a runoff election was held to determine whether Wellington or Oxford would be the official county seat. Oxford residents, suspecting vote fraud, obtained an injunction restraining the county commissioners from canvassing the vote until a hearing could be held before the district court. Mr. Thompson brought the injunction to Wellington on the evening before the commissioners were to meet. He checked into the Frontier House, a hotel operated by Orange Scott Cummins (the future "Pilgrim Bard" of Kansas and Oklahoma). During the night, Cummins stole the injunction from the sleeping Mr. Thompson—who was bitterly denounced as a "basswood puttyhead" by an Oxford correspondent to the *Wichita Eagle*—and Wellington carried the day (*Wellington Monitor-Press*, 24 August 1921; *Wichita Eagle*, 19 April 1872).

[17] Colson, though he was to serve in many elected offices in later years, did not post the qualifying bond and so never actually held this office (see chap. 45).

[18] A number of people in early Sumner County were residents of Sedgwick County to the north; many of these were taking claims for speculation or for possible permanent occupancy later. C. E. Sullivan may have been one of these; a man by that name was one of the first settlers of Kechi Township, Sedgwick County, and contributed to D. B. Emmert's "History of Sedgwick County" in John P. Edwards's *Historical Atlas of Sedgwick County, Kansas,* pp. 7, 9.

[19] George Mack was one of the partners of O'Bannan, who killed George Peay (see chapter 5).

[20] Frank Barrington, one of the co-owners of the trader's ranch on the Chikaskia River (chap. 1) in present-day Chikaskia Township.

[21] C. P. Epps is probably the Epps involved in the killing of William Manning (chap. 7).

[22] "During this time . . ."—Freeman is again vague. In the context of the entire paragraph, the time indicated appears to be the period before Governor Harvey issued his proclamation organizing the county. If this is the case, the contest for county seat was essentially a contest to receive the governor's designation as temporary county seat. At that stage in Sumner County history, the main contenders were Sumner City (soon to be defunct) and the imaginary town of Meridian. Two other towns, Nennescah and Union City, were earlier candidates which perished as town entities before they could make a serious bid. When it came time to choose a county seat by ballot, the contenders were all of those

a proclamation on February 7th, 1871, appointing Meridian as the temporary county seat; in accordance with the prayer of a petition from Meridian, [he] also appointed W. J. Ughler, J. S. McMahon, and J. J. Abell [Abeel], Temporary County Commissioners.

As a matter of fact, Meridian was at this time a purely imaginary town, as its site had not been so much as staked out or stepped off.[23] It was not until July 17, 1871, that the town company was organized. No steps were taken toward providing for the seat of county government at Meridian, and when the commissioners met on June 15, 1871, on the open prairie near the supposed site of the town, they ordered the future business of the county to be transacted at Wellington. After much wrangling between towns and several elections, Wellington became the permanent county seat.[24]

It was now to be hoped that lawlessness would cease and that our county would make rapid strides toward civilization and assume the responsibility

---

mentioned by Freeman, plus Oxford (Richards, "History of Sumner County," *Historical Atlas,* p. 8).

[23] The history of Meridian and the events leading up to Governor Harvey's proclamation of 7 February 1871 need some fleshing out. A. J. Angell, of Leavenworth, Kansas, had the contract to conduct the official survey of Sumner County. In collusion with W. J. Ughler, of Wichita, Angell apparently devised a plan to gain control of the county and profit by selling town lots in the county seat. On 28 December 1870, Ughler, Abeel, and others met Angell on the sixth principal meridian line, about four miles southeast of present-day Wellington. There they formed the Meridian town company, with Angell as president and Ughler as secretary. (Angell's profits on the venture, it appears, were to be funneled through the Kansas Immigration Society of Leavenworth, which was given a half-interest in Meridian, with the understanding that the society would direct all its immigrants to Sumner County.) Angell succeeded in beating Sumner City's representative to an audience with Governor Harvey and persuaded the governor to issue the proclamation as Freeman described it—with Meridian as temporary county seat and Ughler, McMahon, and Abeel as temporary county commissioners. Of these, only McMahon was a resident of any significant length of time, having settled on Slate Creek on 29 July 1870. Freeman is correct in stating that at the time of the proclamation, Meridian was a phantom on the prairie. The original town company did little to rectify that beyond erecting a 14-by-24-foot shanty (the first "court house") in March of 1871. On 15 June 1871 (4 June, according to Andreas, p. 1495), the commissioners agreed to conduct business in Wellington, where more congenial amenities existed. Though Abeel had abandoned the project and resigned as commissioner in June, apparently Ughler made one more effort to organize Meridian on 17 July 1871, but to no avail. None of the original conspirators, it seems, made a dime on their efforts (Andreas, p. 1495; Richards, "History of Sumner County," *Historical Atlas,* p. 8; *SCP Chronology,* 1 January 1880; *Wellington Monitor-Press,* 24 August 1921; a biographical sketch of A. J. Angell appears in Andreas, p. 437).

[24] Efforts to determine the county seat by ballot include the elections of 26 September 1871 and 7 November 1871, when no single town achieved the necessary majority; 29 January 1872, a vote never canvassed by the commissioners; 26 March 1872, which produced the necessity for a runoff election between Wellington and Oxford; and 9 April 1872, when Wellington emerged the victor (Andreas, pp. 1495-96).

placed at her hand with a determined corps of officers. Arrests were made by the officers; the offender tried, his fine being paid, he was set at liberty. Sometimes the party arrested could not pay his fine; then he was taken to Wellington and put in the "cooler." This was a light, frame building, and was not substantially built, and often the prisoner escaped by cutting his way out with his pocket knife or used some implement to break the lock on the door.[25]

Sometimes if the prisoner had committed a grave offense, he was taken to Topeka for safe-keeping, and quite often, the prisoner was arrested, tried, and found guilty of the charges set forth in the evidence; some friend or friends of his would give the necessary bond demanded by the court, and the criminal would watch his chances and "skip the country."

Everything would run along smoothly until the time for trial, when to the dismay of the bondsmen, they were called upon to replenish the county treasury by forfeiting the bond. The criminal is probably by this time enjoying himself in some eastern city, or can be found in some frontier hamlet, and is still engaged in his reckless way of living.

Such is life in the Far West.

[25] The first county jail in Wellington is described as "a wooden affair, constructed out of 4 x 4's spiked and bolted together." It was not replaced until 1878, when bonds were voted for the purpose (*Wellington Monitor-Press,* 24 August 1921). Meantime, it was often the practice to hold prisoners in other buildings. I have read of prisoners' being chained to logs in the livery stable or being held under guard in second-floor rooms above various business establishments. Some prisoners, as Freeman indicates, were taken to Topeka for safekeeping—or, more frequently, to Wichita.

CHAPTER 7

The Killing of Wm. Manning—Epps Surrender and Trial—The
Manning Brothers' Threat—Warrant Issued for Their
Arrest—Deputy Sheriff and Possee Make the
Arrest—The Prisoners Escape.

After the lapse of almost a year the curtain raises, showing many changes
and different scenes. The immigrant still comes from the East to get a home
on the frontier of southern Kansas; the character of society is fast changing,
and at no distant day the law abiding settler will predominate in the community. The county has been organized and municipal officers have been elected,
but justices of the peace and constables seem afraid to do their full duty;
but wait a little while and we shall see the law prevail, but not yet; to settle
a dispute by murder is still not uncommon.

In February 1872, one of my horses had either strayed or was stolen, and
in hunting for it I went to Bluff Creek and there saw a man by the name of
Epps. This man had taken a claim about two miles from my place, and had
built a dug-out and was living there. I found my horse had not been seen by
him and started up the creek to look for it. At this time the settlers had
all taken claims near some creek or river; this was done for several reasons,
viz: the land bordering the streams was confirmed by many as being the best
land, as the richest of the soil was gradually washed to the bottom land or the
land bordering the streams; then again, they wanted this land for its watering
facilities and also for the fuel; the only trees seen here were those on the
banks of a stream; hence, by getting a claim which was watered by a stream,
they would get wood for fuel and trees for sheltering stock both from the hot
sun and from the winter blasts.

After getting about two hundred yards from Epps dug-out, I met a man by
the name of William Manning. This man Manning, in company with three
brothers of his, was keeping a bunch of cattle near the Bluff Creek country
and had wintered them there during the winter of 1871 and 1872.

As Manning came up to me I spoke to him and I noticed his greeting
was not very cordial. I rode on, however, and had only gone a short distance
when I heard the report of a gun in the direction of Epps' dug-out.

I turned and rode back to the dug-out, and found Epps standing in the
door and Manning lying on the ground, near the door, dead. Epps had shot
him, the charge taking effect in his breast; I found afterwards that the cause
of the shooting was occasioned by a dispute or quarrel which Epps and Manning had in a settlement about some hay which Epps had cut and stacked
for the Manning brothers.[1]

[1] As far as I can determine, Freeman's is the earliest extant record of this altercation.

It seems they could not agree on a settlement, each getting angry about it. When they parted it was agreed that they should shoot on sight, and the one getting the lucky shot would be the most fortunate, as far as his life was concerned, at least. Manning was buried two miles south of Caldwell and to-day the place is called Manning's Peak.[2] Epps went to Sumner city and gave himself up to the officers of the law, had his trial, and was cleared,[3] the jury giving in a verdict to the effect that he acted in self-defence, for had he not defended himself, in all probability Manning would have killed him.

Soon after this the remaining Manning brothers threatened the life of Epps; consequently Epps went to Wellington, the county seat of Sumner county, and got out a warrant for the arrest of the three Manning brothers; the deputy sheriff came down to make the arrest and deputed about twenty men to help him, myself included in that number.[4]

The Manning brothers had heard of this and left their home, and went to the house of H. H. Davidson and took refuge in his dug-out. A man with his daughter and child were living in the dug-out at the time.

The deputy sheriff and posse arrived at the dug-out at about two o'clock in the morning, and the deputy sheriff demanded their surrender. They would not surrender for reasons of their own, and told the deputy they would never surrender to us. I suppose they presumed we were a mob of reckless characters and that their surrender would probably mean death for them.

The deputy told them they would not be hurt, but would be tried and settled with according to law; if that was the cause of their hesitation, he assured them that they should have justice; notwithstanding all this they would not consent to a surrender.

D. D. Leahy, writing in the *Wichita Eagle* of 28 June 1932, asserts that the Mannings were Texans, William a Confederate veteran.

[2] The site appears to be the sandstone prominence now called Lookout Point or Look-out Mountain, which Leahy accurately describes as a "nose-like bit of land jutting out of the level prairie across Bluff creek." (*Eagle,* 28 June 1932). *Kansas: A Guide* (p. 463) reports that Coronado may have camped on this bluff. Leahy explains that William's brothers "vowed that his body should not be buried in the hated soil of abolition Kansas and it was taken across the state line into the Cherokee Strip for interment. . . . a resurvey was subsequently made of the state line and the corrected survey put the grave of Manning into Bleeding Kansas." The more than two-mile adjustment of the Kansas border by a resurvey is a matter of record, but the rationale for the burial of Confederate veteran Manning below the state line may be no more than local folklore. Leahy's source was hearsay, since he did not arrive in Caldwell until many years after the event. The story of Manning's burial is repeated, with some variation, in *Kansas: A Guide* (pp. 463-64).

[3] Sumner City, until its demise shortly after 9 April 1872, was located a few miles northeast of present-day Wellington on Slate Creek. The officers before whom Epps appeared are unknown, the town records having disappeared (Richards, "History of Sumner County," *Historical Atlas,* p. 7).

[4] The name of the deputy is unknown to me. He would have been serving under G. A. Hamilton, who was elected sheriff in November of 1871 (Andreas, p. 1496).

I told the deputy I would arrange to get them out if he was willing to have me try. He consented to my proposal and willingly turned the management into my hands; there was a hay-stack near by, so I said we would smoke them out of the dug-out. A couple of men and myself went to the stack and got some hay and twisted it up in a solid bundle, put it into the chimney, and then lit the hay.

We soon heard from them in this manner; they said the woman and child were almost suffocated with the smoke and asked us to put the fire out; the deputy told them the only way to get rid of the smoke would be to surrender. They replied that they would not surrender. I told the deputy to tell them that if they did not, in a few minutes we would let the dug-out roof in on them, which he did. Everything was quiet for a few minutes; then one of them asked to know who the parties were that wanted their surrender. He named the parties over to them, and they finally said for one of us to come into the dug-out and they would try and fix up the matter; we thought their reason for wanting one of us in the dug-out was to keep us from caving in the roof on to them.

We finally agreed to their proposition provided they would let the man out again in case they did not agree to surrender. To this they consented; so one of the men went into the dug-out and they said they would surrender, if we would get C. H. Stone and Mr. Dixon[5] to come to the dug-out.

Rather than give the woman and child further trouble we sent for Mr. Stone and Dixon; these gentlemen were in Caldwell. It was about eight o'clock in the morning when the men arrived on the scene; the Manning brothers gave themselves up to the sheriff's keeping.

He returned to Caldwell, and soon after, the sheriff and two men started to take the prisoners to Wellington.

They stopped for the night at Smith's ranch, which was about eight miles north of Caldwell, on the banks of the Chikaskia river.[6] This ranch had two rooms, and in the back-room was a window considerably larger than the other windows. After supper the men engaged themselves at a game of cards, leaving one idle to act as guard over the prisoners.

No sooner had they began playing cards, when they also began drinking whiskey—the two are usually in company with each other. So it was this time, and the men became very much interested in their game; the drinking was kept up until all, more or less, were intoxicated; and the more intoxicated they became, the more interested they became in their game of cards.

They were having a jolly time, enjoying themselves to their hearts content, drinking and playing, playing and drinking; but the curtain must soon be

[5]Probably either B. H. or Noah J. Dixon, both early settlers and merchants. More details on N. J. Dixon appear in chap. 31, n. 2.
[6]I have been unable to identify Smith's ranch.

drawn, the first scene is almost completed; draw the curtain upon this crowd of hilarity and let us see scene the second.

The curtain raises showing the deputy sheriff and his men, but the Manning brothers, oh, where are they? It seemed they were terrible thirsty, and the water was in the back room; the guard by this time [had] become interested [in the card game] and told them, the prisoners, that they could enter the room and help themselves, which they did; they also took the advantage given them, and opened the window and skipped out. Once more they are free men.

They started for Caldwell and arrived there about two o'clock in the morning; their journey had given each a good appetite; they got something to eat and left town, never to return.

The deputy sheriff and the men that were with him stayed at the ranch all night, and next morning arrived in Caldwell, after the prisoners had fled.

The reader will readily see the class of people usually found in the western frontier towns; we do not intimate that all the residents are of the desperado style, but we say that the rougher element prevails in these towns. In christianized communities, these towns are called hard "places," and, indeed they are hard places, and many will have to surrender their lives to the grim monster death, before our book is finished.

CHAPTER 8

The Buffalo Hunt—Overtaken by a Storm—Taking Shelter in a
Quickly Made Log Cabin—A Woman and Children About
to Perish—The Buffalo Range Reached and Two
of the Party Lost—A Futile Effort
in Searching for Them.

In the winter of 1871, I was living in Butler County, Kansas, eleven miles
East of Augusta. A party of us conceived the idea of going on a buffalo hunt.
As this part of Kansas is nearly all prairie land, the farmer has nothing to
busy himself at in the winter months. In the East, the farmer has fences to
rebuild, wood to cut and haul, timber land to clear, and many other ways of
keeping himself busy through the winter.

On the morning of January 20th, the sun shone bright and clear; the day
bid fair to be a beautiful one. We had made the necessary arrangements to
start on our proposed hunt on that day. So our party, consisting of eight or
ten of our friends and neighbors, including father, brother[1], and myself, bid
farewell to our friends, homes, and familiar scenes, turned our faces westward,
and started for the land of the buffalo, fully expecting to reap a rich harvest
upon our arrival there.

The first and second days of our trip were beautiful ones, but when we
stopped and made arrangements to camp on the evening of the second day,
a dark cloud was visible in the North [, though it] soon settled back as if "it
had not been."

I suggested that we blanket our horses for the night, as there was going
to be a storm. The men laughed at my predictions and said "it had been too
nice a day to think of a North'er so soon." But as a wise man has said "thou
can'st not tell what a day may bring forth," was surely true this time, for about
three o'clock in the morning the wind changed its course from the South to
the North, the heavens were black with angry looking clouds, the wind began
blowing a furious gale which warned us of the approaching storm. For fully
ten minutes the wind could be heard roaring in the distance, and almost in
an instant the storm was upon us in all its fury. About daylight, snow began

---

[1] Freeman's father may have been John Freeman, listed in the 1870 Census for Walnut
Township, Butler County, Kansas (KSHS). A William Freeman is listed in the 1870 Walnut Township Census and in the 1875 Bloomington Township Census (where Freeman
himself is listed in 1875). William was possibly George's brother. Other sons of John
Freeman were James M. and John W., both living with their parents in 1870. John the
elder is not listed in the 1875 Census, but as Freeman indicates in chap. 21, George himself took over his father's farm in Butler County sometime after 1874.

to fall, or whirl rather, as the wind seemed to come from all directions; and turn in any position possible, the snow seemed to blow in our faces. As soon as it was sufficiently light enough to see, we hitched our teams to the wagon and started for the Little Arkansas River, knowing there was plenty of timber there for fuel and shelter; also a cattle ranch, at which place we might find food and shelter if necessary.

Upon our arrival on the Little Arkansas River, we went to work cutting logs, preparing to make us a shelter of some description for ourselves and horses. We succeeded in getting enough logs to make the four sides of a shanty, but what were we to cover it with, was the question. At last some one suggested the wagon sheet. Well, we took the sheet off one of the wagons and tied it over the top of the shanty, thereby sheltering us from snow and wind. We soon had a rousing fire in the center of this shanty, and the boys were singing "I'm always light-hearted and easy, not a care in this world have I."

The weather continued to be cold and disagreeable the rest of the week; the snow had fallen to about the depth of ten inches;[2] as we were very comfortable in our new home, we concluded to camp there until the weather was more favorable. We succeeded in passing the time spent in camp very pleasantly. We had now been in camp from Thursday morning until Sunday. On Saturday the weather moderated to such an extent that Sunday morning found us up by daylight, making arrangements to start on our journey.

Once more we are in our wagons wending our way westward, fully determined to push on until our goal is reached. Little did we dream what the future had in store for our little party, and e'er we would turn our faces homeward, the many disappointments and hardships, the suffering and heartaches some of our little party would be subject to.

We traveled a distance of six miles when we came to the Arkansas River; the severe cold weather had frozen it over, so we could cross over on the ice. There we would leave the last ranch and would necessarily have to lay in a supply of hay and provisions, realizing if we were far from habitation and should have the misfortune to be in another blizzard, we would need a good supply of the necessaries of life.

We traveled until evening when we came to a small log house in which lived a widow with three children; we found them to be in destitute circumstances. She told us they had nothing to eat; before the storm came she had but very little provision in the house, and that during the storm she would

---

[2]The storm and its effects on parties such as Freeman's is reflected in the Eldorado (Kansas) *Walnut Valley Times* for 3 February 1871: "Information reaches us that four or five persons were frozen to death on the Plains during the late storm. The Indians brought in the report. Quite a number of persons who were out buffalo hunting were more or less frozen. Some of them had to have toes and feet amputated. The weather on the plains has been intensely cold and many persons have suffered severely while hunting."

not send her boy from home, for fear he would get lost or frozen. We gave them some bacon, a turkey, a paper of coffee, and some flour.

We camped near the house that night; the next morning we started by daylight and traveled three days in a southwest direction.

On the third day, about two o'clock, we reached the land where the buffalo roamed unmolested, save when an occasional hunter or Indian breaks in upon the scene, either for the sport of killing the buffalo or for the many pounds of delicious meat they get after it is killed.

We selected a good camping place of which I will endeavor to give the reader a brief description. The country here was broken by ravines of greater or less extent, though not perceptible at a glance. These ravines, if followed, would be found to grow deeper and deeper, until, after running their course for an indefinite extent, they would terminate in the valley of some running stream. The land was ornamented with little knolls and an occasional sand hill. These knolls are frequently found with trees or brush of some description growing on top of them.

The knoll selected for our camping place was the only one with trees on it, and it could be seen for miles; besides giving us a splendid view of the surrounding country, it also afforded us the satisfaction of knowing we had plenty of good wood at our command with which we could warm our aching fingers and cook our frugal meal.

After unhitching my horses, watering them and giving them their feed, I took my gun and in company with one of the men, started to hunt for game of some description. We failed to find anything and started to go back to camp when we met two of the boys; I call them boys, but their ages were seventeen and twenty-two.[3] The people of the West have a habit of saying "boys" when many times they really mean old men. They use it as a familiar term, showing the good will and friendly feeling they have for each other.

The boys, too, had started for the purpose of trying their luck at the sight of game. We wanted them to go back to camp, but they said "supper was not ready and they would hunt awhile."

We told them "not to go far, and to keep in sight of the knoll." They replied, "all right," and went on.

It had been a fine day, clear and warm, but the signs were not favorable for a good day on the morrow. A cloud was rising in the northwest, the wind began blowing, and soon the snow began to fall. It was then about 4 o'clock in the afternoon.

After remaining in camp a short time I saw a herd of buffalo coming in

[3] The identity of these young men is uncertain, but because Freeman's way of referring to them in succeeding passages is confusing, I offer the following: one of the boys had a brother and a father in the party; the other boy was his friend and was apparently unaccompanied by relatives.

the direction of camp. I took my gun and went to a sand-hill about two hundred yards from camp. I stationed myself on the hill and waited until they were within shooting distance. I succeeded in killing one and wounding another. One of the men at camp brought a team and wagon, took the buffalo to camp, while myself, brother and the father of one of the boys that had gone hunting, followed the wounded buffalo in hopes we could get a lucky shot at it and succeed in killing it.

After following it until nearly dark we finally concluded to give up the chase and go back to camp. Not noticing in what direction we had started or the many turns we had made, we began to consider in what direction camp would be found.

Neither of us agreed as to the direction we were to go, and I told them if they would remain where they were I would go and hunt for some land-mark by which we might determine where we were and in which direction to take to find our camp. I told them I would fire my revolver off two times in succession in case I concluded we were lost.

After wandering around for some time, not knowing which way to go, I concluded we were lost. I took my revolver from my belt, held it in the air and pulled the trigger once, — twice. The sound rang out in the cold air, leaving an awful stillness, in which I could almost hear the beatings of my heart.

The silence was broken by an answering shot fired from camp and how gladly we turned our steps in that direction. When I shot my revolver I saw the two boys I have spoken of before, about a mile to the north of where I was standing and I supposed they would arrive at camp about the same time we would. To guide us the boys at camp had taken an old fashioned bake oven, fastened it to the end of a ten-foot pole, then made a fire in the oven and held the pole up, thinking we could see the light and thereby reach camp in safety.

The light in the oven made an excellent guide for us and we arrived safely in camp, but very tired and hungry after our long tramp.

After eating our supper, which consisted of coffee, bacon, and bread, we related our adventure to the boys at camp. Then the question was asked, "Where are the remaining boys?" As it was getting late and they had had ample time to reach camp since they were last seen, we concluded to fire our guns, knowing if they were lost and heard the report of the guns they could follow in the direction of the sound and reach camp, and if they were not lost they would probably think all was not right at camp and reach there as soon as they possibly could.

We kept up the firing all night. We had an old army musket and filled it with sand and fired it off. Our efforts were all in vain.

The father and brothers of the lost boys were nearly wild with grief. Daylight found us prepared to go and hunt for the lost boys. A heavy fog hung like a curtain over the horizon; it was very difficult to see a short distance from camp, but we saddled our horses and were soon on what proved to be a fruitless search for our friends.

We started east and were situated in a line north and south from each other. As I mentioned before, it was dark, foggy, and misty, and to keep from getting separated or lost from each other, we were to halloo every few minutes. I was at the north end of the line. I would halloo the next to answer, and so on the entire length of the line of men. The wind was blowing from the north and each could easily hear the halloo above him.

At 12 o'clock I was to fire off my revolver, each of the boys to do the same, but no person to fire two times unless the boys had been found.

After firing our revolvers we started for the same point, and upon arriving there we made a fire, boiled some coffee and ate our dinner.

I have often wished we had fired off our revolvers every few minutes, as the lost boys afterward told me they heard the report of our guns at noon and started in the direction from whence they thought the sound came. After walking a mile or two they listened and could not hear any more shooting, thought perhaps it was imagination, and turned and started back from whence they came.

When our horses were through eating their corn and we had eaten our dinner, we started on our homeward march after this fashion: The man that was on the south end of the line, as we left camp, was to follow his horse's tracks toward camp and we were to follow him, each keeping within hearing distance of each other.

Great anxiety prevailed throughout the entire party concerning the fate of the lost boys. As the day star sank in the west and the night stars came out one by one and the shades of night settled around our little camp, it was with many misgivings that we lay down upon our blankets to rest.

I told the father of one of the lost boys that on the morrow I would take one of my horses, some provisions for myself and horse, and a blanket, and see if I could get any trace of the lost boys. In the meantime I told them to kill enough buffalo to load the wagons, which they could easily do, as the range a short distance from camp was alive with them.

The morning dawned finding me fully equipped and ready for my journey. After drinking a refreshing cup of coffee I bade adieu to the little party I was leaving behind and started on my search.

I rode rapidly in a northeast direction galloping across ravine and plain. Occasionally, as I dashed across a ravine, I would startle a few buffalos from their slumber and cause them to wonder who was this strange party disturbing their peaceful repose.

After traveling all day without the least sign to urge me on, I concluded about sun-down that I would go into camp. A large cottonwood tree was in sight and I turned my horse's head in that direction intending to stop there for the night.

I found, to my good luck, a large cave in the south side of a large sand-hill near the tree, and thought it would afford me a place of shelter.

I unsaddled my horse and found he was very tired after a day's hard travel. I fed my horse, looked around and found some dry limbs to make a fire, cooked my supper, and will here tell the reader that it was not a feast and far from being a famine. After partaking of my supper I lit my pipe and indulged in my accustomed evening smoke.

Oh, how lonely it seemed to me, with nothing to break the monotony of my loneliness save an occasional howl of the gray wolf, and their howl only had a tendency to make me melancholy and have a yearning for my home far away.

It was not a very desirable place to be in I assure you. I had seen places where the Indians had camped but a short time before. I knew unless I should be taken unawares or by surprise that I was prepared for a small band, as I was well armed, having with me two good revolvers, a shot gun, and a Winchester rifle. My dog was some company for me. I put my saddle under my head for a pillow and prepared for a night's rest.

I was tired and weary after my long ride, as all who have been in the saddle all day know how to appreciate a good place to lie down and sleep when the night begins to draw near.

I could not sleep; my thoughts were on the lost boys' condition. I knew they would suffer with cold, as only one had an overcoat on; also that they would suffer from hunger unless they were fortunate enough to kill something to eat.

Morning dawned finding me in the saddle to again resume my search. I started in a southeast direction, thinking I might find their trail in the snow. I rode until noon, stopped and fed my horse, built a fire out of buffalo chips, and made some coffee. I traveled the rest of the day as fast as I deemed best. About dark I heard some one chopping. I rode in the direction from whence the sound came and found it was one of the men chopping wood to make a fire at camp.

I told the boys' father that I had seen nothing of them. He said it was no use to hunt further, for in all probability if the lost boys had not reached a settlement or ranch they were frozen to death.

In my absence the men had killed enough buffalo to load our wagons, so we concluded to start for home on the following morning. In my next chapter I will endeavor to tell the reader more about our trip and the final result of our buffalo hunt.

CHAPTER 9

A Buffalo Hunt—The Homeward March—A Man's Track Found
—Arrival at Wichita—The Lost Boys on Their Journey
Homeward—Nearly Famished with Hunger—
A Friend in Need Is a Friend Indeed—
Returned Safely to Home
and Friends.

The morning dawned finding us in our wagons before it was sufficiently light enough to view the surrounding country.

As we wended our way towards our homes, I could not help but notice how silently our little party trudged along, the father and brother mourning for the lost ones, and looking, perhaps upon scenes and places for the last time but which time could not erase from their memory. Although many years have passed since then, yet when I recall that Buffalo hunt to my mind I am apparently young again, ready for any emergency which may come before me.

We had not proceeded far on our journey, perhaps a mile, when one of the party had the misfortune to lose one of his horses. To all appearances the horse was well when we started, but soon began to reel in walking, and upon investigation it was found to have the blind staggers; it was too sick to travel and rather than leave it there on the prairie one of the boys shot it. The old man came to me and wanted to know if I would haul their bedding and provisions home for them; he said he would burn his wagon rather than leave it there for the Indians. I told him it was useless to burn his wagon as he could have my leaders and take his wagon home with him. He took my front team and hitched to his wagon and we were soon on our road again.

In the afternoon about four o'clock we came to a small creek which we thought we would have difficulty in crossing; one of the boys started up the stream to find a place safe to cross; after finding a fordable place, he by chance saw a man's track, and hallooed to us "here is a man's track." Words would indeed be poor vehicles with which to convey to the mind of the reader how eager we were to see for ourselves and examine the tracks. Our conclusions were that they were the lost boys tracks and were made the following morning after they had left camp; as the snow was thawing we thought it would be useless to try and follow them.

When the father saw the tracks, he gave way to his grief, the tears trickled down his cheeks as he said "my poor boy is lost, and perhaps dead, Oh! how I wish we could find him."

About dark we stopped for the night; our camping place was on the bank of a little stream. The weather was very agreeable overhead. The night was a beautiful one; nothing happened to disturb our rest, save an occasional howl of a coyote or the fluttering of a bird which was startled from its perch in the limbs of a tree.

We were up by daylight and soon on our way; after traveling four days we arrived at Wichita. We made inquiry there of the lost boys, but could hear nothing concerning them.

We camped about two miles east of Wichita that night, and were thirty one miles from home.

The following morning was very disagreeable, a misting rain was slightly falling. The weather had moderated to such an extent that the snow had melted, making the roads slushy and muddy. We did not make a very big days drive that day, only reaching Augusta at night. Our camping place was on the Big Walnut River. We started for home early the next morning.

After driving six miles we met one of my brothers and a brother of one of the lost boys. How glad we were to hear all were well at home, and we were almost overjoyed on hearing the lost boys were alive and that [these two] were now on their way after them intending to bring them home.[1]

We arrived home safely without further adventure, and I will tell you the experience the lost boys had as they related it to me.

"After leaving camp we started north and continued that course for a few hours; after traveling for some time we changed our course thinking we could easily find camp. We had traveled until quite dark before we gave up, realizing we were lost.

"The reader may imagine our feelings when the thoughts flew through our minds, with the rapidity of lightning, that we were lost. How our hearts sank within us, when we would picture to our minds eye our warm fireside, with our father and mother in their easy chair, waiting for our coming. We thought perhaps we would not be found, and we would be left to perish on the western plains. How vividly our past life came back to our memory; what a terrible picture the future presented to us. We prayed that we might escape the hands of the Indians.

"Gradually the actual fact that we were lost and far from habitation, took possession of our senses, and we concluded to act immediately upon that fact.

"We endeavored to press on, hoping to be rescued by our friends, or that we might by chance find a ranch.

"We wandered all night, never stopping to rest and did not realize how tired we were. The next morning was damp and foggy and very difficult to see two hundred yards from us. We knew from the lay of the country that the course of streams here was east, and we thought we would start in that direction.

[1] Freeman does not explain how the people in Butler County learned that the boys were alive and where they were located. Presumably Davis, with whom they took refuge, sent word.

"We had not proceeded far before we came to a small creek or ravine. We thought that by following it we sooner or later would find where it emptied its waters, knowing if we followed its course we would in time reach the Arkansas river.

"We followed the ravine all day, wandering around with it in its meanderings, through hill and plain. About night we came to the terminus of the ravine, or rather where it entered a stream. On the banks of this stream we saw a herd of Antelope; we tried to shoot one, but fate was against us and soon we were left alone, our four footed friends having left us, giving us the right of way and full possession of the creek.

"We had now given up all hopes of reaching a settlement, and our only source of rescue was to strike a ranch on the banks of the creek, or to follow it until we would reach a settled portion of the state.

"The ground was covered with snow, the wind was blowing a furious gale from the north, chilling our bodies; had we had some matches we could have made a fire and one slept while the other kept up the fire; but all the sleep we had was when we could find the south side of a hill; then, as the snow was on the ground we had to make a bed by pulling up dry grass to lie down on; then one of us would lie down with the overcoat over him and take a sleep, while the other one, like a soldier on his beat, would walk around to keep himself warm. After each of us had taken a little nap, we would start on our travels again. We traveled three days without having anything to eat. Oh! how ravenous our appetites were; on the morning of the fourth day my friend gave up in despair. He said he did not care to go any further; he was so weary both in body and mind and he did not believe we would find a settlement; we were nearly starved for something to eat.

"I told him I would never leave him there to perish on the plains, and rather than leave him there I would kill him. I drew my gun on him and I suppose he thought "as long as there is life there is hopes," and he concluded to try and keep up strength and courage.

"We traveled all day; at night we came to a river, which we afterwards found was the Nennescah. We were then 19 miles west of Wichita, and were within one-half mile of a house. Little did we imagine we were so near help.

"Just at sunrise the next morning we again resumed our journey; upon crossing the river and walking up the bank, to our surprise and joy we saw a house; at the sight of the house our strength seemed to leave us, and in order to reach it we were compelled to crawl on our hands and knees.

"When we arrived at the house it was twelve o'clock, and the family were preparing to eat their dinner. Perhaps it would be well enough to say that the ranch was kept by Captain Davis. He and his family moved there in an early day.[2]

---

[2] This appears to be C. Wood Davis, who with his wife and two sons settled in what

"The Captain saw us first, and knew by our emaciated appearances that we were famishing for food.

"He told his wife to clear the table of the provisions; upon hearing this we drew our guns on him and told him we would kill him if he did not let us have something to eat. The Captain told us we could have something to eat, and told his wife to get them some beef soup. He knew we were not in the condition to go to the table, which was well spread with eatables. Mrs. Davis gave each a pint cup half full of soup and a slice of light bread.

"We will never forget the kindness shown us, for they indeed treated us as they would one of their own children.

"Mr. Davis had his team ready to start for Wichita as soon as he had eaten his dinner, but he postponed his trip and stayed home to care for us. We thought several times that we would take his life, because he would not let us satisfy our craving appetite.

"The Captain had been a soldier in the Civil War, and by way of interesting us, he would tell us how the soldier's suffered in the Andersonville prison; also related his experience as a soldier, and of the many fights he had witnessed.

"Had we been in a different condition we would have enjoyed his reminiscences very much, but as we were nearly famishing, our only thought was to satisfy our appetites.

"The night drew on and we began to get sleepy. Mrs. Davis made us a bed; the Captain slept near by and all through the night was ready to wait upon us, giving us soup every hour.

"The next day we were allowed to sit at the table, but ate only what the Captain said was best for us. I presume we were not very mannerly at the table. After dinner was over the captain invited us to go with him to see his stock, stable and corral, which was about one hundred yards distant.

"We first went to the corrals to see the cattle. The Captain was the owner of a large herd of cattle, and was a man that took great pride in his home and surroundings. He took us out for the purpose of showing us his home and possessions.

"After admiring his cattle, we thought we had best go in the house and rest, as we were yet very weak. We rested a couple of hours, had a refreshing sleep, and felt very much better. About four o'clock the Captain had us go with him again; we stayed with him until he had done his feeding.

"After supper we, in company with the Captain and his wife, went to spend the evening with a neighbor living near by.

"The captain related the story of our adventure, how we had come to his house nearly starved and how we had suffered from cold as well as

was to be Viola Township, Sedgwick County (Andreas, p. 1388; Chas. G. Davis in Emmert, "History of Sedgwick County," *Historical Atlas,* p. 10).

hunger. We had the sympathy of the people, and they said we were lucky to find such a man and family to care for us.

"That night we were allowed to sleep without being disturbed; how well we appreciated that bed will never be known as I am unable to fully express myself.

"On the next morning my friends feet were getting very sore, he having had them badly frozen. He could not walk without the crutches which the Captain had been kind enough to make for him.

"We remained with the Captain about ten days, when the boys came for us to go home with them.[3] We were very glad to see them and we had a general hand shaking all round. Nothing would do them but we must tell of the suffering and privations we had experienced since we left home but a short time before, but to us it seemed years since we had started on our buffalo hunt, full of expectations and bright prospects before us.

"Had we known we were to be the victims of such an experience, we would have shuddered at the thoughts of it. But here we are apparently well and happy and have had our share of the sufferings and disappointments of the buffalo hunter.

"Early the next morning we bade the Captain and his family goodby. Thanking them for their heartfelt kindness, telling them they would long be remembered by us, and that we considered it was to them that we owed our lives, for, had they not been so considerate with us, in all probability we would have fared much worse.

"Late in the evening we arrived at Augusta and as we were so near home, we wanted the boys to continue our journey; the boys wanted us to stop over night in Augusta, but we were determined to reach home that night.

"I will not attempt to describe our meeting with father and mother; suffice it to say that we were all very thankful that we were restored to our loved ones again."

I will not tire the reader by relating how each reached his home, nor of the happy meeting afterwards, but will add that one of them lost all of his toes off his feet, and the last I heard of him he was living in Indiana. The other was not badly frozen, but the exposure was too great a strain on his constitution and he died the following fall. This ended the buffalo hunt upon which we started, with our hopes buoyant and our anticipation bright as we pic-

---

[3] The young men had wandered for four days and had been at Davis' cabin for nine days — a total of thirteen days—when Freeman's party reached home. Yet Freeman's party arrived only a week after the boys became lost. I mention this not to impeach Freeman but to reassure the reader, who may have begun to wonder if he had missed something along the way. This is merely another example of Freeman's faulty memory and failure to revise his material.

tured to ourselves the many monarchs of the plains that would give up their lives to satisfy our appetites for the pleasure of killing them.

I have had many a buffalo hunt, and have realized a great deal of enjoyment while chasing them over the plains, and as I recall such scenes to memory, in the language of the poet I feel like saying, "backward, turn backward, oh! time in your flight."

While we were fortunate in having our friends restored to us, yet how many have wandered from their camp and were never found. Quite likely they either died from starvation or were frozen to death, and perhaps many had the misfortune to fall into the hands of the cunning Indian, and were either burned to the stake or suffered a similar death.

About this time the Indians were to be greatly feared. The tide of civilization had gradually driven them west to the plains. Occasionally the buffalo hunter would wander too far and be surprised to find himself surrounded by a small band of the Noble Red Men, who, after taking him prisoner, would discuss by what means they would kill or torture him to death, while the poor fellow would pray to God for help, knowing he would have no mercy at their hands.

Thus ends our buffalo hunt, and the readers may decide with themselves whether it was an enjoyable affair for us or not.

CHAPTER 10

The Murder of Dave Fielder—McCarty Pulls Fielder out of Bed—Fielder Resents
Such Treatment—Fielder gives McCarty a Whipping—McCarty Gets on a
Drunk and Hunts for Fielder—Fielder Goes to Reid's Dug-out—
McCarty Calls for Fielder—McCarty a Murderer and Flees
to the Indian Territory—Public Sentiment Aroused.

Scarcely had one month, one small month passed since the tragedy at Epps
dug-out, which resulted in the killing of William Manning, than the people
received the startling intelligence that another had seen the sun set for the
last time.

Spring was just making her appearance and was donning her robe of vernal
beauty. Little did the victim think that before the bud changed to blossom
that he would be sleeping under the grass with a bullet in his breast.

During the winter of 1871 and 1872, two men by the name of Dan
Fielder and ——— McCarty[1] were batching together in a dug-out, on Bluff
Creek, located about two miles from town. Each I believe had taken a claim
a short distance from town, and as it would be very lonely living alone,
they concluded to batch together and time would not seem so monotonous
for either.

Fielder was formerly from Pottowattomie county, this state, and was a man
about medium size in height and weight, and bore the marks of a gentleman, save in regard to his dress, which partook of the rowdy element. He
was not considered a bad man, was a lover of peace, and still the organizer
of discord. He would shrink from courting danger, and yet when it did come
he was ready to meet it. He was not the man to be imposed on, and would
resent an insult heaped upon him by a friend, in the most quiet and unassuming manner possible.

As McCarty will be presented before the minds of the reader for a considerable length of time, perhaps it would be well to note his many characteristics. No character in this history presents a more remarkable career than
does that of McCarty.

His was a strange character, one which the novelist might gloat over. In
person he was about five feet ten inches in height, straight as a warrior,
well formed [in] chest and limbs, and a face strikingly handsome. His hair and
complexion were those of the perfect brunette, the former laid in ringlets
about his head. His costume was that of a dandy, with the taste and style of

---

[1] A. A. Richards identifies the two as Eugene Fielder and Michael McCarty, though he
does not indicate they shared a dugout (*SCP*, 26 February 1880). Richards used a condensed
version of his *SCP* story in Andreas (p. 1495).

a frontiersman. He was well educated and in manner resembled a cultured gentleman.

Of his courage there could be no question, as it had been tested on several occasions. He was formerly from Texas.[2] His use of the revolver was unerring, and his practice at target shooting would make the people shudder at the daring feats he displayed. At times he would show his skill in shooting at the sole of some boot, and again he would point his revolver over the shoulder of some one who was reading a letter and put a bullet hole through the paper. Numerous were his ways of displaying his skill with the revolver.[3]

There had been no law recognized by the frontiersman beyond the fact that might makes right. The quarrel was not from a word to a blow, but from a word to the revolver, and he who could draw and fire first was the best man.

In the early part of April, 1872, McCarty came in to town and indulged freely in drinking whiskey with some companions of his. He remained in town until late at night when he left town and returned to his dug-out. By this time he was considerably under the influence of the whiskey and was in a quarrelsome mood.

After putting his horse away for the night, he went to the dug-out and found that Fielder had gone to bed. McCarty requested Fielder to get up and Fielder replied that he would not. At this McCarty's evil spirits were aroused and he went to Fielder and caught hold of his hair and pulled him out of the bed, onto the floor. Fielder again sought his bed and McCarty, as before, pulled him out by the hair.

This was too much for Fielder to endure and he resented such treatment by giving McCarty a good whipping, which had a tendency to sober him, and he soon became quiet and went to bed.

Nothing more was thought or said about the trouble by Fielder, and to all outward appearances McCarty too had laid all prejudices aside and said nothing about it. But there was certainly a feeling of revenge being kindled in his heart, only to break out of its place of bondage at the first opportunity which presented itself.

As we have mentioned before, his manner and style were not of the desperado type, nor had he the look of a murderer upon his features, and yet he

---

[2] Richards says McCarty had been a saloonkeeper on the Union Pacific Railroad and fled to Butler County after killing a soldier. From there he came to the Caldwell vicinity. A more contemporary report says McCarty was from Boise City, Colorado, but this account, though closest in time to the event, is unreliable in other important particulars, placing the killing of Fielder in Wichita, for example (*Topeka Daily Commonwealth*, 21 April 1872).

[3] Richards: "His favorite amusement was to lie in bed and shoot through the keyhole in the door. Many stories, of more or less doubtful authenticity, are told of his peculiar habit of shooting off boot heels, coat buttons, etc., for the stranger, just to intimidate him."

proved to be a double murderer and a desperado.[4] Truly we cannot tell by man's appearance what lies hidden in the recesses of the heart. And yet, I believe whiskey was the cause of McCarty's downfall, which terminated in his ignomonious death at the hands of a law-abiding people.

On the following Sunday[5] after the trouble, McCarty was again in town and drank until he became very much intoxicated. Fielder heard McCarty was drunk and imagined he would be quarrelsome, so he left their dug-out, and went to Reid's, thinking thereby to escape further trouble with McCarty. Upon going home and not finding Fielder, [McCarty] went back to town and began making inquiry of Fielder's whereabouts. Some of his friends, not thinking that McCarty held malice against Fielder, told him that Fielder was at Reid's dug-out.

McCarty got his horse and rode in that direction, and it seems, in the still and voiceless night, he wanted to avenge himself of the ill-treatment he had received at the hands of his friend Fielder. He did not stop to consider or realize that it was he who provoked the quarrel which resulted in his supposed ill-treatment.

He took the precaution to roll a blanket about his body in such a condition that it would be difficult for a bullet to penetrate through its thickness and enter his body; this precaution probably saved his life, as will be shown before this chapter closes.

Upon his arrival at Reid's, he called for Fielder and was told by one of the family that he was not there. He got off his horse, holding it by the bridle rein, and called again for Fielder. At this, Fielder said with an oath, "here I am, come in here if you want anything." No sooner had the words left his lips than he was standing, revolver in hand, ready for any emergency.

Fielder was facing the door and in such a position that as soon as the door was thrown open he had a good view of McCarty. As McCarty opened the door, he also raised the blanket to get his revolver; and as he was in this act, Fielder fired, his shot taking effect within the folds of the blanket around McCarty's body, and glanced off without injury to his person. As quick as lightning, McCarty shot several times in succession at Fielder, one of the bullets taking effect in his lung, which caused his immediate death.[6]

McCarty then got on his horse and left town, and was not seen again for several days.

Fielder's body was properly buried by the citizens of town, while tears of sympathy were shed over the newly made grave.[7]

[4]Richards: "He was known to have killed nine men before his arrival in Sumner County."

[5]1 April 1872 (per Richards).

[6]Richards says McCarty fired only once.

[7]The *Wichita Eagle* 3 May 1872 reported that Fielder's sister had arrived in town en route to Caldwell to visit her brother's grave.

Thus another victim enters that long sleep that knows no waking.

Public sentiment revolted at such acts of lawlessness and bloodshed. The question was asked "can a man commit murder and go free and unpunished?" The public mind was thoroughly aroused; it felt that this state of thing was a disgrace to civilization. A change must be made; let it cost what it will. It was coming like the rushing of a mighty wind, soon to burst forth in all its fury.

The law-breaker, the murderer, and desperado must go, or submit to the inevitable will of the people. Crowds of by-standers were talking in undertones of the terrible state of affairs that were now existing in our little town and its surrounding country. Wait, and time will determine when the tide shall turn and we shall realize this fact, that the "right must prevail."

During the spring of 1872, I was elected constable of Caldwell and vicinity, and soon after I was appointed Deputy United States Marshal, under United States Marshal Place.[8]

The offices I held placed me under obligations to be with the rougher element the greater part of my time, and I experienced the many trials the officer had to endure, whether at home in my native town or on the western plains, in pursuit of the horse-thief or murderer.

Many times have I sat in the saddle, day and night, in search of the fugitive fleeing from justice, and have returned to my home, utterly worn out from exposure and fatigue, after a long, weary, fruitless chase.

In my next chapter I will relate to the reader a second shooting by McCarty, and it is said, completed a record in which he killed his ninth man.[9] Had his been a charmed life? Had fate decreed that he should die a shameful death and be denied a decent burial? Me thinks I fear the faint whisperings of the wind as it mournfully whispers, Yes.

---

[8]Neither of these appointments is a matter of record, but the reader is advised that both township and U.S. marshal records are spotty—when they have survived at all. For the same reason I find no record of U.S. Marshal Place, but there is no reason to doubt that Freeman held both offices he claims for himself.

Freeman does not offer any explanation for his failure to attempt to arrest McCarty for killing Fielder, but as he points out in the next chapter, the general sentiment was that Fielder had lost his life in a fair fight.

[9]Freeman is refreshingly careful to attribute seven previous killings to hearsay.

CHAPTER 11

The Killing of Anderson — The Fatal Plug Hat — McCarty's Reckless-
ness — Theories in Regard to the Murder — The
"Last Chance" — The Proprietor.

Time flies, oh, how swiftly, and in its flight many are the changes it brings
and different are the scenes presented to our view. Man plays many parts
on the world's stage. The novelist may fascinate us with his romance of
fiction, but the novelist's dreams fade utterly away when the checkered lives
of men pass before us in their different stages of life, filling our minds with
their wonderful history of adventure, heroism and bravery.

In the chapter preceding this I mentioned to the reader the killing of
Fielder by McCarty, and now, so soon, I must add another victim to the list
of men murdered at his hands. On the following Monday, a week after the
Fielder tragedy, McCarty came into town in company with one Webb.[1] This
was the first time he had been seen in town since his flight into the Territory, after the murder of Fielder. As was his custom, he again indulged
freely in drinking and was soon under the influence of whiskey. He and
Webb went into the store formerly occupied by Cox & Epperson, now of
which J. M. Thomas was the proprietor, and loitered around apparently with
no aim in view; Thomas was busy looking at some goods which a man by
the name of Doc Anderson had for sale.

This man Anderson had been the proprietor of a store in Butler County,
and after closing out a greater part of his goods, he brought the balance to
Caldwell and was trying to make a sale to Thomas.

On his way to Caldwell he stopped at Wellington over night, and while
there, he in company with others bought a plug hat from some party for the
purpose of gambling over a game of cards, the winner to have the hat. Anderson was the lucky man and won the hat; but unfortunately for him that
game of cards, together with the hat, sealed his fate. 'Tis strange upon how
small a pivot our destiny swings.

As Anderson was showing Thomas the goods, McCarty noticed that he
wore a plug hat, (probably this was the first plug hat seen in the town)
and remarked to Webb that he would like to shoot a hole through that
man's hat. Webb said, "no you won't shoot through a man's hat." "Oh no,"
said McCarty, "of course I wouldn't unless the man wanted me to," and just
then Anderson turned round to get more goods when quick as a flash Mc-
Carty shot at him, the ball tearing the top of Anderson's head off; Anderson

---

[1] April 9 — or the following Tuesday — according to A. A. Richards (*SCP*, 26 February
1880). Webb has not been further identified.

fell, and died without a struggle at the feet of his assassin. It is said some one remarked "there McCarty you have killed that man," "well," said McCarty, "he is out of luck, that's all."

McCarty then went to his horse and rode south towards the Indian Territory. Whether he shot at Anderson with the intention of killing him remains to be told, or whether he shot at the hat and accidently hit "his man" also remains a mystery. It was currently reported afterwards as a rumor that Anderson had used his influence against a gang of horse thieves which had infested Butler County, which resulted in the hanging of seven thieves on the Walnut river in one night, and caused such a cleaning up that many left that country in a short time; whether they were guilty of any crime and feared they would be used in a like manner was never known; but the rumor was to the effect that in all probability either McCarty was there at the time and left, or he had friends among the doomed men and swore to avenge their death by killing any party he might find in his ramblings.[2]

It did not matter whether he shot at the hat to show his skill as a marks-

[2] Richards' version is essentially the same, though he names Anderson (otherwise unidentifiable) as a member of the Butler County vigilantes and states unequivocally that McCarty was engaged in stealing horses there and "barely escaped the vigilantes, who put to death several of their [sic] comrades." D. D. Leahy says Anderson came from Douglass in Butler County (*Wichita Eagle*, 27 March 1932). Freeman errs when he states that seven men were hanged on the same night on the Walnut River. During the fall of 1870, eight men were lynched as suspected horse thieves. The local accounts differ in many particulars, but the episodes may be outlined thus: In early November, 1870, vigilantes dispatched George and Louis Booth, Jack Corbin, and Jim Smith, alias Jim Gilpin. Smith/Gilpin was killed in a gunfight at a ford on the Little Walnut River. Corbin and the two Booths were taken at the Booth cabin near the Little Walnut; Corbin was hanged and the two Booths were shot. About a month later, the following were arrested at Douglass under suspicion of being members of a band of horse thieves: William Quimby, Mike Dray, and a Dr. Morris and his son. These were taken from the authorities by vigilantes and hanged in the timber along the Walnut River. Doc Anderson is not mentioned by the Butler County newspaper, even after his death at Caldwell. (*Walnut Valley Times*, 11 November, 2 December 1870, *passim*; Andreas, pp. 1431-32; Jesse Stratford, *Butler County's Eighty Years, 1855-1935*, pp. 14-15; Vol P. Mooney, *History of Butler County Kansas*, pp. 118-19, 228-29, 254-60. The latter contains an extensive reminiscence of the events by W. P. Hackney, who served as attorney for three of the vigilantes.) In short, the seven hangings Freeman speaks of were probably the four which occurred on 1 December 1870. But Freeman is not alone in magnifying the event. Orange Scott Cummins remembered seeing the ropes still hanging on the tree when he passed through in February of 1871, and he distinctly remembered *five* ropes (*Wichita Eagle*, 3 October 1920). Henry N. Fargo, who was in the same company with Cummins, remembered it differently; he claimed to have seen five *bodies* hanging from a tree on the riverbank (*Kansas City* [Missouri] *Star*, 18 February 1900). Freeman, who was not there, may be forgiven his misinformation. At the same time, it is interesting to note that when the Walnut Valley lynchings occurred, Freeman was still a resident of Butler County. Though I do not wish to imply that Freeman was one of the vigilantes, I think it odd that he professes to know so little about what happened there.

man or if he shot to avenge a friends untimely end; it was enough that he committed murder unprovoked by his victim, and he was looked upon by the people as double murderer.

Had he not "killed his man" such a short time previous to the last murder, probably the public would not have been so thoroughly indignant over the affair, but to have a double murderer in their midst and at large, free to roam at his pleasure, was more than they would submit to, and they were determined that such characters must emigrate to some "healthier clime," or take the consequences which were sure to come were they to continue in their lawlessness and murderous inclinations.

Upon the killing of Fielder a dark cloud had begun to gather in the horizon of public sentiment. The time is fast approaching when there must be a speedy reckoning for crime. Fielder is dead; public feeling is warm and needs but a spark more to ignite the flame; the last straw is on the camels back. The killing of Fielder appeared to be a free fight, Fielder assuming the role of a duelist, but the killing of Anderson caused the cloud to arise and, with its black wings hovering over our heads, ready to burst at a given signal. Here was a man killed without any provocation and without even the privilege of defending himself, and without a word of warning.

There were several theories concerning the killing of Anderson. One was that McCarty did not intend to kill him but shot at his hat, as I have before mentioned, to show his skill as a marksman, and his aim being too low, shot the man in the head, the bullet entering the top of his head, leaving about two inches intact.

Another theory was that Anderson had been living in Butler County previous to coming here, and had probably taken a part in ridding the country of supposed horse thieves. Public indignation ran so high that eight men were hung in one night,[3] and many parties, whether they were suspicioned or not, left the country. Whether McCarty was there or was guilty of any crime and left, was not confirmed. Some thought he was avenging the death of some particular friend, and, like the red man of the western plains, killed the first white man he saw.

It was reported that McCarty became conscience stricken and told some parties at a ranch near town, that he had accidentally killed a man in town, and that he was very sorry and wished he could recall that shot, also that if money would call back the life he had taken, he would willingly work all his life for one penny per day. He was by nature a kind hearted man and like his relatives in "ould Ireland" was possessed with great "mother wit." But his love for whiskey caused his ruin and death.

Anderson was killed about four o'clock in the evening; I was not in town

---

[3] Yes, the seven men have now become eight.

at that time and knew nothing about it until the following morning. The evening of the shooting, a man came to my house and called for a man who was living with me. I went to the door and asked him what he wanted; he said he was after the man that was living with me, and for me to be prepared to serve a warrant in the morning. The two men got on their horses and rode in the direction of town.

I was very anxious to know what the trouble was and consequently was restless during the night. I knew both men well and knew they were excited over something unusual.

The night was a very dark one. A party of about fifteen or twenty men went to a ranch located about one mile South of town, on the cattle trail, and called the "Last Chance,"[4] so called on account of its being the last chance where whiskey could be bought after leaving the state line until the line of Texas is reached. The government laws prohibited the sale of and also carrying of whiskies into the Indian Territory.

This ranch was kept by Curly Marshal, an old frontiersman, and said to be a government scout during the war and afterwards an Indian scout under the employ of the government.[5] He was a desperado and made his living in nefarious ways. This ranch consisted of a double log house in which were kept whiskies, provisions, and feed for horses, and was probably established in 1869.[6]

Marshal erected a frame box house near the log house, intending it to be used as a dance hall. He had made arrangements with some women of ill-repute to come from Wichita and aid him in running the hall. The women had not yet put in an appearance; public sentiment was against the starting

---

[4] The Last Chance southbound and First Chance northbound—a saloon name that must date back to the early Jurassic period. This saloon was the successor to the ranch on the Ninnescah just south of Wichita, mentioned in chap. 1 (see n. 6), being frequented and at times operated, it appears, by various members of the same crowd (Andreas, p. 1387).

[5] The most accurate account of the life of John E. "Curly" Marshall is to be found in W. E. Koop's excellent "A Rope for One-Armed Charlie," *True West*, February, 1967, pp. 22-23, 56. Marshall served in the Civil War with Company L, Second Missouri Cavalry.

D. D. Leahy indicates that at least part of Marshall's service as a scout occurred at Fort Harker (Ellsworth County, Kansas). Leahy's reminiscence is largely based on Freeman and is obviously slanted toward the blood-and-thunder audience. According to Leahy, Marshall was with McCarty (Leahy calls him McCarthy) in the Butler County gang of horse thieves (*Wichita Eagle*, 27 March 1932).

[6] This date seems early. I can find no other source which places the Last Chance in Sumner County prior to 1872 (the date of establishment per Andreas, p. 1387), although illicit whiskey sellers, dealing principally with the Indians, are commonly reported at various places along the border before that date (and see chap. 3, n. 4). If Leahy can be trusted, Curly Marshall was the founder of the Last Chance, and in 1869, Marshall was in Wichita, where he had just come from Fort Harker.

of such a house and used all means possible to prevent it. This Last Chance was the favorite resort of the desperado and horse thief.

Curly Marshal was a fine type of physical manhood, standing about six feet in height. Physically he was perfection as a man animal, weighing perhaps about 250 pounds, muscular, well-built, and well proportioned. In appearance he bore the type of the frontiersman: in dress neat but pertaining to the western style of rowdyism.

Together with his extensive acquaintance on the frontier and on the western plains, and the numerous travelers on the trail, he expected at the Last Chance to establish a good business. His physical courage, indomitable will, and unerring marksmanship with the revolver led him to believe that he could over-awe public sentiment.

In our next chapter we will show the reader wherein he was mistaken.

CHAPTER 12

The Shooting of McCarty—Watching the "Last Chance"—Burning the Dance
Hall—Busey Nicholson Captured—McCarty Fights to the Bitter End
The Final Result—Curly Marshal Attempts to
Rebuild the Dance Hall—His Threat—An
Encounter with Newt Williams.

As I mentioned in the preceding chapter, the night was extremely dark, which
was to McCarty's advantage, for had he taken extra caution he might have
escaped to Texas in safety. As I have said before, Anderson was killed on
Monday afternoon about four o'clock; that night soon after dark, a posse of
fifteen or twenty men went to the "Last Chance" ranch intending to get
McCarty, as it was generally supposed he would make that his headquarters
for the night.[1]

These men went up to the ranch and demanded of the proprietor a right
to search the ranch for McCarty, but the proprietor would not give his consent and this fact led them to believe that McCarty was hiding there.

The posse of men were not to be foiled, and rode away in the direction
of town; about two hundred yards from the ranch is a ravine, running in a
southeast direction and finally terminating in Bluff Creek. This creek in its
winding course almost makes an island here, and the ranch is situated near
the center of the ground in this enclosure.[2]

Some of the men went to this ravine, the greater part of them remaining
to watch the ranch, while two or three went to town. The remaining men
were detailed here and there behind the bluffs and closely watched the movements at the ranch. They supposed McCarty would try and make his escape,
and by close watching they could get him. After waiting for some time all
was quiet at the ranch; I presume the inmates were wrapt in slumber; when
the men from the town returned to the ravine, they brought with them two
pails of coal-oil, also a couple of bed quilts.

A part of the men went quietly and cautiously up to the new frame house,
which I have referred to, as being built to be used as a dance hall, and after
saturating the quilts with the kerosene and throwing the remaining oil on the

---

[1] The vigilantes were headed by a Dr. C. A. Rohrabacher, according to A. A. Richards
(*SCP*, 26 February 1880; Andreas, p. 1495). The *Topeka Daily Commonwealth* (8 May
1872) describes the committee as "composed principally of roughs, broken-down gamblers,
amateur horse-thieves, and a few respectable citizens, who, it appears, joined the party in
the heat of the excitement," but does not explain why this aggregation would be interested
in lynching McCarty. The Wellington (Kansas) *Sumner County Democrat* (11 August 1880)
characterizes "Doc" Rohrabacher as "a former convict of the Iowa State penitentiary, and a
man who made his boast of being a rebel."

[2] Freeman's is the most exact description extant of the site of the Last Chance.

house, the quilts were fastened to the sides of the house with pins, and then, quick as a flash, the burning match touched the quilts and all was aflame.[3]

A noise was heard in the building and soon the door was opened, and the inmates began taking out the counter and rolling out the several barrels of whiskey. In doing this they saw the crowd of men and began shooting at them; the firing was returned by the crowd, and was kept up for some time. Fortunately none of the party were hurt, but two of the ranch men that were rolling out the whiskey barrels were hit with buck-shot fired from the crowd, but were not seriously hurt.

The light from the burning building made it almost light as day, and had McCarty been there he could easily have been seen;[4] and as he failed to make an appearance, the crowd went back to town, after leaving two men in the woods near the ranch to watch until daylight for McCarty's appearance.

As soon as the day had dawned, some one brought me a warrant for the arrest of McCarty, charged with murder. I soon had the necessary men to accompany me in my search for the fugitive. Men were sent in all directions, one went to Douglass, Butler County, the home of Anderson, for the purpose of informing his relatives and friends of his death and the manner in which he met it.

On Tuesday night about ten o'clock, forty men from Butler County arrived at my house.[5] Their errand was to assist in capturing the murderer who was yet at large. I told them we had all the men necessary, men who were well acquainted with the country over which we were compelled to travel, and also men who were acquainted with the parties who were supposed to give McCarty assistance.

After remaining a short time and getting something to eat, they started on their return home, and after traveling about eight miles, they went into camp for the balance of the night.

We scoured the country in every direction, rode over hill and plain, up and down the banks of the streams, through ravine and hollow, but all in vain. Our chase was a long weary one to both horse and man, and we were utterly worn out from want of sleep and rest. The search was continued until Wednesday, when we returned to town giving up all hope of his cap-

---

[3]The specific details of the firing of the building are uniquely Freeman's. The fact that the newly constructed dance hall and not the saloon itself was fired is blurred in all of the other early accounts (Andreas; *SCP*). Richards says the "ranche" was burned. One report states that it was a storeroom (*Commonwealth*, 21 April 1872). Harry Sinclair Drago questions Freeman's accuracy, citing a *Caldwell News* report of the burning of the old Last Chance building in 1887. Drago misses Freeman's point that of two buildings at the site, only one was fired (*Wild, Woolly & Wicked*, pp. 230-31).

[4]Richards indicates that McCarty was there and escaped during the melee.

[5]No other version mentions a delegation from Butler County.

ture. But upon returning to town, we learned that his hiding place had been ascertained by the men remaining to watch the proceedings at the ranch.

It seems the citizens wanted possession of the ranch, and as it was a little risky to attempt to get it by force, they laid a plan in which two men were sent to a rock quarry, which is in the Territory, and on the opposite side of the creek from the ranch, and in coming towards town they were to stop at the ranch and get some whiskey. Upon arriving at the ranch they found, to their good luck, only two men in possession of it.

They asked for a glass of whiskey, and when the bar-tender turned his head to get it, they drew their revolvers and ordered a surrender. This little game of stratagem gave them the possession of the "Last Chance," and also the men under the employ of Curly Marshal.

Soon after getting possession of the ranch, some of the men who had been looking for McCarty came, and while holding council as to what would be the proper thing to do, a man by the name of Busey Nicholson[6] came in and asked for a drink of whiskey. He then turned to the crowd and asked where Curly Marshal was. Some one replied that they did not know, but they supposed he was in Wichita.

Nicholson then said a man had given him an order to get five hundred dollars from Marshal. He was asked who the man was that had given him the order for the money. He refused to tell, but finally after much hesitation, told them it was McCarty. The news created considerable excitement among the men, and now they were satisfied the game was theirs.

The next in order would be to ascertain from Nicholson the hiding place of McCarty, and this, he utterly refused to reveal to them.

The minds of the people had become so inflamed over the tide of affairs now existing that they were determined that Nicholson should reveal McCarty's whereabouts or die upon his refusal. A council was held and a rope produced, and Nicholson was given to understand that unless he told them of McCarty's place of concealment and went with them to find him, he would be hung to the joists of the building he was in. He saw that a further attempt at concealment would be fatal, unless he was willing to forfeit his life for that of his friend.

He could see depicted in the faces of the men a look of resolution and indignant determination, foretelling that what they undertook to do, they meant to accomplish. Their looks and manner intimidated him and he told all he knew concerning McCarty, saying he was on Deer Creek about twelve miles South of town. Upon hearing that information concerning McCarty's whereabouts had been obtained, I went directly to the ranch, and arrangements

---

[6] Richards renders the name *"Boosey" Nickleson* and speaks of him as a young man. Beyond Freeman's later encounter with him (chap. 13), I have discovered no other information about Nicholson.

were made to start for McCarty on the following morning about four o'clock.

I was very tired and sleepy, having been deprived of a good nights rest for several days; I went home and soon after I had eaten my supper I went to bed and told my wife to have a cup of coffee ready for me at two o'clock in the morning, and also told my brother to have a fresh horse in readiness at my command.

At the appointed time my wife called me, and having lost so much sleep, I felt I had hardly closed my eyes before they told me it was two o'clock. I said I would lie down again for an hour, and then I could get to the ranch in time to start with the crowd.

At three o'clock I arose and after drinking a cup of coffee I went to get my horse, which I found had broken his halter and got loose; I found him, however, without any difficulty, and was soon on my way to the ranch.

To my surprise I found the men had been gone from the ranch a considerable length of time before my arrival, and as I thought it would be useless for me to try to overtake them, I concluded to ride along at my leisure in the direction they had taken. I had not proceeded far, when I saw the forms of the men coming in the distance, and after going a short distance I met them.

It was afterwards reported, and I learned from good authority, that their reason for leaving the ranch earlier than the appointed time was that their fears were that McCarty would become alarmed at Nicholson's lengthy visit and would change his hiding place, which proved to be the case. Nicholson told me afterwards, that when the men arrived at the place designated by him to be the place of McCarty's concealment and found he had fled, he expected every minute he would be shot.

When they found McCarty had changed his place of concealment the men scattered, going in all directions to hunt him; they had not proceeded far when they saw a horse in the distance, and quietly approached near enough to see it was his horse. It was not light enough to see McCarty and they quietly waited for the coming day, which had already begun to break in the East.

As soon as it was sufficiently light, they saw McCarty lying on the ground, sleeping with his head on his saddle and the lariat rope on the horse, tied to the horn of the saddle.

The men surrounded him and ordered his surrender; this of course startled him, but he soon realized the condition he was in and began shooting at the men with a Sharpe carbine. Here, it is said, one of the most daring and perilous acts took place which has ever been recorded. McCarty's horse was tied to a thirty foot rope, the rope was tied to the saddle; McCarty stood near the saddle and was trying to get his horse in order to make a run. In the mean time he kept firing at the men, and they kept firing at him. One man with more daring and courage than his comrades possessed, saw what Mc-Carty's intentions were, and ran between him and his horse and cut the rope. McCarty shot at him twice during this perilous act, but each shot missed its errand, and he was allowed to return to his comrades unhurt.[7] McCarty finally got a shell fast in his carbine and in his effort to get it out, his right hand was hit with buck-shot, disabling the use of that hand.

I presume he thought as long as life lasts there is hope, and tried to use his revolver in his left hand, but found he must surrender or be killed in attempting to run. He could not use his left hand to advantage and at last, hope left him, and he threw up his hands as a signal of surrender.

The men went to him and the report was that McCarty asked for mercy at the hands of the mob. The men left him in charge of one of the party, and they stepped a short distance away from him and held a consultation as to what they had better do with him. Some were in favor of hanging him, while others favored shooting him, and some of the cooler men were in favor of taking him to the state and give him a trial for his life. While they were discussing about it, some one asked Fielder, a brother to the man McCarty had killed, what he wanted done with McCarty. He told McCarty that ten minutes before, he could have killed him, but now his conscience would not let him become a murderer. Some one asked which one of the revolvers McCarty had killed Fielder with, and after being told, he took it from the scabbard and holding it at McCarty's head, pulled the trigger, the bullet entering his head, killing him instantly.[8]

After their deadly work had been accomplished, they turned and left the body of the murdered man lying as it fell. His body remained unburied at the place of his death until Sunday, when the mother and brother of McCarty arrived in Caldwell and proceeded to the spot where the son and brother had met his death. The body was buried near the battle ground where McCarty received the fatal charge which ended his life.[9]

[7] The daring young man was one Newt Williams, as Freeman later reveals.

[8] Richards gives no details about McCarty's killing, merely saying that the vigilantes found him and "left him lying on the prairie." D. D. Leahy (*Wichita Eagle*, 27 March 1932), whose principal source is Freeman, describes the action thus: "The greatest gun battle in the history of the Cherokee Strip was fought that morning with a single desperado on one side and fifteen determined but cautious friends of law and order on the other." Another embroidered version is contemporary: "[The vigilantes] came on [McCarty] in the night, and although he fought desperately, he was so riddled with bullets that he rattled when he fell" (*Wichita Eagle*, 26 April 1872). Wayne Gard misreads Freeman and asserts that the vigilantes brought McCarty back to town before they shot him (*Frontier Justice*, p. 196).

[9] No other source mentions the visit of McCarty's relatives to the spot, although D. D. Leahy offered this melodramatic flourish: "An aged but still beautiful woman in deep mourning took the body from the prairie a few days later. No one seemed able to discover who she was or whither she had taken the corpse." Richards states that three days

A short time after the shooting of McCarty, eighteen men residing in the vicinity of Caldwell received a notice purported to have been signed by "many citizens," notifying each party that their presence was no longer needed in Caldwell. It would be needless to add that the eighteen men, excepting two, took warning, and deemed it best for their safety to leave the country, which they did.[10] The determination was to rid the country of all parties who expressed themselves as sympathizers with murderers, outlaws, and desperadoes.

A short time after the death of McCarty, Curly Marshal began to make preparations to rebuild a dance hall, in lieu of the one which the reader will remember as having been burned to the ground by the infuriated people, there-by hoping to capture McCarty. Marshal was in Wichita at the time the hall was burned, and when that intelligence reached him, he started for the "Last Chance" alone, as he had to defer bringing the prostitutes that were to aid him in establishing the dance hall.

He remained here for a short time, and in the mean time inquired among his friends for the facts concerning the killing of McCarty, the burning of the dance hall, and the circumstances pertaining to the strategy used by which the "Last Chance" fell into the hands of the posse who were watching for McCarty. Upon learning who the men were that demanded a "throw-up" of his bar tender, Marshal made several threats; one of them was that he intended to kill Newt Williams for the active part he had taken in gaining possession of the "Last Chance."

The reported threat reached the ears of the citizens, and also was reported to Williams. Williams was a man who feared no man, he was quiet and unassuming in his manner. He believed in having the laws of the land enforced for the prosecution of the criminal and was a strong believer in the bible quotation, "an eye for an eye and a tooth for a tooth," and thought it was applicable to the murderer, desperado, and highwayman. He did not court danger, loved peace, and was ready to use his influence to quiet disorder and in upholding the law.

He was courageous and daring in disposition; the reader will remember the daring feat he performed in liberating McCarty's horse by cutting the lariat rope amid a shower of shot and the deadly fusilade of bullets.

---

after the killing, a delegation composed of "Messrs. [B. W.] Fox, Webb [presumably McCarty's companion when he shot Anderson; see chap. 11], Robinson and others went to the territory and buried him decently. The grave was afterward ravished by wolves; and last summer [1879] Mr. Enos Blair [see chap. 43] picked up the thigh bone of a man in that immediate vicinity, which is supposed to be the last of McCarty."

I have sternly resisted the temptation to try to relate this McCarty to the family of Billy the Kid.

[10]The identities of the eighteen are lost. The two exceptions may have been Curly Marshall and Dave Terrill, to whom Marshall sold the Last Chance.

Marshal's indomitable will led him to believe he could establish the dance hall at the "Last Chance" and make his business a profitable one, even though public sentiment was very unfavorable for the erection of the building and the purpose for which Marshal intended it to be used. The citizens deemed it unwise to allow Marshal to establish a dance hall and house of prostitution at the "Last Chance." The country now was infested with horse thieves, criminals who had rushed to the border of the Indian Territory to evade the laws of the eastern states. This class of people were the popular element in society at the "Last Chance;" they made the ranch their favorite resort, in laying off, after they had been on a thieving expedition or had escaped from some frontier town and succeeded in dodging the officers of the law.

This ranch was known by every horse-thief in the south-west, and they knew the proprietor and his associates were friends and associates of the outlaw and desperado.

Marshal's extensive acquaintance with the class of people who were known to frequent the dance hall and visit the houses of prostitution, assured him that his business would be profitable in various ways. He also sold whiskey of the vilest kind to his patrons and friends.

He finally went to Wichita to get lumber to erect the dance hall.[11] In his absence the citizens concluded to prevent him from establishing his house to be filled with the lowest class of prostitutes from the city of Wichita, and the citizens finally agreed that Marshal must live elsewhere or submit to the wishes of the settlers, who wanted peace and quietude to reign throughout the vicinity in which they lived.

The time arrived for Marshals return from Wichita and the people were watching with much anxiety for his coming. One morning about ten o'clock, I was sitting in front of a store in company with Newt Williams conversing about various things, when Williams said Marshal was to return to Caldwell that day; when looking up the road we observed Marshal coming with a load of lumber; as he approached town I attempted to induce Williams to go into one of the stores out of sight, knowing that if Marshal undertook to carry his threat into execution there would be a shooting scrape then and there. But Mr. Williams fearing no man refused to go out of sight, but when Marshal reached town and arrived in the street opposite to where we sat, Williams arose and said; "halloo, Marshal, I want to see you," and revolver in hand approached the wagon. Marshal stopped his team as Williams came up. Williams then said, "I understand, Mr. Marshal, you intend to kill me on sight;" having followed Williams toward the wagon, I now saw there was trouble

[11] The sequence of events has become murky here, but Freeman evidently means that Marshall, determined to have a dance hall, went to Wichita to buy new lumber to replace the burned structure.

at hand and so I at once seized Williams' revolver, and at the same time a citizen on the opposite side of the wagon seized that of Marshal.

The citizen seemed to get Marshal's revolver without difficulty, but Williams clutched his revolver like a vice, and it was by a great effort on my part that I was enabled to remove it from his hand.

The two men were now face to face unarmed. Marshal, being a giant physically, was much more than an equal for Williams, but the dauntless courage of Williams, buoyed up by a spirit of right and backed by public sentiment, made him as courageous as a lion. Few words were spoken, but Marshal was given to understand that it would be impossible for him to erect a building and run such a den of iniquity as he proposed in the vicinity of Caldwell.

While Marshal had been a government scout he had many narrow escapes and had shown himself brave behind the six shooter on many occasions, yet perhaps he had never been so completely overawed by public sentiment. There was but one alternative, and that was to return to Wichita with his lumber and never again be seen in Caldwell. The characteristic bravado having deserted him, the tears of the conquered, unbidden, forced their way down his cheeks. He said if he might be permitted to leave the town, he would never again be seen on the South side of the Nennescah River.

He turned his team around and drove to the North part of the town, unhitched, and fed; he then spent a few minutes hurriedly in closing up his business as best he could, went to his team and hitched up, and was soon on his way to Wichita. In the few minutes allotted him in town, he had sold his ranch interests to Dave Terrill, who run it for some length of time as a ranch and supply store.[12]

Curly Marshal returned to Wichita with his load of lumber, and I presume kept his word sacred, as he was never seen in Caldwell again. He spent several years in Wichita after this, and finally died by disease brought on by his intemperate habits and life of debauchery.[13]

[12] The description is misleading. The Last Chance, as Freeman himself later indicates, continued to be principally a saloon under the ownership of Terrill. Terrill's identification with Caldwell's first saloon has been noted (chap. 2, n. 4).

[13] Marshall died the November following the events of this chapter (*Wichita Eagle,* 28 November 1872, quoted in Koop, "A Rope for One-Armed Charlie," *True West,* February 1967, p. 56). D. D. Leahy says Marshall died in a Wichita livery stable, a pauper, "after prolonged and intense suffering." Leahy also states that Marshall was buried in Maple Grove Cemetery in Wichita and that the U. S. government, in recognition of Marshall's service as a soldier and a scout, erected a marker over the grave.

CHAPTER 13

Busey Nicholson Arrested on Charge of Stealing Cattle—All
Parties in Search of Evidence—Search Proves Futile—
Nicholson Liberated at Pond Creek Ranch—His
Reported Threat—Proposes for Me to
Meet Him at His Camp—Gives
Me a Family Cow.

After meeting the parties who had been on the McCarty chase, and receiving from them the intelligence that it would be useless for me to go further as the course of the double murderer was ended, I was left to infer what I might. But I was led to conclude that the dreadful work was done, and that McCarty was no more. I turned my horse and went back to the ranch and on up to town with the crowd. After we reached town, I found that some of the cattlemen had got out a warrant against Busey Nicholson on the charge of stealing cattle. It had been reported and currently believed that Nicholson had a herd of cattle about forty miles below town, and that most of his herd were stolen stock. Armed with the warrant, and in company with ten or twelve of the cattlemen, most of whom had lost stock, I proceeded to Wild Horse Creek[1] where the stolen cattle were reported to be. Before leaving town I had made the arrest of Nicholson, as he had been stopping in town most of the time. But he seemed anxious to prove his innocence to the cattle owners by going with them and me to where, report said, he was keeping the herd. The cattle owners were also anxious to go and see for themselves whether or not there was any mistake about the matter.

I have often thought that if evidence conclusive of theft had been obtained, that I would have been overpowered, the prisoner taken, and his life sealed then and there. I have always questioned my wisdom in going with my prisoner and these men down into the Territory so far.

We arrived about noon at the place where the cattle were supposed to be kept, but found no cattle or any signs of where any cattle had been kept. It seems that often men's minds become so inflamed that they are hasty to decide a man guilty without evidence or reason. About half the crowd were willing to hang the prisoner as a matter of example, without the remotest signs of guilt; while the other half seemed inclined to consider the matter in a much cooler light and were willing to declare the prisoner "not guilty."

[1] Freeman's commission as a deputy U. S. marshal gave him jurisdiction in the Territory. The Wild Horse Creek mentioned here lies about ten miles north of Skeleton Creek, sixteen miles north of modern Enid. Rolla Wells calls it Wild Horse Dry Creek (*Episodes of My Life,* pp. 42-43).

But all parties were willing that I should turn the prisoner loose. The prisoner himself insisted that I should release him, as he would then be that far on his road to Texas, where he intended to go. But in my mind I was strongly averse to this proposition, for when men's minds become so inflamed, it is difficult to tell what they will not do, and were I to give him his liberty here, it was a question in my mind whether he would reach Texas in safety or be over-taken on his journey and either be shot or hung to the nearest tree. I told Nicholson I would not turn him loose here but would take him back with us as far as the Pond Creek Ranch, which was fifteen miles distant. This was a traders ranch located on the Chisholm Cattle Trail, and men who were recognized by the U. S. Government could use it as a trading place; cattle drovers on their drives from Texas to some shipping point in Central Kansas would lay in a supply of provisions here.

After we had eaten our dinner we started on our way towards home; Nicholson and I were riding a short distance behind the other men, our conversation pertaining in a measure to his arrest, when he suddenly turned to me and asked my reason for not releasing him. I told him I did not think it would be a wise action on my part, for were I to liberate him here, my fears were that he would not reach Texas, as some of the men had shown a disposition to hang him and I knew them to be men of a determined will, and as an officer of the law, I would do my full duty in defending and protecting a prisoner in my charge; and were I to turn him loose here it would seem almost like placing him in the hands of a mob. I thought he would be safe when we arrived at Pond Creek Ranch and there he could go to Texas in company with some cattle drovers who would likely be there on their return from some shipping point. He would then be safe with his own countrymen, and in all probability they would protect him from further trouble. Nicholson seemed satisfied with my reasons and we rode quietly along, Nicholson conversing pleasantly about his home and friends in the "Star State."

Occasionally a coyote or jack-rabbit would cross our path of destination, at which some of our party would show his skill as a marksman. We proceeded on our travel without further adventure and arrived at Pond Creek Ranch late in the evening; there were a number of cattle drovers there to stay for the night beneath sheltering trees, and after passing the evening in the ranch we went to our respective places to rest. Soon after lying down on our blankets, we were in slumber-land and no doubt each dreaming of his happy by-gone days.

The next morning we were to start for Caldwell and before our departure I released my prisoner, gave him his revolver, and after bidding him good-by and wishing him a safe return to his native state, we started on our journey and arrived in Caldwell safely, and found after our absence of a few days, the people had again become quiet after their excitement over the McCarty tragedy, but how long peace and quietness is to prevail remains to be seen, and we fear it is like the rushing of the tide which recedes for a time, only to start with renewed and greater force.

The following summer [1873] Nicholson came up the trail with cattle, going through Caldwell to Abilene for the purpose of shipping the cattle, which belonged to a cattleman in Texas, Nicholson acting as the boss drover of the herd. These large cattle owners seldom go through with the herd, as the drive requires from two to five months traveling and is attended with much exposure. He usually takes the train after the cattle have arrived at their destination, meeting and shipping them to some eastern cattle market. After the employees are hired for the drive, a boss is selected by the owner and he is given charge of the herd, and is usually known by the name of "boss herder."

After arriving in Caldwell, Nicholson, it was reported, had made threats to the effect that he intended taking my life. I became aware of the threat, and upon meeting Nicholson in town I asked him if he had said he would shoot me and why he had made such a threat. He said if I would come out to camp the next morning early, he would explain the circumstances to me.

Their camping place was about a mile and one-half north of town, and they were holding the cattle there for a few days for the purpose of resting them and giving them a chance to graze. I hesitated about going to the camp, for I did not know what his intentions were and thought his purpose was not a good one and this was done to get the advantage of me. I said nothing about it and the next morning I was undecided as to what I had better do; I finally concluded to risk that his intentions were all right, so saddled my horse and rode out to his camp. I had taken the necessary precaution, however, to see that my revolver was in good shooting order. Upon my arrival at camp, I found him eating his breakfast in company with several of the herders and was greeted with the usual good morning. I got off my horse and waited patiently until he had finished eating. Then he got his pony, saddled it, and asked me to ride out to the cattle with him. I consented and we rode quietly along talking about everything excepting that which had prompted my being there. There was a man herding the cattle and we rode up to him, Nicholson telling him to go to camp and get his breakfast.

Now, thinks I, my time has come; we were there on the open prairie alone, and my thoughts were not very bright, but by his manner I did not consider I was a dead man yet. He asked me to ride with him through the herd and look at the cattle; we were almost through the herd when we came opposite a large Texas cow.

He drew rein and stopped his horse, "now," said he, "that cow is a gentle, well broke animal and is a good milk cow; you can take her as yours, she is not mine, but I will make it satisfactory with the owner; I have often wondered if I could ever repay your kindness to me, for if there is any one to whom I owe my life it is to you; for had you not been so considerate when I was under your arrest, in all probability I should not be alive to-day. I have never threatened your life, and I hope we part as friends." I was perfectly surprised and well pleased with his manner. The cow was driven to my place by two of the herders and was all Nicholson represented her to be.

CHAPTER 14

Cowboys' Carousal—The Unseen Midnight Duel—Attempt to
Awaken the Dead—Cost of Burial—
Manner of Interment.

It has been said that "when whiskey is in, wisdom is out," and this maxim has too often proved true in the case of the cowboy and herder. How often has whiskey been the cause of their trouble, and while under its poisonous influence they have been prompted to do many things which, had they been in their sober moments and in full control of their senses, would have caused them to shudder with horror. The world to-day is strewn with wrecks of men who, under the North-east storm of intemperance, have been driven to the rocks.

Whiskey has been the ruin and downfall of many a promising young man who had left his parental home with father's blessing and mother's prayers, anxious to mingle with the outside world, and to participate in the great struggle of life; how bright were his anticipations for the future, how radiant his hopes, alas, only to be blighted.

Whiskey has caused the best of friends to part in anger who have been continually in each others society for years, and shared each others burdens and whispered words of comfort in times of sorrow and bereavement, and finally when under the influence of the social glass, some disagreement, probably of a trivial nature, causes one friend to fall at the hands of the other, and upon regaining his natural senses he finds he is a murderer, is branded a criminal in the sight of people for taking the life of his dearest friend; he gives way to his grief and is inconsolable.

Would that he could recall the effects of that drink, and say, "it had not been;" ah, it is too late, any act committed, or word spoken yesterday, cannot be buried with the past. We may say we forgive, but to forget, never. The act has been accomplished, the words have escaped from our lips, and time alone can obliterate them from our memory.

In the latter part of June, 1872, a party of about twelve men, with a large herd of cattle from southern Texas, passed Caldwell on the trail, and going about a mile north of town, went into camp.

They arrived at Caldwell in the fore part of the day, and as the cattle were weary from their long tedious drive, the men concluded they would rest one day and night, lay in a supply of provisions, and proceed on their journey early the following morning.

In the afternoon some of the men came in to town, leaving the balance of the herders on duty, and after buying the necessary articles wanted for their journey onward, the men indulged freely in drinking whiskey and playing cards.

Caldwell is the first town in which whiskey can be bought after leaving the state of Texas; consequently, the boys get very thirsty for a drink of the ardent spirits, and the result is, as soon as Caldwell is reached, the saloons and grocery stores are visited, and a good supply of wet groceries is bought and often they receive an overdose of that article called whiskey.[1]

Such was the case of the parties referred to, and after remaining in town until night, all returned to their camp, except two of the boys, who were by this time largely under the influence of liquor and were having, to use their expression, "a high old time."

As the evening shades began to draw near, and the twilight hours were rapt in stillness, and the moon beamed forth in her beauty, occasionally the cowboys' yell could be heard to ring out in the clear night air. They kept on drinking and reveling until near the midnight hour, and then they seemed to realize the lateness of the hour and got on their ponies and started for camp.

What scene took place after leaving town is yet a mystery and will always remain so, unless a voice from the dead tells the awful story.

Only the twinkling stars of heaven, and the moon in solemn awe, looked down upon the ghastly scene which took place upon that fateful ride to camp.

Soon after the midnight hour, two shots fired simultaneously were heard by the herders at camp; nothing was thought of it, however, as the presumption was that the boys were returning from town, and it was not an unusual thing for them to fire their revolvers.

No attention was given to the supposition and all was still again, with nothing to break the stillness but the occasional lowing of some animal in the herd near by.

When the "wee sma hours" of the morning began to dawn, the cook arose and began making preparations for breakfast. He could see by the light of the coming day the two forms of the cowboys, lying on the ground a short distance from camp. He supposed they had taken off their saddles, turned their horses loose to graze, and had lain down to sleep. The night had been a beautiful one, and the green grass for a bed and their blankets for a covering made an excellent place for sleeping.

When breakfast was ready, someone called to the boys to get up, and as they did not seem to hear, one of the men went to arouse them from their drunken sleep. Can the reader imagine his horror, when upon touching them, found they were dead, each with a bullet through his heart.

As I stated, it was a mystery, and the facts will never be known, but after a close examination of the boys and their surroundings, the men came to this conclusion. After leaving town they became involved in a quarrel, one threat-

[1] The reader is reminded that Freeman is talking about the first town where whiskey could be obtained, a qualification which does not imply that the Last Chance was out of business.

ened the other's life, and quick as an instant the other pulled his revolver from its scabbard and holding at the heart of his adversary, pulled the trigger, both boys shooting simultaneously at each other. The result was, that both were shot through the heart, dying instantly.[2] It was a life for a life, they had died together and met death in a similar manner.

The men hired a man in town to bury the bodies, paying him twenty-five dollars, and the herd was started north. The man made a box out of crude pine boards, put the boys in it, and buried them about eighteen inches under ground. They were denied a decent burial.

Such was the fate of two young men, who to-day might have been living honorable lives had they refrained from taking the first drink, and perhaps, a mother's prayers goes out for them to-day.

[2] The incident is unrecorded in extant newspapers. The *Wellington Banner* does allude to a mutual killing of cowboys—Frank Moore and James Harris—in its issue of 16 October 1872, but while the location agrees roughly with Freeman's, no other details are given which might reconcile the October event with the one described here.

CHAPTER 15

The Killing of Oliver's Herder—Oliver Refuses to Pay a Discharged Employee—
I Go to Oliver's Camp and Serve Papers on Him—One of Oliver's Herders
Killed—Oliver Pays the Employee and Costs Accrued—In Pursuit
of the Murderer—My Horses and Wagon Stolen.

The fame and notoriety which Caldwell and vicinity had won, was not confined to this immediate country. The flow of immigration from the East set in toward the Arkansas River, the largest river in the state, and finding the most beautiful country their eyes had ever rested upon, they stopped, built their dug-out on the slope of a ravine, a cottonwood cabin on the hill, prairie grass stable close by, and called it home. They were right in calling it home, as what they lacked in social enjoyment they made up in hard labor. With civilization also came horse thieves, hard characters, and peril. The claim hunter from Missouri with two fat horses lay on the prairie with the picket ropes tied to his feet to be sure that he would be in sight of his team when the morning sun beamed out across the broad sea of prairie grass and resin weed.

More settlers came as time passed, and with them brought more horses and a bit of extra strong rope, also a double barreled shot-gun. Then there was peace and afterwards a coroner's inquest held over the body cut down from the spreading branches of the mammoth cottonwood tree.[1]

Some guilty one had to suffer at the hands of the Vigilant's Committee, or in other words be used as an example for the good of others. While I do not uphold the method of the Vigilants, yet it is the only way lawlessness can be subdued in a new country.[2] This country was fast assuming a point in which were two factions, the one belonging to the side of the law, the other against civil government. A few settlers took no part in the contests for the right, being on neutral ground; such people attended strictly to their own business, and they were seldom molested.[3]

[1] Sentences in this and the preceding paragraph are purloined from the *Caldwell Journal* of 1 January 1885.

[2] Freeman omits reference to another lynching which took place shortly after the killing of McCarty (chap. 12). John D. Lynch was hanged in Wellington by vigilantes from the Caldwell vicinity on 28 April 1872. The action, following so closely on the lynching of McCarty, prompted Governor James Harvey to wire acting Sheriff A. A. Jordan to determine whether the militia was needed to preserve order in Sumner County (Probate Court Records, Sumner County, Kansas, *Topeka Daily Commonwealth*, 8 May 1872; Governors' Correspondence, KSHS; T. A. McNeal, *When Kansas Was Young*, pp. 16-20).

[3] Freeman makes it sound as though those who were on the side of the law were the only people molested by outlaws—a sense he surely did not intend.

On the morning of June 5th, 1872, papers were placed in my hands to serve on one Oliver, a cattleman from Texas, who had passed through Caldwell on his way to Abilene to ship cattle from that place. He was then camped about twelve miles North of town on the trail. It seems Oliver had hired a man in Texas to drive cattle to Caldwell and agreed upon arriving there to pay him in coin.

When Caldwell was reached the employee demanded his pay, and Oliver refused to pay in coin but said he would pay him in currency. The reason why the employee was not satisfied to accept currency instead of coin, was probably owing to the fact that at that time there was a small premium on coin, and as their contract stated that he was to receive coin, and as that was the only kind of money used in Texas, he would accept no other. The employer was willing to pay in coin but as there was no bank at Caldwell, it was impossible to pay the debt in coin. [When he] moved on toward Abilene, he was stopped by legal papers.

I took the necessary papers, and in company with the employee went to serve them on Oliver. I supposed we would have trouble with Oliver, for the class of men that worked under him were tough looking fellows, and I presume were as tough as they looked. We rode out to Oliver's camp and arrived there at noon; the herd was slowly grazing in the distance and enjoying their noon rest. The cook was getting dinner and the rest of the men were lying under the wagon in the shade, the horses quietly feeding on the green grass near the camp.

I told the employee he had better remain a short distance South of camp, for I did not know but his going to camp would create a disturbance between the parties concerned. He was willing to comply with my wishes, and when we got within sight of the camp he got off his horse, sat upon the grass near it, and prepared to wait until I should return.

When I rode up to the wagon I asked to see Mr. Oliver, and that person stepped from among the rest of the men and came to my side. I read the papers to him and he said, "all right, I will go with you as soon as I have had my dinner." He asked me to stay with them for dinner, and ordered that my horse be taken and fed.

It seemed he had noticed that a man was in company with me and had stopped a mile or more from camp, and he asked me if the man on the prairie was not the man he had refused to pay; I told him it was the man that had been under his employ; Oliver told one of the herders to go out and tell the man to come to camp and get his dinner. I objected to this, but finally said I would not oppose it if he would promise me he would not mention their trouble; he consented and said he would not say anything concerning their trouble.

The herder went for the man and they soon returned to the camp together, and to my surprise and satisfaction, their trouble was not mentioned during our stay at the camp or on our journey to Caldwell.

Oliver willingly went back to town with us, and we arrived there late in the afternoon. The man Oliver could not have trial that evening, as it was too late after we got to town to do anything about the case.

The town was not supplied with a place in which prisoners could be kept, and it became my duty as an officer of the law, to remain with Oliver overnight, and to have him in court the following morning. I gave Oliver his freedom to go about town, but kept an eye on him so he could not give a slip and return to his camp. We went to bed about eleven o'clock, and Oliver slept very sound, and I presume I did too, for when I awoke the next morning, it was about sunrise and we both got up and dressed and went and got our breakfast.

About seven o'clock a man came from Oliver's camp and said two of his employees had got into a dispute about something, and their trouble terminated in a fight and the result was, one of the men was killed.

This was new trouble for Oliver and worried him considerably; the affairs at his camp were in a terrible plight. One of his employees dead, another fleeing from justice, with the mark of Cain stamped indelibly upon his brow. Oliver's cattle had no doubt strayed far from his camp, and all this with his previous trouble with his employee, confused and disturbed his mind wonderfully.

His cattle and the recent trouble at camp demanded his immediate attention, and consequently he was in great haste to return to his cattle and ascertain the cause of the murder of his employee.

Oliver told me he would pay the money due the man, and also pay all costs that had accrued relative to the suit. This was satisfactory to the man, and after paying him the money and settling the costs, he was allowed to depart in peace.

Oliver went hurriedly to his camp, and after getting the facts concerning the murder, he, in company with others, started in search of the murderer.

The search was long, interesting, and fruitless. The murderer eluded their grasp; they traveled in pursuit for some time, and at last utterly worn out from fast riding and exposure, they returned to camp.[4]

The cattle were soon on the trail again and were driven to their destination by a sadder set of cow-boys, since death had claimed one of their comrades.

Hardly had the words been spoken which liberated Oliver, and sent him to view the death scene at his camp, than a horseman was seen in the distance, riding in full speed and coming towards town. As he neared the little group

---

[4]This incident is unrecorded in extant newspapers as far as I have been able to determine. Given the events which immediately followed, it seems unlikely that Freeman is mistaken about the approximate date.

of bystanders, we saw it was my brother,[5] who was making his home with me, and in his haste, he told us my horses, harness, and wagon had been stolen the day before by two unknown men.

The reader may better imagine than have me attempt to describe with what surprise and consternation I received this startling intelligence.

My one great fear had been realized; I had watched my horses with great care and anxiety, and thus far they eluded the hands of the horse thief.

My horses were my main dependence, and now I was left without a team in a new country, and my condition financially speaking, was such that I could not buy me another team. I had paid $550 for them in Pottowattomie county, previous to my coming here. After paying my little all for them, I could not well stand the loss.

They were large Illinois horses, sorrel in color, and weighing perhaps twelve hundred pounds, and were considered as one among the best teams in Sumner county.

In my next chapter I will relate our experience in chasing the thieves over the western country, and the incidents pertaining to the long, weary chase.

---

[5] Milton Freeman, about fifteen years of age, according to the *SCP* (29 July 1875); but the *SCP* also identifies Milton as the *son* of the owner of the stolen team.

If John Freeman of Butler County was, as I have earlier speculated, the father of G. D., the brother mentioned here could be James M., about twenty, or John W., about fifteen (1870 Census Records, Walnut Township, Butler County, KSHS).

CHAPTER 16

Stealing of My Team and Wagon—My Brother's Story—
His Capture and Release—Thirty-five Men Start in
Pursuit—Trail of Wagon and Horse Found—
A Buffalo Killed—Great Thirst Prevails—
Description of the Lariat.

I will relate to the reader as near as possible, the facts obtained from my brother concerning the stealing of my team and wagon.

On the fifth day of June, 1872, my brother took my team and wagon about four o'clock in the afternoon, intending to go after a load of hay which we had cut and stacked a couple of miles from home.

When he was about one mile from home, he noticed two horsemen coming in the distance and riding in the direction he had picked out as his intended route. Upon nearing the wagon they stopped and inquired of him where they could find a good crossing on the creek. He was near the creek, on the west side of it, and as he turned his head to show them a fordable place, they drew their revolvers on him and demanded the team and wagon.

He told them they had the advantage of him, but if they would lay off their revolvers and step a hundred yards from the wagon, he would fight them and if they came out victorious they could have the out-fit. They laughed at this idea, and told him they did not propose to fight for it when they could have it without. He knew they had him at a disadvantage and realized that further remonstrance would probably make matters worse, so he submitted to their wishes.

One of the men got into the wagon while the other rode in front, and the one in the wagon told him to follow in the same direction the horseman had taken, which was toward the setting of the sun. They traveled until near midnight, when they stopped and asked him if he had any money with which to buy his breakfast. He told them he did not, and one of them gave him one dollar and told him he might get out of the wagon and return home.

He got out of the wagon and started to retrace his steps toward home; he walked very slowly for the first hundred yards expecting every minute to receive a shot from their revolvers. After he had walked a couple of hundred yards he ran until he came to a ravine, then stopped and listened, to see if he could hear the rattling of the wagon going on in the distance; he waited a few minutes which seemed hours to him, and soon the sound was heard.

There he stood, alone on the plains with no human in hearing, and how lonely and solitary he must have felt. The night was dark and he had only the twinkling stars to light him on his way. In the distance could be heard the howl of the coyote, which sounds very lonely in its nature; their howling made him feel and realize his far away condition. He did not know how far they had traveled before stopping.

He looked in the heavens and saw a bright star in the eastern horizon and used it as a guide by which to travel; he walked in its direction until about three o'clock in the morning, when he came to a ranch kept by Major Andrew Drumm,[1] who on learning the circumstances connected with his long walk, told one of his herders to get a horse for him to ride home and he would get him something to eat. After he had eaten his breakfast, he got on the horse and Mr. Drumm generously told him to tell me I could take the horse and ride it to hunt mine. He arrived at home about six o'clock in the morning.

I have mentioned before that I was in town the time he came home, and as soon as possible he rode into town to tell the news.

The people stood spell bound while he was relating it, and as soon as he finished, about thirty-five men volunteered to go with me and try and find the horses and if possible, catch the thieves.

The ladies of the town began preparing eatables for us to take with us, and the proprietors of the stores kindly offered us any thing they had in the line of provisions. Mr. C. H. Stone asked me if I was in need of any money; I told him how much I had and he gave me twenty dollars, saying I might find I was short of funds before my return. He also went to the stable and got a horse and saddle for a young man, and told the man if he did not think he would go and stay with me until I found my horses or gave up the chase, he did not want him to go. He said he would stay with me and never murmur; he kept his resolve and proved to be an excellent companion, and made the arrest of one of the thieves.[2]

[1] Andrew Drumm's association with cattle interests in Kansas and Oklahoma approaches legend; the *Caldwell Journal* (17 May 1888) called him "the Nestor of the cattle business in the Territory." William W. Savage, Jr., in *The Cherokee Strip Live Stock Association,* details Drumm's central participation in that organization. T. A. McNeal (*When Kansas Was Young,* pp. 177-78, 186-88) provides flamboyant accounts of Drumm's skill in the game of poker. In a retrospective version, the *SCP* (29 July 1875) says young Freeman arrived at the home of W. B. King. It also gives King credit for organizing the pursuit and capturing the thieves. G. D. Freeman was indeed without honor in his own country.

[2] Freeman later identifies this young man as Asa B. Overall. Overall, new to the vicinity at this time, became a prominent cattleman and citizen. He married Clara Nyce, daughter of a Caldwell banker, in 1882 (*Caldwell Post,* 1 May 1879, 13 April 1882; *SCP,* 16 February, 16 March 1882; Angie Debo, *The Cowman' Southwest,* pp. 55-56). Overall's activity as a citizen-lawman was not restricted to Freeman's posse. The *SCP* (20 September 1877) reports that two cowboys "got on a bit of a jamboree last week, and assaulted J. M. Thomas and wife . . . [Thomas] was not . . . to be outdone, so wore out a chair over one of them, and Asa Overall knocked the other one into the street with a sap elm board."

We started from town about nine o'clock in the morning on the day of June the sixth, and went to my house to see if my brother knew the men who had stolen the team. He was lying down on the bed and was sleeping soundly when I called him and told him what I wanted. His long walk during the night together with his loss of sleep had caused him great weariness, and when I roused him he seemed so bewildered that I could not make him understand what I wanted to know. He had told my wife all about it before lying down, and she told us all we wished to know.

When we had traveled but a short distance, a mile perhaps, we saw a man plowing; he wanted to know where we were bound for; we told him our business and he said, "by chinkins you shust take one of mine horses and let me have one of yours, for mine will stand the trip better than your horse," and we traded with him and were soon on our journey as before.

We traveled in the direction my brother said they went, and at noon stopped a few minutes to rest our horses and get something to eat, which was eaten hurriedly and we were again on our travels.

We had not proceeded far until we came to a low, marshy piece of land, and upon examination a wagon track was found, also a large horse track. One of the men asked me if it was my horse's track; I examined it and to my gratification I found it was. I am a blacksmith by trade and I had put the shoes on my horses, hence could easily identify the tracks made by my horses.

We followed the trail of the team and wagon until near the middle of the afternoon. The tracks showed we were not very far behind, and we did not travel very fast as we thought we would need the horses' strength and swiftness during the latter part of the chase. Asa Overall and myself were riding a short distance ahead of the balance of the men, and in nearing a ravine we saw some dark looking objects which we thought were horses; we turned towards the men and motioned for them to remain quietly where they were, while Overall and I would ascertain what it was. Upon second thought, I concluded to deploy the men and make a charge towards the ravine. When we got nearer we could see what we supposed to be the horses' heads and after getting within one hundred yards from them, two buffaloes jumped up and ran across the prairie land. When we saw it was buffaloes instead of horses, Overall and myself ran after them. We pursued one of them about one-half mile and shot at it and succeeded in killing it. We now had a chance to get some delicious steak, and we cut several nice pieces of meat off the hump, tied it to our saddles, and started towards the men, and after resting our horses a short time, we started on our journey. We could easily follow the wagon track now, and after traveling until about dusk we came to a spring of water.

This was the first water we had seen since noon, and you may presume how our party relished a drink of the pure sparkling water. We concluded to camp here, as the spring afforded us all the water we wanted, both for ourselves and horses, and the grass was good here, and would make excellent grazing for our horses.

After lariating our horses we made a fire and prepared something to eat. Perhaps it would be well to explain to the eastern reader, what this word "lariat" means. It is derived from the Spanish word "lariata," and means a lasso, or rope with a noose, and is used by the Spaniards in catching wild horses. In the West on the frontier, the lariat rope is carried by all cowboys or plainsmen, and its principal use to them is simply to make their horses secure, or from straying from camp.

To lariat a horse, using the common term of the words, consists in tieing one end of the lariat rope around its neck and the other end is either tied to the saddle or an iron pin, which is driven into the ground, thus making the horse secure and, also giving it the freedom of roaming and feeding to the extent of the rope. The lariat is also used by cowboys or herders to lasso cattle, horses, or anything which commands the throwing of the rope to gain its possession. Some are very skilled in the use of the lasso, performing feats which seem very difficult.

CHAPTER 17

In Pursuit of the Thieves—The Anonymous Letter—Provisions Getting Low—
The Trail Shows but a Few Days in the Advance—Description of the
Buffalo "Wallow"—The Thieves Are Spied—Arrest of
One Man—Waiting for Smith to Come to Camp
—His Appearance and Refusal to Surrender
—Smith Receives Several Shots,
and Rides for Life.

After selecting a beautiful piece of sward for our couch, we took our saddle blankets for covering and our saddles for pillows. Both horses and riders were weary. At first the horses grazed upon the fresh green pasture, but fatigue, more powerful than hunger, soon claimed the mastery, and in a few minutes our little group, horses and men, were wrapped in the sweetest of slumber. One man was left however on detail until midnight, to watch that nothing molested the horses.

Daylight was beginning to make its appearance in the east when our little party began to arouse themselves. Being the first to awake, I arose to a sitting posture and took a hasty survey of our situation. The appearance presented by this sombre looking group of sleepers strongly reminded me of scenes during the war when, after a battle, the bodies of the dead had been collected for interment.

Breakfast disposed of, we saddled our horses and waited until it was sufficiently light to see the trail when we would again pursue in search of team, wagon, and thieves. We had not long to wait, and soon we were galloping over hill and plain, feeling very much refreshed after our good sleep and rest.

Our provisions were running low; we had started with a sufficient supply to last us several days,[1] when we hoped and expected to overtake the outfit by that time. We knew the thieves could not travel with any speed as long as they kept possession of the wagon. We intended, upon finding the deserted wagon and harness, to return to Caldwell, and I would take the stage for Wichita, and there take the train and go to Ft. Larned. I expected to find the thieves at Boyd's Ranch, located about three miles east of Ft. Larned.[2]

---

[1] What happened to all those provisions is a mystery, because only one day has elapsed since the posse's departure: They left on the morning of June 6, and they are now "galloping over hill and plain" on the morning of June 7. Yet Freeman reiterates, two paragraphs further along, "We had traveled a part of two days . . . and now we had nothing to eat but buffalo meat and coffee." The cheerful defense that even Homer occasionally nodded doesn't seem adequate here.

[2] Albert Henry Boyd was a member of the town company which established Larned, Kansas. He settled on a claim near Fort Larned in 1868 and established a trader's ranch,

I have forgotten to mention this fact, as we were preparing to leave my home, a boy came to me and gave me a letter, stating this news, "Tom Smith, and —— Dalton[3] have stolen your team and their destination will be Boyd's Ranch."

We had traveled a part of two days, and as yet nothing had been seen of the wagon or horses. I did not like to start home without some trace of the thieves, but our provisions was so limited, and now we had nothing to eat but buffalo meat and coffee. I did not like to leave the trail and go home with nothing to show for our trip, and I told the boys, I would keep in pursuit, if any of them would remain with me. They replied in one chorus that they had come with me to find my team, and they would stay with me as long as I thought it was necessary to continue the search; and after shaking hands, signifying, "I'm with you until the last," we concluded to keep traveling and follow the trail until we found the wagon, and then we could make further arrangements, and offer suggestions as to what would be the best manner to gain possession of the thieves and stolen horses.

I have before stated that I received a letter telling me which way to pursue after the thieves, but as this letter was an anonymous one, I did not know but what it was used as a ruse to throw us off from the direct course taken by the thieves, so our squad of thirty-five men divided into several different posses and started in different directions.[4] The party of whom I was the leader num-

---

a saloon, and a crude toll bridge across Pawnee Creek to accommodate traffic on the so-called dry crossing of the Santa Fe Trail (Pawnee County Clippings File, KSHS, 1:152-53; *Great Bend Tribune*, 7 October 1956; *Larned Tiller & Toiler*, 11 February 1947). Whether Boyd himself was a member of the horse-thief ring that Freeman later describes is conjectural; at least Boyd's establishment appears to have been a haven for those who were members.

³"Tom Smith" was the youngest of the five orphaned children of Thomas Ford (1800-1850), a former governor and supreme-court justice of Illinois. "Smith" was adopted by Thomas C. Moore of Peoria and took his foster father's surname. Thus, originally Thomas Gord Ford, he became Thomas Gord Moore. (A brother, George S. Ford, appears later in this narrative as "Charlie Smith.") Thomas Moore served in the 139th Illinois Infantry during the Civil War (*Peoria National Democrat*, repr. in *SCP*, 29 July 1875; *Peoria Evening Call*, repr. in *SCP*, 28 December 1882; *Dictionary of American Biography*, 3:520-21).

No further identification of —— Dalton has been uncovered despite my wishful efforts to link the young man to the notorious Coffeyville family of the same name.

⁴The anonymous letter seems like a plot device from a bad play—and so is probably true.

It is not clear why, when they all had been following tracks left by the fugitives, the posse split up into groups and searched in several directions (though I am sure I have served on committees which did things like that).

As opposed to Freeman's tally of thirty-five men in the posse, the *Wichita Eagle* (14 June 1872) reported "some eighteen . . . Sumner County vigilanters" had gone in pursuit of the stolen team.

bered seven men, namely, Ballard Dixon,[5] Asa Overall, Jim McGuire, ——— Sullivan, ——— Dobbs, and ——— Franklin.[6] Some of these men are to-day honorable residents of this county, while some are peacefully sleeping the sleep which knows no waking.

The different parties of the squads, after traveling for several days without any trail or signs of encouragement, returned to their homes.

We followed the trail until noon, and then stopped for a short time and made a fire out of buffalo chips, and proceeded to boil some coffee and fry some buffalo meat. Our horses were lariated to our saddles and were grazing on the green buffalo grass. We were very hungry, and it took a good supply of buffalo meat to satisfy our appetites, and our dinner consisted of buffalo meat alone, save a few swallows of coffee.

When the meat was cooked, we helped ourselves to the mess. One of the men looked at it, and remarked, he would rather starve than to eat meat which had been laid on buffalo chips and cooked. He sat quietly by, while we, old frontiermen, took hold with a relish and cleaned the platter.

We were soon in the saddle again, and traveled until nearly dusk. The country here was full of wolves and buffaloes. We could see great herds of them in the distance and the night air was filled with the howls of the gray wolves. We lariated our horses near camp, and guarded them all night, as we were afraid the wolves would prowl around the camp and might possibly scare our horses and cause a stampede, and then we would be left a foot on the broad prairies and many miles from home. I will relate an incident which occurred at supper time. Our supper consisted of buffalo meat, and cooked in the same manner in which it was cooked for our dinner; the man who would rather starve than to eat meat cooked on buffalo chips, had began to get pretty hungry, for he had had nothing to eat since morning. I roasted a nice piece of meat and was sitting near him, and after watching me a few minutes, he said, "George, give me a piece of your meat, I believe I can eat it." I willingly shared it with him, and after that he did not complain of cooking with buffalo chips.[7] We were glad to have anything to eat, and it did not matter to us in what manner it was cooked.

Soon after starting on the following morning [8 June 1872], we found where the thieves had camped the day before; from the appearances it had been their noon camp, and this gave us renewed strength and brightened our prospects. At noon, we found where they had killed an antelope, and from the appearances they did not seem to be in any hurry, for the grass had been eaten close to the ground by the horses. We hastened our speed, and were

---

[5] C. B. Dixon, whom Freeman profiles in chap. 45.

[6] McGuire, Sullivan, Dobbs, and Franklin are otherwise unidentified.

[7] Freeman likes this anecdote so well that he later tells it about two other blokes (chap. 26).

satisfied we would soon overtake them, unless they abandoned the wagon.

We traveled as long as we could see to follow the trail, and between sundown and dusk we stopped for the night on a high prairie land, and we were without water, unless we would use it out of the buffalo wallows. We used it, however, and also watered our tired horses at one of the wallows. The wallows are to be found throughout the buffalo country, and are about eight feet in diameter and from six to eighteen inches in depth, and are made by the male buffalo in the spring when challenging a rival. The ground is broken in pawing, and if the challenge is accepted, as it usually is, the combat takes place; after which the one who comes off victorious occupies the wallow of fresh upturned earth, and finds it gives a cooling sensation to his hot and bleeding sides. During the shedding season, the buffalo resorts to his wallow to aid in removing the old coat of hair. After a heavy rain these wallows become filled with water, the soil being of such a compact character as to retain it. True, the water is not of the best quality, particularly if the water has been of long standing and the wallow used by the buffalo as a summer resort, but on the plains a thirsty man or beast will not take these facts into consideration, but will make the best of his situation, and will drink and use the water for cooking purposes.

The night was a cloudy one, and after midnight a slight rain had fallen, which made it difficult to follow the trail. After we had proceeded on our journey about twenty miles,[8] we came to a dim road, and could see by their wagon tracks that we were not far behind the thieves. Some of the men had a pack horse, so we changed our saddles, putting them on the horses we had been leading. I told the men that had no lead horse if they were afraid of hurting their horses, they could ride at their leisure, but we, who had fresh horses would ride faster. They all agreed to stay with me, so we started on a run and rode very rapidly for about five miles, when we came to some good water, and we decided to rest our horses and cook something to eat.

We cooked some buffalo meat, boiled some coffee, and after eating our frugal meal, we prepared to proceed on our journey. We rode at a pretty good gait, and about four o'clock in the afternoon we came within sight of the Arkansas River. When we were within one mile and a half of the river, we found the land was broken by hills and ravines. We entered a ravine and halted until we could lay plans to get a view of the country beyond the hill over which the trail crossed and entered the valley.

I finally conceived the idea of tieing a bunch of weeds together and taking them with me and when I was near the top to roll the weeds in front of me, thereby keeping myself from being observed by parties in the valley, in case there should happen to be parties there—and would also afford me the chance to make observations beyond me.

[8]Presumably the next day, 9 June 1872.

I took my bunch of weeds and started for the hill and soon I lay down and crawled upon my hands and knees, carefully pushing the weeds in my advance. Upon my arrival at the summit of the hill, I was surprised to see a wagon in the valley and three grazing horses near by. I could not determine whether the horses were mine or not, but imagined they were the outfit we were after. I saw the river was very high, past fording, and the outfit could not cross, and neither could we so I went back to the men and told them what I had seen and what my surmises were. We decided to go into camp and a couple of us went to the summit of the hill and watched the movements at the wagon.

After remaining on the hill until dark, we entered a ravine, and followed it in its windings until we were within about one hundred yards from the wagon. We also got so near one of the horses that we could have taken it very easy, but I did not care to get the horse until we were ready to get the horses, wagon, and thieves. We went back to camp and we remained in the ravine until about three o'clock in the morning. By this time our horses were considerably rested and had had an abundance of green feed. We were now ready to attack the party and made our arrangements in this manner—two of the men were to take their horses and were to follow the thieves in case they made a run, the balance of the men were to creep on their hands and knees until we were within a few feet of the wagon.

When all was in readiness we followed the ravine until we were about one hundred yards of the wagon; the men on horseback remained in the ravine, while five of us crawled within about fifty feet of the wagon. The grass was about eighteen inches in height and was wet with dew, wetting our clothing through to our bodies and making us very uncomfortable. The night was damp, and together with our wet clothing and chilled bodies, made us wish morning would soon dawn. We quietly waited for daylight to make its appearance, and the hours seemed to drag slowly by. I kept raising my revolver and looking to see if I could see the sights on it, and at last, after examining it I found I could see well enough to shoot. The men were placed in such positions as to surround the wagon, and when the first signs of the coming day made its appearance, I quickly jumped to my feet and commanded the thieves to surrender. Not a sound was heard in the direction of the wagon; I again gave the command, but I received no response. I began to think there was no one in the wagon, and that the "birds had flown," but I made one more effort and yelled surrender. This time a man's head made its appearance, and I ordered him to lie down, he fell like a log and remained perfectly quiet. I then told him to get up, but to hold his hands above his head while he was getting out of the wagon; he did as I ordered, and I do not think I ever saw a more frightened man than he was. He looked around and saw five men, armed with guns and revolvers. I told him to tell the other man to get up and to hold his hands above his head, the same as he had done. He replied there was no one in the wagon. I told him if he did not tell the man to get up, I would give him a load of buckshot. Asa Overall was standing in such a position that he could easily see into the wagon, and replied to me, that there was no one in the wagon but the man who had already surrendered. We closely surrounded the wagon and the man began begging for his life. I told him he would not be hurt provided he would answer all questions asked him. I asked him where the other man was; he hesitated a few minutes, then said he took his horse, swam the river, and went to Boyd's ranch. He also said the other man's name was Tom Smith, and that he had gone to the ranch to get some provisions for them.

Dalton, the prisoner in our possession, was a nice looking young man, about twenty-two years old and less than medium height. He did not bear the looks of a desperado, nor had he the looks of a criminal upon his face. I do not think he was a hardened criminal, as he had not lost his looks of humanity. He was very much frightened and feared he would have to forfeit his life for the crime committed by him.

Two of the men took Dalton to our camp in the ravine, while the balance of us arranged ourselves around the wagon; we hid in the grass and waited for Smith to make his appearance. We were very hungry and thirsty, but did not think it best to go to the camp, so we concluded to wait for Smith. About ten o'clock we saw him in the distance; when he reached the Arkansas River, he took off his coat and swam his horse across the swollen waters, about 400 yards from the wagon; after he had reached the opposite bank he stopped, put on his coat again and rode slowly toward the wagon, apparently as though his suspicions were aroused that all was not right at the wagon.

I intended to let him come up to the wagon and then order his surrender, but I saw one of the men was about to rise, [so] I immediately arose upon my feet and ordered him to surrender. Smith took in the situation at once, and turned his horse rapidly and gave a yell like the Indian on the warpath. As he turned I fired at him with a double barreled shot gun. The shot did not seriously hurt him, as his coat was a very heavy one and the shot did not penetrate through its thickness. We found out, however, that two of the buckshot struck him in the right shoulder and several of the shot took effect in his right arm; the fine shot did not penetrate through the coat.[9]

As he turned his horse he took from his belt a dirk, and began to use it on his horse instead of a spur, and the horse and rider were soon out of the range of our guns; hence the only way to get "our man" was to give chase and run him down, or trust to Providence to place him in the hands of the law.

In my next chapter I will relate to the reader our long, weary chase and the final result of our pursuit after the thief.

[9]Freeman seems to be trying to say that although "Smith" received minor wounds in the shoulder and arm, the coat prevented any buckshot from hitting a vital area.

CHAPTER 18

Arrest of Tom Smith—In Pursuit of Tom Smith—Arrival at Fort Larned—
A Sergeant and Six Soldiers Accompany Us to Arrest Smith—
Description of Boyd's Ranch—The Search—Smith Arrested
and Shackled—Crossing the Swollen Waters of
the Arkansas River—Smith Falls from his
Horse and Is Nearly Drowned—Our
Homeward March—Great
Hunger Prevails.

As quickly as I could I ran to the wagon and cut the rope which fastened one of my horses which the thieves had stolen, and mounted the horse and in haste proceeded after the thief. The land was a level prairie for about one mile, consequently was greatly to his advantage. My horse was rapidly gaining on his in the race, and I intended when I was near enough, to throw the lariat rope and jerk him from his horse. But in this scheme I failed, for Smith was riding for some hills and there he would have the advantage of me, for he could watch for me, he being concealed under the hill, and upon my approach he could shoot me. I saw what his intentions were, and had about given up the hope of getting him, when I saw one of the men [Asa Overall] who had been watching the prisoner, coming on the run, and he too saw what Smith's scheme was, and he ran between Smith and the hills causing Smith to turn his horse in the direction of the river.

I turned and rode back to the wagon to get a saddle, leaving Asa Overall in the chase. When I got to the wagon I found one of the men ready to go with me, and as soon as possible we were in the pursuit. Smith swam his horse across the river, and was riding at full speed on the opposite side. We did not stop to consider the perilous act that lay before us, but hastened on until the river bank was reached. I knew my horse to be an excellent swimmer. We did not take the necessary time to go to the ford, but entered the river at the nearest point within our reach. When my horse jumped from the bank into the river we both went under water. I had taken off my hat and held it in one hand, while with the other I took hold of the horn of the saddle. We had no difficulty in crossing to the opposite side, and as soon as we could conveniently, we got off our horses, pulled off our boots and emptied the water out of them, put them on again and immediately started for Fort Larned, which was located about nine miles from the river.

I had a couple of ten dollar bills in my pocket, which of course were wet, so I took them out and partially dried them before we reached our destination. We rode very rapidly until we reached Fort Larned, and we expected to find

Smith had arrived there in our advance, but upon making inquiry we could find no one who could give us any information concerning him.

We were very hungry, having had nothing to eat since the evening before, and we concluded to go to the quartermaster's store and buy some provisions. While we were in the store a soldier came in and told the quartermaster that Tom Smith had been on the other side of the river and had been attacked by a band of Indians; also that he had been shot at twice, one of the charges taking effect in his arm, and his horse had also been shot. He gave us the necessary information we wanted to know, for he further said that Smith was going to Boyd's ranch to get a fresh horse, and wanted some of the men to go with him and they would give them [the Indians] a fight. We did not pretend to know anything about Tom Smith; but as soon as we had eaten a few bites of lunch set before us, I went to the commanding colonel of the fort[1] and informed him what my mission was, and requested him to let a squad of soldiers accompany me to Boyd's ranch located about three miles East of the Fort.

The colonel sent his orderly to the sergeant with a command to take six soldiers and go with me to make the arrest of Tom Smith. I accompanied the orderly to the sergeant's headquarters, and he soon had six men in readiness. We also had the company of an old scout who expressed a desire to "see the fun." The scout had two fine horses and offered me the services of one of them; I was very much pleased to get a fresh horse, as mine had already begun to show signs of great fatigue.

I looked at the horses, one of them was a beautiful black, while the other was a smooth, sleek sorrel. I suggested that he let me ride the sorrel, but he said I had better take the black one. I did not think he was possessed of the qualities which require great speed, but thought a scout would certainly have good running horses, so I decided to ride the black horse.

When arrangements were made and all were in readiness to start, the scout told me to hold my horse, so that his could run with mine. I made reply that I thought in order to race with him, I would have to use the spur instead of holding my horse back with the rein. He warned me to hold my horse and not let him get the advantage of me, in the start.

No sooner had I taken my seat in the saddle, than my horse was all nerve and dashed away, over the broad prairie on the run; the balance of the men soon gained ground however, and were riding near my side.

[1] The commanding officer at Fort Larned was Captain H. B. Bristol, Fifth Infantry. The post returns show no record of Freeman's visit, and there is, of course, no compelling reason why they should (Fort Larned Records, Post Returns, November 1859-July 1878, National Archives).

When we were about two miles from the ranch, we saw a man leave the ranch, cross the ravine, and go North. Our party halted and I took the scout's field-glass and looked at the man, but could not satisfy myself that it was Smith. But fearing I might be mistaken, I suggested that the sergeant take three soldiers and get the man; and I would take the remaining three soldiers, the scout, and the man that came with me from camp, and proceed to Boyd's ranch and search it. As the sergeant and soldiers left us, one of them, a Dutchman, turned to me and said, "sposen he shoots ven we go to arrest him." I told him if the man made any resistance and attempted to shoot, for him to be prepared to defend himself and get the first shot.

Our party arrived at the ranch and rode to the south door, got off our horses, and entered the ranch. We found to all appearances that the bartender was the only person there, and I asked him if he knew where Tom Smith was; he replied in an indifferent manner that he did not know anything about Tom Smith. I told him I knew better, for Tom Smith was seen about noon going in the direction of the ranch, and also, that Smith said he was going to the ranch. The bar-tender said we could search the ranch if we wanted to. Two of the soldiers went to the back door and stood guard, while one remained at the front door. Perhaps it will interest the reader to have a description of the ranch. This ranch was well known throughout the West, and by some it was presumed to be the hiding place for criminals who were being searched for by the law. The ranch was about twenty feet in width and forty feet in length; the bar-room was in the southwest corner, the balance of the west side was partitioned into small rooms in which was a bunk or bed to accommodate one man. A hall run through the entire building, and the East side was arranged in similar manner to the West. Opposite the bar-room was a room in which was kept saddles and guns.

I told the bar-tender to light a lamp and I would proceed to search the building. The scout took a position in the hall, about midway between the North and South doors. I have forgotten to mention that the building was lighted with only two small windows which were in the South end. The bartender got the light, and I told him to go into the room in advance of me; we searched the entire building and our search proved to be a futile effort. As we returned to our soldier friends at the door, they informed me that the soldiers had arrested the horseman and were going in the direction of Fort Larned. The bar-tender offered us a drink of whiskey; I did not indulge, but the other men seemed to think their livers were torpid and needed a tonic and indulged freely, and I presume they felt much better, physically, after drinking of the stimulant.

We got our horses and started for Fort Larned, and overtook the sergeant when we were about one mile from the fort. As I rode near the group I saw they had Tom Smith, or in other words, "our man." I turned to Smith and made this remark, "It seems that time makes a change in circumstances very quick." He said, speaking to the sergeant, "Do you allow a man to talk in such a manner to one whom you have under arrest." The sergeant replied that he was arrested under my orders, consequently was under my control.

I took the prisoner to the Colonel's office, and when the Colonel came to the door, he said to Smith, "Mr. I think you are caught this time." Smith said I was only a constable and had no authority to arrest him. I showed a commission of Deputy U. S. Marshal, and colonel told Smith I was a U. S. officer and he was in duty bound to help me in making the arrest. He then asked me if I wanted shackles for the prisoner. I replied that I did and he gave me some shackles. I went to he blacksmith and had them properly fastened on Smith. I also obtained a pair of shackles for Dalton. The colonel offered me the services of six soldiers to accompany us on our return to camp, near the Arkansas River; I did not think it was necessary, for our prisoner was securely shackled and I did not think the circumstances required any additional help, other than what our own men were capable of doing. The colonel then asked me if we had a good wagon tongue and a piece of extra strong rope, intimating that if Smith gave us unnecessary trouble, we could put an end to his earthly career by hanging him to the wagon tongue. We were to travel over a prairie country almost devoid of trees; the only trees to be seen were very scattering and grew on the banks of the streams; hence in order to hang Smith, we would probably have to use the wagon tongue, but our intentions was not to commit violence to either of our prisoners, but to take them safely home and give them over to the law, and let them have trial and abide by the decision of the court.

Smith became very indignant over the colonel's jesting remark, and angrily told the colonel he would not dare to use such insulting language in his presence, provided he was free. The colonel replied in a very indifferent tone, saying, "I think when you are a free man again, you will have served a few years in the penitentiary, and I hope you will be capable of following a better trade and one in which you can make a more honorable living than by stealing horses." I presume Smith thought the colonel was "joking on facts," and that it would be best for him to keep still, so he made no reply; but his expression showed a terrible struggle with the inner man, in which to gain the mastery over his rebellious spirit and quell the rage which was being manifested.

The colonel sent several soldiers to a mound a few miles South of the Fort, ordering them to remain there until we had reached the camp, and if we wanted their assistance we were to signal them and they would lend us a helping hand.

As we were on our way to camp I told Smith if any of his friends came to his rescue and offered to do us any violence, that he could easily quiet the trouble, and if he did not he would most assuredly suffer at our hands;

and if necessary we could fight our way through. He said there would be no trouble for there was no one at the ranch. When we were about four miles from camp, Smith's horse was too much exhausted to carry his weight so Franklin let Smith ride his horse; we had to lift him in the saddle and he had to ride side ways, for his feet were shackled together, therefore preventing him from using both stirrups of the saddle. Franklin and I took a "turn about" in riding and we reached the river without any adventure worthy of mention.

The river was yet past fording with a wagon and really it was not safe to cross it on horseback, but we were good swimmers and our horses were also, so we concluded to risk it and endeavored to cross to the opposite side. The Arkansas River is a very treacherous and swiftly-flowing stream; the shifting sands is a great barrier and changes the intentions of many who attempt to cross this perilous water, unless they have great inducement or duty which causes immediate attention and urges them onward across the muddy, foaming waves.

We belonged to that class of people that duty urged onward, and we cautiously entered the rapid running water. Franklin took off his clothing and tied it securely to the saddle on the horse Smith was riding, and he was going to try and get Smith's horse to swim across to the opposite side. It was too weak, however, and we left it standing on the sand bar. My horse was heavily loaded; besides my weight I had a two bushel sack filled with hard tack, twenty pounds of bacon and five pounds of coffee.

As we entered the water I took the bridle rein of the horse Smith was riding, and led it until we got within twenty feet of the opposite bank, when our horses began to whirl. It seems we had unconsciously rode into the whirl, and no sooner had we got within its reach than our horses began to whirl with the tide, and had not the boys come to our assistance with ropes, in all probability we should have been drowned.

The men at camp saw us coming and came down to the river to watch us cross it, and were thoughtful enough to bring a couple of lariat-ropes. When they saw our situation, one threw a lasso over the head of Smith's horse, and the other drew one end of a rope and I put the loop over the horn of my saddle. Then all on the bank lent a helping hand and we were out of our difficulty.

Smith, however, came near losing his life; as the horse started out of the whirl, Smith accidently fell backwards, and had not the shackles caught on the horn of the saddle, he would have been buried beneath the bounding billows of the Arkansas river and thereby escaped the shameless way in which he met his death, a few days after our arrival home. The shackles held him fast and he was dragged out of the water.

It was about six o'clock when we arrived at the camping place of the thieves, and we concluded we would go to our camping place in the ravine. We hitched my horses to the wagon and Smith was helped to get in, and then we started for camp. Upon our arrival there I put the shackles on the boy prisoner, and we prepared supper. We were very hungry and had not eaten any bread for three days, and it tasted very good to our appetites. Our supper consisted of bacon, coffee, and hardtack; and we ate very heartily. Smith was very morose during the evening and did not seem inclined to talk.

My companions and I were very tired after our days work; I was feeling jubilant over the fact that we had good success in capturing the thieves and obtaining my horses again; I imagine I felt as proud as the man whose wife presented him with twin babies; this man had lived the greater part of his life in a new country, and his greatest desire was to see the country populated.

The men who remained at camp during our absence were to act as guard over the prisoners and horses. We feared an attack might be made by Smith's friends, but we were prepared for an active defense in case they had come to our camp. Each man in our party was armed with a shotgun and two revolvers, and two of the men had a Winchester rifle apiece, and the men were a determined and active set and I believe would have given the friends of Smith a warm reception, had they attempted to molest us.

After lariating our horses securely in our midst, and posting the guards for the night, each one of our little party first satisfying himself that his fire-arms were in good order and loaded, spread his blanket on the ground, and with his saddle for a pillow, the sky unobscured by tent or roof above him, was soon reposing comfortably on the broad bosom of mother earth, where, banishing from the mind as quickly as possible all visions of horse-thieves, soldiers, etc., sleep soon came to the relief of each, and we, all except the guards, rested as peacefully and comfortably as if at home under our own roofs or that of our mother's home.

The next morning [11 June] daylight found us in readiness to start for our homes in Caldwell. Our hard tack had to remain behind, however, on account of its not being fit to eat. In crossing the river, it had been thoroughly wet, and the following morning when we went for our hard tack for breakfast, we found it had increased in size and had a powerful smell about it, and it was not fascinating either; so we left it "to perish by the roadside," and we started with no provisions, but coffee, salt, and bacon.

After riding all day we went into camp early in the evening, as that would be the last watering place for fifteen miles; hence we concluded it would be advisable to camp near a good supply of water. Our supper consisted chiefly of water with a little coffee in it, and a slice of bacon for each.

The next morning [12 June] as daylight was breaking in the east we proceeded on our journey. We did not see any game, and now our bacon was consumed; we watched, thinking we might get a chance to kill a buffalo, but we were unfortunate and did not see a buffalo on our return trip. We traveled all forenoon without any water, and at noon we came to a buffalo "wallow," which furnished us a drink. The water was very muddy and filthy looking, and Smith told us to take a prickly pear leaf and put it into the water, and it would settle it so we could drink with some satisfaction. We did this and it cleared the water very nicely, all the dirt adhering to the glutionous part of the leaf. I did not drink any of it until Smith drank a good draught of the water, then as it did not seem to injure him, we drank until our thirst was quenched. We made some coffee and rested our horses until about two o'clock, and we rolled out of camp and began traveling over the plains.

CHAPTER 19

The Hanging of Tom Smith—One of the Thieves Escape—Arrival at a Cattle
Camp—Arrival in Caldwell—The Prisoner Given Trial and Pleads
Guilty Great Excitement Prevails—Smith on the Way to
Wellington, to be Confined in Jail—Smith Taken
from the Constable by a Mob—Smith's Body
Found Hanging from an Elm Tree—His
Manner of Death and Burial.

Those unfortunate persons who have always been accustomed to the easy comforts of civilization, and who have never known what real fatigue or hunger is, cannot realize or appreciate the blissful luxury of a sleep which follows a days ride in the saddle of half a hundred miles or more. After riding until nearly dark, we selected our camping place on the banks of a small tributary of the Chikaskia River. The water stood in small pools and was very warm for drinking purposes. One of the men dug a hole about eighteen inches deep in the sand, and it was soon filled with much cooler water than we found in the pools.

Our horses were lariated near the wagon and they were soon contentedly grazing on the green verdure. We made some coffee and had to content ourselves as well as we could, without any provisions. The low hanging clouds gave us warning that a rain storm was approaching. We gathered some dry limbs and brush to keep a bright fire throughout the night; the brightness of the fire made our watch more cheerful, and the hours seemed to pass more swiftly.

Ballard Dixon and myself acted as guards during the fore part of the night. The prisoners had been submissive, and did not give us any uneasiness; yet we concluded it would be safer for us to guard them closely. About midnight Asa Overall and McGuire came to our relief, and said they would stand guard the balance of the night. We were sleepy, tired, and hungry.

Relieved from our sense of responsibility, and feeling confident that our comrades would perform their duties as guards, which gave me strong assurance of the prisoners safety, we sought our blankets and were soon rapt in slumber. The night was dark, and the little fire kept by the guards blazed very brightly, showing the dim outlines of the horses picketed near the wagon. Before I lay down to sleep I looked about me to see if all was well, and being assured that men and prisoners were sleeping, I felt renewed confidence and slept profoundly during the after part of the night.

I had been confident during our traveling with the prisoners that they would make an effort to secure their liberty should there be the slightest probability of success. Their past career justified me in attributing to them the nerve and daring necessary to accomplish their freedom. How well my presumptions were grounded the reader will know as this chapter progresses.

At daylight [13 June] I arose, and the first thing I did was to go to the wagon and see if the prisoners were there; you can imagine my amazement when I saw Dalton had made his escape. I called to the sleeping men and told them of his flight, and then went to see if the horses were safe. I saw that Dalton had taken the precaution to take his own horse, and when I came back to the wagon the men were in a group, discussing the subject which was uppermost in the minds of every one in camp. I listened to the various theories and surmises advanced by them and derived but little encouragement from their expressions. I hastily saddled my horse and started in pursuit of our prisoner, but who was now at liberty and a free man. A slight rain had fallen during the night and as he had escaped after the shower, I could readily follow his trail. I noticed by his trail that he rode away very rapidly and after following the trail for about three miles, and not knowing at what hour he had escaped, I concluded it would be useless for to follow him. We were only a days drive from Caldwell; the men were getting tired and great hunger prevailed, and I was certain we had the thief who had instigated the theft and was probably the cause of Dalton's taking the active part he did in stealing the horses. My opinion was, that we had better let Dalton go and start toward home as quick as possible.

When I returned to camp the men had made some coffee, had the horses harnessed, and were ready to "roll on." We found the shackles that Dalton had worn were too large for him, and we supposed he had pulled off his boots, slipped the shackles over them, and put his boots on again, thus freeing him, provided he could elude the guards, gain his horse, and ride away.

We had now been two days without provisions and were almost ravenous; at times our thirst was so great that we could scarcely talk above a whisper. We had hoped we might kill sufficient game to satisfy our wants, but our efforts proved futile; we traveled onward however, realizing we would soon reach Caldwell where we could obtain the necessaries of life. We drove as fast as our tired horses could endure, and about noon we came to a cattle camp; the cowboys had eaten their dinner and were preparing to drive the cattle on toward their destination. The men remained about a quarter of a mile from the camp, while I went to it to see if we could get something to eat. The boss herder said they had a good supply of provisions, but he did not want so many men to come to his camp. I saw that his suspicions were aroused, and I suppose he thought we were a band of thieves or highwaymen. I showed him my commission as Deputy United States Marshal and made him acquainted with what I had done; he then said to have the men come and get some dinner.

He called the cook and he soon spread before us a beautiful dinner, and it would be needless to add that we did it justice as far as our ravenous appetites were concerned. I asked the boss what our bill was, and he said "you are welcome to all that you ate, and if he should ever catch the man who had stolen anything from him, he would take the stock and return home, and he would bet that thief would never steal again." We rested about two hours to let our horses graze, then we proceeded on our journey and arrived at Caldwell about four o'clock.

The people were very much surprised when they saw us; I was driving the team, and Smith was riding in the wagon with me. As the men at town saw us coming, they knew it was our outfit before we reached town. My team was well known throughout the country, as a team of their weight was seldom to be seen in the West. The horses were a span of matched sorrels and commanded attention wherever they were to be seen.

As I drove into town the men threw up their hats, and yelled "hurrah for the boys, they have the team and also captured the thief." This caused great excitement, and I feared the prisoner would be taken and hanged. I hurriedly took Smith up the stairs over Thomas' store, and secured the services of some trusty men to guard him. I went immediately to the Justice and told him the facts concerning our capture of Smith, also that the people were manifesting much excitement and indignation over our return, with Smith in our possession.

The Justice told me to send for my brother as quickly as possible and let Smith have his trial and be taken to Wellington, the county seat, that night; for in case he remained in Caldwell, he had an idea that Smith would be lynched by a mob. My brother was sent for and arrived in a short time; I went to Smith and asked him if he was ready for trial, he replied that he was. I took him to the office of the Justice, and was followed by a crowd of excited men. When Smith was asked by the Justice if he was ready for trial, he answered in the affirmative, and my brother was called to the witness stand. His evidence was, that Smith was one of the men who came to him on the fifth day of June, and demanded the team and wagon, also that he was commanded, by Smith, to drive the team for them, and that after traveling about twenty miles, he was released from bondage and given one dollar and told to return home. After hearing my brothers testimony, the Justice asked Smith if he was guilty of the crime as set forth in the evidence; Smith replied, "I am guilty."

The Justice ordered that I take Smith to Wellington immediately.[1] I was fortunate in getting Mr. I. N. Cooper[2] to let me take his team and wagon;

---

[1] The justice of the peace, otherwise unidentified, has held a preliminary hearing and bound "Smith" over for trial in the district court at the county seat.

[2] I. N. Cooper owned a farm one-half mile west of Caldwell (see chap. 4, n. 1) not far

and I secured the services of Perry Haines, Dan Carter, and Dr. Black[3] to accompany us with the prisoner to Wellington.

We started from Caldwell about sundown. The wagon was supplied with three seats, and two persons sat on each seat. I. N. Cooper and Dr. Black sat on the front seat, Cooper driving the team; Dan Carter and Smith occupied the middle seat, Dan sitting on the right side, leaving the hindmost seat to be occupied by Perry Haines and myself. We did not anticipate any trouble unless the excited crowd should follow us from town, but we would occasionally glance back, and was satisfied we were not followed.

As we were nearing the Chikaskia River, Smith put his hand on Carter's shoulder, and was slyly letting his hand slip near his revolver, which was in a scabbard in the belt worn around Carter's waist. I happened to glance in that direction, and saw Smith's hand within six inches of Carter's revolver. I caught the revolver before Smith could get it, and told Carter that it was not safe to carry his revolver there, and that I would keep it for him.

Darkness had overtaken us before our arrival at the crossing on the Chikaskia River known as the stage crossing and located on the claim of J. A. Ryland.[4]

As we neared the river, Smith pointed at the bunch of timber on its banks and remarked, boys I never expect to pass that clump of trees; how well his assertion proved a fact, the reader will learn in the conclusion of this chapter. Whether he had a premonition of his death, I cannot say, but he seemed willing apparently, to meet his death. Before leaving Caldwell he wrote a letter to his brother Charlie, at Wichita, and placed in it forty dollars, telling his brother he did not expect to live long enough to need the money.

When we arrived at the river bottom, we emerged into a road densely grown with tall grass, weeds, and brush; as we entered this our team was stopped, and the forms of about one hundred men gathered around the wagon. Some of the men began to feel for the prisoner; the only way to distinguish Smith from our party was by finding the man who wore the shackles. As they were doing this, Smith raised to his feet and said "I am the man you

---

from Freeman's claim. Cooper appears to have been a power in local Republican politics, though not always as a candidate. He may have been responsible for the ouster of Bat Carr as marshal of Caldwell (see chap. 34, n. 7).

[3] Dr. Black is not Dr. Clark Black, who appears later in this narrative, for the latter did not come to Caldwell until 1879. No other person by that name has been identified.

[4] The old Colson and Ryland spread (chap. 6, n. 5). The stage crossing became known as Ryland's Ford, and Freeman so calls it in a later chapter when referring to the incident described here. Sam P. Ridings (*The Chisholm Trail,* p. 36) locates the crossing at Ryland's Grove, a few miles northeast of Caldwell. Ridings identifies this as the place where the Chisholm Trail crossed, but I believe it was merely the crossing on the stage route from Wellington. The Chisholm Trail crossed the Chikaskia farther north.

are after." I told him to sit down and keep quiet; he did as I directed and at that instant a revolver was placed near my face, and the possessor of it told me if I said anything, I would be shot. I pushed the revolver from my face and told the man not to be so careless, as the revolver might go off. He said he was not careless, and if I did not keep quiet it would go off. A couple of men took hold of Smith and he again rose to his feet; I commanded him to sit down. In an instant a double barreled shot gun was placed in such a position that I could easily see the shining barrels, and I was told if I said one word I would be shot. I saw it was useless to try and defend the prisoner and to keep him from the hands of the mob. I did not care to run any chances for my life, as our party was so outnumbered by the mob, and the shining barrels of the shotgun looked as large as stovepipes, so I concluded it was safer to keep quiet.

Smith was taken from the wagon, and a couple of men took our horses by the reins of the bridle and led them across the river; and then the men informed us that we would be shot if we attempted to cross the river again, until morning.

I concluded the best thing to do was to drive on to Wellington, the county seat of the county, and report to the sheriff.[5] We arrived at Wellington about sunrise [14 June] and I immediately went to the sheriff's office and informed him of the probable hanging of Smith by the mob. The sheriff said it reminded him of a circumstance in which a drunken Irishman was left at a station because he was too drunk to get on the cars; his partner, a Paddy, went to the conductor and told him there was a passenger on board who had been left behind.

We went to the hotel and had our breakfast, and soon the news was

[5] A. A. Jordan was acting sheriff at this time, having replaced G. A. Hamilton, who resigned on 11 April 1872. Hamilton and a group of citizens recommended to Governor James M. Harvey that Jordan be appointed to fill the vacancy (Correspondence Received, Papers of Governor James M. Harvey, KSHS; Richards, "History of Sumner County," *Historical Atlas*, p. 10, states that Jordan was appointed undersheriff on 12 April 1872— an unlikely date, since Jordan was presumably functioning as acting sheriff after April 11). According to one version, Hamilton "at one time refused to go to Caldwell after a bandit, fearing for his life. He shortly afterwards resigned" (*Wellington Daily News,* 11 February 1928). The same source recalls Jordan as "the most fearless and best officer in the history of the county."

A member of Wellington's original town company, Jordan was a one-armed veteran of the Confederate Army who had been a Texas cowboy prior to settling in Sumner County in 1871. Apparently he was unable to post the necessary bond in order to qualify as Hamilton's replacement, and the position was declared open on 9 October 1872. Jordan left Sumner County in 1875 and died in Oregon sometime after 1900 (Richards; *Wellington Monitor-Press,* 24 August 1921; *Daily News;* "Pioneers Come and . . . Pioneers Go," undated newspaper clipping, scrapbook, Chisholm Trail Museum Archives, Wellington).

spread over town, and the hotel office[6] was filled with people, anxious to learn of the circumstances.

I was very sleepy and tired and concluded to seek a little rest, while the team was eating and resting before they were driven to Caldwell. About ten o'clock I awoke and Mr. Cooper was satisfied that his team was ready for our return home, so we harnessed them to the wagon and started for Caldwell. We arrived at the Chikaskia River about the middle of the afternoon, and found Smith's body hanging to a limb of an elm tree; a Justice and ten or twelve men were holding an inquest over the body. We waited until the verdict was given by the jury, which was to this effect: that Smith was taken from the constable by a gang of desperadoes and horse-thieves and hanged for fear he would divulge the secrets of the order to which he belonged.

Whether or not they were former associates of Smith, and feared he had divulged their secrets to the officers, or if the hanging was done by a party who had organized themselves into a vigilance committee, remains a mystery to the community.[7] Smith may have recognized some of his former associates, which caused his eagerness to escape from our hands, but the unfortunate man had fallen into the hands of an infuriated mob, and met a shameful death.

Smith was hanged to a tree whose branches spread their protection over the road and afforded to the weary traveler who had stopped to rest beneath its spreading branches, a cool resting place, sheltering him from the heat of the noonday sun. The limb from which Smith was hung has long since decayed, and to-day the tree may be found, but the limb which supported the body of Smith may be designated by the rough knot in the side of the tree which nature has caused to grow over the place, after the limb had decayed and fallen to the ground.

Smith was buried across the river, almost opposite from the place where he met his death. A large sand hill was selected as his burial place. The grave was dug on the summit of the hill, the body, with the shackles still upon the feet, was placed in an open grave and sand thrown over it, and all that remained of Tom Smith was lost to view.

I suppose if Dalton by chance heard of Smith's sorrowful death, he felt that he had been very fortunate in making his escape before we reached Caldwell. Dalton had made a confession concerning the stealing of my horses. His story was that Smith had been hired by Curly Marshal, whom the reader will remember as the proprietor of the "Last Chance" ranch. Smith was to receive twenty dollars when the team was delivered at Boyd's ranch. Smith got Dalton

[6] As nearly as I can determine, Wellington had but one hotel at this time, Orange Scott Cummins' Frontier House (see chap. 6, n. 16).

[7] One suspects that the mystery was a matter of local collusion, Freeman's included. Why wouldn't Smith's" cohorts merely set him free?

to help him get possession of the horses. Dalton said Smith and himself had secreted themselves on several occasions to get the team. They wanted to get it from my brother, as it was generally known that he did not go armed at any time, consequently they could get the team without any trouble. They watched their chances, and finally succeeded in obtaining possession and the reader knows the result and the ignominious death of Smith. How sad to think that the small sum of twenty dollars was the cause of the crime, and the sad ending of one of the parties concerned. I suppose the twenty dollars Smith put in the letter to be sent to his brother was the money due him at the ranch for stealing the horses.[8]

Dalton said Smith belonged to a large gang of thieves which infested the southwest, who made their living in no other way than by stealing horses. The thieves were scattered throughout the southwest, some staying in Wichita, others at Newton, while those who were in this part of the country made the "Last Chance" ranch their favorite resort; others made Boyd's ranch their headquarters.[9] The country South and West was a vast expanse of land where isolation and wildness brooded. The landscape was unbroken by house or fence, and thus afforded a hiding place for outlaws and criminals who were evading the laws of our great commonwealth.

These thieves and desperadoes often visited the frontier towns and laid in a supply of whiskey. They were often brought before the public minds by some daring feat they would perform, or by a free use of the six-shooter in which some unfortunate man was the victim.[10]

---

[8] The reader will remember that, a few pages earlier, Freeman said the amount was forty dollars. He never looked back. Never.

[9] That such gangs existed appears incontrovertible if for no other reason than the ubiquity of the claims that they did. The gang operating in Butler County has been alluded to in chap. 11, and the gang to which "Smith" belonged does not seem to have been disbanded until several of the members were lynched in Wellington in 1874, a full account of which is given by Freeman in chaps. 26 and 27. Contemporary newspapers yield abundant references to elaborately organized horse stealing. These accounts occasionally border on the fanciful; for example, a story in the *St. Joseph* (Missouri) *Herald* (repr., *Topeka Daily Commonwealth,* 26 June 1872) echoes Freeman's earlier allusion to secret societies with awesome oaths and goes on to assert that these clans were made up of Negroes, Indians, whites, and halfbreeds, each executing that aspect of the theft and disposal for which his racial propensities best suited him. In any case, feeling was generally so high that one does not find it difficult to believe the vigilantes would lynch the thief of Freeman's horses, even though Freeman seemed content to have the offender tried.

[10] A last word about "Tom Smith": His adopted family and friends in Illinois could never quite believe that Tom Moore could be guilty of stealing horses. In 1875, the *Peoria National Democrat* ran a retrospective article in which it described how Tom Moore, walking one day toward Caldwell, was suddenly beset by six ruffians who accused him of horse stealing. Moore offered an alibi but the "frenzied" captors ignored him, and although for a time he kept the six at bay with his muscular prowess, at length they pre-

---

vailed and hanged him—only to find in his coat certain letters which proved his innocence. The *SCP* (29 July 1875) reprinted the article and refuted it point by point.

In 1882 the *Peoria Evening Call* printed a similar article, though this one asserted that Tom, having accepted a ride from a man in a wagon, discovered too late that his benefactor—one Smith—was driving a stolen team. Twenty men captured the wagon and hanged both Smith and Moore, despite the latter's offer to demonstrate his innocence, again by a display of letters he carried on his person. This article, too, was reprinted by the *SCP* (28 September 1882). This time the *SCP* did not offer to refute the story, which, by its melodramatic invention, probably serves as its own best refutation.

CHAPTER 20

Charlie Smith's Threat—The "Last Chance"—The Horse
Race—Smith Attempts to Put His Threat into Execution—
Our New Friends—Arrival in Butler County.

A short time after the hanging of Tom Smith by a mob or vigilance committee, a friend of mine came to me and informed me that my life was in
danger. It seems Tom Smith's brother Charlie of Wichita, Kansas, had said
he was coming to Caldwell, and would kill me on sight.[1] My friend gave me
a description of Charlie Smith, and told me I had better be cautious and not
let Smith get the advantage of me.

About two months after the conversation with this friend, I sold some
hay to the proprietor of the Pole Cat Ranch. This ranch is located on the
cattle trail about thirteen miles South of Caldwell, in the Indian Territory,
and is named after the stream upon whose banks the ranch is built.

One morning I took my team and wagon and started down the trail
with a load of hay for the Pole Cat Ranch. I stopped at the Last Chance
Ranch to buy some corn to feed my horses until my return home. A man
by the name of Dave Terrill was proprietor of the Last Chance; here I will
tell the reader what an odd sign this ranch had for the purpose of advertising
its business. Near the front of the log house was a board upon which was
printed the "Last Chance." This inscription was in such a position as to be
read by those leaving the state, while on the reverse side of the board was
the inscription "First Chance," which was to be read by those coming from
the Indian Territory. The full meaning was that on going South the ranch was

---

[1] That "Charlie Smith" was "Tom Smith's" brother is about the only fact of the former's
identity that is not in dispute. The *Washington Post* of 23 October 1910, in an article
regarding the settlement of an estate, gives "Charlie's" real name as Sewell Ford and identifies him as a son of Thomas Ford, former governor of Illinois (Koop, "A Rope for One-
Armed Charlie," *True West,* February, 1967, p. 65). G. W. Robson, former Caldwell
postmaster and acquaintance of "Charlie," gives the name as Charles Ford and states that
both Charles and Tom were adopted by Thomas E. Moore of Peoria, Illinois (Koop, p. 65).
Still another source—and in these particulars, at least, probably the most reliable—reports
that "Charlie's" real name was George S. Ford and that, after the death of the father, he
was reared by Jonathan K. Cooper of Peoria (*Peoria Evening Call,* repr. in *SCP,* 28
September 1882).

"Charlie Smith" was the proprietor of the notorious trader's ranch on the Ninnescah
(Sedgwick County, Kansas) in 1870, per Andreas, p. 1387 (see chap. 1, n. 6). He lost
the lower portion of his right arm in a shooting accident in November of 1871. (Freeman,
intent in this chapter on building up "Smith" as his fearsome adversary, understandably
does not mention until chap. 27 that the nemesis had only one arm.) Why "Charlie
Smith" held Freeman responsible for "Tom's" death is not clear, but the obscurity of the
motive does not of itself discredit Freeman's assertion.

the last chance the traveler had to get a drink of whiskey until the line of Texas was reached, and it also afforded the first chance the weary traveler had encountered since leaving the Lone Star State.

After this slight digression from my story, I will return by saying as I entered the door of the ranch I passed by a man who answered the description given me of Charlie Smith. I watched him very closely and in a few minutes Terrill took me into the back room and asked me if I knew who the man was. I told him I thought it was Tom Smith's brother.

He said I was right and that Smith had arrived there that morning and had made arrangements to stay there a few days. Terrill said Smith took a fifty dollar bill out of his pocket and said he would kill me before he would have to pay that for board.

Terrill asked me if I had a gun; I replied in the negative, and he said I could have his shotgun, that he would load it and go out of the back door and take it down to the ford of the creek for me. I told him not to load it, but bring the ammunition; also that I wanted buckshot. I got the corn, went to the wagon, (on the way I again passed Smith who was sitting in the door) and drove to the ford where I found Terrill with the gun. I examined it closely and loaded it, and proceeded to Pole Cat Ranch.

I kept a good lookout for Smith, but he failed to put in an appearance. That evening I called at the Last Chance, gave Terrill his gun, and again passed Smith. I was satisfied he would not hurt anyone unless he was under the influence of whiskey, and I concluded he had been intoxicated when he threatened my life and was too cowardly to put his threat into execution, unless he was made courageous by a few drinks of whiskey.

I saw him again in a few days but he said nothing to me, and I began to think it was unnecessary for me to anticipate any trouble, for he seemed wholly unconcerned about the threats he had made. Sly whispers came to my ears concerning his intentions, and I deemed it best to be prepared at all times, so that in the event he did attempt to take my life I would not be taken unawares.

During the summer months [1872] I frequently saw Smith; he made the Last Chance his headquarters, and during his stay in this part of the country he made frequent visits to Wichita and other cities. What his business was we did not know; he was considered a "gentleman of leisure," but before this book closes the reader will read much of his history, and of the disgraceful way in which he met his death.

Sometime in the fall when the leaves were about to clothe themselves with the yellow of autumn, and the flowers which had dotted the prairies with their pretty faces as they peeped from beneath the tall waving grasses had long since died and had been buried under the trodden turf, I happened to be in town when Smith was drunk, and a friend of mine came to me and warned me of the threat Smith had made on that morning, saying that if I came to town that day he would shoot me. The friend urged me to go home with him and remain at his house for a time, and perhaps Smith would leave town and go to the Last Chance.

I did not like the idea of offering myself as a target in which Smith might show his skill as a marksman, so after considering the proposition my friend had made, I concluded to do as he suggested. I went to his house and after remaining until about ten o'clock, I had no desire to remain longer in secretion, so I went up town and found quite an excitement was raised over a proposed horse race.

In the selection of judges for the race, Smith, Jones, James Short, and myself were chosen. Smith and Jones were to judge at one end of the race course, while Short and I were to judge at the other end. After the race was ended, our decision was called for. Jones and I gave our report, but Smith and Short did not say anything concerning the race or what horse had come out victorious.

The crowd dispersed and the majority went to town, some to indulge in a glass of whiskey, and others to loaf and pass the hours in social enjoyment. We had not been in town but a short time, when I heard Jones sing out in clear musical tones, "George can you see?" I looked around and saw Smith coming in the direction where I was standing, with his hand in his pocket. I drew my revolver from the scabbard and held it in my hand near my side. As he came near I heard the click of the hammer of his derringer, as he raised it preparatory to shooting and I watched his arm, and the first movement he gave I intended to shoot him. He approached and stood within a few feet of me for several moments, but the suspense made the moments seem like hours, and I drew a long sigh of relief when he turned and entered a saloon. The saloon proprietor had been watching the proceeding and as they entered the saloon door he said, "you coward why did'nt you shoot him?" Smith's reply was that he only had one load in his derringer, and if it by chance refused fire or if his aim was not true, I would have the drop on him and would cut him to pieces, as I had a dirk in my belt.

He certainly was a mind reader and a good judge of human nature, for my calculations were the same as he represented them to be. I had found a splendid dirk belonging to a cowboy, and I had brought it with me, intending to return it to him should I happen to see him in town, and if Smith had shot and missed me I certainly would have used the knife to the best of my ability.[2]

This circumstance led me to believe that my supposition was correct, concerning his cowardice. I was quite sure he would not attempt to put his threats into execution, unless he was favored with the advantage.

[2]Freeman has apparently forgotten that he already had a revolver in his hand.

He came to live with a family who were living about one half mile from my claim, and it had become generally known that he had threatened my life, and the neighbors were very uneasy concerning my safety, with Smith living on an adjoining claim.

One morning a man with his wife, a wagon, horses, and household furniture, drove to my house and wanted to stay with us. He said they had no place to stay and if we would let him live with us a few days, it would be doing a great favor for them. I asked my wife her opinion about sharing our house with these people, and she seemed to be in favor of giving them the privilege of remaining with us, and remarked that she would be glad to have their company. So it was decided that they should stay with us. We unloaded the wagon and cared for the horses, and before we returned to the house, the man told me why he came to my house. He said it was reported among the neighbors, that Smith had come to live near me so he could have the advantage of me on my trips to town, as he could waylay me and shoot me from ambush. The neighbors had conceived the idea of having [this man] move to my house and accompany me on my trips to town, and perhaps Smith would give up his project.

Everything run along smoothly for a few days; we found the company of our new friends made life very interesting and pleasant for us. Our neighbors were very few and scattering, and my wife yearned for company, and now she was delighted to have these friends with us. The threats Smith had made reached her ears, and she was in continual suspense and anxiety; so great were her fears concerning my safety that she would scarcely give her consent to have me leave home.

Words of warning and new threats made by Smith were whispered in my ears, and at last I became tired of being hounded by this ruffian and forbearance had ceased to be a virtue with me, and I asked myself the question, will my manhood allow me to remain quiet, while this man with his threats and insinuations makes my life one of suspense and peril? No, I would not be classed as a coward or submit to his threats any longer and as it has been said by an illustrious man, "procrastination is the thief of time," hence I concluded I would get my shot gun and horse, and proceed to his stopping place and we would determine which of us could remain here or emigrate to a healthier clime.

I was getting my horse in readiness when our friend came out and asked me where I was going; I replied in an indifferent manner, hardly able to control my agitation, that I was going to take a ride. He noticed I was not in my usual condition of mind, so he entered the house and inquired of my wife, if she knew where I was going. My wife replied that she did not know positively, but her suspicions were that I was going to order Smith to leave the country, and requested him to say nothing to me concerning the matter, and she would try and use her influence to detain me from going on such a perilous errand.

My wife came out where I was and pleaded and begged me not to go; her words convinced me of the rash step I was about to take and of the dangerous role I was about to play; and after much hesitation and consideration I told her [that] her words had probably saved my life, and although many years have passed since she was laid beneath the sod, yet I remember distinctly her pleadings, and I feel like asking God to bless her. Had I gone to see Smith he would have killed me or I should have become a murderer.

My wife's health began to fail; she had not been very well since the Indians had shot Fred Crats, and this, together with the suspense she had endured since Smith had come to Caldwell, sometime in July, had been very trying on her nerves and constitution, and she finally persuaded me to rent our farm to the friends that were living with us, and we moved to Butler County, where my father was living.[3]

After our arrival in Butler County, I received a letter stating Smith's disappearance from Caldwell, and telling me to watch for him. In several days I received more letters concerning Smith's disappearance; I gave them no further thought, as I did not think he would follow me. I destroyed the letters and did not say anything about it to my wife, for I considered the fact and saw it would disturb her peace of mind and could not add any to her pleasures.

We were well pleased to return to our relatives, old neighbors, and many friends and hoped my wife would be greatly benefited by the change.

---

[3]Freeman has telescoped time with a vengeance in this paragraph. Fred Crats was wounded in 1871 (chap. 3). "Charlie Smith" came to Caldwell in July of 1872. Freeman was still in Sumner county in 1873, when Busey Nicholson delivered the cow (chap. 13), and other incidents described in subsequent chapters confirm that Freeman did not move back to Butler County until the fall of 1873 at the earliest. Freeman may be exaggerating the extent to which "Charlie Smith" continued to threaten him. In any case, one's heart goes out to poor Laura Freeman—her nerves suffered the better part of two years, not just a few months, as Freeman makes it seem.

CHAPTER 21

The Drought of 1874—The Grass Hopper Raid—My Return
to Caldwell in 1879—Taking Photographs of the
Cowboys—The Appearances and
Positions Assumed.

The mind of the reader will now accompany us in our ramblings, and note the sorrows and misfortunes which attended us. The autumn months were gone and grim Winter has taken their place. It is now January, 1874. The new year is gladly welcomed and hopes are entertained by us that this will eclipse the preceding years, in the prosperity and development of our State.

In the Spring of 1874 I rented my father's farm, and took my brother as a co-worker in the business transaction. I made a contract with my brother, giving him a share of all the crops raised on the farm. We had into cultivation one hundred and fourteen acres of land. All productions of the soil grew most luxuriantly and gave promise of a bountiful harvest. In June, I bought the interest my brother had in the crop, giving him about three hundred dollars for it. Previous to this, the corn we had planted was waving its green guidons of prosperity in the wind, but in the latter part of June, rain was needed very badly, for the last rain had fallen in May. Vegetation began to wither and die, and the clouds were daily watched by the people, hoping to save the remaining crops, which had up to this time continued to hold their verdure.

The early settlers, like all pioneers were poor, and many of them unaccustomed to rough western life; therefore they were discouraged over the prospect of the coming drought.

The ground became hard and dry, and the heat of the sun's rays parched and dried up the grass and herbage. The streams and water courses were almost devoid of water; in some of the creeks the water had entirely dried up and the cattle were driven for miles in order that they might find a pool in which to quench their great thirst.

The old saying, that "misfortunes never come singly," was verified; the suffering occasioned by the continued drought was increased by the appearance of the grass hoppers. On August the first, the sun was darkened by the clouds of grass hoppers, which came from the north-west, from the Rocky Mountain region, miles in width and scores of miles long.

The greater part of these pests passed on, but the small portion of them that did alight almost covered the earth, in some places making drifts from two to four inches deep. Then the remaining vegetation disappeared, and every green thing shared the same fate, and disappeared from the face of the earth.

The crops did not diminish their appetites and the leaves and twigs were eaten from the trees and shrubs. Fields and gardens were devastated and left bare. The earliest planted corn was the only crop the farmers harvested, and it was thought by some that this was not an act of mercy by the grass hoppers but a necessity compelled them to leave it, for it was too tough for their mastication. The plague continued through the summer and fall. The continuation of the drought caused want, much suffering, and distress among the people. Immigration began to be reversed, and many who were able financially left the country; those who would not, and could not leave, were compelled to appeal to the charitable public for aid. Our sister states responded generously, and car loads of corn, flour, potatoes, and clothing were sent to the relief of the almost famishing families.[1]

On the fifth day of September, the first rain since May was gladly welcomed by the people. The summer had been an uncommon hot and dry one, and in the fall many were stricken with death, and the ague, commonly called chills and fever, was a prevailing disease throughout the country.

In September, the illness of my wife terminated in her death, and I was left prostrated with grief with four motherless children, the youngest a babe six months old.[2] In my hours of affliction, my sister kindly came to my aid and took my family of little children home with her, and filled a mother's place in caring for them. She kept them about two months, when her health began to fail, and finally she told me she could no longer keep the children, for her health was not sufficient to care for so large a family of little ones. I told her if she could keep them a short time I would try to find a home for them or make arrangements to bring them home. This she willingly did, and I was perplexed and undecided what to do. I was placed in very straitened circumstances and could not pay money for their keeping and I was not competent to take them home and alone share the responsibility of filling the place vacated by the death of their mother and give them the attention and care which children need in their early youth.

After giving due consideration to my conflicting thoughts, realizing my situation, I thought the best thing for me to do was to get married and then I could have my children at home.

---

[1] Scarcely a single printed old-timer's reminiscence fails to mention the drought and grasshopper invasion of 1874. Moreover, like Freeman in the closing paragraph of this chapter, everyone seemed to perceive it as the absolute nadir of hard times—a combination of natural forces that could not possibly occur ever again, particularly after the land became well populated. Much of the general information in this chapter is lifted or loosely paraphrased from Richards, "History of Sumner County," *Historical Atlas.*

[2] Laura A. Pool Freeman died on 17 September 1874. The children were Rhoda, age nine; Elihu, age six; Oscar, age four; and the baby, Susan (Pension Records, National Archives; 1875 Census, Bloomington Township, Butler County, KSHS).

Freeman's residence in Caldwell, 1881

I will not weary the reader by relating the experience I had in finding a suitable companion, or of my courtship and marriage; suffice it to say, I found a most admirable woman and we were "made one," and on our way to our home stopped at my sisters and got the children.

I was well acquainted with the lady I married, and my suppositions were that she would make an excellent wife and mother, and since living with her for fifteen years I have realized that she possessed excellent qualities and filled the place of a mother in my home.[3]

The following spring I again rented my father's farm and the season was a very favorable one; consequently, I reaped a very bountiful harvest for my labor. In the mean time I traded my land near Caldwell for a farm in Missouri. I did not care to change my location, so made another trade; this time I obtained land in Butler county.

Soon after trading for my Butler county farm I took possession of it and we were living quite comfortably and laying up a few pennies for old age.

My health began to fail and I was advised by the physicians to change my locality, and [told] in all probability I could be greatly benefited by the climate of Colorado. Acting upon their advice I traded for land in Colorado, and fully intended to go to that healthful climate; but circumstances over which I had no control prevented my going on my proposed trip.

Late in the fall [1878] I purchased a daguerreo car and started west, traveling through small towns, stopping several days in a place to take photographs, and in this method I paid my traveling expenses.

I traveled through the winter months and finally reached Caldwell in April, 1879. I opened out a photograph gallery[4] and did a profitable business among the "cowboys," who were anxious to get a photograph of themselves in "cowboy" style to send to their friends living in the eastern states. Some

[3] In December, 1874, Freeman married Emmaline Covert at the home of James Covert near Walnut City (Pension Records, National Archives). Further particulars may be found in the Editor's Introduction.

[4] Freeman's return to Caldwell is noted in the *Caldwell Post* of 1 May 1879: "Mr. Geo. Freeman, one of the old boys of '72 is here with his Photograph Gallery. Geo. came to Caldwell in '71."

Freeman was in partnership with a man named Brodie, probably the Brodie of Augusta mentioned in chap. 25, but it is not clear whether Brodie actually came to Caldwell with Freeman or was merely a partner by virtue of a cash investment. A George Beodie— possibly a typographical error for *Brodie*—is listed as one of the signators of the petition for incorporation of Caldwell as a city of the third class. So is Freeman (*Caldwell Post,* 8 May 1879).

The newspaper ad for Freeman and Brodie's atalier contains the following unattributed verse: "Come ye youthful and ye gay. / Bring the wrinkles and the gray, / Secure your shadows while you may, / But don't forget to bring the pay." By December, Freeman was back in business as a blacksmith (*Post,* 18 December 1879).

of their styles were novel in the extreme. Some of the boys would wear a large sombrero and have several revolvers hanging from a belt worn around their waist, others would be represented in leather leggins, two large Texas spurs on their boots, revolvers in hand, and looking as much like a desperado as their custom and appearance would admit. Often I would be required to take a photograph of a "cowboy" and his horse; some of the attitudes were very ludicrous and displayed wonderful equestrianism; while some of their positions had a dignified appearance, yet the observer would notice the dignity was assumed for the time being.

After remaining in Caldwell a month I received the appointment of Constable to fill a vacancy, and in the spring election I was elected to fill that office.[5]

I found that during my absence from Caldwell many changes had taken place, and in the meantime Caldwell had not stood still, but kept on enlarging her borders and taking in every thing that came within her reach.

The seasons had been favorable for several years previous and immigration began to flow west as it had in the early seventies. The railroad had now reached Wichita,[6] sixty miles north-east of Caldwell, and the farmers found a ready market for grain. Cattle were shipped from Wichita instead of from Abilene.

The Indian territory was now the home of the "cowboy," and this vast grazing ground was filled with cattle. The Texas cattle and ranch interests took on vast proportions, and the "cowboy" of yesterday finds himself rated in commercial circles at twenty-five, fifty, one hundred and two hundred thousand dollars.[7]

More permanent and costly homes are being built, and a new Kansas is being developed, and the drought and grass hopper raids are a thing of the past.

[5]The date of Freeman's appointment to fill the vacancy is uncertain, but it appears to have occurred more than a month after he returned to Caldwell, for he is not named as a constable in the newspaper until January of 1880, and that reference does not indicate how long he had been serving as such (*Caldwell Post,* 8 January 1880). In the spring of 1880, he successfully ran on the Republican ticket. Two constables were elected; the other was Dan W. Jones, who figures in this book later (*SCP,* 5 February 1880).

[6]The comment is misleading. The railroad had reached Wichita back in 1872. In 1879 it had reached Wellington, about twenty-five miles northeast of Caldwell.

[7]Most of this paragraph comes verbatim from the *Caldwell Journal* of 1 January 1885, which accounts for the anachronisms. The fortunes in cattle—at Caldwell—were yet to be made in 1879; the "vast grazing ground" of the Territory was still four years away from the first lease by the Cherokee Strip Live Stock Association.

CHAPTER 22

Indian Raid on Kiowa—A Party in Search of Horse Thieves—Listening to the Tales
of an Old Buffalo Hunter—Arrival at Kiowa—A Man Killed by Indians—
A Log House Used as a Fort—Twenty-one Indians Killed by
One Man—Reinforcements, and Preparations
Made to Follow the Indians.

In the latter part of August 1872,[1] I received a letter from a party at Wichita, Kansas, stating that forty-four horses had been stolen from some employees of the railroad company, and also some government horses from Fort Larned, and the report was that five thieves had stolen the entire outfit and were traveling south and would probably take the horses to Texas.

A party of eight men were organized to go with me to search for the thieves and horses. Several of us had conceived the idea of going on a buffalo hunt and now we concluded to take a wagon with supplies sufficient to last us several weeks, also a good supply of ammunition, and in case of a failure to capture the thieves, we would take our proposed hunt.

The first day [29 July] we travelled about thirty-five miles, and went into camp near a spring of water. We found we were very tired and hungry, for we had not stopped to get anything to eat since morning. Our camp fire was built and preparations were made to get our supper.

We had, in our company, several men who might be called "tenderfeet." They had recently come from the east and were not accustomed to rough western life, and especially as to the exposures of the camper and buffalo hunter.

We old frontiersmen were willing they should be initiated in a romantic way and learn as much as possible of life on the frontier and be able to fully understand and appreciate this life to its fullest extent; they must take "some bitter with the sweet," and must not complain if the larger proportion of it is the bitter.

Our crew was a jolly set of men and the first night we enjoyed ourselves hugely. After supper we listened to the tales told by an old buffalo hunter [W. B. King], of adventures among the Indians, and learned much of the art of killing the buffalo. Perhaps many of the readers will presume there is no art in being a successful buffalo hunter, but in this you would be mistaken, for it is certainly an accomplishment to be successful nine times out of ten in causing these monarchs of the plains to fall from a shot fired from your carbine.

[1] Actually the latter part of July, based on the date of the raid on Kiowa, Kansas, discussed later in this chapter.

They are difficult to kill by shooting them in the head, as the form of the fore-part of the head is oval shaped and will glance a ball, and then their forehead is covered with such a thick mass of hair and so closely matted that it is seldom a bullet penetrates through its thickness; consequently the experienced hunter never shoots at the forehead, but aims just behind the shoulder, the shot generally taking effect in the lungs, which either causes its death or disables it until a ball can be planted into the heart.

After digressing from the principal part of my story I will now resume to the "stopping place" and endeavor to interest the reader by relating the many facts which occurred during our trip.

The next morning [30 July] we were in our saddles and on our way, ready and eager for what might be in store for us. The general direction taken by us was nearly due west. We were riding along without interruption or incident to disturb our progress, until we had traveled ten miles perhaps, when we suddenly came upon some government soldiers who were on their way from Fort Reno[2] to Fort Larned, and we made inquiry of them as to whether they had seen any men with horses travelling south-west. They replied in the negative. We were now about five miles east of Kiowa; this was a small supply ranch and located on the territory line about fifty-five miles west of Caldwell.

We arrived at Kiowa about nine o'clock in the morning and to our amazement found but two remaining families in the ranch, and one of the men, Mosley by name, had been killed by the Indians.[3] Upon inquiry we found that the northern Cheyennes had passed through that country about daylight on their way from the Indian territory to the reservation in the northern territories recently occupied by that tribe,[4] and in traveling they killed or would

[2]Freeman perhaps means Fort Sill. Fort Reno was not yet established in July of 1872 (see chap. 25, n. 2).

[3]Only two families—the Leonards and the Lockwoods—are mentioned in the other extant accounts of this raid. Later, Freeman implies there were more families than these, but he does not overtly contradict himself as he is sometimes wont to do.

Paradoxically, no contemporary newspaper reports of the incident are extant as nearly as I have been able to determine. The other principal sources dealing with the Kiowa raid (see below) were written well after the fact by persons who were not on the scene and therefore must be read with judgment reserved. Freeman must be considered the best extant authority despite some minor lapses.

Mosley (E. H. in Andreas, p. 1531; Ed S. in Andreas, p. 1384) was a trader who had located on the Medicine Lodge River in the spring of 1872. He had previously operated a trader's ranch near what would later be the town of Wichita in the late '50's or early '60's. T. J. Dyer calls him Capt. John Mosley, perhaps confusing him with a cattleman by that name who flourished in the 1880's. Further, Dyer confuses the 1872 raid on Kiowa with the 1874 raid on other Medicine Lodge settlements (*Old Kiowa In History and Romance,* p. 5).

[4]Freeman has, in retrospect, confused the raiders with Dull Knife's group (or with

take possession of all stock found on their route, and also killed a number of persons and caused much suffering; many homes were devastated and houses and stables burned by these "Government Pets."

The women and children were very much frightened and one of the children, a boy about six years of age, had handled one of the guns to good advantage when the Indians attacked the house that morning.

The families had assembled together in a log house, and soon after Mosley was shot, [Mr.] Leonard realized that he must fight to the bitter end, and contrived a plan of getting the drop on the Indians by climbing upon the joists of the house and picking out one of the pieces of wood used as chinking between the logs, and by putting his gun through this opening he could use it to a great advantage. His wife [stayed] below and loaded the guns for him to shoot, and how well he succeeded in keeping them at bay and their final hasty departure was told to me by an Indian trader; he said the Indians told him Leonard killed twenty-one Indians[5] and that all his shots were true and each Indian was shot in the head.

A short time after this we found the dead body of an Indian, and, as the trader had said, he was shot through the head, the charge taking effect just above the right eye.

While we were thus engaged in conversation about the murderous work of the savages, five men came up to us and informed us that they were Kansas State Militia men. The man claiming to be lieutenant was acquainted with W. B. King, my former partner and an old buffalo hunter. King introduced the lieutenant to me, and upon the information given him, by King, that I was a Deputy U.S. Marshal, I observed a change of countenance in the man and also noted his actions were those of a man who was not at ease; and his conversation ceased entirely.[6]

It was now about noon, and after eating our dinner we held council to know what was best to do. The Indians had gone into camp about two miles from Kiowa, and their tents could be plainly seen by climbing to the top of the house. They had chosen as their camping place a fine location in the Horse Shoe bend of the Medicine Lodge river.

After our consultation it was considered by all that we had better remain

---

one of the migrations of 1877 or 1878), one of the few instances where he seems to succumb to the old-timer's propensity for translating some thug he once knew into Jesse James. This was not Dull Knife's band but rather a mixed batch of Kiowas and Osages (John Davidson to Assistant Adjutant General, Department of Missouri, 10 August 1872, in Fort Supply, Letters Sent, Vol. 28, cited in Robert C. Carriker, *Fort Supply,* pp. 71-72).

[5] One Osage and two Kiowas were killed (Carriker, p. 72). The exaggerating trader has not been identified. Note that Freeman reports seeing only one body.

[6] Actually there was no organized Kansas militia at this time, though Freeman's suspicions do not appear to have been triggered by that knowledge (Correspondence Received, Governor James M. Harvey, KSHS).

where we were until night and for the men to take their families to some canyon for safety, and we would go to the Indian camp and surround it. Their location was greatly to our advantage, the banks of the river, where the Indians were, was about four feet high, and it was about two hundred yards across the bend. Our intentions were to surround the camp by remaining under the banks and use this as a fortification, and by firing upon them we presumed it would not be a difficult matter to drive them from their camps and ponies.

When we made it known to the families what our best judgement was and what our intentions were, we found they were very much opposed to it. Their plan was for a couple of us to go and get the soldiers to come to their aid and for those remaining to secret themselves in the houses and be prepared in case another attack was made by the Indians.

It was finally decided that the plan was a favorable one, and Newt Williams and myself were selected to go for help. We saddled our horses and were soon on our journey. After traveling about five miles we came to the Cedar Mountains; we rode to the top of them and by looking through our field glass, we could see the Indians, and by watching them a few minutes, we saw they were taking down their wigwams and preparing to move; we remained on the mountain until we saw them start in a south-west direction,[7] and after they had traveled as far as the eye could see, we were satisfied they would not molest our new found friends again.

Our horses were very much fatigued and we concluded to remain where we were until morning. We went down to the canyon and there, in the valley, found excellent grazing for our horses and also a good camping place, with plenty of cedar limbs to build a fire.

At dawn on the following day [31 July], we were ready for our journey to Kiowa, and upon our arrival we related what had been seen by us. Upon receiving this information the party were in favor of following the Indians and attacking them, with the exception of Newt Williams, King and myself; our reasons were that they had now one night's travel in advance of us and we did not consider it a wise project to interfere with them, but as the majority of the party were in favor of pursuing them, we finally agreed, but very reluctantly, to accompany them.

We found the few scattering people were willing to join us in an enterprise which promised to afford them an opportunity to visit just punishment upon their enemies.

The frontiersmen of the Kansas border, stirred up by the numerous massacres committed in their midst by the savages, favored our project, and we made arragements to start immediately.

---

[7] The southwest direction of travel should have reminded Freeman when he wrote this that the Indians could hardly have been Dull Knife's Cheyennes.

CHAPTER 23

In Pursuit of the Indians—The Appearance of the Lockwood
Family on the Trip—The "Arkansaw Traveler"—The
Sound of the Coming Buffalo—Keeping the
Buffalo from Ruining the Corn Field
—Strange Actions of the
State Militia Men.

No person who has not lived on the frontier and in an Indian country can correctly realize or thoroughly appreciate the extent to which a frontiersman becomes familiar with and apparently indifferent to the accustomed dangers which surround him on every side. It is but another verification of the truth of the old saying, "familiarity breeds contempt."

After the necessary preparations were made, we proceeded on our journey. Our party would have been a good sketch for the artist pen. I was riding near the head of the column of marching men, and as I would occasionally glance backward toward the line of gallant men, it was with much difficulty that I would refrain from laughing out loud. The sight was equal to any circus parade I have ever seen. Old Mr. Lockwood was thus represented: he rode on a mule without a saddle, or, to use a common expression, he rode "bareback;" on his head was a cap made of a coon skin; he wore a pair of Indian moccasins on his feet; his "weepen" was an old musket and had the appearance of taking an active part in the Revolutionary war. One of the Lockwood boys was armed with a muzzle loading rifle, and the other, a double barreled shot gun, with only one lock on it; both of the boys were bare headed and were without shoes or boots, and like the old man Lockwood, they rode "barebacked." They were very anxious to get started and their manner was very amusing. I imagined they would be equally as glad to get home again, especially if there would be any fast riding to do or if the Indians should give us a chase. We wanted them to get all the fun there was in it, [so] we rode rapidly for about five miles. Our "bareback" friends seemed to enjoy the ride very much, and as we advanced in the distance they could be noticed in riding "sideways." We kept riding at pretty good speed until about noon, when we stopped and went into camp. We were now about seventeen miles from Kiowa.

After we had drank a cup of coffee and were comparatively rested after our ride, we decided it was useless to try to follow the Indians, as we had not traveled one half day and had seen nothing to encourage us in our pursuit, so we turned our faces in the direction of Kiowa.

The "bareback" riders did not seem to be in as much haste as they had been before dinner, and after traveling a little in the advance of them we stopped and waited until they overtook us; then we told them they must ride with us, for some of the Indians may possibly have remained and were hunting buffalo, and in case they should happen to see them, they would, in all probability, be scalped by the savages. They rode near us for a little while, and it was soon noticed they began to lag behind again; finally they got off their mules and walked. To have a little amusement one of the men asked them why they did not ride and keep up with the crowd. One of them replied: "We would as leave be killed by the Indians as to be split in two by a mule." This created a laugh, and as we knew there was no danger of being "killed by the Indians" we rode on and left them, but was soon overtaken by the old man, who said he "could stay with us, for he was as tough as the mules back, and if the mule could stand it to be rode barebacked, he could stand to ride it so, as he was the oldest." We indulged in another hearty laugh and lessened our speed, for, at our rate of rapid riding, there was certainly great danger of the old man getting "split in two" before we would reach our destination.

We arrived at Leonard's ranch about five o'clock in the afternoon. After supper we talked of starting on the morrow in search of the thieves, but some of the party were not favorable towards going any farther as we had been delayed for several days,[1] and in all probability, the thieves had nearly reached Texas, and, after a lengthy conversation, we concluded to give up the chase, and then after letting our horses rest for a couple of days, we would hunt buffalo and return to Caldwell.

Our new friends, the Lockwood's, told us they had not seen any buffalo for three or four weeks, and we would have to go some distance west to find them.

Old man Lockwood lived about one-half mile south of Leonard's ranch, and he was an oddity to be sure. He had ten children and had formerly come from Arkansas, and in my mind, the old gentleman and the farmer represented in the "Arkansaw Traveler" are very similar persons in appearances. The song entitled "The Arkansaw Traveler" was a favorite piece of music in the home of the Lockwood's. The old man and his family were living on a claim, and he had planted a considerable part of his land to corn, and the crop gave every evidence of a bountiful yield of corn in the coming Fall.

We camped at Leonard's the following night [Aug. 1 or 2] and I shared my blanket with King; our bed was made on the green, mossy, buffalo grass, and after lying down we were soon in the land of dreams. It was just that uncertain period between darkness and daylight on the following morning, and I was lying enjoying the perfect repose which only camp life offers, when I was startled by a shake from the hands of King; he told me to put my ear to the ground and I could hear the sound of the coming buffalo. I did so,

---

[1] In terms of days and nights mentioned in the text, the party had been delayed at Kiowa only two days; but, as the reader has perceived by now, Freeman tends to use time in a relative way.

and I could distinctly hear the sound, and the very earth seemed to quiver beneath their tread. King said they were probably about three miles away, and that their course was in the same direction taken by us on our Indian chase.

When the sun was about one hour high we looked in the distant west and saw a moving cloud of dark objects, which, upon closer observation as they came nearer to our camp, we could easily determine what the black looking objects were. It was the largest herd of buffalo I had ever seen, and they probably numbered by the thousands.

When we saw their course was towards Lockwood's claim we thought we would mount our horses and endeavor to keep these huge monsters out of the corn field.

In traveling, if not grazing or alarmed, the buffalo usually move in single file, the column generally headed by the champion of the herd, who is not only familiar with the topography of the country, but whose championship in the contests entitles him to become the leader of the herd. He maintains this leadership only so long as his strength and courage enable him to remain the successful champion in the many contests he is called upon to maintain.

In traveling they follow their leader "through thick and thin," to use a common expression, and it is useless to attempt to change their course after the leader has advanced in the chosen direction.

We took our guns and went to the corn field and succeeded in turning their leader in his course. We shot and killed a number of them as they would pass us on their travels, and before a great while had a good supply; in fact we had a sufficient amount to load our wagon, and it would be unnecessary to go further on a "buffalo hunt" as we could have all we wanted without hunting for them.

It was about noon before the last buffalo passed the field, and after they got beyond the hill, located about one mile [west][2] of the Leonard ranch, they stopped traveling and began grazing quietly along with as much ease as though they were thousands of miles from human habitation.

We were well pleased with our mornings work and concluded to go to the ranch and get dinner, and then we would remove the hides from the buffalo slain by us and select the pieces of meat we wished to take home with us, load up our wagons, and prepare to start towards home the following morning.

While one of our party was getting dinner, one of the party rode out to the dead buffalo and cut a fine piece of delicious steak from the loin, and we enjoyed our dinner very much. It as the first time our "tender foot" friends had tasted buffalo meat, and they relished it exceedingly well.

[2]Freeman says east, but other details in this and the succeeding chapter indicate that *east* is a typographical error.

The five men who claimed to be State Militia men were still with us, and after our dinner was over I noticed they had congregated together in a group and seemed to be talking in undertones, and the man who claimed to be a lieutenant had been intently watching our movements for several days.

Soon after this incident King and I went to water our horses and prepare them to ride to the buffalo herd in company with the other men of our original party, and in conversation with King I told him I did not think the men were Militia men, but my fears were that they belonged to a set of horse thieves. The horses they were riding were above an average sized horse, and I could not help but think that they were stolen stock.

King laughed at my apprehension and said I must be mistaken, for he knew the man claiming to be the lieutenant and he did not think he was of that character. The reader will hear of them in my next chapter and of how my fears were confirmed.

CHAPTER 24

The Colonel and Mrs. Leonard Shoot a Buffalo—The Wounded
Buffalo Gives Them a Chase—A Laughable Episode—The
Return to Caldwell—Lockwood's Mules Are Stolen—
Arrival in Wichita in Search of the Thieves—An
Exciting Race After the Thief—Capture of
Thieves and They Receive Sentence.

In opening this chapter I must refer to incidents in the preceding one, and the reader will go with me in imagination to the scenes which took place during our dinner hour, and at a time when we were saddling our horses preparatory to going to the buffalo herd. The herd was on the opposite side of the Medicine Lodge River, and was about one mile from the ranch, which is located on the east side of the river; consequently the buffalo were on the west side of the ranch and also across the river. Here I witnessed one of the most laughable incidents which has ever occurred within my knowledge, and yet it was occasioned with much danger to the parties concerned, and after the danger had passed we enjoyed the sport with the originators of it.

As we prepared to go to the herd, Colonel Connoble,[1] one of our party from Caldwell, asked a lady if she would like to ride out to the herd, and if she would he would unload our spring wagon, and he would drive out with the team. She replied that she would like to see the buffalo, so it was settled that they should go in the spring wagon. The Colonel unloaded the spring wagon, and with a lady on the seat with him and with his trusty gun by his side, they proceeded to the top of the hill and there they could get a good view; also a splendid shot at the loitering buffalo.

After gaining the summit of the hill they noticed a large, shaggy fellow near them, and the Colonel drew his gun and shot it. To his surprise and gratification the buffalo fell and to all appearances was dead. The Colonel was very much pleased with his good luck, and was telling the lady he "had always been considered a good shot." As he drove to his game he was feeling very jubilant and made the lady think she was highly honored to have the privilege of riding with "Col. Connoble."

When he had driven within fifty yards of the buffalo, it suddenly jumped up and started for them on the run. The Colonel turned the horses as quickly

---

[1] Connoble, as events will show, was one of the greenhorns in Freeman's party. He appears again in chap. 40, where he accompanies Freeman and Bent Ross to Pond Creek to arrest a horse thief (in July, 1872, actually previous to the adventure here recounted). Connoble operated a grocery store for a time at Caldwell (*Wellington Banner*, 25 September 1872) and was a member of the ill-fated Barber County expedition which resulted in the death of Reuben Riggs in December of 1872 (see chap. 6, n. 9; *SCP,* 5 February 1880).

as he could, and the first cut with the whip the horses received, Mrs. Leonard tumbled backwards into the spring wagon; her feet were resting on the spring seat, and in her efforts to regain her position, her feet were kicking the Colonel in the back, while he was bent in the shape of a rainbow, striking the horses at every jump.

For about three quarters of a mile the country was a level prairie, and the race was an even one; the Colonel's hat had fallen off his head and his iron grey locks were flying in the wind. He did not take the time to glance backward to see if the enemy was following him, but looked onward and had his thoughts on every thing except the woman bumping up and down in the back part of the wagon.

The buffalo began to gain on the horses, and had either of the horses stumbled and fell, the buffalo would have been the victor, and the spoils would certainly have belonged to him.

We had been watching the race, and now as the buffalo was gaining ground we saw something must be done, and done quickly, too, or the wagon was liable to be upset by the angry antagonist. We started and our intentions were to run between the buffalo and the wagon, thereby changing his course, as he was sure to attack the first enemy seen. We run our horses between the fleeing party and the pursuer, and as I passed the buffalo I drew my gun and fired a shot at him, and we finally killed it.

The Colonel did not stop but supposed the angry buffalo was in pursuit of him, and he kept running the team up hill and down; and when the banks of the river was reached he dashed on, splashed through the water and did not draw rein until the ranch door was reached. All this time the lady was lying in the back part of the wagon and was laughing to her hearts content.

We followed in the direction taken by them and arrived at the ranch soon after they had reached it. We indulged in a good laugh over their funny escapade, and the lady told the Colonel she did not care to go on a hunting expedition with him again, and that he should have known better than to drive up to a buffalo until he was certain it was dead. The shot fired by Colonel Connoble only stunned the buffalo for a few minutes and had maddened it. The buffalo are very vicious when they are wounded and will always attack the enemy unless they happen to be shot in the loins, disabling them in such a manner as to interfere with their locomotion.

Breakfasting before the stars bade us good night, or rather good morning, daylight found us ready for our homeward march towards Caldwell. I will not weary the reader by describing our journey, but will say we did not meet with any adventure or incidents worthy of mention.

About six weeks after our return home the old man Lockwood came to Caldwell and informed me that four of his mules had been stolen, and his suppositions were that they had been taken to Wichita. I engaged the services of Newt Williams to accompany me in search for the thieves and stolen property.

We left Caldwell on the evening of the same day I received the warrant, and after traveling all night we arrived in Wichita the next morning about daylight. The night was a beautiful one and the moon shone her mellow light over hill and dale, and seemed to cheer us on our way. The distance to Wichita was about sixty miles and we had to ride at a rapid gait in order to arrive there and search the stables before time for feeding the horses. We had an idea the thieves had either sold the stock or would start early for some other town in which they could dispose of the mules at a bargain.

Soon after our arrival there we made inquiry concerning the stock, and then went to the several livery stables to look for the stock we were hunting. Finally after we had wasted considerable time in looking through the barns we went to West Wichita[2], and there upon entering a feed stable we noticed a man run out of the back door. We gave pursuit and fired several shots at him, but he made good use of his lower extremities and soon reached the Arkansas river. This did not check him, but he jumped into the water and was soon on the other side; then in his flight he started down the river and was soon lost from our view.

We could not ford the river on our horses so we hurriedly ran to the bridge, a few yards above us, and we were soon on his trail. We followed the river bank for several hundred yards and finally found him in a brush heap, where he supposed he was hidden from sight. We arrested him and took him back to Wichita and put a guard over him, then went in search of the other thief. We searched a number of houses where we supposed he would be found and failing to meet with success we went into a saloon and there found "our man." The man proved to be the lieutenant of the men [who] represented themselves as state militia men.

We took him to the jail for safe keeping and then searched for the mules; by this time old Mr. Lockwood was with us and he was very much pleased with our success so far, and when we found the mules he was happy.

Court was in session in Wichita, and the men were given trial and found guilty and sentenced to the penitentiary; one for the term of five years and the other for seven years. The curtain closed upon the scene and the prisoners were left to meet the fate the judge had decreed to be theirs, and I presume in after years they realized the truth of the familiar saying, "The way of the transgressor is hard."[3]

[2]West Wichita was a small community on the west bank of the Arkansas River, directly opposite Wichita itself. A bridge (to which Freeman refers in the next paragraph) had been constructed this same year, 1872, which spanned the river and linked the two communities (Emmert, "History of Sedgwick County," *Historical Atlas,* p. 10).

[3]The two men arrested were S. F. Howe and William White. The sentences were not

A short time after this incident a U. S. marshall went to Texas in search of the thieves of whom we were in pursuit when we reached Kiowa and there found the ill fated families and the murderous Cheyenne Indians of which we gave mention in a preceding chapter.[4]

The stolen horses were found but the thieves had escaped, and no clue could be found which would lead to their capture. Two of them were arrested by me and assistant. These men were the same whom the reader will remember as having received their sentence at Wichita for stealing Lockwoods mules.

The men claiming to be militia men were none other than a band of thieves, and they had in their possession at the time we were at the Leonard ranch, horses which had been stolen from a man living near Belle Plaine, Kansas. Some time previous I had had a description of the horses and was offered a reward for the capture of the thieves and horses.

The horses were probably sent to Texas or taken there by three of the party, while the "Lieutenant" and one of the men stood near the vicinity of the Leonard ranch watching a chance to steal Mr. Lockwood's mules. The much wished for opportunity came, the mules were stolen, and the reader has learned of the result and the sentence of the "Lieutenant" and the "state militia" men.

---

five and seven years but three and five, which prompted the *Wichita Eagle* to observe, *contra* Freeman, that "the way of the transgressor is not so hard, after all" (26 September 1872). The *Eagle* account does not mention the efforts of Freeman and Newt Williams but gives all the credit to Sedgwick County Sheriff John Meagher (see chap. 42, n. 14). John was the brother of Mike Meagher, about whom more is heard in succeeding chapters.

[4] The sense of this paragraph skirts on the ambiguous. The "ill fated families and murderous Cheyennes" were, of course, found by Freeman and his party at Kiowa. What the U. S. marshal found in Texas is described in the next paragraph.

CHAPTER 25

Indians on the War Path—The Frightened Settlers Flee to Places
of Safety—Fortifications Built at Caldwell—Men Organized
into a Force to Protect the Town—Four Freighters
Killed—The Finding of Pat Hennessey's
Body by W. E. Malaley—
The Rude Funeral.

In opening this chapter the reader must turn backward with me to the year
of 1874 and to the month of July.

The year 1874 was a most disastrous one to Kansas at large, but doubly
fatal to Sumner county. During the years of 1872 and 1873, thousands after
thousands of immigrants were attracted thither by our delightful climate and
magnificent soil, so that by the spring of 1874 there were no less than 8,000
actual settlers within the county limits.[1]

In [a] preceding chapter I have related to the reader facts concerning the
drought and the grasshopper raid, and have, briefly, pictured the suffering and
distress which was occasioned by these visitations, and now, to add to the already stricken people, rumors were afloat that the Indians were making trouble
at Fort Reno.[2] This is a military fort, kept up by the government, and is
located about one hundred and ten miles south of Caldwell, in the Indian Territory. The northern Cheyenne Indians had threatened an outbreak, and rumors had been afloat all spring and had occasioned much uneasiness among
those who pictured in their imagination the savage arrayed in war paint and
feathers.

On July the 15th [6th] report came to Caldwell that two freighters had been
murdered and [a] third one burned alive by the Indians a few miles south of
Caldwell.[3] This startling news created quite an excitement on the border and

---

[1] This paragraph is taken verbatim from Richards, "History of Sumner County," *Historical Atlas*, p. 9.

[2] The grasshopper invasion had not yet occurred; it came in early August.
Fort Reno was not established until 1875. Its location was two miles south of the
Cheyenne-Arapaho Agency, around which trouble was indeed brewing in 1874. Freeman's
anachronistic reference is ascribable to his source, Richards. Freeman skims various facts
and language from Richards in several of the succeeding paragraphs.

[3] The date is generally confused; Richards says it was July 5, but contemporary newspapers indicate clearly that the news of the freighters (Pat Hennessey and others) arrived
in Caldwell with Indian Agent J. D. Miles on July 6. Part of the confusion is occasioned
by the fact that the Indian panic hit Caldwell in two waves—the first on July 4, when
credited rumors were received from parties unknown that an attack was imminent; the
second in the early morning hours of July 6, when Agent Miles arrived with the informa-

many were very much frightened and caused much anxiety for the frontiers-men concerning the safety of their families.

On the evening of July [6th] Agent J. D. Miles arrived in Caldwell from Fort Reno. He came with his family, driving as fast as his horse could run, and halted in Caldwell long enough to say the reports were true, that the Indians were on the warpath and that he and his wife were fleeing for their lives.[4]

The wildest consternation prevailed among the people. A few old soldiers organized themselves in a body and prepared to protect the town. Scouts scoured the southern border. Many were the hearts that sank when they heard the shot fired from a gun or revolver and the warning cry, "The Indians are on the warpath, run for your lives," awakened them from their slumbers.[5]

Couriers went from house to house and from town to town carrying the dreadful news. In most cases the people availed themselves by putting into use any wheeled vehicle in which to convey themselves and families to supposed places of safety.[6]

---

tion that freighters had been killed some sixty-five miles to the south (*SCP,* 9 July 1874). Freeman's date, July 15, is so far off the mark that I have simply corrected it in the text on the theory that nothing valuable to the reader is gained by preserving an obvious aberration.

[4] John D. Miles that summer had taken over the Cheyenne-Arapaho Agency, which was located about 110 miles south of Caldwell in the Territory. A Quaker, Miles none-theless perceived that only military presence would forestall the trouble which was building at the agency. Increasing harassment and provocation by the war-minded element of the Cheyennes led Miles, with family and staff, to leave Darlington for Kansas, where Miles hoped to persuade General John Pope at Leavenworth to provide military protection and to aid in checking the territorial incursions of white hunters and livestock rustlers, the chief causes of the Indian grievances (Flora Warren Seymour, *Indian Agents of the Old Frontier,* pp. 242-45; *Topeka Commonwealth,* 8 July 1874). The excessive panic which Freeman, as have others, attributed to Miles is possibly overstated and probably unfair, for Miles had, after all, discovered the murdered Hennessey and, in addition, thought he had reason to believe the hostiles were heading toward Caldwell. (His assessment of the situation is printed in the *Walnut Valley Times,* 10 July 1874—evidently reprinted from another source but unascribed.) Miles's administration is given full and sympathetic treatment in Flora Warren Seymour's *Indian Agents,* pp. 234-56; Sam P. Ridings provides a balanced and complete short treatment of the agency and the events leading up to the so-called Outbreak of 1874 (*The Chisholm Trail,* pp. 148-60).

[5] A correspondent from Caldwell, writing in regard to the false alarm of July 4, described it thus: "Saturday after noon some of our people became a little excited [at] the news of five hundred Indians only five miles off on the trail. "'Oh! then there was hurry-ing too and fro, / And tremblings of distress; / And cheeks, all pale, which but an hour ago, / Blushed at the praise of their own lovliness.'" He concludes by saying: "But lo! the romance of border life was knocked into pi when it was ascertained that instead of being the dreaded savage . . . it was a very innocent looking herd of Texas cattle" (*SCP,* 9 July 1874).

[6] John H. Folks, editor of the *SCP,* left Wellington for Caldwell in the early morning

Major Miles arrived at Wellington about midnight and gave a report similar to the one he gave in Caldwell. About twenty men, old soldiers and citizens, armed themselves and started to help protect the town of Caldwell.[7] Men organized into a force also came from Oxford, Belle Plaine, South Haven, and Guelph [township].[8]

The fleeing settlers met in Wellington and camped there in a body. Hundreds were camped upon the banks of Slate Creek about one-half mile from Wellington.

The remaining citizens of Caldwell were prepared to defend themselves in case of an attack, and fortifications were built of barrels and boxes which were filled with dirt and placed in such a position to serve as a protection against the wiles of the noble redman. The military companies never saw service, as the hostile Indians were not accommodating enough to come nearer than sixty miles to Caldwell.

Many of those who deserted their homes returned in a few days, and many others, having turned their faces toward the east, never saw fit to return to their new homes, while others returned after several years, thinking the danger, which the frontiers were subject to, was now passed, and peace and contentment would be the controlling element.

The year 1874 was calamitous in more ways than one. The Indian scare drove hundreds of people from our county and occasioned the loss of much

hours of July 7. He later expressed surprise at "the wholesale exodus of the settlers on Bluff creek and the lower Chikaskia, which we met on the road" (*SCP,* 9 July 1874).

[7] The Wellington delegation included W. P. Hackney, C. S. Brodbent, A. W. Sherman, L. K. Meyers, J. A. Kirk, T. J. Riley, James Stipp, Joseph M. Thralls (see chap. 26, n. 8), W. E. "Elzie" Thralls, and John H. Folks. The other members are unidentified (*SCP,* 9 July 1874). When they arrived in Caldwell, they learned that a government supply train, anticipating attack, was corralled at Pond Creek Station awaiting weapons and reinforcements, which the station proprietors, J. C. and Lou Hopkins, had come to Caldwell to secure. The Wellington delegation, with the exception of Folks, decided to escort the Hopkins brothers back to Pond Creek. They saw no Indians, but they did have a face-off with eight men who vainly attempted to bully them out of a Sharp's needle gun one of the party was carrying. Joe Thralls would recall that two of the party of eight would be hanged not many days afterward at Wellington (quoted in McNeal, *When Kansas Was Young,* pp. 17-18; W. P. Hackney's and C. S. Brodbent's recollections of this incident appeared in the *Wellington Monitor-Press,* 24 August 1921). The two unfortunates were Freeman's nemesis, "Charlie Smith," and Bill Brooks; the events leading up to their hanging are recounted in chaps. 26 and 27.

[8] The Belle Plaine delegation numbered fifty (or one hundred, depending on the version), and they were organized to the nines under the command of Colonel H. C. St. Clair, with J. M. Reitz acting as captain, Ed. C. Jeffries as lieutenant, and Thomas Donohue as orderly sergeant. When they passed through Wellington the evening of July 7, they were cheered and suppered by the citizenry; but on July 8 when they arrived, all pomp and circumstance, in Caldwell, they received "unmerited jeers." Caldwell had decided she could look after herself (*SCP,* 9 July 1874, 18 March 1880).

property. The drought made crops a failure, and the grasshoppers finished what little vegetation remained; the granaries were empty, and the coming cold, bleak winter was staring the people in the face; woe, despair, and discouragement was depicted upon their countenances, and had not the charitable public sent them succor and aid many would have perished from hunger and cold.

The consequences of these disasters were that a large proportion of the settlers lost faith in the state of Kansas, and the tide of immigration was reversed from what it had been. Many were so poverty stricken that it was common to see a horse and a cow harnessed together to pull the wagon and a few household goods, including a feather bed, upon which six or eight children were seated; the load being too heavy for the poor old horse and cow to pull, the man was compelled to walk, in order that he might be able to shake the Kansas dust from his feet forever. We will presume these people were seeking the provender in the home of "wifes people."[9]

Those that remained by dint of skillfull management and stolid endurance have held the fort and are to-day, valuable, honored, and wealthy citizens of our county. Many others, after enduring the hardships of the frontier life, have been laid to rest and are now peacefully sleeping their final sleep.

It is strange, indeed, how panic stricken the people will become and rush pell mell to supposed places of safety. Many of the old veterans who have braved the fusilade of bullets and the clash of the saber, in the late civil war, were among the first to rush from their country and let the noble redman have entire possession, had he wanted it, and like our "Robinson Crusoe" be the monarch of all he surveyed.

The "Indian scare" did not extend on the border alone, but reached far in the interior of the State. The excitement almost reached Topeka, and in the counties of Sedgwick and Butler the excitement was nearly equal to that of the border counties.[10]

I was living in Butler county at the time, and the people there were terrorized with the reported outbreak. Everyone seemed to think his place would be the first attacked by the murderous Cheyennes on their departure from their homes in the Indian Territory.

I was in the field cutting oats when the news of the outbreak reached Augusta, and a man came running to my place and gave me the warning. He was very much excited and begged me to go and find out if the report was

[9] I have encountered this expression innumerable times in newspapers of the '70's and '80's. "Going home to the wife's people" was the wry description of those who quit Kansas and went back east.

[10] For *excitement* read *panic.* Though the Topeka newspapers do not indicate any local apprehension, they do report migrations of frightened people from southern Sedgwick County (north of Sumner) into Wichita (*Topeka Commonwealth,* 14 July 1874).

substantiated by facts; he said that the people had congregated themselves together in Mr. Brodies corral,[11] and they had sent him to me to request me to go and ascertain if the report was true and to report to them immediately. Their reasons for wanting me to act as scout was because I had traveled the road to and from Caldwell so often that I knew of places in which I could secret myself and thereby escape from the hands of the Indians.

I told the man I would go provided he would take my place as one of the binders, and that I did not have any faith in the report, and I knew how excited the people would become under such circumstances, for I had a little experience myself about a supposed Indian outbreak at the time Fred Crats was shot, of which the reader will remember.

I took my horse and started on my errand, and after proceeding about ten miles I met a man who had just came from Wellington. He reported how the affairs were there and that upon investigation there was nothing of it, and upon hearing this news I went back and found some of the people hid in the brush near their rendezvous. I related to them what I had heard and they quietly went back to their homes in contentment.

In Sumner county, the people had scarcely returned to their homes and got settled again to their usual routine of living when the second alarm was given. The report even went so far as to say South Haven had been burned and the Indians were now on their way to Caldwell and were burning buildings and killing people on their route. One man said he had just came from South Haven, a town twelve miles east of Caldwell, and had seen the burning buildings and the farmers' haystacks afire; this created another rushing of the people, and it was soon found out that the report was false, and South Haven had not been burned and an Indian had not been seen within her borders or nearer than sixty or eighty miles.[12]

The report of the murdered freighters, however, was true. Whether they were surprised while encamped and killed by the murderous Indians is a mys-

[11] Brodie was possibly Freeman's partner in the photography business some five years later (see chap. 21, n. 4).

[12] The rumors and concerns lasted several weeks, at least through the end of July, but I am unable to date the rumor of the burning of South Haven, although I have seen it elsewhere. Exemplifying the extent of rumor is a letter from the town of Douglass in Butler County, where Freeman was residing at the time. The correspondent reports that on July 8 a bootless and hatless man, "frightened nearly out of his senses," rode into town in the middle of the night and raised the cry that Indians had fired the town of Belle Plaine (in Sumner County, some thirty-five miles northeast of Caldwell and about eighteen miles southwest of Douglass). The man, who lived eight miles east of Belle Plaine, claimed he "could plainly see the fire from his house." The extent of reaction in Douglass as a result of this alarm ranged from the skeptical to the panic-stricken. Though "a few turned over and went to sleep again," many fled the city. "Mr. Wise took [some of] the people in, squalling babies and all. . . . One old lady wailed out, 'I knew there would be war when I saw the comet'" (*Walnut Valley Times,* 17 July 1874).

tery and has not been fully determined in the minds of the people. There were many theories advanced relative to the murder, and at this late date many of the old settlers regard the theory advanced that the freighters met their death at the hands of the Indians, as a myth. One good reason for their doubts is this: Had the Indians been on the warpath and killed the parties in the manner in which one of them was found, it would be reasonable to suppose that his scalp would have been taken by the Indian by whom the man was killed. According to the belief of the Indian tribe, a warrior's bravery is known by the number of scalps taken; consequently, it would be reasonable to suppose that the warrior would have added this scalp as a trophy of his greatness.[13]

In the month of July, 1874, Pat Hennesey [Hennessey] in company with three companions[14] were engaged in hauling government freight, consisting of various kinds of provisions, from Wichita, said freight to be delivered at some government post located on the Caldwell and Fort Reno [Fort Sill] trail.

When the freighters arrived at Buffalo Spring, a ranch whose proprietor was Ed Mosier,[15] they concluded as it was early to go into camp, to travel on

---

[13] Suspicion lay on a band of horse thieves who were stealing from the Indians, the settlers, and even from the official mail service (see chaps. 26 and 27). C. S. Brodbent was still convinced of their guilt in the matter as late as 1921 (*Monitor-Press*, 24 August 1921), but George Rainey (*The Cherokee Strip*, pp. 151-53) musters evidence to the contrary, as does Sam P. Ridings, who considers further debate to be closed (*Chisholm Trail*, p. 444). The suspicions may have been fostered by General Pope. The *Topeka Commonwealth* claimed Pope was "inclined to attribute all outrages . . . alleged to have been committed, to white horse thieves disguised as Indians" (repr. *SCP*, 2 July 1874).

[14] The number of men with Hennessey varies in the literature from two to three. Freight drivers George Fant and Thomas Calaway are the only two mentioned by William Matteson (see n. 17 below), who claimed to have been with the party that buried the two.

The third companion seems ultimately attributable to Agent Miles's report, which stated that four men, including one Reed, were found murdered at the site (*Walnut Valley Times*, 10 July 1874; *Topeka Commonwealth*, 14 July 1874). Since Miles's party saw only the body of Hennessey, the others having been buried already, Miles was reporting from hearsay.

This odd man is a difficult ghost to lay, however. Even such a careful work as Robert C. Carriker's *Fort Supply* (p. 89) repeats the "three companions" version. A writer in the *Arkansas City Dispatch* (repr. *Caldwell Journal*, 10 January 1889) claimed the fourth man was "a passenger, a tenderfoot from Boston, who had a morbid desire to kill Indians." (However, this account is so inaccurate in all other respects that the tenderfoot hypothesis probably should be returned to Boston unopened.)

Pat Hennesey, about whom considerable ink has been spilled, was one of those men remembered chiefly for the manner of their dying. Little is reported about his life other than the fact that he was a freighter. The *Topeka Commonwealth* (10 July 1874), in recording his death, observed that he was "formerly sheriff of Christian county, Illinois." Old-timers remembered him as a responsible, friendly man and described him as having red hair (Rainey, p. 143; Ridings, pp. 434-35).

[15] The name *Ed* is unique to Freeman; Burr Mosier is the name given in the con-

and they would probably reach the location which is now known as Bull Foot Ranch. These ranches are located on the stage line running from Wichita southwest into the Indian Territory, and are in distance about eight miles apart.[16] Probably darkness [overtook] the freighters before arriving at Bull Foot Ranch, and they concluded to camp for the night on the divide, about one mile from the ranch.[17]

What happened during the night will probably never be known, save by the parties who were present. This we know, that the freighters met a sorrowful death at the hands of some murderous fiends.

I will give the reader the facts concerning the finding of Pat Hennessey's body by Wm. E. Mallaley [Malaley], who kindly gave the writer a correct statement of the sad affair. Mr. Malaley is an honorable resident of Caldwell, and is an extensive cattle dealer and owns considerable real estate property.[18]

temporary newspaper accounts and in at least one official record (*SCP*, 6 August 1874, among others; Trial Docket of James A. Dillar, Justice of the Peace, Wellington Township, Chisholm Trail Museum Archives). Mosier had operated Buffalo Springs Station since October, 1873.

[16] The various stations south of Caldwell are referred to frequently enough by Freeman that I offer the following table of distances for the convenience of the reader. The table is taken basically from the *Caldwell Commercial* of 20 May 1880, modified to reflect the names of locations as Freeman gives them (e.g., Haines Ranch appears as Bull Foot). Locations marked with an asterisk (*) were not the sites of stations in 1874.

From	To	Miles	Nearest Modern Town
Caldwell	Pole Cat	12	Renfrow
Pole Cat	Pond Creek	14	Pond Creek
Pond Creek	Skeleton (or Baker's)	21	Enid
Skeleton	Buffalo Springs	16	Bison
Buffalo Springs	Bull Foot	8	Hennessey
Bull Foot	Little Turkey*	4	———
Little Turkey*	Red Fork	4	Dover
Red Fork	Kingfisher	10	Kingfisher
Kingfisher	Cheyenne Agency	21	Concho
Cheyenne Agency	Fort Reno*	2	———

The Wichita Agency (at Anadarko) was 40 miles below Fort Reno.* Fort Sill was 35 miles below the Wichita Agency or 185 miles from Caldwell.

[17] This is Freeman's reconstruction of events. The attack on the freighters occurred during daylight hours, according to William Matteson, who reported seeing the skirmish from a distance of about two miles before he retreated to Buffalo Springs. Matteson was an employee of Vail & Co., contractors for mail delivery to the Territory (Rainey, p. 146). Rainey fixes the date of the attack as July 4.

[18] Malaley also gave Sam P. Ridings at least part of his version of the story, which differs in some particulars from Freeman's but not in any fashion that necessarily impeaches Freeman, Ridings, or Malaley himself (unless one believes the improbable circumstances that Malaley always told the story in exactly the same way and that Freeman and Ridings would retell the story exactly as Malaley told it to them.) William E. "Billy" Malaley, though an Alabamian by birth, enlisted in the Union Army during the Civil War in order to escape the cruel uncle who was rearing him. Malaley served in the Eleventh

W. E. Malaley

Mr. Malaley in company with Indian agent J. Miles of Fort Reno, J. A. Covington, his wife, and others[19] were on their route from Fort Reno to Caldwell, and upon their arrival at the Red Fork Ranch, they were told by the ranchman that the Indians had been making trouble between that point and Caldwell, and cautioned them of the impending danger of traveling on the trail.

The company were not frightened, however, and after watering their horses proceeded on their journey. They had traveled about eight miles, when they saw the remains of a wagon at the east side and perhaps a hundred yards from the trail. They also saw a pile of corn and oats still smouldering; the fire had almost consumed the wagon, leaving the corn and oats still burning. Mr. Malaley thought he spied a man's feet protruding from the pile of smoking grain. Contrary to the wishes of the party, Mr. Malaley went to the ruins to ascertain if his suppositions were correct; to his horror he saw he was not mistaken. The shoes were not burnt from the feet, and he took hold of them and pulled the blackened and charred remains of a man from the pile of smoking grain. The flesh had been almost burnt from his legs and arms, and the body presented a most sickening appearance; the intestines were dragging from the abdomen.

The body was examined to ascertain the cause of the unfortunate man's death. One bullet hole was found to have penetrated the left leg just above the knee. A close examination was made of the wagon, and the party came to the conclusion that Hennessey had been tied with his hands to one of the hind wheels of the wagon and his feet to the other, then the body was covered

---

Indiana Cavalry. During his later life he was a U. S. marshal, and it was in that capacity that he accompanied J. D. Miles and his entourage to Kansas at the time of the outbreak. Shortly thereafter he became engaged in the cattle business and eventually became active in the Cherokee Strip Live Stock Association. During the '80's he was a resident of Caldwell; he lived in later years in Hennessey, Oklahoma. He is reported to have been such a good rider that Cherokee Strip cowboys said of bad horses, "Billy Malaley could not ride that horse" (Ridings, pp. 100-15).

[19] J. A. "Amick" Covington was married to Sarah (or Sallie) Darlington, daughter of Brinton Darlington, J. D. Miles's beloved predecessor as agent to the Cheyennes and Arapahos. Covington was the first agency clerk there and served some years with distinction in a most difficult post. One of his duties was teaching the Cheyennes to handle teams and wagons in order to freight agency supplies from Kansas railheads (see chap. 38, n. 2), and for a number of years he accompanied and supervised the Indian freighters on such missions (Ridings, pp. 104, 134-36, 172-74, 185, 437). Covington moved to Caldwell in August of 1882, where for a short time he engaged in the grocery business in partnership with William Morris. Covington also functioned as Caldwell agent in charge of freighting for the Cheyenne-Arapaho and Kiowa-Comanche agencies (*Caldwell Commercial,* 17 August, 24 August 1882). The exact makeup of the Miles party is uncertain; it did include Covington's wife and daughter as well as other civilians, accompanied by a small military escort of three or four, including a driver (Rainey, p. 148; Ridings, pp. 104, 437).

with corn and oats taken from Hennessey's wagon, and the whole set on fire.[20] The result was as I have given it. Some of the party were in favor of leaving the body and others did not want to leave it unburied. But it was decided to bury it, and preparations were made to dig a grave. They had nothing to dig the earth with except an ax, which Mr. Malaley took and cut the earth, while the other men cleared away the earth with their hands. After digging the grave as deep as they could with the ax, the dead man was laid in it and the men filled the grave by throwing the dirt in with their hands.

The party found provisions and pieces of harness scattered around the wagon. Nothing was seen of the other freighters by Mr. Malaley, but when he arrived at the Buffalo Springs Ranch, upon inquiry he found that Mosier and a companion by the name of Bill Brooks[21] had taken a wagon from the ranch and proceeded to the place of the massacre, and taking the bodies of the three freighters, had buried them near Buffalo Springs Ranch.[22] In what manner they met their death Mr. Malaley did not ascertain. He asked Mosier and Brooks why they did not get Pat Hennessey's body and bury it at the same time they got the other bodies. They replied they did'nt have time.[23] Mr. Malaley received the information that the three freighters were killed about fifty yards from Hennessey, and east of the trail. He did not see the teams which belonged to the murdered men.

Pat Hennessey's grave is in the Oklohomo country, about ninety miles

---

[20] Ridings's version (p. 438) mentions no bullet wound; indeed, he asserts that the Miles party found no evidence of violence upon the body, apart from the obvious ravages of the fire. Rainey, the ultimate purist in detail, offers a very different version of the manner of Hennessey's binding and how the grain came to cover the body: One of Hennessey's hands was bound to the front wheel of the wagon, the other hand to the rear wheel. Then brush was heaped around and set ablaze. When the rear wheel burned through, the wagon collapsed, partially covering the body and spilling smoldering grain over a portion of the body that remained exposed. When the tragedy was discovered, the grain was still burning. Rainey bases his description on interviews with eyewitness Matteson (p. 147).

[21] William L. "Bully" Brooks was a member of the gang of horse thieves plaguing the area at the time. His fate is described in chap. 27. Brooks's career was checkered. He served as marshal in cow town Newton, Kansas, in 1872, but before a year had passed he had degenerated into a killer and thief at Dodge City. The best account of Brooks's activities may be found in Nyle H. Miller and Joseph W. Snell, *Why the West was Wild*, pp. 51-59.

[22] William Matteson claimed to have been one of the party which retrieved the bodies of Fant and Calaway and brought them back to Buffalo Springs for burial (Rainey, p. 147). He had left for Caldwell before the Miles party arrived, which may explain why Malaley did not mention him (Ridings, pp. 438-39). It is unlikely that Malaley was mistaken about Brooks's presence, given Bully's reputation and his sensational death not long after. Indeed, Burr Mosier would testify that Brooks was at Buffalo Springs Ranch at the time in question (*SCP,* 6 August 1874).

[23] Matteson said they did not want to handle the body because it was so badly burned (Rainey, pp. 147-48).

South of Caldwell. An enterprising town has been laid out near the place which marks the spot on which the murder was committed, and the town bears the name of Hennessey, in honor of the unfortunate Pat Hennessey, whose rude funeral was solemnized by the presence of four parties.[24] There was no shroud or coffin, no priest nor tolling bells.

Pat Hennessey left a widow with four children living near Manhattan, Kansas. The family were left in destitute circumstances.[25]

In later years a stone was placed at Hennessey's grave with the following inscription, "Pat Hennessey, killed, July 13, 1874."[26]

[24] Malaley, of course, plus three unidentified others.

[25] I can find nothing to corroborate the survivors.

[26] Rainey—who cared passionately about such details and whose words therefore have weight—said the only stone marker that ever existed was the one he saw in 1889, which read, simply, "P.H. 1874" (p. 149). July 13 is incorrect in any case.

CHAPTER 26

The Stage Stock Is Stolen—The Secret Told to A. M. Colson—
He Organizes a Party to Pursue the Thieves—A Fight with
Buffalo Hunters—A Flag of Truce—Great Hunger
Prevails Among the Party—A Jack-Rabbit Shot
and Divided—The Thieves Are Spied—The
Fight—The Escape of the Thieves—
Capture of Seven Mules and
Three Horses.

A short time after the death of Pat Hennessey, word reached Caldwell that the Stage Company had lost nearly all their stock, and a reward of $400 was offered by the Stage Agent, John [L. T.] Williamson, for the capture of the stock.[1] About the time the Stage stock was stolen, Bob Drummond also lost a fine race horse and a pony; the presumptions were that the thieves who had stolen the Stage Company's horses had also stolen the race horse.[2] Numerous horses belonging to the settlers were missing, or had "strayed too far" from civilization so that all traces of them were lost.

The Stage line was owned and controlled by [Vail & Co.],[3] and its starting place was Caldwell; and Fort Sill, a place 180 miles away, was its point of destination. Stage ranches were located all along the line, furnishing fresh

---

[1] The systematic theft of the company's livestock was already under way before Hennessey was killed. Four company mules were stolen from Judd Calkins' livery barn in Caldwell and four more from the Skeleton Creek stage station on the night of June 29. Other stations were to have been pillaged, but the Indian uprising described in the previous chapter delayed execution of those thefts. The company, which had only recently been granted a U. S. mail contract, was to begin operation on July 1. The reward offered was three hundred dollars, but Freeman might have been thinking of the remark attributed to one of the thieves when he heard about the reward: "Oh, hell! We will not take them back for four hundred dollars, when we got six hundred dollars for stealing them" (*SCP,* 6 August 1874). Freeman incorrectly identifies the stage agent as John Williamson.

[2] The presumption was correct. The thief was identified as a gang member, Jasper "Granger" Marion. At least Marion was riding Drummond's horse when he escaped from a posse on July 21 (*SCP,* 6 August, 27 August 1874). Bob Drummond was an early settler in the Caldwell vicinity; his spread was located near the Chikaskia River, where the horse thieves had raided several farms in recent weeks.

[3] Freeman says it was the Southwest Missouri Stage Company, but this was the previous contractor, whose employees, if not its management, were behind the efforts to so deplete by theft Vail & Co. livestock that Vail could not fulfill the mail contract recently awarded it (*SCP,* 6 August 1874). Vail & Co. is the name generally given for the new company, although George D. Rainey (*The Cherokee Strip,* p. 137) states that it was organized as the Southern Stage Company. Freeman's confusion may spring from the similarity of names, then. In any case, he compounds the confusion in a later chapter; I have emended the text in both passages.

A. M. Colson

horses for traveling and supplying food and shelter for both man and horses.

Near the latter part of July,[4] Dr. [P.] J. M. Burkett, a doctor and drug-gist of Caldwell, called A. M. Colson, a resident of the town, into his office and told him to get up a crowd and try to capture the thieves, who were to pass the Devore place, twelve miles west of Caldwell, with the stolen stock at about nine o'clock the next morning.[5]

Mr. Colson asked Burkett of whom he received the information. Burkett declined to reveal the name of the informer, but finally, after asking Mr. Colson to "never give it away," he told the secret[6] and stated that the thieves had been holding about thirty-five head of horses and mules in the "black jack" near Turkey creek, located in the Indian Territory about seventy-five miles South-west of Caldwell.[7] Burkett said the thieves would pass Devore's place with the horses and continue North-west in their travels; their desti-nation would be either Larned or Fort Dodge. Upon receiving this informa-tion, Mr. Colson concluded to get up a party and go to the place designated by Burkett and endeavor to capture the thieves and get possession of the stock. He immediately went to the North of Caldwell, to the Chikaskia river, and

---

[4] 15 July 1874 (*SCP,* 30 July 1874).

[5] That Dr. Burkett chose Colson to confide in is probably as much as anything an indication of Colson's recognized leadership ability, for Colson had no official status; his public achievements were still ahead of him. "The Devore place twelve miles west of Cald-well" would have been the homestead of H. J. Devore on Bluff Creek, where Devore settled in 1872 (*Caldwell Commercial,* 15 February 1883). Devore's place was located near the Ellsworth Cattle Trail in Harper County (*SCP,* 30 July 1874). Andreas (p. 1364) is clearly in error when it indicates that Mr. Devore did not settle in Harper County until 1876.

[6] A. C. McLean was Burkett's informant. McLean by 1874 was proprietor of the in-famous Last Chance Saloon south of Caldwell. Despite the information he provided Burkett, McLean was later arrested along with the others for being a member of the horse-thief gang. Yet in the early morning hours of July 30, when three of his cellmates in the Wellington jail were taken from the guards and lynched, McLean was spared. D. B. Em-mert and William Ross of Sedgwick County later claimed that McLean was not lynched because of past kindnesses and favors he had done members of the vigilance committee. Whatever the reason, some measure of justice was done, for McLean was tried and ac-quitted in Wellington Township before Justice James A. Dillar on 6 August 1874 ("His-tory of Sedgwick County," *Historical Atlas,* p. 9; Andreas, p. 1387; Criminal Docket of James A. Dillar, Chisholm Trail Museum Archives). McLean was heard from again in 1884 when a group of vigilantes in the northwestern United States advised him to quit the territory; it seems McLean had offered as a reference the name of a Caldwell man who, despite the acquittal in '74, would not attest to McLean's *bona fides* (*Caldwell Journal,* 4 September 1884).

[7] Freeman errs. At the trial of A. C. McLean, Burkett testified that the stolen animals were being held near Pole Cat, about twelve miles below Caldwell. (They had earlier been held at Turkey Creek, near Mosier's Buffalo Springs Ranch.) Further, Burkett does not mention thirty-five head of stock; he mentions four mules. Burr Mosier testified to seeing ten animals—eight mules and two horses—in the thieves' possession (*SCP,* 6 August 1874).

engaged the services of some of the settlers and all together mustered up a crowd of seven men, namely, Frank Barrington, Alex. Williamson, Bob Drummond, —— Force, John Williams, and A. Livingston;[8] the men were detained from starting until quite dark, and after traveling for some time they reached Fall creek where they were joined by Ballard Dixon and George Perringer, citizens living on Fall creek. The night was extremely dark; the company of men got bewildered in the darkness; and, after traveling for some time up hill and down, they concluded they were lost and the best thing for them to do was to stop here until daylight; here Ballard Dixon and George Perringer forsook the party and returned to their homes.[9] The little company of men began to make preparations to rest until morning. They made themselves as comfortable as their circumstances would allow and slept on the prairie, using mother earth for their bed; as soon as it was sufficiently light enough to view the surrounding country they saddled their horses and started on their journey, and soon after they arrived at Major Andrew Drumm's ranch, where the party ate breakfast; here they were joined by "Buffalo" King and soon after by Sheriff John Davis from Wellington, with a company of ten men.[10] Upon their arrival at the Devore place, they were surprised to learn from one of the family that the thieves—three in number—had passed there the day before, driving and leading ten head of horses and mules. The question was asked: Where are the other twenty-five head of stock?[11] It was presumed that the original stock had been divided, a party of men each taking a bunch and going in different directions; their intent was, it is supposed, to dispose of the stock, get their money, and return to Caldwell.

The party who were in pursuit of the horse thieves started in a North-

---

[8] Colson went to the Chikaskia River vicinity for help because many of the settlers in that vicinity "had suffered from the depredations of the thieves," as the *SCP* (30 July 1874) explains it; but then, of course, the Chikaskia River would probably be the first place Colson would have thought of anyway. That is where he and Ryland had settled when they came to Sumner county. That is where he had old neighbors he could count on. Apart from Barrington and Drummond, the posse members have not been identified further; the same thing is true of George Perringer a few lines down. Although no one says it directly, it seems obvious that Colson, after learning of the thieves' plan, telegraphed the sheriff at Wellington, who asked Colson to gather men for a sheriff's posse. *SCP* (30 July 1874) indicates that the sheriff had information and went to Caldwell to meet others who were "in on the secret."

[9] *SCP* (30 July 1874) describes Sheriff Davis' party as the one that got lost during the night.

[10] Sheriff Davis started with only six men (*SCP*, 30 July 1874). John G. Davis of Oxford was elected sheriff on 5 November 1872 to fill the unexpired term of George A. Hamilton, whose office A. A. Jordan had unsuccessfully bid to fill (see chap. 19, n. 5). Davis was reelected on 5 November 1873 but resigned in 1875 before his term was up.

[11] They are in Freeman's imagination. As explained in n. 7 above, there were never more than ten animals to account for.

west direction, following the Ellsworth cattle trail. Perhaps it would be well to give a description of this cattle trail. As the tide of civilization crowded West, and settlers settled here and there on their farms of 160 acres of land, the Chisholm trail was in the center of a civilized country; hence the trail must be disposed of and a new one established further west. The new trail made connection with the former one at Pond creek, Indian Territory, and angled across the country in a North-west direction; its destination was a town located near Larned, on the Kansas Pacific Railroad. This town was called Ellsworth, and the trail was designated by the cattle men as the "Ellsworth trail."[12]

After the men had traveled a short distance they rode upon a herd of buffalo and each man endeavored to kill the greatest number of these mighty monarchs, until the horses were very much wearied from the chase. The party were unwise in doing this, for by doing so they had lost the trail of the thieves. They did not realize the condition of their horses until after the chase was over; then they saw the disadvantage they were in and rode slowly on; some of the party, however, walked a greater part of the way. When they neared the Chikaskia river the trail was again found and the party traveled on. We will not attempt to follow them in their many turns, but will say that the trail was again soon lost, and the party traveled a part of two days without trace or track of the thieves. It had been ascertained by the men upon starting from Devore's, that the thieves had a wagon along with the outfit; this could be easily followed as long as it was kept in the road, but after leaving it the tracks were difficult to discover. The party left the Ellsworth trail and traveled in a North-west direction and traveled for two days with the trail of the stock thieves. The party had started with a good supply of whiskey, and so long as that article lasted the men were ready and eager to push on after the thieves, but when the last drop had been drained, the spirits and energy of the party began to wane, and one by one the men left until the little band numbered but ten men. Five of these men were from Wellington: namely, John Botkin, Neal [T. C.] Gatliff, Joe Thralls, John Davis, the sheriff, and one whom I have forgotten.[13] The five men who started from Caldwell were:

[12]Freeman distorts the emergence of Ellsworth as a cattle town by linking it with the closing of the Chisholm Trail. The Ellsworth Trail, forking off at Pond Creek as Freeman describes it, was used as early as 1871. Ellsworth was a competitor of Abilene as a cattle town and not an expedient heir to the trade as Freeman implies. In 1874, the year of the present narrative, Abilene was out of the picture, but the Chisholm Trail terminus at Wichita was still doing good business. So, incidentally, was Ellsworth.

[13]Only four of the remaining ten were from Wellington, the four whose names Freeman did remember. Two of the Wellington men who had started with the posse returned home. These are identified only as Stevenson and Abrell (*SCP*, 23 July 1874). John Botkin served in Company G, Seventh Iowa Cavalry, during the war. He worked on construction of the Union Pacific Railroad before he settled in Kansas in 1870. At the time of

W. B. King, A. M. Colson, Frank Barrington, Alex. Williamson, and ——— Force.[14]

This band of ten men were determined to follow on and succeed, if possible, in catching the thieves and getting possession of the stock. They arrived at Kingman[15] about noon and ate dinner at that place; this was the last meal they ate until four days afterwards. After they had been without food for one day and a half, Mr. Colson shot a jack rabbit; a fire was quickly made out of buffalo chips, and some of the men removed the hide from the rabbit, then the rabbit was laid on the buffalo chips and roasted; the party had no salt, hence the rabbit was to be eaten without that article of seasoning. As the meat lay frying on the fire, T. C. Gatliff looked on with utter disgust and remarked "he could'nt eat it, fried on buffalo chips." There would be no trouble attended to this, for the remaining nine men were ravenous and could quickly dispose of Gatliff's portion, but when the rabbit was cooked, it was divided into ten pieces and distributed among the ten men, who ate it quickly and wished for more. Gatliff ate his share without a murmur.[16]

From Kingman the party traveled west until they reached Sand Creek, where they struck the trail of the thieves again.[17] This time they had found a

this episode, he was a farmer (*Portrait and Biographical Album of Sumner County, Kansas*, pp. 431-33). Thomas C. Gatliff (Freeman calls him Neal) was a Wellington grocer who had lived in Sumner County since 1871 (Andreas, p. 1499). Gatliff was the official complaining witness against the gang members who were later arrested in Caldwell (Criminal Docket of James A. Dillar). Joseph M. Thralls was Wellington town marshal and a deputy U. S. marshal at this time. He was to become one of the most outstanding lawmen of the Southwest, a legend in his own time though forgotten in ours—probably because he never killed anyone and thus failed to engage the interest of the dime-novel crowd. Thralls was sheriff of Sumner County from 1880 to 1884. He served as Wellington's mayor from 1917 to 1927. A Thralls adventure, only slightly distorted, may be found in T. A. Mc-Neal's *When Kansas Was Young* under the title "An Early-Day Murder and Man Hunt" (pp. 133-36); see also "Recollections of a Frontier Sheriff" (pp. 16-20) in the same volume. A biography of Thralls is in preparation. Thralls was the older brother of W. E. ("Elzie") Thralls, sheriff in Garfield County, Oklahoma Territory, during the 1890s.

[14]There were six, not five, from the Caldwell area. Freeman has omitted one John Williams (*SCP*, 30 July 1874).

[15]Kingman, Kansas, in 1874 consisted of "a hotel, a schoolhouse, a small (and very small) court house, a store and two or three small residences," which is not too bad considering the town was only four months old (Andreas, p. 1527). The account in *SCP* mentions only a dwelling somewhere in the center of Kingman County (30 July 1874).

[16]Again, Freeman's favorite local-color anecdote. It seems unlikely that Gatliff, old settler that he was, would have been fastidious about a buffalo-chip barbecue.

[17]Sand Creek in northeastern Barber County. The *SCP* (30 July 1874): "On Sunday the sun shone fierce and hot, yet they did not quite despair but voted to make another day's effort. Meeting a boy who was driving some cattle out of Barbour county, they learned that a party answering the description of the thieves had encamped the night before on Sand creek, fifteen miles to the west."

camping place of the thieves, which showed the fact that they had used pieces of a wagon for fuel, for the men found burned remnants of a wagon bed with pieces of old iron scattered around the recent camp fire.

The little party tired, hungry, and almost utterly worn out from exposure and fatigue traveled on, and, when they neared the Nennescah River bottom, the eyes of the men scanned the bottoms, and at last an exclamation of surprise escaped the boys, when one of them said, "Boys, there's our outfit," and in looking near a draw two men were seen going toward the camp, about which a number of horses were grazing. At this agreeable intelligence, the men were elated because of their good luck and nervous because they feared the thieves would become aware of their presence and make a hasty departure. The party decided to run, and if possible, obtain a position between the two men and the camp. Their plans once laid, the party dashed on the run toward the camp, but the two men reached the camp before the party could head them off. The men at camp began to fire at the party, and a general battle ensued, in which both parties indulged. After trying to get possession for nearly a half day, the party from Caldwell took a handkerchief and made a flag of truce and run it up so that it could be seen by the men at the camp.

This had the desired effect, and the men consulted over the matter; finally they had a meeting, when to the surprise of both parties, they saw they had had a wrong impression, for the men at camp were a party of buffalo hunters who mistook the ten men for Indians. The affair was settled without further trouble. The party of ten men said the buffalo hunters stood them off, and it was strange that none of the men were hurt by the numerous bullets that were flying.[18]

The party had now lost one-half day of valuable time and another half day was spent in finding the trail of the thieves, which was found but soon lost again. They were near a draw or ravine, and the men got off their horses and hunted in the ravine to find where the wagon had crossed. The only manner in which the trail could be found would be to part the tall grass of rank growth. This the men did, and succeeded in finding the tracks made by the wagon through the damp ground. The party were now west of the Ellsworth cattle trail and south of the Nennescah River, and were traveling in a northwest course. It would be wearisome to follow them in their many changes of directions, hence [we] will not attempt it. Now we find them pursuing a different course. The party had conceived the idea of striking the Medicine Lodge and Wichita wagon road and there the trail could be followed, or the tracks could be easily seen in case the thieves crossed the road.[19] They crossed

[18] To my knowledge Freeman is the only extant source for this plausible misadventure.

[19] The *SCP* account of 30 July 1874 indicates that the posse managed to keep the trail after locating it on Sand Creek. Freeman's version, retold after many years and second

Elm Creek near Medicine Lodge; it was here Mr. Colson killed the jack rabbit which was divided between ten hungry men. How ravenous their appetites must have been as they had now been several days without provisions. No doubt they relished their frugal meal. The horses had become weary and exhausted from hard riding, and it was necessary for the men to walk a part of the time in order to rest the weak and tired horses. W. B. King walked a greater part of the time as his weight was about two hundred and fifty pounds, and his horse was almost too weary to travel and carry the weight of Mr. King. A man could outwalk the poor, tired beasts and it would be useless to urge them in a run.

When the party reached the sand hills near the Arkansas River, an abundance of wild plums were found growing on the sand hills; as the men caught sight of the fruit, they hastily left their horses and began picking and eating the plums; they had now been one day and a half without any nourishment and nearly four days without a sufficient supply of food to satisfy their appetites.

After eating all the plums their appetites craved, the men once more resumed their weary chase. The signs of the thieves' camping places satisfied the party of men who were following them, that they were getting nearer and nearer to the object of their search and for [which] they had suffered the privations of hunger and thirst in order that the thieves might be captured.

When the men came within sight of the Arkansas River, a settlement was within one mile and a half,[20] and the men, with the exception of Mr. Colson, wanted to go to one of the houses and try to obtain some provisions. Mr. Colson told the men he was in favor of keeping on in the chase, for the signs were that they were not a great distance behind the thieves. He also said he thought he could get along without provisions for about twenty-four hours longer, and he was certain that by that time they would have the thieves in their possession; finally Mr. Davis, the sheriff, agreed to Mr. Colson's suggestions, and said he would favor pushing on in search of the thieves. After much talking, it was agreed to take a vote on the question, whether they

hand in the first place, garbles the sequence somewhat but probably renders at least a poetic truth about the difficulties of this pursuit. The posse caught up with the thieves near the Arkansas River. Had they been following the Medicine Lodge-Wichita road, they would have reached the Arkansas River at Wichita itself, and nobody contends that this was the case. Indeed, the *SCP* reports that contact was made on the Atchison, Topeka & Santa Fe railroad line "twelve miles west of Garfield in Pawnee County"—some 80 miles northwest of Kingman as the crow flies.

[20]The settlement was probably Garfield. Fort Larned lay about seven miles north, so the thieves were apparently heading for Boyd's ranch (see chap. 17, n. 2, and chap. 18), although there was some testimony that they planned to sell the stock (to settlers, presumably) along the Arkansas River (*SCP,* 6 August 1874).

were to travel on in pursuit of the thieves, or go to the houses and obtain food. The result was, four of the men went to a house to get provisions, two men to the Arkansas River to get a drink of water, leaving four men to wait until their return. While the four men were talking they noticed about three-quarters of a mile away, some stock resembling horses, grazing on the grass. The horses were watched, and in a short time a man came out of a ravine and drove the horses under the hill out of sight. These actions aroused the suspicions of the men, and they concluded they were the thieves, which they knew from the recent signs could not be very far in their advance.

The men waited for Williamson and Force to return from the river, then they said, "Colson, you are the lightest, you run and get the other men." Mr. Colson started to get the men who had crossed the river and gone to the settlement; when Mr. Colson reached the bank of the Arkansas River, the men that he wanted were on the opposite side, probably one-half mile from Mr. Colson. He hallooed to them but could not make them understand him. He tried to inform them what his errand was by the signs and maneuverings which he underwent for their benefit; he would take off his hat, wave it, beckoning for them to come to him, then he would turn his horse quickly and dash off, thinking thereby to inform them what he meant and what he wanted; the men stood and looked in amazement and wondered if Colson had gone crazy, or what was the cause for his strange movements; finally John Botkin came across and together with Colson went through performances similar to what Colson had, and, after much difficulty these men succeeded in inducing the three men to cross the river, when Colson informed them that the thieves were near and were making preparations to travel again.

The five men rode as rapidly as they could in the direction where the thieves were supposed to be camping. As the party neared the wagon they saw the other five men of the party ride up to the wagon and begin firing at the thieves. After several shots had been fired, the five men rode up to their party; the firing was returned by the thieves, who had by this time jumped into the wagon to which two mules were harnessed. One of the party had been slightly wounded in the affray, and the other two applied the whip to the frightened mules, and they left the party far behind.[21] The horses could not

---

[21] Freeman's version is obviously derived from Colson (who has rather the best part in the play here). Minor discrepancies are found between Freeman and the *SCP* (30 July 1874). For the reader who wishes to compare, the *SCP* account follows, beginning at the point just after the settlement was sighted: "Four of the party set off to forage for themselves and comrades who had halted to await their returning. Believing that they were nearing the fugitives, Sheriff Davis crept up the slope to reconnoiter. He was joined by the veteran King, and the two watched a small herd of buffalo until they were transformed into mules

endure fast running, and, in fact, they could not run faster than a good man on foot. The party of the thieves were pursued, however, by three or four of the party, and, becoming alarmed, [the thieves] quickly untied the two horses which they were leading [and] made their escape.[22] One of the horses was the race horse which had been stolen from Drummond.[23] Their horses being fleet runners, it was not difficult to escape from the party of men, as their horses were too tired to travel far. The party tried to obtain fresh horses in the settlement, in order to give the thieves a chase. Some of the settlers that had heard the firing, had started to see the fight. These men were met by the thieves and were informed that the party after them were horse thieves, and the men could not for some time change the opinions held by the settlers, hence a horse could not be procured until it was too late to give the thieves chase.[24]

Three of the men hunted and gathered together the mules and horses that had taken fright during the firing of the guns. The stock had been hobbled, but they had become so frightened that it was with much difficulty that the boys could accomplish their errand and bring the stock to a halt sufficiently for them to be driven back from whence they came. Information was received that the names of the thieves were —— Williamson, "Hurricane Bill," and "Red"; this man was a blonde with red hair and moustache, hence his name "Red"; what his real name was I never knew, nor did I know that of "Hurricane Bill."[25] These men had been temporary residents of Caldwell. "Hurricane Bill" and Williamson were in the wagon and escaped on the two horses. It was supposed by many that the wounded thief gave the information which implicated many of the residents of Caldwell as accomplices in the

---

and horses; and when a man came out of the ravine, they knew they had found their game. The best armed men were gone. Two men were dispatched to bring them in, and finally a third to hurry them up. In the mean time, the first man discovered was joined by a second and the two hitched up the team and drove away with two led horses. Fearful that the whole party would escape, Davis, King, and Williams resolved to charge the camp. Approaching from behind a hill, they rode in to find a yellow-haired thief in charge, who lost no time in an attempt to escape by mounting a horse. Foiled in that attempt he broke out on foot and by great leaps distanced his pursuers and—got lost on the sand hills. The spoils were four valuable mules belonging to Vail & Co., and two horses. The rest of the party coming up, the pursuit of the wagon was resumed."

[22] Editorial emendations to clarify ambiguity.

[23] As noted above, one of Drummond's horses was used in the escape.

[24] This delightful Keystone Kops sequence is not mentioned in *SCP.*

[25] The three men who escaped were apparently the man known as Red, Jasper ("Granger") Marion, and Jerry Williams. If Hurricane Bill Martin is the desperado Freeman was thinking of, nothing in the testimony at McLean's trial links Martin with this particular group or operation (*SCP,* 6 August 1874). Moreover, Hurricane Bill had an iron-clad alibi: he was in jail in Wichita (*Topeka Commonwealth,* 14 July 1874). "Williamson" may be a corruption.

stealing of the stage company's stock. It was rumored that the wounded man was rounded in by some of the party and to them made a confession[26] implicating Charles Hasbrook [L. B. Hasbrouck], Bill Brooks, one arm Charlie Smith, Jud Calkins, Dave Terrill, and others.[27] He also gave the names of the two men who had made their escape. "Red" reported they were to receive three hundred dollars for stealing the stock.[28] It was afterwards reported and published in the newspapers that the stealing was instigated by the [Southwest Missouri] Stage Company, thinking in this way the [Vail] Stage Company would become discouraged and throw up the contract for carrying the mail, and they would step in and fill it for them. [Vail & Co.] bid in the contract at eleven thousand dollars, while the [Southwest Missouri] company had been receiving a much larger sum, and the last bid made by them was seventeen thousand dollars; [Vail & Co.] was given the contract, and the result was their stock was stolen near the beginning of the first trips made by them through the Indian Territory.[29]

The party were elated over their good luck in securing the stock, and of the information received; they probably concluded the information received from the thief was more profitable to the community than the harm which he had done, and, as the party were tired, thirsty, hungry, and much fatigued, the vigilance of the guards proved not sufficient to keep the prisoner; it was

[26] The *SCP* (30 July 1874) version mentions no wounding and attributes information gleaned by the posse to effects left in the abandoned wagon. The wagon also contained supplies—sugar and coffee—which had been part of the ill-fated Pat Hennessey's cargo. Granger Marion later claimed he had salvaged the supplies with the knowledge and consent of Agent J. D. Miles at the scene (*SCP,* 27 August 1874).

[27] L. B. Hasbrouck was Caldwell's first attorney (Andreas, p. 1503). The *SCP* (6 August 1874) described him as "a young man of varied talent, good address and liberal education" who was "recognized as the legal adviser and a head center [*sic*] of an organized band of thieves." Hasbrouck had been accused of stealing a cow from one Seymour Dye in 1872 but was acquitted, a circumstance received with much bitterness in Sumner County (*Belle Plaine Democrat,* 22 August 1873). Judson H. Calkins operated the Caldwell livery stable from which four of Vail & Co.'s mules were stolen. Bill Brooks, "Charlie Smith," and Dave Terrill have been introduced heretofore. Terrill was very likely related to B. N. Terrill, who is squintingly associated with the management of the Southwest Missouri Stage Company (*SCP,* 6 August, 20 August 1874). The others to whom Freeman alludes would include only A. C. McLean.

[28] The amount was $600 (*SCP,* 6 August 1874).

[29] The many emendations are offered to spare the reader from a wickedly scrambled series of wrong names wrongly attributed. The purist is invited to consult an unedited version of the text and go quietly daft on his own.

reported he escaped from the crew of sleeping men.[30] The men returned home after an absence of ten days; the party divided at Slate Creek; the Wellington men returned to their homes, while those living in Caldwell traveled in a southeast direction, and reached home on the tenth day after leaving Caldwell.

[30] As indicated earlier, Freeman is the only source which mentions a prisoner. There may have been a prisoner and he may have escaped; but given the emotional climate in Sumner County, the rationale that the posse "probably concluded the information received from the thief was more profitable to the community than the harm he had done" seems specious. It would be easier to believe that they lynched him on the spot than that they had quietly let him go. At this writing I do not believe there was a prisoner.

CHAPTER 27

A Vigilance Committee—The Sheriff and Two Hundred Men
Surround Caldwell—Capture Dave Terrill, Jud Calkins,
L. B. Hasbrouck, Bill Brooks, and Charlie Smith—The
Prisoners Taken to Wellington—Three Pris-
soners Are Hanged by a Mob—A Banquet
Given by Agent Williamson—Four Hun-
dred Dollars Divided Among
Ten Men.

The numerous deeds of lawlessness and horse stealing in the south-west portion of Sumner county had occurred so frequently that in order to suppress
it something must be done by the citizens of the county. To catch a thief
[and] try him by a process of law was a slow method to render justice to the
law breaker, besides costing the county a large sum of money. A quicker and
surer way of meting justice to the horse thief was contemplated by the settlers. As a result, the entire southwest part of the county was organized into
a vigilants committee, whose purpose it was to rid the country of horse
thieves, and if necessary to accomplish this they would indulge in dealing with
the thieves according to the rules and regulations of the law over which Judge
Lynch presided.[1]

The adage, "Where there is a will, there is a way," seldom fails to be
realized. so it was with the vigilants; they had an indomitable will and a power
behind the throne of Judge Lynch which always found the way to accomplish
their mission.

The citizens at Caldwell knew nothing about the catching of the horses
[by the posse] until the men had returned from their trip after the thieves.
It was not generally reported among the residents of the town. At a late hour
in the night the town of Caldwell was surrounded by a crowd of men num-

[1] Freeman does not exaggerate the magnitude of the problem or the resolve of the
settlers. Corroboration may be found in the *SCP* for 30 July 1874 under the headline "A
Speck of War." The editorial states in part: "Horses and cattle by the thousands have been
spirited away during the past three years, and so perfect has been the manipulation of the
thieves that but few have ever been recovered. If pursued they fled for protection and shelter
to the Indian Territory where our citizens could not follow them, and thus escaped the
vengeance of justly incensed and exasperated settlers. . . . Depredations became more
frequent, and no farmer's stock was safe. This was the condition when the people began
to organize for self protection. Vigilance committees were formed, composed of men fear-
fully in earnest. . . . Courts of justice had been appealed to, so frequently in vain, that a
resort to a summary manner of dealing with them was resolved upon. The thieves, too,
armed and even fortified themselves in Caldwell, and threatened the destruction of everybody attempting their arrest. They thus invited the doom that evidently awaits them. The
people are fully aroused and mean business."

bering about two hundred. The sheriff was in charge of the men, and it was soon reported what their object was. They were after the parties implicated in the stealing of the stage stock.[2] After surrounding the town, the sheriff proceeded to make the arrest of the parties. Jud Calkins was found at the City Hotel, of which he was proprietor;[3] Hasbrouck was found at the Last Chance ranch, located one and one-half miles south of town;[4] Bill Brooks had taken refuge in a dugout on the Fall Creek, where he was arrested by the sheriff's posse;[5] Dave Terrill was found three miles northwest of town, at the house of Deacon Jones;[6] Charlie Smith was on Deer Creek, about twelve miles south of town. Smith was arrested the following day, and was taken while procuring wood for the camp. He was surprised to find himself in the presence of the sheriff's posse, who were standing with guns drawn, requesting him to surrender.[7] Hasbrouck heard the men coming and ran into a cornfield, which was immediately surrounded by the men, who waited until the approach of daylight when they arrested him.

The actions of the sheriff's posse caused great excitement among the residents of the town; some of them secretly left it and did not return for several days, while others left it never to return; whether they were guilty or not remains a mystery.[8] A doctor had informed the sheriff of the information he had received when the men surrounded the town;[9] the doctor requested

[2] The sizable force, which the *SCP* reports at 150, was occasioned by the expectation that the suspects would resist arrest with gunfire (see n. 1 above). Sheriff Davis and his group entered Caldwell at 2 A.M. on 28 July and began the search for the various parties for whom warrants had been issued the previous day by Justice James A. Dillar of Wellington. As it turned out, only Bill Brooks threatened armed resistance, but even he surrendered without an actual fight (*SCP,* 30 July 1874; Criminal Docket of James A. Dillar, Chisholm Trial Museum Archives).

[3] Freeman is the sole source I have found for Calkins' proprietorship of the City Hotel, while the newspaper accounts identify him only with a livery stable. Freeman renders Calkins as Calking.

[4] A. C. McLean was arrested at his home near the Last Chance; Hasbrouck, as Freeman later points out, was arrested in a nearby cornfield (*SCP,* 30 July 1874).

[5] Two other men who were with Brooks and had threatened resistance were captured, disarmed, and released (*SCP,* 30 July 1874).

[6] J. L. "Deacon" Jones was, with Terrill, associated with Caldwell's first saloon (see chap. 2, n. 4). In 1881 he was operating a hay ranch near Grand Lake, Colorado, and was remembered fondly by the editor of the *Caldwell Commercial* (27 January 1881).

[7] The *SCP* (30 July 1874) reports that "Smith" was twenty-five miles away in the Territory when fifteen men from the posse caught up with him.

[8] I have been unable to identify these people or even corroborate their departure, but the probability that such departures occurred seems high. Perhaps a remark from the *SCP* of 20 August 1874 is revealing: "Relieved from the terror of [the] presence [of the outlaws] the people of Sumner County breathe easier. For the first time in years they feel that their property is safe."

[9] This is obviously Dr. P. J. M. Burkett, mentioned in the preceding chapter, but the sense of the clause eludes me. Burkett, of course, was the man who passed along the infor-

the sheriff to place guards around his house, which he did, leaving five men as guards for several days, or until the doctor could pack up his goods and settle his business affairs in order that he might be able to leave the country. It seems the doctor feared the men implicated in the stealing, or their friends, might attempt to take his life. This fear occasioned great anxiety and fear on the doctors mind and as quickly as he could, he bid farewell to Caldwell and hied himself away to a healthier clime.[10]

The prisoners were taken to Wellington and given a preliminary trial.[11] Terrill and Calkins were liberated on a habeas corpus.[12] Charlie Smith, Bill Brooks, and L. B. Hasbrouck were found guilty and confined in the county jail to await the convening of court.[13] These men remained in jail one night

---

mation which led to the marathon pursuit (chap. 26) and ultimately to the arrests catalogued here.

[10] Burkett was evidently under threat (see n. 12). He moved to Wellington immediately after the arrests were made, and it appears he intended to make that his home. How long he remained there is uncertain, but by 1880 he was living in Silver Lake, Indiana (*SCP,* 6 August 1874, 5 February 1880).

[11] They were not tried immediately. On July 28, Brooks, Calkins, McLean, and Hasbrouck were brought before Justice Dillar. The charges against each of them were the theft of seven mules from Vail & Co. at Caldwell (though it appears that only four had been stolen there) and for being "members of an organized band of thieves opperating [*sic*] in this and adjoining counties." Dillar's docket shows that on the twenty-eighth each "was called before the court and the prosecuting witness [T. C. Gatliff] and county atty. both being absent this cause is continued until Wednesday morning [July 29] at 9 o'clock." It is interesting to note that no warrant had been issued by Dillar for "Charlie Smith," yet he was arrested and, on the evening of July 28, placed in the Wellington jail (Criminal Docket of James A. Dillar; *SCP,* 30 July 1874). Dillar, being a township justice, would have conducted a preliminary hearing to determine whether the accused should be bound over to the district court for trial.

[12] No warrant had been issued for Dave Terrill, at least by Dillar, and from the newspaper account it appears Terrill was never formally charged with theft or conspiracy. Calkins was not released on a writ of habeas corpus but rather on bond, and this release was not granted until Wednesday, July 29, so it would appear that Calkins spent the night of the twenty-eighth in jail with Brooks, Hasbrouck, "Smith," and McLean. Bond was approved pursuant to Dillar's granting Calkins a continuance on his trial to August 5. Dillar's records do not show the amount of the bond, but the *SCP* reports it as $500 "straw bail." Apparently no sooner was Calkins released than he teamed up with Dave Terrill and made threats against the life of Dr. Burkett. On a complaint by Burkett, Dillar issued a warrant for the arrest of Terrill and Calkins, but they fled to Wichita, where they successfully hid from pursuers (Criminal Docket of James A. Dillar; *SCP,* 30 July, 6 August 1874).

[13] They were never tried or bound over for trial. Dillar's docket shows no entry for the twenty-ninth, when Brooks' and Hasbrouck's trials were set. On the thirtieth Dillar recorded in each case that it had been dismissed due to the death of the defendant.

A. C. McLean was tried, but not until August 5. The testimony of Dr. Burkett and Burr Mosier (reprinted in *SCP,* 6 August 1874) was sufficient to acquit McLean. Their

and a part of two days. The second night, the 30th of July, will be ever immemorial in the minds of the earlier residents of Wellington, and also to the settlers who were living throughout the country during the month of July, 1874.

About the twilight hour,[14] horsemen armed with guns and revolvers were seen near the town of Wellington; one by one the number increased until the crowd probably numbered three hundred men. Near the midnight hour the men marched with muffled tread to the jail in which were confined the three guilty men. The jail was broke open and the prisoners were taken out. The crowd quietly marched to [Slate] creek south of Wellington, probably one mile from the town, and the prisoners were hanged to a tree near the main road from Wellington to Caldwell.

It was reported by citizens of Wellington, who saw the mob as they marched through the streets, that the silence was unbroken by word or whisper, and the men resembled an army marching on duty. Everything was done in an orderly and systematic way; the foot steps of the entire crowd seemed to be marching to a "right," "left," "right," "left" order. The prisoners were marched between two men, each file having one of the three prisoners.[15]

---

testimony would likely have caused Brooks and Hasbrouck to be bound over for trial—as well as "Charlie Smith," assuming he were ever charged and tried. In any case, no matter how the successful flight of Terrill and Calkins may have affected Sumner County tempers, the acquittal of McLean *after* the lynchings is significant. Certainly the acquittal did not inspire a sense of frustration with the courts and provoke the lynchings as some observers have suggested. The lack of spontaneity in the lynchings may be judged by a remark in the *SCP* of 23 July—five days before anyone was arrested and two days before Sheriff Davis and his posse had returned from their odyssey of pursuit: "There is a tree with a convenient limb near the Slate creek bridge that promises to become historical." See also the last three sentences of n. 1 above, from an editorial obviously written before the hangings actually occurred.

[14] To keep the record straight: the vigilantes gathered on the evening of the twenty-ninth and moved in on the jail after midnight, the morning of the thirtieth.

[15] This eerie precision, so contrary to the hysteria of the cinematic lynch mob, is verified in the *SCP* (6 August 1874): ". . . the full moon rose on Wednesday evening, climbed a cloudless sky and smiled down upon a scene of almost unusual quiet . . . , when the ominous tramp, tramp of marching horsemen broke upon the stillness of the night; and soon . . . could be seen a long line of mounted men, preceded by a small body of footmen, marching swiftly, yet in the most perfect order directly toward . . . [the jail]. As the head of the column approached the calaboose, the short, sharp cry of halt! rang out upon the stillness of the night, and the click of carbines was heard. . . . fifty horsemen broke from the ranks and instantly surrounded the calaboose, dismounted, disarmed the guards and possessed themselves of the key. The doors were thrown open and the prisoners brought out. During all this time not a word was spoken. The silence was oppressive. . . . They marched in the direction of Slate creek bridge. . . . not even a dog barked, and the slumbers of the nearest families were not disturbed. The cavalcade disappeared in the gloom, the tramp, tramp of the marching column died away in the distance, and stillness reigned supreme."

Hasbrouck asked permission to speak before the hangmans noose was placed around his neck, but this request was denied him; whereupon he began talking and requested that the awful manner in which he was to meet his death be never reported to his parents, who were living in one of the eastern states.[16] While he was talking the noose was put around his neck, and he was swung into eternity. Hasbrouck was a young man possessed with great intelligence, had won the reputation as being a smart lawyer, and practiced in the courts of Sumner County until the time of his arrest and death.

Charlie Smith was a brother of Tom Smith, who had, some time previous, been hanged at Rylands Ford on the Chikaskia River. He had only one arm, having lost the other either by an accident or in a fight with an adversary. The Smith brothers were respectfully connected with relatives in Illinois. It was reported that they were the illegitimate sons of one of Illinois' most noted men, officially speaking.[17]

Bill Brooks is one of the men who, it is claimed, helped to bury the two freighters who met their death in company with Pat Hennessey. It was reported that Brooks pled for mercy at the hands of the mob, but he was to receive none and was hung with Hasbrouck and Smith.[18] It is the supposition that Brooks and Hasbrouck stole the race horse and pony from Bob Drummond.

The men were left hanging until the following morning, when their bodies were cut down and taken to Wellington, when they were placed in the old court house. The bodies of the dead men were laid side by side upon the floor, and to shield their ghastly faces from the gaze of the passing people, a blanket was spread over the bodies, covering the faces.[19]

They were buried in rude coffins near the old cemetery, and the graves are pointed out to the recent settlers as the last resting place of the three horse thieves who were hanged by a mob on Slate Creek.

But little remains to be told; suffice it to say this hanging had the desired effect; horse thieves took a leave of absence and quit their haunts in Sumner county. They learned, by the example of Hasbrouck, Bill Brooks, and "one

[16] To the best of my knowledge Freeman is the only extant source for the words and manner of the men at the time they were hanged.

[17] None of the Illinois sources previously cited (see chap. 17, n. 3, and chap. 20, n. 1) gives indication that "Tom" and "Charlie Smith" were anything else but legitimate sons of Governor Thomas Ford. The rumor regarding illegitimacy may be attributable to "Charlie" himself, who, perhaps in bravado, made that claim (G. W. Robson in *The Frontier Echo,* 17 March 1876, quoted in W. E. Koop, "A Rope for One-Armed Charlie," *True West,* February, 1967, p. 65).

[18] "The distorted features of Brooks gave evidence of a horrible struggle with death. The other men looked naturally, and evidently died easily" (*SCP,* 30 July 1874).

[19] The details are essentially the same as those recalled by Joseph M. Thralls (*Wellington Monitor-Press,* 24 August 1921).

armed Charlie" Smith, that the people were determined to suppress lawlessness, and if they continued in the practice of horse stealing, they were liable to meet a similar death to that of the three prisoners.[20] The consequences were the thieves did not know who to trust and all men were suspicioned as belonging to the vigilants committee of the Southwest. So strongly were the people organized into this society that in case of a necessity an hours ride would collect, without difficulty, a company of men numbering several hundred. Thus the reader will see with what uniformity the settlers worked together to suppress lawlessness and to encourage men of law, energy, and enterprise to visit our country, settle down, and cast their fortunes with us.

The stock belonging to the stage company was restored to the agent. The stock numbered seven head of mules and several horses.[21] A short time after the capture of the thieves and horses, the agent for the stage company, L. T. Williamson, gave a banquet at Wellington, inviting the ten men who had effected the capture of the mules; the three hundred dollars offered as a reward for the stock was divided among the trusty and tried men, each receiving an equal share of the money.

This sum would not pay them for the horses they had ruined while searching for the thieves, notwithstanding the exposure, starvation, and fatigue which the men had suffered, while they were riding over the western plains, enduring the privations of the plainsman without food or drink.

The greater part of these ten men are still residents of Sumner county; by their energy and pluck they have accumulated a small fortune, and we presume their intentions are to live the rest of their years in "Sunny Kansas."

---

[20] What Freeman has said is evidently true with regard to highly organized bands of thieves. Horses continued to be stolen in Sumner county from time to time—indeed, one of Freeman's was stolen in 1880 (see Editor's Introduction)—but the incidents were isolated and individual.

[21] Davis' posse (see chap. 26) recovered six mules and two horses (*SCP*, 30 July 1874).

CHAPTER 28

[L. L.] Oliver Shoots a Shoemaker of Caldwell—Facts Concerning
the Murder—Citizens Become Enraged—Efforts to Hang
the Murderer to a Sign Board—Men of Cooler
Judgment Interfere—At Midnight He
Is Taken and Lynched—The
Burial of the Body.

Scarcely had the people of Sumner County, Kansas, settled down to the usual routine of life, scarcely had the excitement caused by the hanging of Hasbrouck, Smith, and Bill Brooks quieted, before we are again called upon to witness a dreadful tragedy, in which two men are the unfortunate victims. This time it was not the Texas desperado, the dreaded horse thief, or the duelist that has met death. It is the laboring man bending over his work, unmindful of the vengeance which is being kindled in the breast of the enemy, who wantonly murders his opponent.[1]

It was a beautiful morning, the 20th [19th] of August, 1874; the sun broke in beauty over the undulating prairie. The day was exceedingly warm, the sun was hot, but its rays were tempered by a gentle breeze.

Men and women were going forth on some business errand, or were lounging lazily in the shade of the building, chatting socially and conversing of recent events, when the crack of a revolver rang in the air,[2] and the hushed and startled citizens looked this way and that in order to learn from whence came the sound and who was the victim and victor.

Very soon the mystery was solved by the appearance of a young man holding in his hand the still smoking revolver. Immediately a dozen or more of excited citizens were at the scene of the murder and had the murderer in their possession. The facts obtained concerning the shooting were these.

T. T. [L. L.] Oliver,[3] a young man, a temporary resident of Caldwell, had been drinking whiskey and carousing alone in hours of dissipation until he met a shoemaker living in the town who also liked the influence of whiskey,[4] where-

[1] The nineteenth of August, per the *SCP,* 27 August 1874, and the *Arkansas City Traveler,* repr. in the *SCP,* 3 September 1874. Freeman says the twentieth.

[2] Two shots were fired, according to the *Traveler.*

[3] Freeman shows T. T. Oliver, but the *Traveler* and the *SCP Chronology* (1 January 1880) have L. L. Oliver. Oliver was twenty-four years old and had been in Caldwell about a month.

[4] Although the *SCP* of 27 August 1874 names him Fred Voss, both the *Traveler* and the *Chronology* identify the shoemaker as Frederick Ricer. The *Traveler* further indicates that Ricer, from Ellington, Missouri, had been a resident of Caldwell only since the previous May. He is characterized as "a German, of quiet and inoffensive manners generally, but given to getting on a spree every now and then."

upon they both entered the saloon and drank to the health of each, and the consequences were that the two men became very much intoxicated and had a hilarious time together.

When the shoemaker was partially sober, he went to his shop and began to work at his trade. L. L. Oliver entered the shop for the purpose of buying a pair of boots. After priceing the different pairs of boots, he selected a pair which suited him and the men differed about the price, which Oliver said was too high. The shoemaker would not sell them as cheaply as Oliver offered to pay for them, consequently a dispute arose and a quarrel ensued.[5]

Finally Oliver told the shoemaker he would not buy the boots, and, turning he went out of the shop. The shoemaker was thus free, so he began mending a pair of boots, giving no more thought of the dispute with Oliver. This person, however, was harboring an ill feeling against the shoemaker, and to avenge himself of the wrong which he supposed had been inflicted upon him, he resolved to kill his opponent. He walked back to the shoe shop, and looking in, he saw the shoemaker at work near the door. He quietly drew his revolver and, pointing toward the unsuspecting shoemaker, sent a bullet crashing through his body. He saw the form of the shoemaker sway and fall, then he turned and left him writhing in the agonies of death.

The citizens' minds became inflamed over the cruel, cold-blooded murder. Had the victim been implicated in any manner by giving just cause for the action on the part of Oliver, the people would have viewed the murder with consideration, but the facts relative to the shooting were without just cause for the terrible crime, hence public sentiment revolted at the circumstance that so cruel a murder should be committed in their midst. A crowd of excited men took hold of Oliver and showed a determination to hang him to a sign board, but men of cooler judgment interfered with this project by remembering the presence of the gentler sex and the children of the town.

Oliver was guarded by men of principles and good judgment, and had the murderer been removed from the town, in all probability, his life would have been spared, but the enraged people in the community were determined Oliver should pay the penalty of the crime he had committed by dying the death of a felon.

About the midnight hour a moving of dark objects could be seen near the place occupied by the criminal. They [entered] the house, got possession of the man, and went in an easterly direction; after going about one quarter of a mile they [congregated] in a group, and as the summer moon in full glory was rising majestically above the dark treetops, she looked upon a dreadful picture. The

[5] Freeman is the only source known to me for the cause of the quarrel, and it must be remembered that his version is hearsay since he was living in Butler County at the time the event occurred.

body of young Oliver was hanging from the limbs of a tree, his feet dangling in the air; his expression bore marks of a conquered hero, his face assumed a look as if calling for mercy at the hands of his enemies. The deed has been done, the law "an eye for an eye" had been filled.

The body of the murderer was left hanging during the night, and the spectral scene was looked upon by stars that have shown in the cloudless firmament—there was a wailing wind like a funeral dirge sweeping through the trees; sad, unearthly music it sighed and moaned, and whispered forth, dying away in faint prolonged surges over the distant prairies.

The body of the shoemaker was laid away to rest near the bodies of Fielder and Anderson.[6]

The following morning after the dreadful double tragedy, the citizens repaired to the place of the lynching which took place on the little creek, a few rods east of Caldwell,[7] and cut the rope which held the body swaying between the heavens and the earth, and placing it in a rude box, buried it beneath the grassy turf and the last sad rites were over.

Thus ends another chapter where whiskey was king and caused the untimely death of two of its victims.

[When] the growing youths take warning and think wisely on the crimes committed within our county, and then resolve to "touch not, taste not, handle not" the intoxicating beverages, then we can truthfully say, intemperance does not exist.

---

[6] Metaphorically speaking, anyway. Ricer, a widower, left two small children; it is possible, then, that he was buried in a pauper's corner of the cemetery, and it is likewise possible that Fielder and Anderson were buried in the same section; but my observation of the disposition of estates suggests that Ricer's grave site would have been charged against any property or salable possessions he left when he died.

[7] Spring Creek, per the *Traveler.*

CHAPTER 29

Description of the First Election at Caldwell—Scenes at the
Polls During the Election in 1872—Votes Challenged—
The Final Result—A Caldwell Stage Driver Put
a Young Lady into a Swill Barrel—The
Barrel is Kicked Over—The
Girl's Appearance.

To make this history a complete work on the early days of Caldwell, I must record the early elections at that place. The first election held at Caldwell was in the early part of November, 1871. The election was held for the purpose of electing township officers.[1]

I do not think I would be exaggerating were I to say that all voted who were inclined to do so. I did not hear any questions asked relative to the residing place of the voter. I presume the only question asked was whether the voter was a resident of America. I know there were votes cast by men whose homes were in New York City, and other voters who lived as far South as Mexico. I do not think that any town polled a larger vote in its early infancy than did the town of Caldwell.[2]

Everything went as merry as a marriage bell; whiskey was the most popular article in demand; the saloons and grocery stores had replenished their stock of wet groceries prior to the day of election. The day gave them a good business and added many quarters to their pocket-books.

An occasional shot was fired from a revolver in order that the day might be celebrated according to the western style of celebrating the day of election. The usual festivities of drinking whiskey, horse racing, and target shooting was indulged in by the cow boys.

---

[1] The reader is reminded that the first township election was coincident with the first county election—the special election of 26 September 1871—but the voting place for the area which included Caldwell was at Colson's and Ryland's ranch (see chap. 6). Here Freeman is talking about the first election held in Caldwell itself—7 November 1871. For that election the county commissioners had provided additional voting precincts, one of which was the town of Caldwell (*Oxford Times*, 21 October 1871).

[2] Such relaxed voting procedures are not unique in the history of frontier elections. Caldwell had nothing to gain one way or the other, but a community vying for designation as county seat, for example, would have obvious incentives for the strays and transients to cast a ballot. In fact, after the special election of 26 September 1871, the people of Belle Plaine were accused of just such chicanery; the *Oxford Times* (Oxford was also a candidate for county seat) published a parody of "The Battle Cry of Freedom," which was dedicated to the Belle Plaine ballot box: "We will count 'em once again, boys,/We will count 'em once again/. . . . We will swindle while we can,/And count seven for each man." The *Times* contended that 384 votes were illegally cast at the rival city (30 September 1871).

The silence would sometimes be broken by some one throwing an old oyster can into the air, when some one would fire at it in rapid succession to ascertain how many balls he could put into it before the can fell to the ground; again was the can thrown into the air, giving another party a chance to show his dexterity with the six shooter.

After the votes were counted, the voters requested the newly elected men to contribute ten or fifteen dollars to a whiskey fund. The new officers donated the required sum of money, and all adjourned to a saloon where the money was squandered in drinking and gambling until the "we sma hours" began to dawn upon the scenes of revelry and dissipation.

On one or two occasions it took the participants several days to sober up. Some of the officers elected were men who very often indulged in drinking a glass of whiskey, and generally when the time comes for the officers to use their influence and authority in quelling disturbances of various kinds, they are found to be under the influence of whiskey and unfit to fill their office in a manner becoming an officer.[3]

The second election of township officers was held at Caldwell in the month of April, 1872.

Caldwell was the only town in Sumner County which did not contend for the county seat, consequently representatives from Belle Plaine and Wellington were sent to Caldwell to electioneer for their respective towns contesting for the county seat.[4]

The voters at Caldwell favored Wellington as the location of the county seat for several reasons: First, it was the nearest town contending for the county seat; secondly, it was near the center of the county, and it was a fine location to make a prosperous business center.

The evening before election day the representative from Belle Plaine arrived in our little hamlet.[5] It was readily seen that whiskey was his controlling element. He was feeling jubilant and had a good word for everyone with whom he conversed.

The men from Wellington were pleased to see the delegate from Belle Plaine, and the citizens of Caldwell treated him freely to whiskey. He was

[3] Freeman shifts in midcourse from a specific statement to a generalization. As far as I can determine, the list of township officers elected that November is not extant. The generalization speaks for itself.

[4] It is difficult to determine exactly which 1872 election Freeman was thinking of. Township officers were normally elected in February, city officials in April. A special election for county seat was held in March, 1872, when Belle Plaine was still in contention; but at that election Belle Plaine was eliminated, leaving only Wellington and Oxford as contenders in the runoff election of 9 April 1872 (Andreas, p. 1496). Thus it is impossible to point to one election which fulfills all of Freeman's stated elements: an April election; an election for township officers; a county-seat election involving Belle Plaine.

[5] This representative has not been identified.

feeling pretty lively on the following morning; when the polls were opened he was escorted to the place of voting, and as he manifested a desire to challenge votes he was taken into the room where the election was held. He was very much under the influence of Caldwell whiskey, and I presume lost the tickets he had brought with him from Belle Plaine,[6] for as soon as he entered the room he began searching his pockets for the tickets, and when he found he had lost them, he became very angry and said he had been robbed. This assertion created a laugh among the prominent men at the polls, which had a tendency to increase his anger. One of the citizens told him he ought to do something for his town; and in order to have a fine time, he was told that Mr. C. H. Stone was intending to vote and that he was not entitled to become a voter as his wife was living in Wichita.[7] The gentleman from Belle Plaine said he would challenge C. H. Stones' vote, also that he would not let anyone vote who was not a legal voter. The township justice was acting as one of the judges of election.[8]

When C. H. Stone came to vote, a couple of men led the drunken delegate to the judges, where he challenged Stones' vote; the justice asked the delegate his reason for challenging Stones' vote; the delegate replied, "that C. H. Stones' wife was in Wichita, and that Stone was not a legal voter." The justice said to Stone, "what do you think of that?" Mr. Stone said, "I am one of the first settlers in the town, and consequently I intend to cast my vote." The justice said he would have to swear in his vote, and Stone replied, "all right," and held his hand up to receive the oath, when the justice said, "Mr. Stone, will you swear to treat the crowd of voters and not slight one man?" Mr. Stone agreed to the proposition, and his vote was cast into the ballot box. The judges of election adjourned the order of business for ten minutes, giving every man a chance to go to the saloon and get a drink. The majority thought the judge had found the correct method in which to determine whether a man was a legal voter.

In a few minutes the polls were opened again and men cast their votes into the ballot box with greater assurance of giving Wellington the victory than the preceding voters had before getting their drink of whiskey.

The Belle Plaine man did not rally round the polls any more that day, and when the time appeared in which darkness hovers over the horizon, he had forgotten it was the day of election, challenging votes, or of his stolen

[6] At this time ballots were not provided by the election officials. Instead, ballots were printed by the various factions and offered to voters outside the polling places.

[7] Stone, one of Caldwell's founders, was notorious for his absentee status (see chap. 5, n. 2).

[8] The justice may have been B. W. Fox, but this man's proclivity for liquor suggests the justice who was called Yank (see chap. 39, n. 6), possibly A. E. Badger.

tickets, but was peacefully resting in a drunken sleep, free from the cares of this life, on the floor of one of the out-buildings.

He was left to his own thoughts and to sober up at leisure. The following morning he was ready to return to his native town and expressed himself as enjoying himself immensely while in this vicinity, but notwithstanding this, he seemed anxious to bid the citizens of the town farewell, and departed with the well wishes of the Caldwell people for his future success in electioneering for county seats.

In the early days of Caldwell's history, long before the mighty steam engine came thundering over the prairie, the coaches filled with the immigrant and land speculator whose destination was at some enterprising frontier town, a stage line run from Wichita, making connections there with the "iron horse," and carried the speculator, immigrant, and traveler to the several towns which were in close proximity to the stage route. This line run southwest from Wichita, and Caldwell was the end of that division; another division made connection with the Caldwell stage and furnished transportation to some point in the Indian Territory. The stage carried the United States Mail and an occasional passenger, but very few availed themselves of this expensive manner of transportation. Money was considered a luxury by a majority of the pioneer settlers, and by many the fare from Caldwell to Wichita, which was six dollars, was considered very unreasonable; consequently, the settlers used their own teams and conveyances to travel to and from Wichita. There was those however who had to patronize the stage company, having no other means to travel except in this way.

The incident which I am going to relate happened during the first few months after Caldwell's connection with Wichita by the stage line.[9] The driver of the stage was a young man addicted to the habit of drinking whiskey. The settlers in and around Caldwell made the necessary arrangements to have a little social pleasure by giving a public ball, all men invited who cared to "trip the light fantastic toe," and the consequences were that the larger proportion of the crowd were a class of disorderly and drinking people.

The stage driver was in town on the evening of the ball, and he, being a lover of that fascinating art known as dancing, concluded to avail himself of the present opportunity and seek the company of some young lady to accompany him as a partner to the ball room.

He had been drinking since his arrival in town and the result was that

---

[9] Again, the date is clouded. I opt for June of 1872, when a triweekly stage line was established which ran from Wichita through Belle Plaine and Wellington to Caldwell (*Topeka Daily Commonwealth,* 6 July 1872). The mail route to which Freeman alludes was established in 1873 but did not offer stage service to Fort Sill until 1874—and Freeman did not live in Caldwell in 1874 (Rainey, *The Cherokee Strip,* p. 137).

when the hour came for him to appear for the young lady, he was very much intoxicated. The young lady was working at the City Hotel.[10]

The young lady declined to accept of his company, on account of his drunkeness. He considered her refusal as an insult, and as a solace, he went to the saloon and sought to drive evil thoughts and care from his mind by filling himself full of whiskey. He was so drunk the following morning that a new stage driver was in demand and the stage made its accustomed trip, but with a new driver however.

About noon some one went to the stage driver and told him if he did not stop drinking and "sober up" he would be discharged as stage driver. This information had the desired effect upon the driver and about five o'clock in the afternoon, he was sober enough to go to the hotel and get his supper.

As he entered the door of the hotel, he saw the young lady who had refused to go to the ball with him go into the back yard, with a pan of dish water to empty into a swill barrel. He quietly approached unknown to her, and as she was in the act of emptying the water into the barrel, he took hold of her feet and gently dropped her head first into the barrel [of] swill, then turned and ran away.

I was standing in the door of the blacksmith shop, and saw the whole proceeding,[11] and, in company with a man who was also a blacksmith, I ran across the street to get the girl out of the barrel. The barrel was over flowing with dishwater and refuse from the kitchen; the girl was kicking and struggling to get out of her predicament, when we arrived on the scene. Had I not understood the blacksmiths trade and been accustomed to handling kicking animals, I should have used much hesitancy in venturing so near the barrel. We saw it useless to attempt to pull her out by the feet, so we tripped the barrel over, girl and all. She was nearly drowned, and wallowed around in the dish water and finally succeeded in gaining "terra firma." When she wiped the greasy water out of her eyes sufficiently to see us, she began to "read our title clear," and almost tore up the ground in her rage. We protested our innocence and related the circumstances to her; she kept up her abusive talk, until quite a crowd of people arrived on the scene. Some of the people laughed, and I could not help but laugh to see the girl standing with her dress bedaubed with dish water, her hair filled with coffee grounds, potatoe parings, and dirty grease.

[10] The City Hotel, Caldwell's first, was erected in the spring of 1872 and destroyed in 1885 during the city's rash of arson and mysterious fires (*Caldwell Journal*, 15 October 1885; see chap. 43, n. 7). Neither the young woman nor the driver has been identified.

[11] The City Hotel stood on the southeast corner of Fourth and Main streets, facing east. The blacksmith shop was apparently on the opposite side of Fourth, between Main and Market, facing south; thus the activity behind the hotel was in full view. Freeman operated a blacksmith shop at or near this vicinity after his return to Caldwell in 1879. His co-worker is unknown to me (*Caldwell Post*, 18 December 1879).

The men became very indignant over the affair and had not the landlady come to our rescue [and] confirmed our statement, we would have probably been used in a rough manner by the bystanders. But when they found the stage driver had put the girl into the barrel, they went to a saloon, found him, and the trouble was settled by treating the crowd to all the whiskey they wanted to drink.

CHAPTER 30

Cowboys Attempt to Take the Town—The Marshal Deputizes
Six Men to Assist in Making Their Arrest—George
Flatt Alone Takes Them—The Sixshooter
Does the Dreadful Work—The
Coroners Jury Decide
the Case.

Justice had been swift and certain in her dealings with the three horse thieves hung on Slate Creek, one-half mile South of Wellington. After a period of comparitive peace and prosperity throughout Sumner county, we are again called upon to witness the scene of a double tragedy, which occurred in the town of Caldwell, in the month of July, 1879.

Caldwell has become a notorious western town; her fame as the home of the cowboy, desperado, and gambler has been spread abroad throughout the land. People living in the eastern states shrink with horror and tremble with fear, when they first enter the town on a business transaction; the traveling salesman, commonly called the drummer, hastens to leave the town; he meets the hardware and dry goods merchant, the druggist, groceryman, and saloon keeper, greets them hastily, shows them the articles he sells, talks very glib and flattering for a few minutes, succeeds in making a sale, bids the merchant good-bye, and hies himself away to a more quiet town. All this is accomplished in a very few minutes; very often, however, before his departure, he witnesses a bloody encounter between the cowboy and marshal of the town, or a pitched battle between the citizen and a band of desperadoes.[1]

The reader will accompany me to the town of Caldwell. The summer has gone, the first bright sunny days of July are here.[2] The day is a balmy and breezy one, such as are usually seen by the residents of sunny Kansas. The evening zephyrs fanned the cheek of the blushing maiden and made nature seem more lovely and pleasing to the aged. The children were running to and fro in their frolics, unmindful of what the future had in store for them.

Near the middle of the afternoon two cowboys, whose names were Woods

[1] Freeman exaggerates the quality and frequency of these "pitched battles." Caldwell was a tough town, but the "bloody encounter" was scarcely a daily event. Freeman's inflated statement is of the kind which has, perhaps, encouraged the hyperbole of some modern historians. As Robert. R. Dykstra has shown, Caldwell saw only thirteen homicides during its cow-town heyday (1879-85), with the greatest number—three—occurring in 1881 (*The Cattle Towns*, p. 144).

[2] Somebody should have revoked Freeman's poetic license. He knew very well that in July summer hadn't departed Kansas. The date of the episode he is girding up to tell is 7 July 1879.

185

[Wood] and Adams, came riding into town armed with several six shooters; they rode in front of a saloon, hitched their horses, and entered the door of the saloon. They passed the time in drinking the vile stuff known as whiskey. Soon their evil nature was aroused, and they appeared like demons in human form.

The quietness of the town was soon broken by these inebriates, and the peaceful citizens were startled by the shots fired from the six-shooters of the cowboys. After filling themselves with whiskey, they proceeded to "take the town." They mounted their jaded horses and rode at full speed up and down the streets, firing their revolvers at what ever their evil dispositions dictated.

The constable of the town became tired of these things and proceeded to make arrangements for the arrest of the cowboys. The cowboy yell, and daring disposition they manifested, terrorized the constable and intimidated him to such an extent that he was afraid to attempt their arrest unless he had a sufficient number of men to assist him.[3]

He appointed six men to assist him, and among that number was George Flat [Flatt], who was known as a man possessed with great nerve and courage; he was also an unerring marksman with the six-shooter;[4] John Wilson was also appointed to act as a leader with George Flatt. Wilson was considered a good man behind a six-shooter and was a man with an indomitable will, and possessed that character pertaining to the order of the desperado.[5]

The leaders, Flatt and Wilson, went to the saloon and found the cowboys,

---

[3] The constable was W. C. B. "Wash" Kelly, whose regular occupation, in partnership with T. H. B. Ross, was management of the St. Nicholas Hotel (*Caldwell Post*, 19 June 1879).

[4] Freeman is, as far as I know, the sole source for the number of men in the posse. George W. Flatt's regular vocation at the time he was enlisted into this posse is uncertain. In February he had bought the Occidental Saloon from James Moreland (*Caldwell Post*, 27 February 1879), but something apparently went sour: by July the Occidental was again under Moreland's management. Details of Flatt's life subsequent to his sudden prominence in this affair are given in the succeeding notes and chap. 31. A detailed account of his brief year of glory may be found in Miller and Snell, *Why the West was Wild*, pp. 163-70.

[5] John Wilson was the official deputy constable under Kelly (per *Caldwell Post* of 10 July 1879). Wilson's primary livelihood was earned as a sign painter and paperhanger (*Post*, 2 January 1879). He was also a sometime saloon employee, his most recent connection being with the Occidental, possibly under Flatt's brief ownership (*Post*, 24 April 1879). He was a frequent fiddler at the community dances and in dance halls (*Caldwell Journal*, 11 December 1884). Wilson was in and out of trouble with the law until the time of his death. In 1880, a few months after his trial in a particularly scandalous bastardy case, Wilson married Aggie Reed, the plaintiff in the aforementioned lawsuit (*Post*, 18 March, 19 August 1880). He was killed at Wellington on 6 December 1884 by W. T. Edwards after an argument following a card game. His obituary said that his family, a wife and two children, "will probably be as well off without him as with him" (*Journal*, 11 December 1884). For Wilson's role in the Talbot raid, see chap. 41, nn. 7, 10, 15.

George Wood and Jake [Jack] Adams, in conversation with the saloon keeper.[6] Wilson went around the building and stood near the back door of the saloon; Flatt entered the front door; I stationed myself near the door opening onto the street, and was sitting outside the door talking to a friend.[7] When Flatt entered the saloon he went to the bar and called for a glass of whiskey; he placed his six-shooter on the counter[8] and quaffed the whiskey; then one of the cowboys went up to the bar and called for some whiskey, and after drinking it gave a Texas whoop. This whoop is commonly called "a cowboy yell," but as the sandy complected Texan was the originator, its proper name would be a Texas whoop. It would be needless for me to attempt to describe it to the eastern reader; I presume all who have lived in the West are familiar with it. I will say this, however, that the whoop has a blood-curdling sound and terrifies one who is unaccustomed to its sound.

After the cowboy gave a whoop, Flatt indulged in another drink, and answered the whoop in true Texas style. The cowboy drew his revolver on Flatt who backed towards the front door; the cowboy followed with his revolver drawn within six inches of Flatt's face. As Flatt stepped out the door, the cowboy said "throw up;" as quick as a flash Flatt jerked his revolver to the head of the cowboy, and as he was saying "I don't have to," fired several shots in quick succession;[9] the cowboy's partner jumped out of the door where Flatt

---

[6]For Jack Adams, Freeman shows Jake. The saloonkeeper was Jim Moreland, and the saloon was Flatt's short-term property, the Occidental.

James M. Moreland was in the saloon business until he left Caldwell sometime in 1880. On 16 March 1881 in Marion County, Kansas, Moreland was arrested for highway robbery. Before he could be tried, he escaped. He spent the next five years in New Mexico, returning to Caldwell in March of 1886, apparently free of prosecution, for no information in that regard is recorded (*SCP,* 24 March, 28 July 1881; *Caldwell Journal,* 11 March 1886). Of Moreland's departure from Caldwell, Stephen E. Smith recalled, "Jim Moreland ran away and his father, with an axe, demolished bar and pool tables" (marginal notes to *Midnight and Noonday,* p. 281). Moreland's brother was Patten "Pap" Moreland, who ran restaurants as well as rooming houses under the name *Moreland House* at various times in Wellington and Caldwell. Pap's wife was fondly known to many Texas cowboys as Mother Moreland (*Caldwell Post,* 9 January 1879; *SCP,* 21 July 1881; *Caldwell Commercial,* 24 February 1881; *Caldwell Journal,* 30 April 1885).

[7]According to the *Caldwell Post* of 10 July 1879, Wilson entered through the front door and walked to the back of the room. Flatt entered by the front door and stopped at the bar near the front of the room. The *Post* does not mention Freeman or any other member of the posse (if that was Freeman's role—he himself is ambiguous about it). Freeman's official responsibilities in the dustup at hand depend on the actual date of his appointment as constable (see chap. 21, n. 5). The township normally had two constables; Wash Kelly is the only one named by the *Post* (see n. 3 above) as being involved in this incident, so Freeman's status—he says he "stationed himself" by the door—is not clear, and one would have to conclude that his ambiguity is deliberate here.

[8]The *Post* (10 July 1879) says Flatt kept both his pistols concealed behind him.

[9]Both Wood and Adams started for the front door, "but Flatt, seeing their object was

was standing, and, I presume, intended to get one of the horses and make his escape; but his fate was sealed, for as he approached Flatt, that person was on the alert, and he fired at the cowboy, who reeled to the sidewalk and fell into the street in the agonies of death. The one Flatt shot first, turned and ran out the back door and fell mortally wounded.[10] He suffered from the effects of his wounds about thirty minutes, when death came to his relief and ended his sufferings and checkered career.

The cowboy that was lying in the street was found to be dead; and upon examination, one of the fingers on his right hand was missing; it was found, however, and the revolver that he held in his right hand, upon investigation, was found too, minus the trigger; and strange as it may seem, the hammer still remained standing, which proved the fact that Flatt had shot the cowboy as he was in the act of pulling the trigger of his revolver, the ball striking his forefinger, tearing it from his hand, and on the same bloody errand tore the trigger from the revolver, leaving it cocked with the hammer standing.[11]

Flatt was very much excited after he had shot the men, and his intoxication seemed to leave him; he pointed his revolvers toward a plank in the sidewalk and emptied both barrels, firing six or eight shots into one spot in the sidewalk.[12]

Great excitement prevailed throughout the town. The men rushed to the scene of slaughter; darkness had settled over the bloody scene, and excited men were questioning the propriety of the murder. Flatt was so excited that he ran out into the middle of the street and would allow no one to approach him.

---

to get between him and the door backed out right in front of them; on reaching the door they both leveled their six-shooters on him demanding his arms; Flatt replied: 'I'll die first;' and at that instant one of the fellows fired; the ball grazed the temple of one W. H. Kiser.... Flatt then drew both his pistols . . . and fired with the one in his right hand at the man who had got farthest out the door." (Thus the *Post*, 10 July 1879; but see n. 19 for a version which questions whether the cowboys in fact ever fired a round from their guns.)

[10] "The man who stood in the door and shot first, received a ball in the right side, which passed straight through his body, from the pistol in Flatt's left hand; the man returned the fire at Flatt, and then turned and fired at Wilson, who was closing in [from] the rear; the ball glazed Wilson's wrist, making a slight flesh wound; Wilson returned the fire so rapidly that the man failed to get his work in, although he is said to have been an expert with a six-shooter. Wilson's first shot took effect in the right hand of the fellow, and the second in the abdomen just below the short ribs, from which he fell, shooting Wilson in the thigh as he went down" (*Post*, 10 July 1879).

[11] *The Post* account (n. 10) suggests Wilson's bullet did the work on the gunman's hand; Freeman was an eyewitness. Take your choice. The *Post* describes the wound thus: The bullet took off "the end of the forefinger, and also the trigger the finger was on" and penetrated "the body in the upper part of the right breast . . . which caused him to drop heavily to the sidewalk," where he "died almost instantly."

[12] The plausible post-crisis agitation displayed by Flatt, as described here and in the next paragraph, is not found in the *Post* version.

Finally I succeeded in getting near enough to talk to him. I told him the people upheld him in his actions, and I requested him to be quiet and not fire any more shots. He held out his hand and quickly withdrew it, then offered it to me again; I took his hand, and he asked me if I would stay with him. I told him I would, and that I did not apprehend any trouble. A crowd assembled, and among it were sympathizers of the dead cowboys. Some of the citizens feared an outbreak in which the sympathizers would seek to avenge the cowboys death by shooting Flatt or some of the assistants of the constable. Citizens were armed with revolvers and shotguns. Suddenly the report of a gun was heard, and the excited men rushed helter skelter and hid themselves behind buildings and boxes, and secreted themselves from the shower of bullets they expected would follow after the enemy had fired the first shot. Their flight was unnecessary, as the shot was fired accidently, by [Clay] Hollister, who was approaching the crowd.[13] On his way to the crowd he passed between the saloon and a building, and his shotgun was accidentally discharged. The crowd of men thought the shot was fired by friends of the dead men, and had Hollister been in the street, he would in all probability have received his death wound at the hands of friends, who would have been mistaken in their man.

As soon as the excitement was quieted, Flatt entered the saloon of which Jim Moreland was proprietor; it was the same saloon in which the bloody encounter took place, and in which Flatt had been the victor and double murderer, thus adding two more victims to his list of nine men, said to have been killed by him;[14] he went to Moreland and accused him of befriending the cowboys and urging them on in their devilish work; his manner terrified Moreland, and he ran out of the saloon and went to his home.[15]

[13]The *Post* does not record this accidental discharge. Cassius M. "Clay" Hollister was to become Caldwell's second mayor, elected in October, 1879, to fill the vacancy occasioned by the death of Noah J. Dixon (see chap. 31, n. 2). During his term as mayor, Hollister would be arrested by the city marshal, George Flatt, for assaulting Frank Hunt (who also appears in a subsequent chapter). Though Hollister, after his term as mayor, was in trouble with the law off and on for various misdemeanors, he ended his career as a deputy U.S. marshal, making several noteworthy arrests and, in connection with some of those arrests, engaging in what appear to be provoked gunfights in alliance with Caldwell Deputy Marshal Ben Wheeler (who is discussed in chaps. 34-36). Hollister was killed on 18 October 1884 while attempting to apprehend one Bob Cross near Hunnewell, Kansas. A detailed account of Hollister's public life as mayor and lawman may be found in Miller and Snell, *Why the West was Wild,* pp. 221-31, from which the foregoing information is drawn.

[14]Freeman is the sole source that I have been able to locate for Flatt's head count. It may be noted that he was probably not a "double murderer" in this instance, one of the kills belonging to John Wilson.

[15]Wellington's *Sumner County Democrat* (9 July 1879), quotes Caldwell's Noah J. Dixon (see chap. 31, n. 2): "Flatt, who thought Moreland had given one of the cowboys a pistol, bursted open the front door of the saloon with a chair. The inmates rushed out of

Some of the citizens of the town went to a barber who extended his sympathies with the cowboys, and who had been suspected of encouraging them in their daring acts and desperadoism. The barber ran into a restaurant followed by the inflamed men; a riot ensued, but no one was seriously hurt in the affray.[16]

The dead desperadoes were herders belonging to some cattle outfit located in the southwest part of the Indian Territory. They had probably been paid by their employer, and had come to Caldwell to have a fine time. The report was afterwards circulated that they had rode until within ten or twelve miles of Caldwell, in company with a cattleman,[17] and had informed him that they were going to kill some one before they left town.[18]

The cattleman stopped for dinner at an acquaintances and told his friend that he must hasten on to town, and if possible, prevent the cowboys from putting their threat into execution. He recommended the boys as being hard workers and quite unoffensive when at work; but their appetites for whiskey was so strong that they would get on a spree occasionally, when their evil dispositions were brought to view, and their character assumed that of the western desperado.

Their last ride decided their fate; and drinking whiskey had been the cause of their death. Their evil habit had caused them to go step by step toward the awful gulf of ruin, until they reached the brink, and not halting in their downward career, took the last step which landed them in the gulf of darkness, ruin, and terrible death.

The morning sun beamed with brightness upon the spot, where the night before, a bloody tragedy had taken place. The town was unusually quiet; the people talked in undertones when referring to the double murder which had been committed in their midst.

An inquest was held over the bodies of the dead cowboys, and the jury

---

the back door, when Moreland was met by Flatt and prostrated by a blow on the head with a revolver."

[16] John T. Baldwin, according to the *Post* of 8 January 1880, was Caldwell's first barber; but Clate Hayden, a black man, may have preceded him. Hayden began to advertise in the *Post* as early as 29 May 1879. In any case, the bearding of the barber as well as the ensuing riot are unremarked in the pages of the *Post* or the *Democrat.*

[17] Wood and Adams "had just arrived from the Chickasaw Nation with Johny [*sic*] Nicholson with a herd of cattle, had been discharged and came in for a spree" (*Post,* 10 July 1879). Nicholson may have been the cattleman to whom Freeman alludes.

[18] The *Post* reported: "It is rumored around town that the man giving his name as Jack Adams . . . has a sister living in Rice county, this State, and he was heard to remark the evening before the shooting took place that he intended going up there and kill her husband before he left the State."

gave in a verdict that the men were killed by George Flatt in self-defence, acting as an officer in the discharge of his duty.[19]

The citizens of the town gave the remains proper burial in the old cemetery, northeast of the town. The remains were followed to their final resting place by a few friends and associates, including a number of the citizens of the town.

Thus two more men are added to the list of victims killed by the power of rum.

[19] J. M. Thomas (see chap. 45), Caldwell Township justice of the peace, conducted an inquest that night. The next morning, the six-man jury returned a verdict essentially as Freeman puts it. County officialdom was not to be denied its authority, however: "Coroner J. H. Folks arrived about forty-eight hours after the fatal shooting; summoned a jury; raised the bodies which had been buried, and held another inquest, with about the same result." The *Democrat* (16 July 1879) examined Folks's records and reported: "The pistols, in the hands of Woods and Adams when the shooting commenced, were produced in court and identified. Not a chamber in either was empty, which would indicate that neither of the men fired a shot." Did Flatt and Wilson gratuitously murder Wood and Adams? (If so, Flatt must also be responsible for inflicting the two wounds on Wilson, to say nothing of poor Mr. Kiser.) Though the hypothesis is tempting, it does not seem likely that the truth would have gone unreported, particularly by Coroner Folks's *SCP,* no matter what the jury might have been inclined to do by way of protecting the officers. The *Democrat*'s Caldwell correspondent (presumably Noah Dixon) assured skeptics that "it is as it should have been." As far as Caldwell was concerned, perhaps the best postmortem of all was rendered by the *Post:* "As to parties coming into our town . . . and getting on a 'high lonesome' for the purpose of 'taking the town,' why that has played out. Evidence of that fact was plainly demonstrated last Monday evening." Caldwell had yet to become acquainted with Jim Talbot.

CHAPTER 31

Caldwell Becomes a Railroad Town—The Town Incorporated
and Officers Elected—The Notorious "Red Light" and
Proprietor—The Killing of George Flatt—
Theories Concerning the Shooting.

The period of triumph began in 1875. The grasshoppers and Indian scare of
Sumner County is being talked about by the world; meanwhile Caldwell is
getting ready for a great future. In the summer of 1880, a branch of the
Atchison, Topeka, and Santa Fe R. R. was extended through the county,
and Caldwell was the terminus of the railroad, thus giving her the name of
a cattle town. Caldwell, being situated at the head of the great Chisholm
trail and so near the center of the grazing fields of the Indian Territory,
found the trade of this vast interest poured into her lap. In the year 1880,
the first shipment of Texas cattle was made from Caldwell. After the advent
of the railroad, for a year or two the city was a pretty tough place for a
peaceable citizen to live in, but as the "survival of the fittest" is a law of
nature, it was not broken in this case.[1]

Caldwell was incorporated as a city of the third class in July, 1879, and
elected the following officers on August 7: N. J. Dixon, Mayor;[2] J. D. Kelley,
Sr., Police Judge;[3] J. A. Blair, F. G. Hussen [Husson], H. C. Challes, A. C.
Jones, and A. Rhodes [Rhoades], councilmen.[4] She also had marshals and a

[1] In this paragraph Freeman again makes free if clumsy use of the *Caldwell Journal*
article of 1 January 1885. The critical sentence, with which Freeman ends this paragraph,
reads in the *Journal* thus: "After the advent of the railroad for a year or two the city was
a pretty tough place for a peaceable citizen to live in, but as the survival of the fittest is
a law of nature it was not broken in this case and the Red Light, variety theater, bawdy
house, gave up to the home, the church and school." The full statement was anachronistic
for the period Freeman was to discuss in this chapter, so he merely cut off the part that
didn't fit, leaving generations of readers to wrestle with the puzzling construction that
resulted.

[2] Noah J. Dixon, a dry-goods dealer who had held many other offices in Sumner County,
died on 23 September 1879, less than two months after his election as Caldwell's first
mayor (Andreas, p. 1503; *Caldwell Post,* 2 October 1879).

[3] James D. Kelly, Sr. for a number of years remained Caldwell's police judge as well
as township justice. His son, J. D. Kelly, Jr., was the first editor of the *Caldwell Post*
and Caldwell's first city clerk. Kelly, Jr.'s name is omitted from Freeman's list of city
officers because at that time the clerkship was an appointive rather than elective office, as
was the post of city marshal.

[4] John A. Blair, one of Caldwell's pioneer settlers, is the subject of a biographical sketch
in chap. 45. F. G. Husson, a tinsmith by trade, operated a hardware store. He left Caldwell
some time prior to 1882 (*Post,* 2 January 1879; Andreas, p. 1237). H. C. Challes was
involved in a number of Caldwell business ventures, including the City Meat Market and,

cooler.[5] Then she began to grow as western towns grow, and with her prosperity came the "Free and Easys," a brick hotel, bank and opera house, also the old "Red Light" and the Varieties.

The building known as the "Red Light" was a house of ill-repute; in connection with it was a dance hall. This building was erected by [George] Woods of Wichita, and that notorious character, Mag Woods, with ten or twelve prostitutes, made it their abiding place.[6] This house was the orig-

in partnership with one of the notorious Spear brothers, the I. X. L. Saloon. Challes, during his tour as councilman, was also Caldwell's first street commissioner. Reelected in 1881, he was part of the council faction which caused the resignation of Mayor W. N. Hubbell (see chap. 41, n. 6). Challes was energetic in boosting Caldwell as a cattle town, going into the Territory in the spring of 1880 to meet northering cattle outfits and trying to induce them to Caldwell. Challes also claimed to have opened a trail that year from Persimmon Creek to Pond Creek, the effect of which was to funnel herds on trails farther west over to the Chisholm Trail and so to Caldwell (*Post*, 2 January, 11 December 1879; 8 January, 27 May, 1 July 1880; 7 April, 28 July, 8 September 1881). A. C. ("Lengthy" or "Long") Jones was a blacksmith and an early settler of Caldwell. In addition to his Caldwell trade, Jones for a time shoed horses at the various stations between Caldwell and Fort Sill, Indian Territory, on the Pan Handle Stage Route. He was reelected to the city council in 1880 (*Post*, 2 January, 9 January 1879; 8 April 1880; 4 August 1881). Jones's new shop on East Sixth Street may have figured importantly in the Talbot raid (see chap. 41, n. 16). Jones served in the Tenth Indiana Infantry during the Civil War (*Caldwell Journal*, 27 March 1884). Abraham (or Abram) Rhoades at the time of his election to the council was proprietor of the Haines House Hotel and operator of a hack line to Wellington and Wichita. He was later operator of a rock quarry and a member of that much-maligned brotherhood the lightning-rod salesmen. Upon the death of Mayor Dixon, Rhoades functioned as acting mayor until the election of Clay Hollister (see chap. 30, n. 13). In 1880 he was an unsuccessful candidate for mayor. Rhoades served twice as township constable, the first term during the Talbot raid (see chap. 41) in which, with Freeman, he played a minor role (*Post*, 2 January, 9 January, 2 October, 16 November 1879; 15 January, 1 April 1880; 13 October 1881; 9 February 1882).

[5] The new city government appointed George Flatt marshal. Flatt had a succession of deputies, including Dan W. Jones, who was one of the suspects in his murder, and Samuel Rogers, who was with him at the time he was killed (*Post*, 4 September, 25 September 1879; 8 January 1880). The calaboose was built in the fall of 1879 and "dedicated" on November 5 (*Post*, 6 November 1879).

[6] The *Post* of 22 April 1880 noted the advent of the Red Light with irony: "George Wood's two-story building has been removed from Wichita to Caldwell. It is being erected, we presume for convenience sake, near the calaboose." I can offer no definite date for the opening of the Red Light; Woods was issued a dram-shop license in May, and a correspondent to the *Post* of May 20 reports visiting the Red Light "out of curiosity" on the previous Saturday, May 15. Mag Woods herself arrived several months earlier, in August of 1879, setting up temporary facilities just outside the city limits (*Post*, 4 September 1879; 20 May 1880). Sam P. Ridings (*The Chisholm Trail*, p. 473) locates the Red Light on the north side of Fifth Street, facing south, between Cheyenne and Arrapahoe Streets—or two blocks east of the main business district. This location is further confirmed by its relationship to the house rented by Jim Talbot (see chap. 41, n. 3). Bill O'Neal's map of Caldwell

inator of much disorder, bloodshed, and deaths; whiskey was kept for sale in the building; after the cowboy had reached Caldwell after his long dusty drive, the proprietor of the herd would usually pay him his dues, and in company with his companions he would visit the "Red Light," fill up on the vile whiskey sold there, then he was ready to "take the town." The citizens of Caldwell are, in a measure, responsible for the deeds committed in this house of prostitution. Had the officers and citizens never tolerated the erection of such a building and given the necessary license for such a nefarious business to be carried on in their midst, the town would not have been compelled by the home and society to cleanse the name of Caldwell from the stain that had blotted her fair name.[7]

About this time there were no less than ten or twelve saloons, and together with the "Red Light" house of prostitution,[8] and with the society which assembles at such dives, is it a wonder that the town was called a "tough place" by people who were unaccustomed to such a state of society as that which existed in Caldwell at this time?

It was not an uncommon sight to see the women of ill-repute parading the streets, mingling with the innocent girls of the town and vicinity and luring many unfortunate victims to the "Red Light," where they were either robbed

---

(*Henry Brown,* p. 86) places the Red Light at the corner of Fourth and Chisholm, a block north and a block west of the site described here.

[7] In this Freeman echoes what editor J. D. Kelly, Jr., prophesied on 8 April 1880 in the *Post:* "Everyone, having lived on the frontier, knows what [a dance house] means. It is a hotbed of vice, it is the favorite place for murders, assault, and drunken ribaldry. . . . If you want the revolver cracking and the bullet doing its deadly work in your midst, if you want to have the most degrading men and women making the night hideous with their hellish orgies, if you want to pollute the air which your wives and mothers breathe, just tolerate a dance-house in your midst." Kelly's words were seconded by an anonymous correspondent to the *Post,* who claimed to know of the evils of dance houses (or hurdy-gurdies) from the early days in Cheyenne. Kelly's dire prophecy was fulfilled in every aspect, beginning with nocturnal gunfire disturbing the peace almost at once and ending with a series of deaths, the last of which was Marshall George Brown's in the Red Light in 1882. Thomas Josiah Dimsdale, *The Vigilantes of Montana,* p. 11, reports similar violence as endemic to dance houses; Joseph G. McCoy, *Historic Sketches of the Cattle Trade of the West and Southwest,* p. 139, observed, "Few more wild, reckless scenes of abandoned debauchery can be seen on the civilized earth, than a dance house in full blast." The phenomenon is interesting, if not altogether understandable. Caldwell had saloons—and most of the businessmen acknowledged them as a necessary adjunct of the cattle trade. Caldwell also had prostitutes and houses of prostitution before Mag Woods and her girls arrived. But combining liquor and prostitution under one roof seemed to produce the worst kind of libertine hell raising if there were added that awful catalyst—dance. A black day for Terpsichore.

[8] Another such house existed in the opposite side of town—but, presumably, with no dancing (*Post,* 13 May 1880).

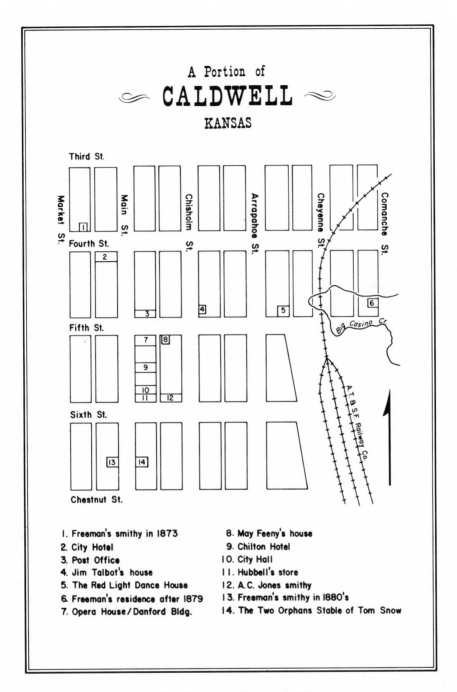

A Portion of
CALDWELL
KANSAS

Third St.

Market St.

Main St.

Chisholm St.

Arrapahoe St.

Cheyenne St.

Comanche St.

Fourth St.

Fifth St.

Sixth St.

Chestnut St.

Big Casino Cr.

A.T. & S.F. Railway Co.

1. Freeman's smithy in 1873
2. City Hotel
3. Post Office
4. Jim Talbot's house
5. The Red Light Dance House
6. Freeman's residence after 1879
7. Opera House/Danford Bldg.
8. May Feeny's house
9. Chilton Hotel
10. City Hall
11. Hubbell's store
12. A.C. Jones smithy
13. Freeman's smithy in 1880's
14. The Two Orphans Stable of Tom Snow

Caldwell in the 1870s and 1880s

and pitched into the streets or squandered their money while under the influence of their vile whiskey, only to "sober up" and find they were "busted." Then their hatred for the place is being manifested in various ways; they begin to shoot at sign boards, ride up and down the street firing off their revolver promiscuously, and the final result is, either the death of the offenders or an officer is shot down while in discharge of his duties.

The "Red Light" was notorious throughout the west; Wichita lent her worst characters to become its inmates. The house and inmates is said to have accomplished the ruin of several of Caldwells brightest young girls, who to-day, had they not listened to the "song of the tempter," might have been filling the exalted position of a noble wife and mother.[9] How many happy homes have been destroyed and innocent lives blasted, by the influence of this house of prostitution?

The cowboy is not a terror as many suppose him to be. They are inoffensive and social in nature; they are not bad men unless they are filled with whiskey. Many of them work month after month on the drive and right the herd through storm and sunshine, then they must have a "lay off" and the employer pays them their wages; they bid farewell to camp life and the familiar scenes of life in its monotonous cares, and hie themselves away to the frontier town to indulge in the luxuries which that little hamlet may possess. They meet with companions of former acquaintance, visit the various saloons and gambling holes, probably lose the larger porportion of their money, then as a last resort, visit the houses of ill-fame and lose their remaining "little all." The dance hall affords them amusement; the air is filled with the echo of their lewd songs. Their drinking is continued; the fun grows fast and furious. The night is passed in debauchery and delights such as the "Red Light" offered. The early morning air is filled with the reports of the revolver fired by the drunken inmates of the house. Ever and anon can the unearthly yell of the cowboy be heard by the citizens, who are aroused from their slumbers by these lesser types of humanity.[10]

The general consequences of such proceedings was that the cowboy would commit some serious offense while under the influence of whiskey and would either leave town with the marshal in pursuit of him, or he would be tried and fined ten, twenty, or twenty-five dollars. His companions would generally come to his rescue, pay his fine, and after he was released, the cowboy,

[9]How many local girls were actually enticed into becoming inmates is not the sort of data one can reasonably expect to find in contemporary newspapers. One case was reported because the young woman later committed suicide, but although she was a prostitute, she does not appear to have been affiliated with the Red Light (*Post,* 26 May 1881; *SCP,* 2 June 1881).

[10]Freeman may well be speaking from the heart here. He lived on Comanche Street, less than two blocks from the Red Light.

together with his friends, would get the drop on the marshal, and to use the phrase familiar in the wild west would "take the town." "Taking the town" usually consisted in riding up and down the streets, shooting at sign boards, at the glass window fronts of the stores, ordering whiskey at the muzzle of the six shooter, riding their horses on the pavements and hotel verandahs; and in fact they were at liberty to run things their own way. Sometimes the citizens would arm themselves and attempt to quiet the "boys," and generally a riot would ensue, a pitch battle would take place, oftentimes ending in bloodshed.

For several years the drunken "cowboys" would "take the town" at their pleasure;[11] the citizens finally became tired of this accustomed dramatic performance and were determined to protect her officers and citizens from the desperate deeds enacted by the "wild and wooly cowboy." A marshall and an assistant were appointed[12] and men were deputized upon special occasions to help the officers in discharging their duties.

The quiet manner which had been assumed heretofore in attempting the arrest of the desperado was to be a thing of the past, and now a new method was put into practice, which may be described in this manner: A wise officer before making the arrest would watch his chances and "get the drop on his man" by placing his six shooter within a few inches of the desperadoes head and demand him to "throw up;" nine times out of ten the desperado will throw up his hands, but occasionally a daring fellow will jerk his revolver from his belt and "throw up" with a bullet fired at the officer. It was not uncommon to see a "cowboy" with several "six shooters" in his belt,[13] the belt carrying from fifty to one hundred cartridges. So the reader will conclude that in case of an emergency the "cowboy" is prepared for a fight.

The position of a marshal is not to be greatly envied. He is in the midst of peril at all times and especially so when he attends to his duties. However

[11] The frequency with which Caldwell was "taken" is not a matter of record; it seems clear that the local newspapers, perhaps out of a sense of civic boosterism, did not report every disturbance as long as no one was killed or wounded. It seems equally clear that for a few months after the Talbot raid in December, 1881 (see chaps. 41 and 42), Caldwell had the reputation of being a town that could be taken. The reader may judge for himself how much allowance to make for irony in the following comment, written six months after the Red Light opened: "There have been but two fights in town this week. Now, the next fellow who says we are not getting civilized down here is liable to get hurt" (*Post,* 11 November 1880).

[12] The appointment of a marshal, of course, was the consequence of the city's incorporation and not necessarily a desperate reaction to violence, as Freeman makes it seem.

[13] ". . . several 'six-shooters' in his belt" sounds like exaggeration. Getting the drop on one's man makes good sense but poor cinema. I suspect that Freeman's version is closer to the mark than the celluloid conventions, though Flatt's own temerity in bracing Wood and Adams when they had the drop on him makes him a dubious candidate for introducing this new procedure.

successful he may be in the discharge of his duties, he can hardly expect to be a favorite amongst men or an ornament to society. There is always a class of people who give their sympathy to the desperado and are ready to keep the blame upon the officer, never realizing the existing state of affairs.

The familiar saying, "Fight the devil with his own men," was confirmed in the case of marshal George Flatt.

Flatt was a drinking man and when under the influence of whiskey he was looked upon as a "holy terror." He proved himself to be a man of down right bravery and a shrewd observer of men and nature. He was very seldom known to be perfectly sober, and when sober was said to be as cowardly as he was brave when under influence of whiskey. He was formerly from Texas and, like most of the Texans who visited Caldwell, was a lover of strong drink and a frequent visitor of the "Red Light." His general associates were a rough class of people as well as a low class of humanity. When his temper was aroused he was as ferocious as a tiger, and [he] had a strong spirit of revenge which marked his daily characteristics. He had an evil looking eye which betrayed the inner man. He was an expert shot with the revolver, combined with great dexterity and alertness.[14]

His love for whiskey and drunkeness made it necessary to discharge him from his office as marshal of Caldwell. A new officer, with three or four assistants, entered upon their new and perilous duties.[15]

Flatt's discharge from office seemed to irate him to such an extent that the new officers seemed apparently to be in great fear of him. He continued to carry his "six shooter" contrary to the city laws,[16] and it was reported that

---

[14]Flatt seemed to get by on his reputation after the shootout with Wood and Adams. The only other recorded instance I have found of his firing his pistol occurred during his term as marshall when he and a deputy went to disarm one John Dean, who was carrying firearms contrary to city ordinance. The upshot is excerpted here from the *Caldwell Post* of 30 October 1879: "Mr. Dean getting wind of their intentions . . . mounted his horse and started out of town firing his revolver promisquously. The marshal started in pursuit and commended him under arrest . . . [Dean] answered . . . with a shot from his six-shooter. At the crack of his pistol the marshal and deputy ['Red Bill' Jone] turned loose with their six-shooters. Dean, being mounted and moving pretty lively, the distance between the parties became so great, the marshal and deputy being pretty well out of wind, they did no very accurate shooting, although they emptied their revolvers at him before he got out of the corporation."

[15]No record of Flatt's discharge is extant. Nyle H. Miller and Joseph W. Snell provide persuasive evidence that Flatt served out his term—to April of 1880 when a new council was elected and a new marshal appointed (*Why the West was Wild,* p. 166). Flatt's successor was William Horseman (see n. 20 below; see also Miller and Snell, pp. 232-42, for details of Horseman's career as a lawman).

[16]Ridings (p. 490) reports that Flatt claimed to fear for his life from the enemies he had made while he was marshal. Thus he not only refused to quit carrying his guns, he armed himself with as many as three of them.

upon one occasion, one of the deputy marshals ordered Flatt to lay down his revolver. Flatt replied that he could come and get it, and held his revolver toward the officer; he was in the act of reaching for it; Flatt cocked the revolver and, pointing it toward the officer, said "take it." The officer knew any attempt to "take it" would mean certain death for him; consequently he made no effort to do so. Flatt was not afraid of the officers, and he knew the entire police force were afraid to arrest him. He continued to rule the officers with his supremacy, until one morning about half past one o'clock, in the month of June, 1880. Flatt was walking along on the pavement in company with [Charles L.] Spear,[17] when the stillness was broken by a shot fired from a revolver; instantly the night air resounded with probably a dozen shots in quick succession, and Flatt fell mortally wounded,[18] his crimson life blood oozing from his wounds and staining the plank pavement he had so often trod while endeavoring to assume the duties of an officer and living simply as a citizen of the town. The night was dark, and beneath the light of the twinkling star in the heavens, Flatt's life ebbed away, and his body was carried by kind friends to the home of his wife. I will not dwell on the sorrowful scene which took place when the loving wife embraced the body of her husband; suffice it to say, the wife received the sympathy of the people in the community in her hours of bereavement and sorrow.[19]

The murder of Flatt was very mysterious. The building opposite to where he was killed was perforated with balls, and the evidence showed they were

[17] It was the morning of June 19, less than three months after Flatt's term as marshal had ended. In addition to Spear, Samuel H. Rogers was walking with Flatt, Spear walking a little ahead and Rogers about a step behind Flatt himself. Rogers, as has been noted, was Flatt's onetime deputy and was still a member of the city police force on the night of the murder (*Post*, 24 June 1880).

[18] The first shot was fired from a shotgun, not from a revolver, per Freeman, as medical testimony would show at the inquest. The shot was fired so close to Rogers' ear that it deafened him, coming from behind and a little above him, as if "from the awning." Rogers also said that "at the first report" he saw "sparks fall off Flatt's head." Both Rogers and Spear testified that the succeeding shots were all fired from the opposite side of the street, about a dozen altogether. Neither Rogers nor Spear was wounded in the fusillade. Flatt fell after the first shot; four no. 1 or no. 2 buckshot had penetrated his spinal column (*Post*, 24 June 1880).

[19] Flatt married Fannie Lamb in September of 1879. On September 22, Mr. and Mrs. Dan Jones entertained the Flatts and another couple at the St. Nicholas Hotel—thus the only social note involving Flatt between the time of his marriage and his death included one of the men suspected in his killing. Flatt was twenty-seven at the time of his death (*Post*, 18 September, 25 September 1879; *Why the West was Wild*, p. 166).

On 23 June 1880—four days after Flatt's murder—Fannie Flatt gave birth to a baby boy. The newspapers yield little about the widow in the months following. In April of 1882, she and a Mrs. Bates opened a dressmaker's shop in Caldwell. Sometime thereafter Fannie married a man named Muntzing. The child—Georgie Flatt—died on 2 April 1883 (*Caldwell Commercial*, 24 June 1880; 20 April 1882; 5 April 1883).

fired from several different directions. A warrant was issued for the arrest of the marshal and assistants, and they were given trial; but no conclusive evidence could be found which implicated them as the murderers.

It was currently reported and believed that the officers were afraid of Flatt; none of them were courageous enough to arrest him, and they knew they did not dare to meet him face to face in a fight; and it was presumed by many that a plan was laid in which Flatt must give up to the inevitable.

They took him unawares and at a disadvantage; for he was walking quietly along not dreaming of danger or his premeditated death by the unknown parties who sought to kill him. One theory of the shooting had been that the police force had decided that Flatt must die; and they had arranged themselves at different places along his route to his home, and at a given signal of one shot by one of the officers, the balance of the officers were to shoot and kill Flatt.[20] It was well they took this precaution, for Flatt would certainly [have] fought to the last had he had a show for his life, and as it was, when he was found after death he had a death grip on his trusty revolver; before he died, which was almost instantly, he had the presence of mind to clutch his revolver.[21]

[20] After a long inquest by Coroner John H. Folks, the following were arrested on June 25 and taken to Wellington for preliminary hearing: Mayor Mike Meagher, Marshal William Horseman, policemen Frank Hunt and James Johnson, Constable Dan Jones, and George W. McFarland and R. H. Collins. After a week-long hearing before Justice I. N. King, on July 3, Meagher, McFarland, and Collins were discharged. Horseman, Jones, Hunt, and Johnson were bound over for trial; Charles Spear and Samuel Rogers were arrested for complicity in Flatt's killing. The latter action prompted W. B. Hutchison, editor of the *Commercial,* to observe: "a coroner, however stupid, and the veriest Dogberry of a justice, it would seem to us, could not fail to discover from the testimony that Spear and Rogers had no more to do with killing Flatt than the mullet-head the county is so unfortunate to have for an attorney [Charles E. Willsie was by general consensus an inept county attorney]" (*Commercial,* 1 July, 8 July 1880; *SCP,* 8 July 1880). The following circumstances probably cast suspicion on the officers: on the night of the shooting, the first persons to appear after Flatt fell were Meagher, Horseman, Johnson, Hunt, and Jones, the latter carrying a rifle or shotgun. All appeared within minutes after the firing. At the inquest Johnson testified that on the evening before the shooting, Flatt pulled a revolver on him and threatened to "shoot his feet off." Flatt also allegedly pulled his gun on Marshal Horseman (*Post,* 24 June 1880). The following October, Frank Hunt was killed by a hidden assassin (see chap. 32). William Horseman was tried in district court and acquitted on 22 April 1881. Charges against all others were then dismissed. Satisfaction with the outcome was general in Caldwell, but the *SCP,* of which Coroner John Folks was editor, observed: "It seems to have come to pass in Sumner County that a man who looks at a stolen horse goes to the penitentiary without hope of salvation. But when he kills his fellow-man, he goes through a farce of a trial then becomes a hero" (*Commercial,* 28 April 1881; *SCP,* 5 May 1881). For postscripts to Flatt's murder, see chap. 32, n. 4, and chap. 42, n. 13.

[21] This is the stuff of which legend is made. Nobody else records this reflex by Flatt. The doctors who performed the postmortem examination reported that Flatt was killed instantly by pellets which severed his spinal cord (Caldwell *Post,* 24 June 1880).

CHAPTER 32

Frank Hunt Slain—Who Fired the Fatal Bullet—The Theories
Advanced—Description of the "Red Light Saloon"—
George Woods the Proprietor Is Killed—Charlie
Davis the Slayer of Woods—Inmates of
the "Red Light" Seek "Richer
Fields"—The Old Land
Mark Gone.

The citizen of Caldwell who hied to his daily occupation at an early hour on the morning of October 12 [9], 1880, was greeted with the phrase peculiar to the wild, wild west, "another man for breakfast."[1] It was ascertained that Frank Hunt, acting as one of the assistant marshals of the town, lay dead at a dwelling house on Main Street.[2]

No definite information could be learned concerning the shooting of Hunt. It seems he was sitting in one of the windows of the Red Light house of prostitution. The inmates of the house were on the floor dancing. The festivities were at their heighth; everything was going merry; the influences of whiskey was being felt by many, when sharp and clear on the night air was wafted forth the deadly crack of the revolver. Who now was the victim who received the bullet? Who now fired the fatal shot? The former question could only be answered by those immediately present at the Red Light. The latter question remains a secret to this day. The inquisitive mind would naturally wonder what was the cause and who the perpetrator of the deed. Theories were at once afloat; some thought that it was some friend of the notorious Flatt, who presumption said met his death at the hands of the police force of Caldwell, while others thought it may have been the finale of an old, long standing grudge. Suffice it to say the mystery has never been unraveled. The only certainty was, Frank Hunt was a corpse and the assassin was at liberty.[3]

[1] D. D. Leahy reported that W. B. Hutchison, editor of the *Caldwell Commercial*, "had a hobby of saying after each killing in town, 'Another man for breakfast'" (*Wichita Eagle*, 28 June 1932). I offer Leahy's statement of the origin of the phrase, even though I do not recall ever seeing the line in any issue of a paper edited by Hutchison in Caldwell.

[2] Hunt was not a member of the police force at the time of his death (the night of 8 October 1880), having been discharged on October 4. The *Commercial* and the *SCP* (14 October 1880) report Hunt was let go because of a reduction in the size of the police force, but an anonymous correspondent to the *Wellington Wellingtonian* (3 July 1884) claimed that Hunt was fired for intruding in a private squabble and pistol-whipping several men.

[3] Hunt, sitting at "the north window" of the Red Light, was struck by a single shot fired through the open window from outside. The bullet entered Hunt's left side, puncturing

Hunt was one of the police at the time the notorious George Flatt met his death, who rumor said was killed by the police force. Some attributed the killing of Hunt as a sequel to the killing of Flatt.[4]

But a few months had passed since the death of Flatt. The early freshness of spring had passed away and the bloom and the glory of summer had departed, the time of the year when the apple trees are laden with their rosy treasures and the summer darkness of the woods are varied by the appearance of the yellow leaves.

The autumnal moon shed her soft light upon the man who, with murder in his heart, cautiously approaches the open window of the Red Light dance hall; he crouches low in the shadow, and when he reaches the exact spot or at the desired time, he holds the deadly revolver toward the visitor of the hall, pulls the trigger, then turns on his heel and walks quickly from the scene.

Hunt lived a few hours, suffering intensely, but thought he was not mortally wounded. He clung to life tenaciously, and when he could no longer hope, he died without a murmur on his lips and succumbed to the inevitable fate of all humanity.[5]

---

his stomach and liver (*Post*, 14 October 1880). The *Commercial* reported that "during the evening Hunt had some difficulty with one of the cyprians belonging to the house, and considerable bad blood was engendered between Hunt, the woman and her 'man.'" David Spear, a seventeen-year-old youth, was arrested and ultimately charged with the murder; the Red Light night watchman, one "Lumis or Loomis," was found by a coroner's jury to be an accessory before the fact (*Post*, 14 October 1880; Miller and Snell, *Why the West Was Wild*, p. 244 [see pp. 242–46 for a history of Hunt's brief career]). Spear was given a preliminary hearing before Justice J. M. Thomas (see chap. 45) and discharged. The *Commercial*, whose editor, W. B. Hutchison, was a member of the coroner's jury, observed: "The impression seems to be among many that Lumis is the man who perpetrated the crime. That he knows all about it, we are firmly convinced, but that he did the work we do not believe. And here the matter must drop and perhaps for all time" (14 October, 28 October 1880).

[4] So said "One of the Ladies of Caldwell" in a letter to the *Wellingtonian* (3 July 1884). In its issue of 23 December 1880, the *SCP* reported an interview with one William Thompson, being held in the county jail as a state's witness in the killing of George Flatt: "He expressed the opinion that the man who actually killed Flatt is dead . . . [Hunt was killed on Oct. 8]. He says that he has been repeatedly threatened with death if he testifies in court." Whether Thompson was attempting to avoid assassination by pinning the crime on someone already dead or whether Hunt was actually the killer of Flatt will probably never be known. In any case, I have found no record of Thompson's having been murdered later on. Muddying the water further is the *Post*'s assertion on 6 July 1882, "George Flatt was killed to satisfy a grudge. Frank Hunt was killed for the same reason," but no particulars are offered. As is frequently the case, one suspects, what appeared in official records did not always square with what was commonly known, and nobody now living can tell where the truth lies.

[5] Hunt was shot on Friday and died the following Monday. Spear was arrested on Hunt's "*ante mortem* statement." Frank Hunt, from Missouri, went to Caldwell about a year before

The scene changes once more. We are again called in imagination to the noted Red Light. Oh, the deeds of crime which have been committed within its walls of iniquity and shame. Many are the crimes and murders which have been caused by its immoral and vile influence.

Since its erection in 1879 [1880], we have witnessed many revolting scenes and much depraved humanity. This infamous den was erected in [1880] by George Woods, a noted man from Wichita, Kansas. The house was a two story building; the front was furnished as a saloon, of which George Woods was the proprietor. Upon the front window the following words were inscribed, "Red Light Saloon."

Mag Woods, the notorious woman known as Woods wife, was the proprietress of the dance hall, which was run in connection with the saloon. Wichita lent her worst inmates to become inmates of this hall, and part of the population of Caldwell.

On August 18, 1881, a visitor and patron of the Red Light, by the name of Charlie Davis, had trouble with one of the female inmates,[6] when George Woods interfered in behalf of the woman, which caused a quarrel between the two men. Davis pulled his revolver and shot Woods, killing him almost instantly. Davis got his horse and left town, going to the Indian Territory.[7] A reward was offered for his arrest, but he was never captured.[8] George

---

his death. He served on the Caldwell police force during most of his residence, being characterized as an officer who was "strictly temperate, quiet and unobtrusive, prompt and strict in the discharge of his duties." He was twenty-seven years old at the time of his death (*SCP*, 14 October 1880; *Commercial*, 14 October, 1880; 1880 Census, as cited in Miller and Snell, *Why the West Was Wild*, p. 244.

[6] The girl was Lizzie Roberts, shown in the 1880 Census as twenty years old and a "dancer" at the Red Light (Caldwell Township, KSHS). According to the *Post* (25 August 1881), Davis and the woman had lived together for some time. About five weeks prior to the night in question, Lizzie left Davis and went to live at the Red Light. The altercation of the eighteenth occurred when Davis tried to get her to leave with him.

[7] Davis shot Woods from a distance of about three feet with a Colt improved .45. The bullet passed through Woods's body and lodged in a partition behind him. Woods lived long enough to tell his wife to "'catch Charley Davis and prosecute him to the full extent of the law,' and . . . to keep all the propery, and do the best she could, and be a good girl." Davis either was captured or gave himself up to Marshal John Rowan, who turned him over to another person to guard. Then, according to one version, learning that Woods "was dead or about to die," Davis escaped from his guard and fled town (*Commercial*, 25 August 1881; *Post*, 25 August 1881).

[8] Mag Woods offered a reward of five hundred dollars and Governor John P. St. John offered one thousand dollars. In February of 1883 word arrived in Sumner County that Davis had been arrested in Albuquerque, New Mexico Territory, but the *Commercial* of 15 February 1883 reports that the "arrest" turned out to be a ruse by Davis and a henchman to collect and split the reward, Davis believing that the witnesses were scattered and could not be found to refute his claim of self-defense. Davis was captured later that year and returned for trial. On 14 September he was found guilty of manslaughter in the third degree

Woods was buried in the city cemetery, and his wife erected a handsome monument to his memory.[9]

For some time after the death of Woods, the business of the noted Red Light was on the decline. The proprietor was now dead, and the visitors were few, as the tide of civilization came West bringing with it men of morality and influences of a christianized people. The citizens became aware of the immorality and bad influences brought about by this den of prostitution. They also saw that its presence caused the worst characters to visit the town, and their visits occasioned much disorder, revelry, and murder.

The citizens devised means to rid the city of the Red Light building and the female inmates, thinking in this manner to suppress much lawlessness, dissipation, and bloodshed. In a short time the city authorities realized the building as a city nuisance, and the noted Mag Woods and her followers left the city, perhaps only to find richer fields in which to establish her infamous business.[10]

----

and sentenced to three years in the state penitentiary (*State of Kansas* v. *Charles Davis, Clerk of the District Court, Sumner County, Kansas*; *SCP*, 27 September 1883, repr. in *Caldwell Journal*, 4 October 1883). Of Davis himself little is known. The *SCP* (25 August 1881) reports: "It has been stated that he is the son of a railroad manipulator and politician of some note in this section of the state." The *Commercial* (25 August 1881) states that Davis came to Caldwell from Texas the previous fall and was known as a quiet, temperate man who seldom carried a gun. Woods was remembered as "honorable and upright in all business transactions," though not "a very useful or ornamental member of society" (*Commercial*, 25 August 1881).

[9] George Woods, "the grand mogul of the demi monde," was obliged to share the monument with Fred Kuhlman, murdered in July of 1881 in an argument over one of the girls at the Red Light's Hunnewell branch. A Wichita marble firm erected "an elegant monument . . . composed of two columns . . . made of Knoxville, Italian and Vermont marble. . . . Altogether . . . a fine specimen of the marble cutter's art"; the piece had "taken the premium" at the 1881 Sedgwick County Fair and cost $550 (*SCP*, 25 August 1881; *Post*, 7 July 1881; *Wellingtonian*, 8 December1881; *Commercial*, 5 January 1882). The monument has not survived to the present day, the old cemetery having been plowed under to become a modern wheat field. In addition to the indignity of sharing a tombstone, George Woods's mortal remains were allegedly dug up by David Sharp and George Spear in order to steal a diamond stickpin which was buried with Woods's body. The theft was revealed after Spear's death (see chap. 41), so only Sharp was charged, and he was later acquitted (*Commercial*, 18 May, 15 June 1882). Spear (older brother of David Spear, who was suspected of killing Frank Hunt) became proprietor of the Red Light after Woods's demise. However, Spear probably only managed the house under Mag Woods's proprietorship (*SCP*, 22 December 1881; George Spear plays a role in chap. 41).

[10] As the previous note indicates, the Red Light did not close permanently as a result of George Woods's death. Although the city council declared it closed as a public nuisance, it was back in full swing within two weeks of the council's action (*Post*, 25 August, 8 September 1881). Such public pressure as Freeman describes did not occur until Marshal

The suppression of this den of iniquity had the desired effect; the visits of the rougher element of society became less frequent, as their old resort was no longer a land mark in the growing city and their associates were gone to try their fortunes in the new country in the direction of the setting sun; they too turned West, in order that they might "grow up with the country" and, amid their wild companions, seek the pleasures in the drama of life.

George S. Brown was slain there in June of 1882 (see chap. 33). At that time the property was purchased by means of a public subscription, which prompted W. B. Hutchison to observe: "Several of our religious friends have bought out the Red Light, but it is presumed that they will not run it after the usual style because the 'young ladies' have gone to Wichita." The subscribers offered the property for sale, "house and lot . . . separately or together." A combine eventually bought the building to use for grain storage and moved it away from the original lot. By 1886 it had also served as a telephone exchange and an implement warehouse. *Sic transit gloria mundi.* Mag Woods returned to Wichita to open a new salon there. The Red Light girls, it was said, either opened private houses or moved to Wellington or Hunnewell, at which place a dance house still flourished (*Commercial*, 22 June, 29 June, 13 July, 24 August, 1882; *Post*, 6 July, 13 July 1882; *Journal*, 1April 1886). The shutdown of the Red Light did not end prostitution in Caldwell, of course; Stephen E. Smith noted that "Poley Bright's place took the place of the old Red Light" (marginal notes to *Midnight and Noonday*, p. 298).

CHAPTER 33

George Brown Appointed Marshal of Caldwell—The Arrival of Two
Texas Men—They Drink Whiskey Freely—George Brown
Enters the Building Known as the "Red Light"—The
Marshal Shot and Killed by the Texans—The
Flight of the Murderers—Sad Scenes at
the Home of Marshal Brown.

In the year of 1882, George S. Brown was appointed City Marshal of Caldwell.[1]

Brown was a young man of an exceptional good character, had a fair education, and [was] unaccustomed to mingling with the rougher elements of society, especially of the drunken cowboys and daredevils which visited the western frontier towns. He was by nature fearful of meeting the adversary or foe, but his characteristics showed him to be a true gentleman, a lover of peace, and his dealings with a man were in a quiet and unassuming manner.[2]

The new marshal entered upon his duties amid the well wishes and congratulations of his friends. Had he dreamed of the destiny awaiting him, he would have recoiled with alarm and shrunk from obeying the duties which he would be compelled to assume so long as he held the office of marshal and endeavored to fill the office satisfactorily to the people.

The fate of the marshals since the corporation of the city had been anything but pleasing to the City Council. The rough element had prevailed, and the marshals must, under the circumstances, either give way to the desperado, or take the consequences if he endeavored to suppress riots or [ordered] the law-breaker to desist his free use of the sixshooter.

Marshal Brown was unfit to fill the office of marshal.[3] The man to fill

---

[1] His official appointment began 10 April 1882, but he had been acting in that capacity since at least early March (*Caldwell Post*, 13 April 1882; *Caldwell Commercial*, 9 March 1882). Brown had come to Caldwell about two years previously. For a while he operated a cafe called the Oyster Bay (see Editor's Introduction, n. 4). Later he went into business as a gunsmith. He was a single man about twenty-eight years old (*Post*, 30 October 1879, 12 May 1881; *Commercial*, 29 June 1882).

[2] After Brown's death, the *Commercial* (29 June 1882) characterized him as "quiet and courageous." That he showed courage in his last official act is beyond dispute, but his courage gains in luster if, as Freeman says, Brown was by nature "fearful of meeting the adversary."

[3] If one reads between the lines of contemporary newspapers, Brown's fitness to be a lawman was apparently a matter of question to persons other than Freeman. W. B. Hutchison of the *Commercial* chided the Caldwell citizenry: "It is idle to prate about the inefficiency of the officers, when the people whom they serve neither give them physical nor moral support. . . . Pay a salary sufficient to secure the services of a competent officer,

the office should have been one who was accustomed to western life, and moreover, should be a man ready to lay down his life at any time, for no prophet could foretell the moment when the marshal would fall, shot by a law-breaker and drunken desperado. A man was wanted and needed who knew no fear, whose highest ambition was to be dreaded by man, and who rushed to the front of battle or where duty calls, with caution and determination to come out of the conflict victorious.

On the morning of June 22d, 1882, two Texans rode into the town of Caldwell.[4] They put their horses in the livery stable and immediately went to a saloon where they filled themselves with the vile stuff known as whiskey. They soon made themselves conspicuous in the eyes of the citizens by the various feats which they displayed with their sixshooters.[5]

At last they seek the noted "Red Light," kept by the notorious Mag Woods, and there they indulge in drinking more whiskey and enjoying the society of the inmates of this vile den. They annoy the passing citizen by their profane and obscene language, and frighten the wives of the citizens who live in that immediate neighborhood, by the frequent firing of their sixshooters.

Finally the marshal goes to the "Red Light," and attempts the arrest of the Texas men.[6] The proprietor informs the marshal that the parties are

and when once secured, stand to his back like men" (29 June 1882). The castigation, though aimed at public "avarice and cowardice" (more fully explained in n. 10 below), admits that Brown's lack of competence was being used by the public to rationalize his death. Compounding Hutchison's scorn was the observation of the *Dodge City Times*: "The discipline of the [Caldwell] city government is probably lax. Once the ribald or dissipated class are allowed the least freedom, soon the condition of the town becomes chaotic. Caldwell suffers from the odium of having once been 'taken' [by Jim Talbot in December of 1881; see chaps. 41 and 42]" (repr. *Commercial*, 6 July 1882). Bown's problem may have been one of timing: under ordinary circumstances he may have had the ability to function satisfactorily as a law officer but lacked the stuff to prevail when rowdies viewed the town as easy to tree. On the other hand, as will unfold, Brown's adversaries in this instance were exceptional by anyone's standards.

[4] These men are called J. D. "Jess" and Steven Green, Ed and Jim Green, Ed and Jim Been, and Edward and James Bean, the latter apparently being the correct cognomens. They are also described as half-blood Indians, French Canadians, Mexicans, and escaped convicts from the Texas State Penitentiary. Whatever else they were, they were mean. Jim Bean claimed that "he and his brother together had killed eighteen men, not counting negroes." The Texas Rangers called them "decidedly the gamest desperadoes in Texas" (*Commercial*, 29 June, 26 October 1882; *Post,* 19 October 1882; *Wellingtonian*, 26 October 1882; *SCP*, 29 June, 9 November 1882).

[5] Freeman is apparently embellishing here. Marshal Brown confronted the pair because one of them had been seen with a weapon, contrary to city ordinance, according to the *Commercial*, 29 June 1882.

[6] The *Commercial*, 29 June 1882, indicates that Brown was accompanied by Constable Willis Metcalf. Of Metcalf, D. D. Leahy remembered: "Willis Metcalf lived in Wichita

up-stairs, and the officer starts to make the arrest. Some of the inmates of the house had seen the marshal coming in the direction of the "Red Light," and guessing his errand, the information was made known to the Texas men, who took a position near the head of the stairs and waited for his presence to be made known to them by his asking them to "throw up."

The design of the house and the plan upon which the stairs were erected was such that the Texans were concealed from the view of Marshal Brown or any person that came up the stairway. When the marshal arrived near the head of the stairs, the attempt was made by him to arrest the men. Quick as a flash they fired three shots in succession at the form of the marshal, who reeled and fell to the landing below.[7]

Quickly the Texas murderers ran down the stairs, out into the street, and across to the livery barn, where they obtained possession of their horses and rode rapidly in the direction of the Indian Territory.

Scarcely had the report of the deadly revolver died away before a crowd of excited citizens visited the scene of the murder and viewed the remains of the dead officer.[8] The news spread rapidly over the town, and the sister of Brown was notified of his death. A number of the dead officer's friends tenderly carried the body to the home where the almost heartbroken sister awaited in sorrow to receive it.[9]

The murderers of G. S. Brown made their escape and are still at large. They were pursued by the citizens, but the twin murderers had the advantage,

---

before and after serving as an officer at Caldwell. He was a dude who wore earrings. . . . He concluded in the early nineties to become a soldier of fortune and went to South America where he butted into some local revolution. When that was over he joined Garcia, who was causing the Spaniards some trouble in Cuba. When Havana surrendered to the American guns in 1898 he made himself chief of police in that city and finally, by some wizardry he . . . wriggled himself . . . into a commission in the regular army of the United States. The last time I had a letter from him he was a major in command of a unit of coast artillery at the fashionable city of Newport" (*Wichita Eagle*, 4 April 1932). Metcalf also served as a deputy sheriff under Frank Henderson in 1884 (*Wellingtonian*, 3 July 1884).

[7] The *Commercial* reported that Brown, after reaching the second floor, asked the man with the pistol to give it up; a brief scuffle ensued in which Metcalf was engaged by the other man while Brown pinned the armed man's hand against the wall. A third man came out of a room and distracted Brown, whereupon the armed man turned his wrist sufficiently to shoot Brown in the head. Covering Metcalf with the weapon, the first two men fled. Only one shot was fired. A detailed account of Brown's short career is given in Miller and Snell, *Why the West Was Wild*, pp. 57-66.

[8] What they saw was "the body of George Brown at the head of the stairs, his face covered with a clot of blood and his brains spattered on the wall and floor of the building, while the gore dripped through the floor to the rooms below" (*Commercial*, 29 June 1882).

[9] Fannie Brown, George's sister, kept house for him. The *Commercial* of 29 June 1882 gives a detailed description of her grief quite consonant with Freeman's here and in succeeding paragraphs.

as they had left town before a posse was organized to pursue them, and while the citizens were scouring the adjacent country, the murderers were over the hills and far away.[10]

The official life of G. S. Brown had been short. But a few short months before, in the early spring time, he took the office of marshal; scarcely had the freshness and verdure of spring passed away before he was called to lay down his life and enter the quietness of a sleep in which there is no dreaming and from which there is no awakening.

The sister of Marshal Brown was very much affected by the death of a brother in whom she centered all her affections. It was a sad parting for her when she saw all that remained of her brother buried deep within the bosom of mother earth. Fannie Brown turned in sadness from the grave; it was then she felt her loneliness and knew of her broken home which awaited her coming. Her grief was almost unconsolable, and in the sad hours of her affliction, amid kind and loving friends she found extended sympathy and condolence.

Several years after the death of her brother, Miss Brown married an honorable citizen of Caldwell, and they are both to-day living in the city. The husband is classed among the influential business men of Caldwell.[11]

[10] The murderers were not still at large at the time Freeman wrote *Midnight and Noonday*, and no posse of any consequence immediately engaged in pursuit. The Beans fled to the Territory, where their escape was fostered by Cherokee Strip cattle outfits, including the T5, with which they had come up from Texas. (Oliver Nelson was a herder at the time and reported how the news of the murder reached the cow camps. See Angie Debo, *The Cowman's Southwest*, pp. 90-91.) Pursuit was delayed when Mayor Colson's orders to commandeer saddled horses standing at hitching racks were countermanded by the horses' owners, "under advice of some of our *best citizens*," according to W. B. Hutchison, who added, "If it is one of the necessary concomitants of the through cattle trade that any ruffian a cattle man has a mind to employ can come into our town, shoot down an officer, . . . and then be allowed to escape through the cupidity or timidity of any number of citizens, then we are paying too dear a price for the cattle trade" (*Commercial*, 29 June 1882). The Beans were found about four months later near Decatur, Texas. Though surrounded by Texas Rangers, the brothers offered resistance. Edward was killed and James severely wounded. Despite his wounds, James was taken to Wellington for trial. He lingered in the county jail for nearly two weeks before he died. He had been wounded in fourteen places, including the head, where a No. 2 buckshot had entered his forehead and lodged in the back of his skull (*Post*, 19 October 1882; *Commercial*, 9 November 1882; *SCP*, 9 November 1882).

[11] Less than a week after the death of her brother, on June 25, Fannie Brown married Samuel Swayer, a local dry-goods merchant (*Commercial*, 29 June 1882). The timing does not seem indecorous, given the day and circumstances.

CHAPTER 34

Must the Officers Be Hunted Down?—Who Will Be the Next?—
A Remedy in Which Law and Order Will Prevail—"Bat"
Carr and Henry Brown Appointed to Fill the Office
of Marshal—Characters of the Men—They Are
Looked upon as "Holy Terrors"—Peace and
Good Will Reign Supreme—"Bat" Carr
Removed from Office—Henry Brown
and B. F. Wheeler Appointed.

Since the direful tragedy of Caldwell in which Marshal Brown had met his death, the citizens were awakening to the pressing facts which were staring them in the face. "Must the officers be hunted down and shot like wild beasts in the forest? Must wantonly murders become daily occurrences?" were the queries of the law-abiding and law-upholding citizen. The questions were answered most emphatically—No. The pitcher goes often to the fountain, but it is broken at last. The longest lane comes to an abrupt and unexpected turning, or, the lane is a mighty long one that has no turning. The city laws and regulations must be upheld and supported, either by submissiveness on the part of the law-breaker or at a cost of his life's blood. Life was becoming perilous to live; the officer and citizen were in suspense and anxiety. Who would be the next to die at the hands of the assassin? The elements of character displayed by the border desperado was terrible to contemplate. They rushed in the city, took the town, hunted the officers, and shot them down,[1] then riding as swiftly as the wind, they crossed the Indian Territory line, reached Texas, and escaped the hands of the law of our enterprising and law-abiding citizens.

The desperado, oftimes branded with the mark of Cain upon his brow, visits our quiet town, and before leaving it, he becomes a transgressor and usually eludes the officers by reaching the adjacent territory, which is usually filled with criminals, out-laws, and murderers. Once in the Indian Territory they are safe and free from molestation, but occasionally, however, they meet their match and they are taken in by the officers. The first thought of the law-breaker is, "How and where can I escape?" which is answered by the second thought, "Flee to the Indian Territory." Under the circumstances which were existing, a remedy must be found in which their plans can be outwitted. What was to be the remedy? At last the city mayor, A. M. Colson, together with

---

[1] Freeman lays it on rather thick here. George S. Brown was the only officer shot down in the line of duty in Caldwell. Both George Flatt and Frank Hunt were former officers, and their killings had no conclusive relationship with their previous efforts to maintain order.

the city councilmen, after devising various methods and different operations, concluded to send for a marshal who was recommended as a good man for that position.[2]

The new marshal was a stranger in the city, but he soon won the admiration of the citizens by his pleasing manners and good discipline. He soon won the hearts of the children, boys and girls, and many times has he been seen crossing the street with girls five, eight, and ten years old hanging to his side, holding his hands, chatting and laughing merrily with this pleasant man who proved to be a fierce, determined officer and a leader of men.[3]

The name of the new marshal was B. [P.] Carr, and usually answered to the name of "Bat," given him by his intimate friends. He was a man weighing perhaps one hundred and eighty pounds; was well proportioned, probably five feet, eight inches in height. His manner was pleasing to the ladies and agreeable to the gentlemen. His dress was without fault; he was usually seen dressed in a uniform of dark navy blue, with polished gilt trimming and brass buttons.[4] On his finger he wore a handsome ring set with precious stones; in his hand he carried a polished cane and upon his breast a large silver star with the words, "Bat Carr, Marshal," inscribed upon it.[5] He took special pains to get

[2]The source of the recommendation has not survived, but it is not unlikely that the sponsor was Mayor A. M. Colson himself. The search for a marshal to replace the slain George Brown was not protracted. Indeed, Carr was appointed on 27 June 1882, just five days after Brown's death (*Caldwell Commercial*, 29 June 1882).

[3]Freeman extols the new marshal here but calls him "a necessary evil" in the next few lines. Carr was the first outsider to enforce the law in Caldwell—and, according to the newspapers, was no respecter of resident over nonresident when it came to executing his duties, an evenhandedness which probably did not endear him to some citizens of Caldwell. In addition, it was clear from the beginning that the new marshal was expected to keep order, even if "a little bit of fine shooting" were required. In short, Caldwell had lost her innocence and had turned to the gunfighter to keep the civic peace (*Caldwell Post*, 13 July, 27 July 1882).

[4]As unromantic as it seems, Caldwell's first "professional" marshal wore a brass-buttoned uniform and not modified cowboy attire such as marshals wear in the movies. At the time of his appointment, Carr was variously identified as "from Texas" and "formerly of Osage Mission." His Texas ties are attested by the fact that he owned property in Colorado City, Texas, and was married in Dallas. Not long after his appointment at Caldwell, the *Commercial* described him as "a quiet, unassuming man. . . . there is that look about him that at once impresses a person with the idea that he will do his whole duty fearlessly and in the best manner possible" (*Commercial*, 2 June, 6 July 1882; *SCP*, 6 July 1882; *Post*, 9 November 1882, 4 January 1883). A detailed account of Carr's five months as Caldwell's marshall appears in Miller and Snell, *Why the West Was Wild*, pp. 91-97. Freeman mistakes Carr's middle initial, writing *B. O. Carr*, an error perpetuated by those modern historians whose principal source is Freeman. One B. O. Carr served as county attorney of Butler County (Freeman's home county) in1867-68; this may explain Freeman's confusion.

[5]The citizens of Caldwell presented Carr with "a brace of fine six-shooters" only two weeks after his appointment "in appreciation of [his] services." Perhaps the citizens were

acquainted with the citizens, who, as they became more intimate with him, learned to respect and honor him for his good moral character. He was strictly temperate in his habits and was generally found at his post of duty. I have given a big description of the new marshal as he appeared daily in his costume and manners; now I will endeavor to picture him when he assumed the role of the conquerer. No character in this history presents more peculiarities than that of "Bat" Carr. His whole nature was enigmatic; his traits of character were peculiar. He was, apparently, at once the polished gentleman and the daring frontiersman, shrinking from and courting danger at the same time; large in his own estimation, yet modest and most unpretentious among his associates. He was a lover of peace. His heighth of ambition was to be feared by men. He took great pride in having his name looked upon with terror and dismay by the cowboy and desperado. He had a perfect knowledge of human nature and could unravel the hidden mysteries of the plots and schemes laid by the cowboys. Carr was looked upon as a necessary evil to straighten the lower class of humanity which paraded the streets of Caldwell.

His assistant was a man similar in character to Carr, with the exception that he seldom smiled, was sober, candid, and determined in expression and mind, therefore was not familiar with the children, or a man with whom the ladies loved to converse. He dressed neatly, was gentlemanly, and won friends immediately upon his arrival in Caldwell.[6]

----

chafing under W. B. Hutchison's charges that they had poorly supported the late George S. Brown (see chap. 33, n. 3). The presentation speech, as reported by the local papers, smacks strongly of guilt feelings: "The people of Caldwell don't mean that you shall be assassinated . . . by reason of being unarmed" (*Commercial*, 13 July 1882). Also suggested is a bit of timorousness in the face of this professional gunfighter: the guns were given "as a token of [Caldwell's] confidence in your ability to protect [the guns] from being used for any purpose other than the defense of the city and [its] peace and quiet" (*Post*, 6 July 1882). In October, Carr was presented with the famous badge (not the mundane silver star Freeman speaks of). It was "solid gold in the form of a shield suspended from a plate at the top by chains." On it was lettered in black enamel: "Bat Carr, City Marshal of Caldwell." It cost seventy-five dollars (*Post*, 12 October 1882). Not to be outdone, Carr returned from a brief absence with "an elegant gold-headed, ebony-stock cane" inscribed "Presented to A. M. Colson by B. P. Carr." The *Post* saw this as appropriate evidence of "the personal friendship which exists between [our mayor] and his chief assistant" (9 November 1882).

[6]Freeman is alluding to Henry Newton Brown, whom he is about to introduce by name. Carr's first assistant, also appointed on 27 June, was B. B. Wood, brother to Sumner County's surveyor. Brown, according to Sam P. Ridings, rode into Caldwell and, an unknown, secured the job as assistant marshal on the strength of his demeanor in applying to the mayor for it (*The Chisholm Trail*, pp. 492-93). However, the *Caldwell Journal* of 8 May 1884 reports that Brown was hired on the recommendation of Bat Carr, who had known Brown when the latter was a deputy sheriff in Oldham County, Texas. Brown also claimed to have been the marshal of Tascosa, Texas. What he did not report, apparently, was that he was better known as Hendry Brown, an associate of Billy the Kid during and

These men were efficient officers and forcibly upheld the law at all hazards. They were ever ready for the desperadoes lawless conduct and took delight in an engagement which they were determined to prove the most powerful in producing the intended effects. The result was, the officers were looked upon by the public as men with force of character which was not altogether assumed. Their determined expression, energy, and unerring shot with the six-shooter won for them a name of fame, both at home and abroad. They were looked upon by the cowboys as a "mighty terror," and soon learned they meant business and were not there for their health; consequently, quietness reigned supreme in the city of Caldwell, where once the cowboy held full sway and possession and was the monarch of all he surveyed. There was no trifling with these marshals; when aroused they were like the fearless tiger of the wild jungles of Africa. These men were constantly on the alert, and when a man was requested to "throw up," it was at the muzzle of a cocked sixshooter, and the offender could read the expression of the marshal, which meant, "surrender or die." While Carr was looked upon as a holy terror, strange to say, while he was the marshal of Caldwell, he was not called upon to kill his man when arresting a man or suppressing a riot.

Marshal Carr and Henry Brown, the assistant, made a different town of Caldwell; it was no longer known as a rough place, the home of the wild and wooley cowboy, the haunt of the desperado, and the favorite resort of the horse thief. These outlaws soon learned the conditions under which they could visit the town in which they were to respect the wishes of the citizens and desires of the officers, whose word was looked upon by the rougher element as law and was not to be broken.

The result of this was that Caldwell began to take rapid strides toward becoming an enterprising and influential business center; she is becoming the metropolis of Kansas, and her future destiny is written in letters of gold. New enterprises are started every day, new buildings are being erected, new people arrive in the town to cast their fortunes with the frontier settler. Railroads, school-houses, churches, and neighbors can be found now, where the Indian, buffalo, coyote, and skunk held unmolested possession then.

The past of Caldwell has been dark and gloomy, the present shows the cloud with the silver lining, and the future is bright with promises that will be realized in a grand and glorious manner.

---

after the Lincoln County War. Born in Rolla, Missouri, Brown was about twenty-five years old when he arrived in Caldwell (*Commercial*, 6 July 1882; *Journal*, 8 May 1884). Brown's unusual term in Caldwell law enforcement has been the subject of much fictional flapdoodle offered as straight history. A reliable and detailed account may be found in Miller and Snell, pp. 67-84. Bill O'Neal's *Henry Brown: The Outlaw Marshall* offers a comprehensive treatment of Brown's life but often relies heavily on hypothesis and conjecture not always identified as such.

Marshal Carr held dominion over Caldwell's interests until December 2, 1882, when he was removed from office, and the assistant, Henry Brown, was appointed to fill the office vacated by Carr.[7]

Henry Brown had an assistant appointed by the name of B. F. Wheeler, formerly from Texas. Wheeler was a man above the average height of men, was well built and proportioned, a perfect blonde, and appeared more to the desperado style than that of a cultured gentleman, although he was gentlemanly

---

[7] Freeman's allusion to Carr's removal from office is echoed by D. D. Leahy (*Wichita Eagle*, 4 April 1932): "Bat Carr left Caldwell under a cloud of some sort that I have never heard explained." Freeman's date, December 2, is contradicted by other evidence. The local newspapers merely compound the mystery of the why and how of Carr's separation as marshal. They report that he left Caldwell during the week of 9 December 1882 for the purpose of getting married (which he did, on 27 December in Dallas), but the expectation that he would return is clearly indicated. Yet on 21 December 1882, Henry Brown was appointed marshal, with no published indication of Carr's resignation or termination (*Commercial*, 21 December 1882; *Post*, 28 December 1882, 4 January 1883).

The story that Brown, desiring the marshal's job, intimidated Carr into resigning is told in various places; the ultimate source of that rumor appears to be Caldwell old-timer Joe Wiedeman, whom Harry Sinclair Drago interviewed (*Wild, Woolly & Wicked*, p. 264). Wiedeman's version also appears in a newspaper article, "Hendry Brown: Marshall and Murderer," *Caldwell Messenger* (8 May 1961) by Chester C. Heizer. My own experience with Wiedeman's published recollections has left me skeptical; wherever it has been possible to compare Wiedeman's statements with historical record, I have found the record contradicts Wiedeman. But even if the intimidation had occurred, it would account only for Carr's resignation of the office (and there is no record of that) but not for the lingering rumor that he was removed from it.

My own theory is that Carr was fired by the Caldwell City Council on the complaint of local politician I. N. Cooper. The *Post* of 28 December 1882 reports: "About the maddest man we have seen for some time was I. N. Cooper on last Thursday [21 December]. He had just discovered that Battie Carr had shot his pet dog, a valuable shepherd, and one that a fifty-dollar bill would not have purchased." The same issue of the *Post* reports that on the very same Thursday, 21 December, the council appointed Henry Brown marshal. At the time of the appointment, Mayor Colson was in Eureka Springs, Arkansas, and so not available to referee this dispute (if dispute it may be called). Carr himself was out of town and thus could offer no defense. The shooting of the dog, which evidently had occurred some time before Cooper learned of it, was probably not capricious; the *Commercial* recounts Carr's killing "a mad dog" on Main Street on November 30 and adds that "this is the second mad dog seen here within the past two weeks" (*Commercial*, 7 December 1882). Whether Cooper's dog was the one shot on November 30 or another shot as a result of concern over mad dogs is, of course, uncertain. But I humbly offer in evidence the hypothesis that Carr's nemesis was not the gun-totin' Henry Newton Brown but merely an irate and politically potent dog lover.

Whatever the circumstances may have been, Carr was obviously unabashed. Early in 1883 he appeared in Wellington, where he settled for a time and, on at least one occasion, served as a special policeman. As late as December of 1883, he was trying to acquire land near Caldwell (*Wellington Wellingtonian*, 15 February, 28 June 1883; *Commercial*, 20 December 1883).

in deportment and dress, yet he bore the rougher marks of humanity by expression and carriage of form.[8]

These men kept law and order in the city, hence were efficacious in filling the office. They were looked upon as gentlemen of good habits and moral character. Neither of the marshals were men who frequent the saloon nor enjoy the festivities of the dancing hall, similar to the one located in the "Red Light" building.[9]

Henry Brown married one of Caldwell's brightest young ladies, who had long been one of the leaders in society and a favorite of her associates and acquaintances.[10] They lived happily together for some time, when her heart was almost broken by the startling intelligence of her husband's tragical death.

The marshals were reappointed to fill the office, and filled it satisfactorily for several years.[11] But, alas! their sad and mournful ending.

---

[8]Ben F. Wheeler—alias Ben Robertson, alias Ben F. Burton—appears in the *Post* as early as 19 October 1882; thus the stories that Brown, after becoming marshal, sent for or imported Wheeler for the assistant's job are incorrect (see Ridings, p. 495; Nellie Snyder Yost, *Medicine Lodge*, p. 91). When Brown was appointed acting marshal during Carr's absence in October, Wheeler was appointed his temporary assistant. The *Post* of 26 October 1882 described Wheeler thus: "[He] has the sand, as the boys say, to stay with the wild and woolly class as long as they are on the war path." Wheeler was again named Brown's assistant on 22 December 1882, the day after Brown was made marshal in his own right (*Post* , 28 December 1882).

Wheeler—or, more properly, Robertson—was from Rockdale, Texas. He had a wife and four children in Texas and a wife and infant child at Indianola, Nebraska. He was twenty-eight years old when he came to Caldwell (*Journal*, 8 May 1884). His exploits while Caldwell's deputy marshal are detailed in Miller and Snell, pp. 625-29.

[9]Freeman is speaking in a relative, metaphorical sense here. The Red Light was closed long before Brown and Wheeler were appointed (see chap. 32, n. 10). Freeman's statement can scarcely be credited as the inspiration for some of the apocrypha which has grown up around the Red Light and Mr. Brown. Harry Sinclair Drago recounts a mass arrest made at the Red Light by Brown and Wheeler, again citing Wiedeman (see n. 7 above)—*Wild, Woolly & Wicked*, p. 265. Nellie Snyder Yost reports that Brown himself closed down the Red Light and that Mag Woods set fire to it before she left town (*Medicine Lodge*, p. 92).

[10]Brown married Alice Maude Levagood on 26 March 1884. Miss Levagood was the adopted daughter of Mr. and Mrs. Richard Rue of Caldwell. (Rue was a brick manufacturer.) Maude Levagood appeared in Caldwell in June of 1882 upon completing her studies to become a teacher. During the 1882-83 academic year, she taught school at the Wichita Agency, Indian Territory. The next year she taught in Anthony, Kansas (*Commercial*, 15 June 1882, 17 May 1883; *Post*, 31 August 1882; *Journal*, 27 December 1883, 27 March 1884).

[11]Brown and Wheeler served 17 months: from December, 1882, to May, 1884.

CHAPTER 35

The Marshals of Caldwell Attempt to Rob the Medicine
Valley Bank—Brown Shoots the President—Wheeler
and Wesley Shoot the Cashier—A Ride for Life—
Robbers Driven in a Pit of Water—Surrender
—"Boys I Am into It with You, I'll
Go Out and Die with You."

In the early part of May, 1884, Marshal Henry Brown and his assistant, B. F. Wheeler, left caldwell for the purpose, claimed by the marshals, of searching for horse thieves for whom a large reward had been offered. The marshals intended to be gone for several days, hence it would be necessary to appoint a marshal to fill the vacancy until Brown and Wheeler returned from their hunt.[1] A few days after their departure the people of Caldwell were shocked with the intelligence of an awful crime committed at Medicine Lodge, a town located in Barber County, about sixty miles west of Caldwell. In this crime the two trusty and respected marshals of Caldwell were involved. The citizens were particularly interested in the affair; and the facts of the awful tragedy were told by our citizens Ben. S. Miller, Harvey Horner, Lee Weller, and John A. Blair, who went to the scene of the crime to ascertain a true statement of the sickening affair.[2] When the terrible news reached Cald-

---

[1] The *Caldwell Journal* (8 May 1884) reports that Brown and Wheeler were allegedly seeking a murderer in the Territory for whom a $1,200 reward had been offered. They received the mayor's permission to be absent from the city for a few days. The appointment of an acting or temporary marshal, as Freeman recounts, is unreported. Freeman's "early part of May" is slightly inaccurate. Brown and Wheeler appeared in Medicine Lodge on April 30.

[2] The "facts of the awful tragedy were told by our citizens." Freeman is alluding to the report made by Blair and Horner when they returned to Caldwell. This appeared in a Sunday extra edition (4 May 1884) of the *Caldwell Standard* and was sent to subscribers along with the regular weekly issue of 8 May 1884, where it may be found today on the microfilm. (For that reason, subsequent citations of the *Standard* extra appear here under the 8 May 1884 date. The *Standard* extra was extracted and published in the *Wellington Wellingtonian* (8 May 1884), and this reprinting survives on microfilm in a much more legible form than the film of the *Standard* offers.) Freeman obviously saved a copy of the extra as a memento, for virtually all of this and the succeeding chapter is directly quoted or loosely paraphrased from that source.

Benjamin S. Miller received a telegram from the mayor of Medicine Lodge reporting the involvement of Brown and Wheeler. Why Miller was chosen to receive the news is conjectural (William Morris was the recently elected mayor of Caldwell), but Miller had connections in Barber County dating back to 1878 when he first came to Kansas from New York. In 1884 he was president and director of the Caldwell Publishing Company, which had purchased the *Caldwell Post* and *Commercial* and merged them into the *Journal.*

well, these gentlemen left on an early train for Medicine Lodge and arrived there about ten o'clock in the night. The town was all excitement; the citizens were nervous about the arrival of strangers in their city, but luckily for our citizens they were met at the train by two friends, Mayor [Charles H.] Eldred and Dr. Moore, formerly from this place,[3] who soon put them on good terms with the men of Medicine Lodge.

The facts reported to us are as follows: The marshals left Caldwell and were joined by two pals, Smith and Wesley by name,[4] and they immediately

---

Miller was a stockman, at one time president of the Cherokee Strip Live Stock Association, but in his Andreas biography (p. 1504) he makes a special point that, early in life, "he filled the noble position of cook for the cowboys." In later life Miller settled in Oklahoma City (*Caldwell Messenger*, 8 May 1961). Miller's book *Ranch Life in Southern Kansas and the Indian Territory as Told by a Novice* recounts his beginnings in the cattle business. Miller also appears in Reginald Aldridge, *Life on a Ranch*.

S. Harvey Horner (Freeman or the typesetter rendered it "Harvey Homer") came to Caldwell in 1879 and opened a drugstore. A successful candidate for several offices, including mayor, Horner also served as a representative to the Kansas Legislature (*Portrait and Biographical Album of Sumner County, Kansas*, pp.404-405). A biographical sketch appears in Andreas, p. 1504. Lee S. Weller was a former railroad conductor on the run between Caldwell and Newton. He located in Caldwell in 1882 (*Commercial*, 9 June 1881; 23 November 1882). John A. Blair is the subject of a profile in chap. 45. According to the *Journal* of 8 May 1884, on May 2, Miller and Blair went to Medicine Lodge "to give their sympathy to the bereaved families"; Weller and Horner went "to look after property that belong to them," though the *Journal* does not indicate the nature of that property. The *Medicine Lodge Cresset* (8 May 1884) throws some light on the matter: "a party who came over from Caldwell last Friday [May 2] claims he had loaned Wheeler $300 in currency and a gold watch valued at $625 and a diamond pin valued at $50 or $60." Horner sold jewelry in connection with his drugstore. According to the *Standard* (15 May 1883), the watch belonged to Weller, who had lent it to Wheeler. The valuables were not recovered.

[3] Eldred, long active in the Cherokee Strip Live Stock Association, was vice-president of the organization at the time of its dissolution (William W. Savage, Jr., *The Cherokee Strip Live Stock Association*, p. 51, *passim*; Edward Everett Dale, *Cow Country*, p. 204). Dr. W. H. Moore moved from Caldwell to Medicine Lodge, where his son was register of deeds, in 1882 (*Wellingtonian*, 12 January 1882).

[4] William ("Billy") Smith, about twenty-eight years of age, was foreman of the T5 range in the Cherokee Strip. Although the newspapers at the time of his death could report no known record or reputation as an outlaw for Smith, Oliver Nelson claims that Smith had ridden with Billy the Kid and, during Nelson's acquaintance with him, dealt in stolen horses (Debo, *The Cowman's Southwest*, pp. 117, 170-71, 189, 208; Nelson offers many anecdotes about Smith, with whom Nelson worked on the T5). Smith was described as "an undersized man with dark complexion and rather a hardened expression of countenance" (*Cresset*, 1 May 1884). John Wesley, about thirty-one and "having several aliases," for a short time prior to the robbery worked as a cowboy on the T5. No record of criminal activities was offered by the press except that he "was always considered a hard citizen." He was described as "rather under medium size," with "an evil, reckless expression of countenance." Both Smith and Wesley were Texans (*Journal*, 8 May 1884; *Cresset*, 1 May 1884; Debo, *The Cowman's Southwest*, p. 189).

went in the vicinity of Medicine Lodge, not for the purpose of hunting horse thieves, however, but on a terrible mission in which a foul crime was commited.

They camped west of Medicine Lodge in a grove on the Medicine River. The next morning was shrouded in mist, and about ten o'clock a slight rain was falling, making the roads slippery and filling the ravines with water.[5] No one seemed to notice the four horse men as they approached and rode into town from the west. They stopped in the rear of the Medicine Valley Bank building; two of the horses were hitched by ropes, and Smith, holding the third, was sitting on the remaining horse. Wheeler went in the building at the front door while Brown and Wesley went to a side door and entered the bank.

It is presumed the men did not anticipate a meeting with obstacles and failure in the attempt made by them to rob the bank, but supposed the officers in the bank would yield readily to their command of throw up; whereupon they would take the money and depart with their treasures, riding rapidly to a place of safety. The old adage "The best laid plans of mice and men, gang aft aglee" may be applied appropriately to the schemes of the robbers.

The bank president and cashier[6] had been notified that an attempt would be made to rob the bank, and these two gentlemen talked over the matter and concluded to make no preparations to guard the bank. The note received by these men was written by "I Bar" Johnson, and stated that an attempt would be made to rob the bank, and in order to save their lives, the warning said they must not resist the commands of the robbers; hence, it was agreed by the officers to throw up conformably and take the chances on recapturing the money in case of a robbery.[7]

[5] The newspaper accounts report that a hard rain was falling when the four entered town. Freeman's "light rain" belies his own statement that the ravines were filling up. In this last, he is foreshadowing the flooding which would force the outlaws to abandon their defensive position in a ravine after they fled from town (*Cresset*, 1 May 1884).

[6] The bank president was E. Wylie Payne, a stockman as well as editor of the defunct *Barber County Index*. Payne's biography appears in Andreas, p. 1523. George Geppert, the cashier, was also a member of the hardware and lumber firm of Geppert & Stone. A biographical sketch appears in Andreas, p. 1523.

[7] The wives of Payne and Geppert acknowledged that the men knew a robbery had been planned, but it does not appear that they knew the day or time (*Standard*, 8 May 1884). W. C. "I Bar" Johnson would testify after the fact that he had communicated a warning to Geppert, among others, concerning information he had obtained from Billy Smith about a design on the bank. It appears his warnings were not conveyed by note, contrary to what Freeman indicates. Johnson was a member of the Eagle Chief Pool, located adjacent to the T5 in the Cherokee Strip (*Cresset*, 8 May 1884). The fact of the forewarning has given rise to a number of theories, myths, and general speculation, among which is the account, here given, of the bank officers' vague plan to recapture the money (*Standard*, 8 May 1884). One of the more spectacular stories is attributed to the would-be robbers themselves: Geppert, being short in his accounts by ten thousand dollars, arranged the robbery; Payne, who was supposed to be out of town on the day of the heist, spoiled

Wheeler entered the building and presented his revolver at Mr. Geppert, the cashier, and told him to "throw up his hands." At the same time Brown covered Mr. Payne, the president, with the same order. Wesley said nothing. It is believed that his part of the terrible business was to cover and kill, if necessary, the clerk Mr. ———, but luckily for him he had gone to the post office with the Harper mail and was not at that time in the bank.[8]

Cashier Geppert threw up his obedience to Wheeler's command, and after a moment of pause, he turned to see what Mr. Payne was doing; then Wheeler fired, shooting the cashier through the body. When Brown heard the shot fired by Wheeler, he immediately after shot president Payne.[9]

Mr. Gepperts expiring effort was directed toward throwing on the combination of the safe and gave conclusive evidence of the fact that they had received a notice of the intended robbery, for had he had no previous knowledge of the attack, it would be hard to believe that a man having received two fatal shots, one supposed to have been fired by Wesley, would turn directly to the safe and, with the last motion of his nerveless arm, turn a lock on the propety of which he was guardian. The dead body of the cashier was found near the combination of the safe, sitting in the vault with his lifes blood streaming and crimsoning every thing about him.[10] Faithful to the last, his expiring thought was of the property in his charge, and with the shadow of death hovering over him he staggered to the vault, threw on the combination, and sank into eternity.

Payne received but one wound at the hands of Marshal Brown. The shot staggered him; he fell from the shock and was found on the floor of the bank, writhing and groaning in the terrible agonies of death. He lived long enough to make a statement, saying Brown was his murderer and that Wheeler and Wesley killed Geppert.[11]

---

the plan by going for his gun when the robbers appeared (McNeal, *When Kansas Was Young*, pp. 157-58). The newspapers support Freeman in the statement that Payne and Geppert had agreed, if robbed, to surrender.

[8] The clerk's name is also omitted in Freeman's source, from which the foregoing paragraph is taken verbatim (*Standard*, 8 May 1884). I have been unable to identify the clerk by other means.

[9] According to the *Journal* (8 May 1884), the bank officers' plan to offer no resistance misfired when Payne's "positive character . . . asserted itself" and he went for his gun instead, whereupon "Brown shot him, and Wheeler shot Geppert while that gentleman had his hands up!" Freeman is faithful to his source, which indicates—on Payne's *ante mortem* statement—that Wheeler shot Geppert when the latter turned to look at Payne; then Brown shot Payne (*Standard*, 8 May 1884). Payne was wounded by Brown's revolver, not his Winchester, as Bill O'Neal suggests (*Henry Brown*, p. 129).

[10] Geppert was indeed wounded twice, and the general hypothesis is that Wesley fired the second shot. All sources agree on the disposition of Geppert's body.

[11] Payne died the next day, Thursday, May 1 (*Journal*, 8 May 1884).

While the shooting was going on, Smith was in the rear of the bank in charge of the horses. When the firing was heard in the bank, the marshal of the town,[12] observing Smith and thinking all was not right in the bank, opened fire upon Smith with a six shooter. When Brown heard the shots fired by the marshal, he became uneasy and ran to the door of the bank, took in the situation at once, and opened fire on the marshal with his Winchester, firing three shots. Smith began shooting at the marshal and everybody else he could see.

Brown, Wheeler, and Wesley, failing in their attempt to gain possession of the money and realizing they were murderers in the sight of the law and outlaws upon the face of the earth, and to escape the justice and fate which awaited them, realized the only chance for them was to flee from the town of excited people and, if possible, find refuge in the canyons which would serve as a place of concealment until the excitement was over.[13]

The robbers ran for their horses, which they had great difficulty in loosening, the ropes having become taut in the rain. Their horses once loose, they mounted them and rode as fastly as their horses could run. Wheeler had purchased a fast horse before he left Caldwell, and it ran with good speed for a short distance, but after running several miles it began to show signs of fatigue and was completely wearied out, so the horse was abandoned; in order to escape, two men must ride one horse, all going in a southwest direction.[14]

The country southwest of Medicine Lodge is very rough and broken with deep canyons and ravines. The robbers were so closely pursued by the excited citizens of Medicine Lodge, that they left their horses and ran into a canyon, which was immediately surrounded by the men, who crowded the robbers deeper into the recesses of the canyon until they were driven into a hole— a pit in fact, filled with water.[15] The robbers were defending themselves from the shots fired by the inflamed citizens by shooting at them with their Winchesters and revolvers. At last, they are standing in water waist deep and have become benumbed and cold, and a surrender is necessary. Some of the posse have returned to the town for the necessary articles to bring an immediate

[12] Sam Denn was the city marshal (Miller and Snell, *Why the West Was Wild*, p. 77).

[13] Apparently the plan was to follow the main road and to make for "the breaks of the gypsum hills" due west of town. According to the *Journal* (8 May 1884), the misadventure described in the next paragraph sent them into a canyon for refuge. The *Cresset* (1 May 1884) reported that the outlaws took to the canyon because some of their pursuers were cutting off their route of escape to the south.

[14] According to the *Journal* (8 May 1884) "one horse began weakening." There is no mention of its being abandoned.

[15] Thus the *Standard* (8 May 1884). The site is further described as "a small pocket, thirty or forty feet deep, with only one exit, that by which [the fugitives] entered. The bottom of the canyon was covered with water from a foot and a half to two feet deep, and it was raining hard and water running down the sides." The outlaws held out there for two hours (*Journal*, 8 May 1884).

Captors of the Medicine Lodge Bank Robbers

surrender. Only nine men are guarding the canyon in which the robbers had retreated.[16]

Brown was the first man to give up. He called out to the attacking party and proposed to surrender [if] they would protect him from violence. The promise was made, and Henry Brown, the man whom our people have always thought so brave, walked out of the hole into which he had been driven and laid down his gun. The assistant marshal, Wheeler, came out second, Wesley third; and finally Smith, the only game man in the band of robbers, the only man that seemed to realize the fraility of a promise of protection after their awful deed, walked out of the pit, saying, "Boys I came into it with you, and I'll go out and die with you."[17] Ah! if they only could have realized the terrible fate which awaited them, of the awful doom and death which was to be theirs, how differently would have been their intentions, and how they would have fought to the bitter end, resolving to die game. Their role as actors in the drama of life is not yet over; would that we could draw the curtain, closing the scene in all its horror from the gaze and minds of the public; would [we] could spare the facts of the heart sickening affair from the young wife of Marshal Brown.

It will be our business in the next chapter to give the account of the sorrowful death of these men upon whom the Medicine Lodge people had vowed to seek vengeance for the death of their honored citizens.

[16] According to the *Cresset* of 8 May 1884, those who returned to town were George Friedley and Charley Taliaferro, who "came in for reinforcements." The men who remained at the canyon and to whom the outlaws surrendered were Barney O'Connor, Vernon Lytle, Alec McKinney, Lee Bradley, Roll Clark, Tom Doran, John Fleming, Wayne McKinney, Howard Martin, and Nate Priest—ten in all, not nine, as Freeman states. Freeman may have been misled by the famous photograph of the captors; Nate Priest was not present for the picture. (Nor was Howard Martin. George Friedley, one of those who went for reinforcements, does appear, however, completely confusing the issue for Freeman and posterity.) Whether Friedley and Taliaferro went for reinforcements or—as Freeman says— "the necessary articles to bring about an immediate surrender" is moot, but an indication of what those "necessary articles" might have been is given in Nellie Snyder Yost, *Medicine Lodge* (p. 96): barrels of kerosene which could be emptied over the edges of the ravine and set aflame.

[17] The order of surrender and Smith's words are unique to Freeman's source among the contemporary accounts I have been able to locate (*Standard*, 8 May 1884). Freeman appears to be on his own from this point to the end of the chapter.

CHAPTER 36

The Robbers Taken to Medicine Lodge—Photographs Taken—Letter
Written by Brown to His Wife—The Mob Attack the Jail—
Brown Shot—Wheeler Wounded—Three Robbers
Hung—Sentiments of the People.

The robbery was attempted about ten o'clock in the morning. The robbers were brought into town by the nine men to whom they surrendered, at about one o'clock in the afternoon. About three hours after the terrible crime was committed at the bank, the robbers were shackled and put into the calaboose, the only jail in which the prisoners could be confined.[1] The prisoners were furnished with dry clothing and properly cared for by the citizens. During the day, a photograph was taken of the four prisoners, and a good picture was obtained of all except Wheeler; his features were so drawn that they looked unnatural.[2] It is stated that when the time arrived for the prisoners to stand so that the photograph could be taken, our former brave city marshal got down on his knees and implored for mercy. Is it possible that this is the man who held Caldwell in terror so long?[3]

The men were furnished with paper with which they might write any word to friends or relatives they wished. Brown wrote an affectionate letter to his

[1] Freeman slightly distorts the sense of his source here, which reads, "The robbers were . . . put in the calaboose, the only jail they have in that county" (*Caldwell Standard,* 8 May 1884). The point appears to be that Medicine Lodge had only a rude city lockup but no county jail, contrary to what one might expect in a county seat. The distinction between a calaboose and a jail reflects a usage I have found often in Wellington newspapers. Violators of city ordinances, chiefly drunks, were housed in the calaboose (see chap. 6, n. 25, for a description of Wellington's calaboose—which doubled as the county jail until 1878). Violators of state laws were placed in the county jail—typically a wooden structure built around an iron, cagelike box.

[2] The comment on the likeness of Wheeler is a direct quote from Freeman's source. The photograph in question has been reproduced wherever the Henry Brown story has been told.

[3] The original is a bit more pungent: ". . . our former brave (?) city marshal got down on his knees, grovelling in the dirt, begged for and implored mercy. Great God! can this be the man who held Caldwell in terror so long?" The admission of Brown's rule by terror is interesting. While Brown lived, the Caldwell papers breathed no hint of this. Laudatory comment—in print—is characteristic. But former Caldwell resident D. D. Leahy remembered: "Few people who cared for their lives argued orders from Hendry. He was rather overfond of making business for the undertaker" (*Wichita Eagle,* 4 April 1932). Even when discounted liberally for exaggeration the comment reveals something of the citizens' state of mind. Under the Brown-Wheeler regime, four men were killed while arrests were being attempted. Brown himself killed two of them: the Indian Spotted Horse (see chap. 38) and Newt Boyce, a gambler. Not a host of killings, but enough to be intimidating (*Caldwell Commercial,* 12 April 1883; *Journal,* 17 May, 22 November, 20 December 1883).

223

WESLEY BROWN   SMITH   WHEELER

The Bank Robbers of Medicine Lodge

young wife, telling her of his incarceration, crime, and his doubts as to the probability of meeting with her again.[4] Wheeler tried to write, but failed in the attempt; the facts were plainly shown that he had'nt the nerve to put his thoughts on paper.[5]

About midnight the calaboose was surrounded by a crowd of men numbering about three hundred; they disarmed the sheriff and opened the jail, intending to take the prisoners and lynch them to the nearest tree.[6]

When the door was opened, Brown rushed out, having got free from his shackles; he only ran a few yards, however, when the night air was filled with the sound of the guns fired at the fleeing man, who fell with a pound of lead distributed through his body. Wheeler too was free from his shackles and also started on the run; he proved to be the fleetest runner of the two men and ran farther than Brown, perhaps one hundred yards, when he too fell. He had been shot in the right arm, which was badly shattered; two fingers of his left hand were shot away, and his body was pierced by three Winchester balls.[7] He made a confession, but it was never revealed to the inquisitive public.[8] Wheeler implored for mercy, and it is said his cries were so loud that they were heard half a mile away. The doomed man begged piteously to be spared until ten o'clock the following day, and said he would give away many things

[4] Brown's letter has been reprinted frequently and need not be reproduced in full here. In addition to the remarks Freeman summarizes, Brown told his wife he "did not shoot anyone, and did not want the others to shoot anyone." He also told her to "keep the Winchester." He was referring to the rifle presented to him on 1 January 1883 by Mayor Colson on behalf of the citizens of Caldwell. It was gold mounted and engraved, with a silver plate on the stock bearing the inscription "Presented to City Marshal H. N. Brown for valuable services rendered." Brown had been marshal less than a month. (*Caldwell Post,* 4 January 1883; *Journal,* 8 May 1884) Brown had the weapon with him on the Medicine Lodge raid; it then passed through various hands down the years but is now in the possession of the Kansas State Historical Society at Topeka.

[5] The *Standard* of 8 May 1884: "Wheeler was furnished with paper and tried to write, but he couldn't do it. Hadn't the nerve."

[6] Some details differ in the *Medicine Lodge Cresset:* the mob came about nine o'clock in the evening. Wheeler, Smith, and Wesley were taken to be hanged "to an elm tree in the bottom east of town" (1 May 1884).

[7] Per *Standard,* 8 May 1884. No other contemporary source gives the nature and number of Wheeler's wounds—or the weight of the lead in Brown's body. The four prisoners had been bound together thus: Brown to Wesley with leg shackles, Wheeler to Smith with handcuffs (the sheriff had only one set of each). Wesley slipped off his boot and then the shackle; Smith, whose hands were small, slipped the cuffs. Thus when the cell door opened, all four men were free to run (*Cresset,* 8 May 1884).

[8] Though Freeman's source mentions a confession, D. D. Leahy, who discussed the matter with fellow journalists T. A. and Joe McNeal (both residents of Medicine Lodge at the time of the incident), concluded that no confession was taken from Wheeler (*Eagle,* 4 April 1932).

that would interest the community at large.[9] The excited mob could not wait, and Wheeler was not spared an hour, but was swung up with Smith and Wesley. Smith showed more nerve than either of the other men and seemed unconcerned in reference to the awful death he was to die. He died without a murmur and was game to the last.[10] Wheeler was hung with a lariat rope. Brown, by his attempted escape, met a more preferable death than by hanging; probably he anticipated what his end would be and preferred to die by being pierced with bullets, than a death by the hangmans noose.

At the request of the gentlemen from Caldwell, the bodies of Brown and Wheeler were exhumed, and the boys reported that the features of the dead men were as natural as if they were merely asleep. The bodies were shrouded and buried in pine coffins. Their last resting place is just over the line of the Medicine Lodge cemetery.[11]

"I Bar" Johnson came into Medicine Lodge and made a sworn statement to the general effect that about five weeks before the terrible tragedy, Wheeler and the others came to him and urged him to enter into the plot to rob the bank. He refused to do so, and they told him that their intentions were to rob the bank anyhow and that if he squealed they would kill him. He said that

---

[9] These details, as reported in the *Caldwell Standard* (8 May 1884), would undoubtedly serve to comfort those who had been bullied or intimidated by Wheeler in the past. More restrained descriptions of Wheeler's terror appear in the *Cresset* (1 May 1884) and *Journal* (8 May 1884).

[10] Smith's gameness is generally recognized.

[11] *Standard,* 8 May 1884. This report firmly establishes that all of the outlaws were buried at Medicine Lodge. As might be expected, local legends to the contrary grew up. Nellie Snyder Yost (*Medicine Lodge,* p. 159) quotes an elderly resident of Medicine Lodge who said that before Brown could be buried, his wife claimed the body, placed it in a lumber wagon, and took it back to Caldwell for burial. Bill O'Neal cites Robert R. Foster, who reports a comparable story told by his grandmother (*Henry Brown,* p. 151, n. 16). It is understandable, however, that Alice Maude Levagood Brown should figure in the legend; her innocent plight teases at the imagination. It is clear that she had no inkling of Brown's plan to rob a bank—his letter to her speaks eloquently to that. In all of the hullabaloo following the revelation of the scandal, Maude gets only a few lines in the *Caldwell Journal* of 22 May 1884, and most of those she paid for herself: "Mrs. Henry Brown will be at her residence on north Main street from 9 till 11 a.m. and from 3 till 5 p.m. each day, commencing with Saturday, to show the furniture to persons wishing to buy. The entire furniture of the house is for sale." The same issue of the *Journal* reports that down at the drugstore, S. Harvey Horner—who brought back from Medicine Lodge Ben Wheeler's coat and "a piece of rope with which Wesley was hung" (*Journal,* 8 May 1884)—was raffling off "Henry Brown's fine silver-bitted bridle." The *Standard* (15 May 1884) explained that the proceeds were to go to the young widow. Maude Brown does not appear in the Caldwell papers after May 22. Apparently she joined her foster parents, the Rues, who had moved to Dakota Territory the previous year, for her correspondence to the probate court regarding the settlement of Brown's estate was sent from Devil's Lake, Dakota Territory (*Journal,* 16 August 1883; O'Neal, pp. 149-50, 152, nn. 23 and 24).

he notified Geppert and Payne that an attempt at robbery would be made, and that the robbers would order them to throw up their hands, and that if they complied, they would not be hurt.[12]

At this time, and in this connection, it might be proper to state the council of Caldwell took notice of the affair by drafting and adopting the following resolutions, which were found in the city clerk's book, and are as follows:

"Mr. Mayor and gentleman of the council: Your committee[13] to whom was referred the matter of drafting resolutions, expressive of the sentiments of the people of Caldwell in regard to the Medicine Lodge tragedy, have had the matter under consideration and submit the following report:

> WHEREAS, Two men in whom the Government and people of Caldwell have heretofore reposed great trust and confidence, have to the unutterable amazement and mortification of our citizens, proved themselves murderers, robbers, cowards and villains of the worst type, by their criminal attack on the Medicine Valley bank, of Medicine Lodge, Kansas; and the wanton murder of Mr. Payne and Mr. Geppert, President and Cashier of said bank, and
>
> WHEREAS, We recognize in the untimely death of Mr. Payne and Mr. Geppert not only an irreparable loss to the city of Medicine Lodge and Barber county, but by loss to Kansas of two of the best citizens of which our State could boast; and
>
> WHEREAS, We recognize the fact that the two men who were the murderers of Mr. Payne and Mr. Geppert had received a large degree of credit, by reason of their employment by this city as peace officers, we deem it due to the citizens of Medicine Lodge that we should take some official notice of the terrible crime that has so shocked their community in regard to the terrible deed. Therefore be it
>
> *Resolved,* by the Mayor and councilmen of the city of Caldwell that the people of Caldwell are horrified by the awful deed which so tragically ended the lives of Mr. Payne and Mr. Geppert, and that they extend to the citizens of Medicine Lodge, and especially to the families and intimate friends of the gentlemen, their deepest and best sympathies in their unconsolable loss, that the people of Caldwell keenly feel the disgrace which her former officers, by their desperately criminal conduct, have brought upon our community. That in no manner whatever, do our citizens entertain any semblance of sympathy for the depraved creatures who have proved themselves the worst enemies of civilized society. And while our people deplore the necessity for lynch law in any case, they do most heartily approve of the summary manner in which the sturdy men of Medicine Lodge administered justice to the scoundrels who so rudely brought death and sorrow to their door.[14]

---

[12] See chap. 35, n. 7, for particulars of Johnson's statement.

[13] The drafting committee consisted of Councilmen M. H. Bennett (see chap. 45), O. Beeson, and J. W. Dobson (*Journal,* 8 May 1884).

[14] The version of the resolution here given differs from that printed in the *Journal* of 8 May 1884 in only one word. Where the "city clerk's book" reads "the people of Caldwell . . . feel the disgrace," the newspaper reads "the people of Caldwell . . . feel the obloquy." Given the choice, make mine *obloquy* every time.

It seems the resolutions are unsigned, and they show quite plainly that the committee was not very well experienced in drafting resolutions,[15] but the sentiments shown seems plainly to be "an eye for an eye and a tooth for a tooth."

[15] I am unable to explain what Freeman found deficient in the resolution.

CHAPTER 37

A Man Borrows a Shot Gun and Leaves the Country—A Warrant
for His Arrest—I Search for the Offender—The Trip to
Arkansas City—We Spy the Thief—A Chew of
Tobacco—I Make the Arrest of the Man—
The Return to Caldwell.

In the year 1880, a man living near Caldwell borrowed a shot gun from a
friend of his, and after obtaining possession of it he left the country, taking
the gun with him. After waiting a certain length of time for the man who
had borrowed the gun to return it, the owner of it swore out a warrant for the
arrest of the guilty party.

As I was an officer it became my duty to find the offender, arrest him,
obtain possession of the much coveted article, and return it to the owner.[1]

I left Caldwell in the early morning and started East, and my intentions
were to proceed to the town of Arkansas City, located in Cowley County,
Kansas. After I had traveled about two miles East of Caldwell, I met Dr.
Black of that town,[2] and I requested his company in making my journey to
Arkansas City.

Dr. Black readily consented to go with me, so he got in the buggy and
we started on our journey. We traveled all day, and about sundown in the
evening we arrived in Arkansas City. I looked around, thinking perhaps the
man was in the city, but my effort to find him proved futile, so we concluded
to remain in the city until morning, when we would again resume our search
for the man and the gun.

We had our team taken care of for the night, and we took in the sights
which were to be seen in the small town of Arkansas City. That was before
the days of the western booms, and Arkansas City had not been boomed as she
has since; hence it was not difficult to view the sights, and in a very few
minutes we had seen everything of any note and were ready to retire for the
night.[3]

---

[1] A warrant would have been issued by a justice of the peace. No record of this warrant
has survived, and since, as Freeman will recount, the matter was settled out of court, no
prosecution to the district court would have occurred. The Caldwell newspapers are silent
on this matter, and so Freeman's is the only extant account.

[2] Dr. Clark Black, of Caldwell. Black came to Caldwell in January of 1879 and thereafter advertised himself as a "Physician and Accoucher," with his office at his residence, a
mile and a half east of town. (*Caldwell Post,* 16 January, 23 January 1879).

[3] Arkansas City's growth began the year previous, in 1879, when the AT&SF arrived.
Arkansas City then became a shipping point for supplies to Indian Territory. Thus that city's
boom began a year earlier than Caldwell's, which started in 1880. Still, Freeman and Dr.

On the following morning we were in readiness to look for the man who had stolen the gun. We drove our team to the state line, a few miles South of the town, but failed to receive any information concerning the object of our search. As we were returning to Arkansas City we met a man traveling on the road and made inquiry of him and described the team and men whom we were hunting to him. He said he had seen two men with a team corresponding with the description I gave, traveling on the road East of Arkansas City, and they were perhaps one mile East of the town when he saw them. He gave us information concerning the crossing on the Walnut River and told us if we would drive rapidly we would probably reach the men at the river crossing.

We started in hot pursuit in the direction given us by the man, and when we came to the river to our surprise we saw the party for whom we were searching. When we arrived on the river bank, they were about midway across the stream and had stopped the team, which were drinking of the cool water.

We waited until the opposite bank was reached by both parties, when I drove my team alongside of the wagon and asked the men for a chew of tobacco. The man that was driving stopped his team, and the man with the gun handed me the requested "chew."

After taking the desired amount, I gave him his tobacco and asked if he wished to sell his gun, and at the same time held my hand for it asking him for the privilege of examining it. Not thinking what my object was in getting possession of the "deadly weepen," he handed it over to me. When I had gained possession of the gun, I felt confident that I would have no trouble in arresting the man. Without suspecting my intentions, the man asked me if I wanted to buy or trade for the gun.

I replied that I did not think I did, as I had gained the possession of it and that I had a warrant for his arrest, charged with stealing the gun. He was taken completely by surprise, and when the facts began to dawn upon him, he began to laugh and he said it was the "slickest arrest he ever heard of."

He asked me if I had a gun; I replied that I had "neither a gun, revolvers, pocket-knife, or a chew of tobacco." He thought it was a strange thing on my part to go in pursuit of a thief and carry no weapons to use in making the arrest or in self-defense. I told him that was not my manner of securing an arrest, and I had always found it advisable, and it was more satisfactory to me, to deal gently with a law breaker and endeavor to secure his arrest without demanding a "throw up" before I was ready, to have him "throw up" probably with a six shooter leveled at my head and within a few inches of

---

Black could not have found much to see; by 1882 the population of Arkansas City was only 1,356 (per Andreas, p. 1597).

my face. I have found this, that in order to accomplish a successful arrest you must be a correct reader of human nature; consequently, it will be necessary to "know your man" and deal with him as his case of human nature may demand.

It is foolish for an officer to risk his life when attempting to arrest a drunken cowboy or desperado. Nine times out of ten when a demand is made by the officer commanding a "throw up," the command is met with a volley of shots fired from the hands of the offender, the shot sometimes taking effect in the head or breast of the officer, and he dies while at his post of duty and while endeavoring to quell disturbances and in attempting to make the arrest of a desperate and lawless citizen of the United States.

The man whom I had arrested got in the buggy and we drove back to Caldwell and was greeted with much warmth by the owner of the gun. The difficulty was settled satisfactorily by the interested parties without calling the case before a court.

Years after this occurrence, when I was in Arkansas City, I met the man who had stolen the gun,[4] and he asked me for a chew of tobacco, and as he did so, he referred to the time when I asked the same favor of him and secured his arrest in such a quiet manner. He said he had never heard of such a case and concluded if all officers would adopt my method of arresting a criminal, there would be less bloodshed and murders committed and a less number of murderers and assassins at large.

[4]It is possible that this meeting occurred in 1885, when Freeman was in the vicinity of Arkansas City with his contingent of Boomers (see Editor's Introduction).

CHAPTER 38

The Indian's Custom When Traveling Among White Settlers—
Women Terrorized When Alone by Hearing, "How, John?"—
Young Lady Refused to Give the Indian Food—Spotted Horse
plays with her Golden Locks—Her Father Comes to the
Rescue—The Marshal Undertakes to Make Him
"Throw Up"—Fires over His Head—"Hold
on John, Me Getting my Gun"—Death
of the Indian and His Burial.

After the advent of the railroad to Caldwell, all government supplies for the Indians was shipped to that place. Heretofore Wichita had supplied the freighter with his load of provision for transportation into the Indian Territory to be delivered at the several Indian agencies.[1]

The white man for many years had hauled the freight to the Indian reservations, and in doing so, he had endured the storms of winter and the heat of the summer, while Lo, the poor Indian, lived a life of idleness and laziness, and I might add, a life of ease and luxury, all at the expense of the government. The Indian passed the hours in hunting, lounging around in the tepee, apparently enjoying a life filled with satisfaction and comfort. The agent gives them their allowances of provision every month; each Indian, little and big, receive a certain proportion of the provisions which the white man had hauled for hundreds of miles.

The idea was conceived, finally, and put into execution by the leaders of our government, in which the Indian could haul their own freight. They had large herds of ponies; the government furnished wagons and harness and provided [that] the Indians would haul the freight and thus save the expense of hiring the white man.[2] The Indians were pleased to visit the state and

---

[1] Freeman oversimplifies the matter somewhat. Arkansas City was also an agency shipping point from 1879 to 1882 (see chap. 37, n. 3). The shipments from Wichita began in 1872 and continued as long as that town was the railhead nearest the Territory. In 1879, when Wellington became a terminus, supplies were shipped from that location (as well as from Arkansas City). Caldwell supplanted Wellington in 1880 and on 1 July 1882 also supplanted Arkansas City, Caldwell becoming the exclusive shipping point at that time (*SCP,* 22 June 1882).

[2] Freeman apparently wants it both ways. On the one hand, he stresses the hardships suffered by the freighters delivering supplies to idle Indians; on the other hand, he chafes at the loss of revenue for freighters when the Indians began hauling their own supplies. Actually, the use of Indian freighters did not altogether eliminate the necessity for using white freighters. For example, supplies were stacked up at Caldwell in 1881 for lack of transport, whatever the color of the freighter (see chap. 2, n. 7). On the other hand, the Indian freighters took on an increasingly large portion of the traffic; the *Caldwell Post*

the numerous towns along their route. An interpreter was sent with each band to secure their freight for them[3] and to keep them from troubling the white people with whom they would come in contact in their travels.

As they traveled to and from Wichita, they would usually stop at the dwelling houses situated along the road and beg provisions from the settlers. One of the strong characteristics of the Indian is an inclination to beg articles of food or wearing apparel. Many times they steal articles of clothing, conceal them under their blankets, and afterwards either trade it, sell it, or adapt to their own use. They seldom wore a protection on their heads, but occasionally one might be seen wearing a hat many sizes too large for him, and a squaw with a parasol of some bright color held above her head as a shield from the rays of the hot sun long, long after the day star had hidden himself below the horizon.

The Indian has a peculiar manner of walking; their feet are encased in a pair of beaded moccasins, which give no sound of their approaching footsteps. Their tread is so light that upon their approach, you are usually taken by surprise to find their presence so near; you are greeted with their manner of salutation, "How, John." The friendly Indian extends his hand and grasps yours with vise grip and assures you that he is a good Indian; then he wants "corn for ponee, chuckaway for pappoose" and continues begging until he is either driven away or the door closed and locked.

Many times when these pests are passing through the country, the husband and father of the house are from home, either in the field at work or away from home on business. The Indian approaches with such quietness that the women folks are surprised and terrorized at the sight of their dusky faces. The fact dawns to the minds of the women that they are alone with the savage. They are so frightened by the presence of the Indian that they lose self control and probably their common sense. The Indian, as usual, offers his hand saying, "How John?" and the trembling woman takes the offered hand saying, "How?" The small amount of the English language possessed by many of the Indians leads them to think that "How John?" is a proper greeting to a white person, whether male or female.

The terror which seizes the wife when alone, when receiving the greeting, "How John?" causes her many times to donate any article of the household that the Indian may chance to demand. A few cases have occurred in which the housewife has given all of the flour, coffee, sugar, and other eatables

reports in July, 1882, that 115 wagons came in that month from the Cheyenne-Arapaho Agency alone (*Post,* 13 July, 20 July 1882). Three years later the *Caldwell Journal* (1 January 1885) states that freighting to the Territory "keeps from forty to one hundred men and teams busy all the time."

[3]See chap. 25, n. 19: J. A. Covington of the Cheyenne-Arapaho Agency was the first to help the Indians undertake this mode of freighting.

which her home possessed. This was done simply to get rid of poor Lo in a friendly way.

The Indian, like other animals, plainly recognizes the fact that white women alone are suddenly seized with fear when he is seen at the door. Sometimes, however, when neighbors are near, or in towns, women are courageous enough to refuse the demands made for grub by the Indians.[4]

On one of these occasions a case like this occurred in the town of Caldwell. Indians had come to Caldwell for government freight or freight for themselves, but the freight not having arrived, they were compelled to wait in camp near the town for its arrival.[5] While there, they concluded begging would be in first class order. One of the Indians, Wild [Spotted] Horse by name, went to the house of Ephriam Beals[6] on one of these begging expeditions; not seeing any man in the house, and thinking Mr. Beals was away from home and that the women [were] alone, he demanded that the young lady, daughter of the household, should get him something to eat. She refused pointedly. Whereupon he seized her by the hair and attempted to force her to grant his request. At this time Mr. Beals, being in an adjoining room, came out and pushed the Indian out of the door, followed him out, and, seizing a spade which lay in the yard, was about to strike him with it, when someone passing by went into the yard and caught the uplifted spade as the Indian was unwrapping his revolver from the blanket which he carried. The Indians by this time concluded it was best to leave and go down into town.[7]

Whereupon Mr. Beals reported to Marshal Henry Brown what had hap-

[4] The intrusions of Indians as Freeman describes them are echoed in most particulars in the *Journal* of 17 May 1883, but the culprits are identified as Pawnees. The *Journal* states: "The Indians belonging to the Cheyenne and Arapahoe and the Kiowa and Comanche agencies never come here except on business, and while here conduct themselves in a manner to give no offense to any one."

[5] The Indian involved in the succeeding episode was not in Caldwell for purposes of freighting, according to the *Journal* of 17 May 1883; he was in town at his own pleasure.

[6] Freeman calls the Indian Wild Horse, contrary to the *Journal* and *SCP* stories of 17 May 1883. I have emended the name throughout. Ephriam H. Beals, a farmer, moved to the Caldwell vicinity in 1880. In November of 1882, he took up residence in the city in order to give his children the benefit of the schools. He died 7 March 1884 of consumption (*Post,* 30 November 1882; *Journal,* 13 March 1884).

[7] Freeman's version differs from the principal newspaper account in several details. According to the *Journal* of 17 May 1883, Beals was at home sitting down to breakfast with his family when Spotted Horse entered the room. Beals ordered him to leave, which he did, but he soon after reentered the house and "put his hand on Miss Beals' head." Beals again ordered him to leave, "at the same time applying an opprobrious epithet to him." Spotted Horse pulled a revolver, whereupon Beals suggested they settle things outside. That is where one Grant Harris found them, Spotted Horse brandishing a pistol and Beals menacing with a spade. Harris reproached Spotted Horse for attacking an old man. Spotted Horse gave Beals a "volley of abuse . . . in good plain English" and left the premises. As for Spotted Horse's "going into town" thereafter, Freeman apparently means the business district. The

pened and that the Indian was carrying a revolver, which was contrary to city ordinance. Marshal Brown went to hunt for Mr. Indian, and finally found him in Mr. Wm. Morris' grocery store.[8] After leaving the house of Mr. Beals, from some source the Indian had received a drink or two of "fire water" and was "Big Injun and Bad Injun."[9] The marshal approached the Indian with revolver in hand, and pointing it toward him, demanded him to "throw up." The Indian, either not understanding what the marshal meant or not being willing to submit, refused to accede to his demand. The marshal, thinking to frighten him, fired his revolver twice just above the Indian's head, which only tended to irate him and cause his desperate courage to raise. He saw there was a chance for a fight. The whiskey had aroused his savage disposition and all the passions and vices of his savage nature.

The novelist in his books of beautiful and pleasing romance may picture the Indian as an innocent, simple-minded character and adopt for him the "noble red man" in place of the name of a savage. Those who have lived on the frontier for years do not address the Indian as the "noble red man"; their character and cruel disposition is too well known, and they are designated by the people simply as the Indian.

When the marshal fired at the Indian, instead of surrendering to the officer, he began unwrapping his revolver and said, "Hold on John, wait, me get my gun." At this statement the marshal saw the Indian was ready for a deadly contest, so he fired at the Indian before he had time to shoot his revolver. The shot took effect, and tore the top of the Indian's head off.[10]

Beals house was in town—on Market Street north of Fifth. The *SCP* (17 May 1883) reports that Spotted Horse—"regarded as a reprobate by the whites and as an outlaw by the Indians for years"—had made such incursions into homes many times before, brandishing a pistol and making demands.

[8] Morris, a member of the troublesome city council of 1881-82 (see chap. 41, n. 6), was mayor of Caldwell for one term, 1884-85. He had become mayor in April, shortly before the Medicine Lodge raid (see chap. 35, n. 2).

[9] The *Journal* reports that Spotted Horse and his wife "helped themselves to breakfast" at the Long Branch kitchen (the employee present offering no objection) before Spotted Horse went, alone, to the Morris grocery. If Spotted Horse did in fact have liquor, perhaps the Long Branch—principally a saloon—was where he got it. On the other hand, a correspondent to the *Wellingtonian* (3 July 1884) claims that Spotted Horse was already drunk when he entered the Beals home.

[10] According to the *Journal,* Brown met Spotted Horse at the grocery store and asked the Indian to accompany him to J. A. Covington, who could serve as a translator. (Covington was a former Darlington Agency employee living in Caldwell; see chap. 25, n. 19). When Spotted Horse refused, Brown "took hold of him," whereupon Spotted Horse "commenced to feel for his revolver." Brown pulled his weapon and told Spotted Horse to stop. When he did not, Brown commenced firing at him. Brown fired four shots, the last striking Spotted Horse in the head at the hairline and emerging from the back. He lived about two hours. Joe Wiedeman, who claimed to have witnessed the incident, said that Brown shot Spotted Horse without warning while the latter was fumbling for the pistol Brown had asked him to

When the shooting occurred there were several Indians near the store; they hastily mounted their ponies and rode to the camp about one and a half miles from town. There were probably one hundred Indians at the camp, and great excitement prevailed throughout the camp.[11] Some of the citizens of the town feared an outbreak among the savages, and the marshal was greatly censured by the timid people for creating a disturbance by killing the Indian. Those who were inclined to fear the cunning savages were very uneasy and filled with anxiety, when they realized the character and disposition possessed by the Indian.

In a short time some of the Indians came into town, accompanied by the dead Indian's squaw. They did not manifest any spirit of revenge and said, "Spotted Horse was a bad Cheyenne."[12] Their expressions led the citizens to believe that Spotted Horse's death was not greatly mourned by the tribe to which he belonged.

The citizens of Caldwell gave the body of Spotted Horse proper burial at the city's expense. Several of the Indians attended the burial services and expressed themselves as satisfied with the actions of the city marshal and of the burial of Spotted Horse.

While the Indians seemed satisfied with the burial given Spotted Horse, his immediate relatives expressed a desire to kill his pony and place it on his grave in order that the animal might accompany him when he reached the "happy hunting ground." This custom was contrary to the rules of modern civilization; the request was refused.[13]

They remained several days in camp south of town and, according to their custom, held their pow-wow's or times of lamentation, but manifested no disposition of revenge toward the people of Caldwell. All seemed satisfied that Spotted Horse was dead, as none of them considered him very much credit to the tribe.

---

produce (Chester C. Heizer, "Hendry Brown, Marshall and Murderer," *Caldwell Messenger,* 8 May 1961).

[11] *Journal:* "The squaw, . . . upon hearing the first shot fired, hitched the horses to the wagon and drove off . . . toward the Territory." The newspaper makes no mention of an Indian encampment near the town.

[12] Spotted Horse, a Pawnee, not a Cheyenne, was killed on May 14. On May 22, a small contingent, riding in two wagons, arrived at Caldwell to claim the body. It would not appear, then, that the large encampment of Indians was within a mile and a half of the city, as Freeman claims (*Journal,* 24 May 1883).

[13] Spotted Horse was buried in the Caldwell cemetery. The group of Pawnees who came for his remains "opened the grave, but finding the body too much decomposed to permit of its removal they went through with their customary rites, replaced the body and filled the grave. Mayor Colson gave the Indians all the assistance he could, for which the Indians expressed great satisfaction." They left Caldwell "for home" on the following day (*Journal,* 24 May 1883).

CHAPTER 39

Court in Session Before a Justice in Caldwell—Steaming Up the
Lawyers—Bent's Ludicrous Plea to the Court—The Justice
Furnishes Money to Treat the Crowd—A Second Trial—
A Novel Way of Giving in a Verdict—A Third Case
Before the Justice Court.—The Justice Gets
Drunk—The Case Settled by Paying Ten
Dollars—The Editor of the *Sumner
County Evening Post* Publishes an
Article on the Drunken Justice—
A Challenge to Fight a Duel—
The Editor Declines to
Accept It.

The bell rings, the curtain rises, showing scenes which are not based upon fiction, but actual facts which actually occurred in Caldwell during the years of 1872 and 1873. Caldwell, not like the novel hero, born of poor but respectable parents, was not born at all. It was like Topsy, "just growed,"[1] and while its population was waiting for a speedy realization of their most cherished hopes and seemingly visionary prophesies, they are in the midst of jocund merriment. The adage for children, "Satan finds some mischief still, for idle hands to do," may be applied to men, whose life is complicated with entire idleness and the love of strong drink.[2]

Life becomes monotonous to the idler, the cowboy, and the Texas steer; for him no longer has it the charms it once possessed. His loneliness in creased when he looks at the immensity of the unpeopled prairie, the infinite sketching of the plains, unbroken by tree or shrub, by fence or house; and he gathers together all of his ideas, in which he may plant something new and present it before the minds of the people. It has been said, "Idleness is the work-shop of satan," but whether his royal highness ever condescended to enlighten his clients, by giving them an opinion, remains a mystery.[3]

I have briefly recorded the dark, gloomy days of Caldwell's early history. This history embraces many scenes of riot and discord, and many unfortunate victims are sleeping beneath the green turf, whose death can be attributed

---

[1] This observation was taken verbatim from the *Caldwell Post,* 1 January 1885.

[2] The foregoing statement appears to be the theme of this chapter. Freeman, like a medieval cleric, seems to have felt the necessity for an uplifting moral to justify his humorous anecdotes. The result, as the reader will see, makes for a strange mixture of tones.

[3] If it is of any comfort to the reader, I am as puzzled as you are. The argument is difficult to follow, and the point obscure. I suspect that this paragraph is another example of poorly grafted plagiarism, but I could not find the source.

to the free use of the six-shooter, or hung by unknown parties; and whiskey, indirectly, may be said to have been the cause of much disorder, bloodshed, and many deaths.

In this chapter I will give the reader an idea how court was held in the early days of Caldwell's history. The incident that I am going to relate was probably instigated by some one belonging to that class of idlers to whom I have referred and was gotten up as a scheme in which the participants could play a good joke on the justice of the town.

This mans name was [B. W.] Fox; and he was the first justice elected after the township had been organized.[4] Fox was a doctor and kept a drug store in Caldwell. The trial of which I am going to relate was held in the drug store. Fox was a man of an excellent reputation and filled the office of justice of the peace very satisfactory.

There had been no trials for a few days, and people concluded it was getting pretty dull in court matters and the lawyers were getting out of the practice of quoting Blackstone; so a little plot was laid in which they were to have some fun over a sham trial. The instigators of the plan did not let either of the lawyers into the secret. One of the men swore out a warrant before the justice for the arrest of one of the parties, who was into the secret, and brought it to me to serve. I knew of the joke perpetrated, so I arrested the man and subpoenaed ten or twelve witnesses for the trial, all of whom were into the secret. While I was serving the subpoena, the leaders of the joke were getting the lawyers ready for action by treating them freely to whiskey, or to use their expression, they were "steaming them up." When they were "steamed up" about as high as they could be under control of the men, I called the court to order.[5] The witnesses were sworn to "tell the truth." Good order prevailed while the witnesses were giving their evidence, and after all the testimonies were given to the court, a few minutes were needed in which the lawyers could add a little more "steam." Court was adjourned for this purpose and the crowd entered the saloon. It was expected the lawyers would make a lengthy plea for their clients, and a high gauge of "steam" would be necessary in order to have a fine time.

In about thirty minutes court was again called to order, and every one in the court room became silent. The lawyer on the defense was a very small

[4]The first township justices were M. H. Lester and George Mack (see chap. 6), but they were elected at the special election of 26 September 1871 and may have declined to qualify in view of the impending regular election on November 7. B. W. Fox was Caldwell's first physician and one of its earliest justices of the peace (Andreas, p. 1503). When he left Caldwell is uncertain; he died at Taylorville, Illinois, in 1875 (*SCP,* 29 July 1875).

[5]Why Freeman (a township constable at the time) would, in effect, determine when court should convene and—as he states later—request order from the spectators is inexplicable.

man and usually went by the name "Yank;" he had a large share of self conceit and placed great stress on his ability as a lawyer.[6] He could make a good speech when he was well "steamed up."

The lawyer for the state having waived the opening speech, "Yank" took the floor and made a lengthy plea in defense of his client, but as soon as his "steam" began to be exhausted he weakened and took his seat. All the while "Yank" was speaking, the other lawyer was indulging in drinking whiskey every few minutes, and the consequences were that he was "steamed up" to the highest notch in the gauge and yet had some to spare.

He was a large man, weighing perhaps two hundred and fifty pounds;[7] [he] was well known through the west; he served the office of deputy sheriff of Cowley county before he came to Caldwell and was elected several times to act as an officer of Sumner county. By his intimate friends he was known by no other appendage but simply "Bent," and in referring to him in this chapter, we will use the name which is familiar to his many friends. He was a man of good reputation and had many excellent qualities as a citizen.

As "Bent" arose to take the floor vacated by his opponent, I saw the crowd was about to burst out into a laugh; I requested order and they were soon quieted; "Bent" had on such a powerful gauge of "steam" that his locomotion was badly interfered with, and he took hold of the counter and tried to steady himself while making his plea. After speaking a few minutes, he turned to the justice and, looking at him steadily in the face, raised himself to his entire height by standing on his tiptoes, and said, "Now Mr. Court, as the people say bind him over, you must say bind him over, and God says bind him over, and I say, By G—d, bind him over."

While "Bent" was finding a seat, the audience were yelling and applauding the speech made by him. The justice began to look at the lawyers, then at the witnesses; meanwhile the crowd were hurrahing and shouting to the extent allowed them by their vocal organs.

The justice hesitated a few minutes, then the secret began to dawn, and he saw through the whole plans and knew the easiest and quickest manner

---

[6] The identity of "Yank" is uncertain. He was, by 1873, a justice of the peace, as Freeman reports later. Thus he may be A. E. Badger, who also figures subsequently in this chapter.

[7] This was T. H. B. ("Bent") Ross, who has appeared before in this chronicle and will appear again (see chap. 5, n. 8, for a synopsis of his career; see also chap. 40). Ross's girth was frequently noted in the Caldwell press; W. B. Hutchison (no sylph himself by all accounts) referred to Ross in print as "Fatty" Ross (*Caldwell Commercial,* 7 July 1881); and on the occasion of Ross's receiving the Democratic nomination for the office of probate judge, the Republican *Post* (16 September 1880) waxed poetic: "If only rotundity/With solemn profundity/Could gain you the day T.H.B.,/You'd be sure of election./But now, on reflection,/your chances are slim, do you see."

to settle it. He saw it was a joke on him, for he had used all the dignity he could muster and looked very wise throughout the trial. He put his hand into his pocket and drew out a couple of dollars and said, "Gentlemen you all know I do not drink, but you can take this and do as you wish with it, and I hope it will pay all costs which have accrued relative to this trial."

No dismissal of court was necessary, and the crowd went to a saloon and drank to the health of justice Fox, each one feeling it was good to be there.[8] The reader will readily draw his own conclusions concerning the object of the trial. Whiskey was the ruling element, and the man who very often treated his friends and companions to a "social glass" was the most admired and looked upon as the champion of the crowd and in the community at large. The man who drinks, and carries a fat pocket book, and contributes largely towards treating his companions, is always favored among that class of people so long as his money and generosity lasts; but let the dark hours of adversity come to his abiding place and share a large proportion of his life, then these friends flee from him, leaving him to share his hours of misfortune and disappointments alone. They "want full measure for all their pleasure" but do not want his woe.

How many men in after years, when taking a retrospective view of their life, wish when [they] started to spend the evening with wild companions, either at the saloon or club, they had heeded to the advice of mother, sister, or the wife; and how often, thoughts similar to these words come rushing to [their] mind: "the fondest hopes I cherished, all have faded one by one."

I will now relate the facts concerning a trial held before the second justice of Caldwell.[9]

The evidence as shown in the suit was that W. B. King and John Turner went on a buffalo hunt together, and while they were out hunting a horse was found, and each man claimed the right of possession. Turner was the successful man, however, and got possession and took the horse home with him. King replevined the horse, and the result was a trial before the justice court. Turner and King wanted a trial by jury to determine who would have the right of possession of the horse.

After the jury were selected the trial proceeded; and peace reigned throughout the trial until the jury were ready to give their verdict to the court. The jury demanded their fees before they would proceed to give in their decision. The plaintiff and defendant both refused to pay the jury fees. The jury stood

---

[8] Adolph Roenigk used the foregoing anecdote in his *Pioneer History of Kansas.* He attributed it to "a book written by a resident of Caldwell, Kansas," another example of Freeman's name being left out.

[9] This justice was assuredly A. E. Badger, though how he may be called the second justice is not at all clear. Both Badger and B. W. Fox were Caldwell Township justices during 1872 (*King v. Turner,* Clerk of the District Court, Sumner County, Kansas).

firm in their resolution, and as the hour was getting late court was adjourned until the following morning at ten o'clock.

I was constable and was ordered to take the jury and keep them from having any conversation with any one until their verdict was rendered to the court. I engaged a comfortable room and got their suppers for them. Everything was passing pleasantly along until about nine o'clock in the night.

One of the jurors was a clerk in C. H. Stone's store,[10] and [Stone] wanted the clerk to go to Wichita early the next morning to haul a load of supplies from that place to Caldwell. Mr. Stone came to me and wanted me to dismiss the clerk, who was acting as juror. I told Mr. Stone I could not dismiss him until the jury gave their decision to the court. This did not satisfy the merchant, so he went to see the justice about it.

In a short time Mr. Stone and the justice came to me and the justice said the clerk could tell him what his decision was, and he was not to give in the decision until the jurors received their fees. This was satisfactory to the remaining jurors and the clerk went with Mr. Stone, and early the next morning he started on the road to Wichita.

The following morning I took the jurors into the court room, where the parties concerned paid them their fees and waited for their verdict. The justice and the five jurors gave in their verdict, giving the plaintiff possession of the horse. The defendant appealed the case to a higher court.[11]

The reader will conclude that we were badly in need of a little knowledge relating to the profession of law. Caldwell, like all the towns on the frontier, had to "live and learn"; in the learning, her officers would often afford a great deal of mirth and amusement for those who were inclined to be merry.

In the year of 1872 [1873], a man by the name of McClain [A. C. McLean] brought suit against me for the sum of sixty-eight dollars.[12] This man McLean was the proprietor of the Last Chance Ranch. He was in debt to me for the sum of eight dollars, and before the time of the suit he said he had the advantage of me, as the justice was a particular friend of his.

McLean sued me on Monday and the suit was to be tried on the following Saturday. I sent to Wellington and employed J. Wade McDonald, of Wellington, as my lawyer in the trial.[13] On Saturday morning the justice began to

[10] For identification of C. H. Stone and his store, see chap. 2, n. 1. The clerk is otherwise unidentified.

[11] The jury in the justice court awarded the horse to plantiff King on 10 September 1872. In April, 1873, Turner appealed to the district court but did not prevail. He was out $76.65 in court costs; the horse was valued at $15 *(King v. Turner)*.

[12] Freeman gives the year as 1872, but his later reference to John H. Folks's publishing the *Sumner County Press* at Wellington pinpoints the year as 1873. Folks did not begin the *SCP* at Wellington until May, 1873. A. C. McLean is treated in chap. 26, n. 6. To the best of my knowledge no record of this suit against Freeman has survived.

[13] J. Wade McDonald served as Sumner County probate judge from 1873 to 1875 and

indulge pretty freely in drinking whiskey, and about ten o'clock he was pretty well "steamed up." I went to his office and told him I wanted a change of venue. He said, "(hic) (hic) why can't the suit (hic) be tried before me?" I told him he was too drunk to attend to the case. He said, "(hic) you may write up the necessary papers for a change of venue, and I'll sign it." My lawyer had not arrived yet, and I wrote the business papers and took them to get the justice's signature; he gave a couple of faint hic's and said he was not able to sign the article, but if any one would sign his name for him he would be very much pleased. No sooner had he finished speaking than he fell off his chair and lay in a drunken stupor.

I knew our suit could not be tried that day and that it would be proper and right that we should pay due respects to the court. We considered over the matter and finally decided the best way to pay our respects would be to take proper care of the justice; so we took him to a livery barn and tucked him away in the feed room and left him lying on the floor of the oat bin.

As I was leaving the barn, I met Mr. McDonald and John T. Showalter[14] at the door; they alighted and had their team taken care of by the employe of the livery stable. Judge McDonald asked me how I was getting along with my trial. I replied that I presumed my chances were pretty good and that the prospects were not favorable concerning the time for trial, for the justice had entered a trance, and in all probability he would not recover from its effects for several days. The lawyer went to the feed room and looked at the justice and returned to me, and shaking his head, said sadly, "There is no chance for a trial to-day, that poor fellow has taken an overdose of 'red eye,' consequently he must sleep off the effects."

While I was engaged in conversation with Judge McDonald, Mr. McLean approached us and asked me how much I would give him to settle our suit without bringing it for trial. I replied that I would not give him anything. A fellow townsman who was standing near turned to McLean and asked him how much he would take to settle it. Mr. McLean replied that he would settle it for ten dollars in cash; whereupon the man gave him ten dollars and took a receipt for the money received, also a written statement giving dates of the

---

as county attorney from January of 1875 until June of 1876, when the office was declared vacant by reason of McDonald's moving from the county (Richards, "History of Sumner County," *Historical Atlas,* pp. 9-10).

[14] John T. Showalter, a Wellington attorney, came to Sumner County in 1872. He was elected register of deeds for one term in 1876. In addition to practicing law, he was involved in the livestock business (Andreas, p. 1501). On one of his cattle-buying expeditions to Sherman, Texas, he was mistaken for one of the James boys, which prompted the *SCP* (9 March 1882) to jibe that Showalter "always was a hard looking citizen."

first acquaintance I had with Mr. McLean and certifying the payments of all debts up to the present date.[15]

McLean took the ten dollars and went to a saloon and [invited] the by-standers to come on and have something to drink. Before McLean left the bar, he had squandered all of the ten dollars, excepting fifty cents, which he said must be paid to the justice for the trouble and care he had experienced since the case had been brought before that honorable personage.

This justice was the lawyer I have mentioned who took part in the joke played on Justice Fox. This was lawyer "Yank," who took the case in behalf of the defense and plead his mightiest plea, and after court adjourned, he, in company with others, drank to the health of Justice Fox.

The day was a dull one in court business, there being only five law suits before the other justice. Mr. McDonald was employed as lawyer on all the cases, and at night I went to him and asked what his charges were against me. He replied that it had been a poor day for law suits, as one of the justices was drunk. He also said that his time had been well improved during the day, and he would not ask anything from me, as my case had not been called for trial; consequently I paid nothing, excepting the ten dollars, which I afterwards paid to the man who had settled with McLean.

Thus ended a day in which the lawyers were the victors, they having received the good will of their client, who treated them to an extra glass of whiskey, and they were also the fortunate ones, as I presume their pocket books were well filled with bright sheckels of silver, or a sufficient amount of currency to pay a board bill at a fifteen cent restaurant.

A few days after Judge McDonald's return to Wellington, the "Sumner County Press," published at Wellington, contained an article supposed to have been written by the editor, J. H. Folks.[16] The article was something similar to the following, if not quite the same language: "While we were in the town of Caldwell, we met our friend and fellow townsman, John T. Showalter, who was quietly waiting for the justice to sober up so he could have a lawsuit."

This article insulted Justice "Yank," and he immediately sent a written

---

[15] I am unable to identify Freeman's obliging friend.

[16] John H. Folks was a member of the town company which founded Oxford, Kansas, in 1871. He operated a newspaper, the *Oxford Times,* from 1872 until 1873. In May of that year he began the *Sumner County Press* at Wellington, which he edited until 1881, when he sold the paper to A. A. Richards. Folks was county coroner from 1878 to 1882, during some of the bloodier episodes described in this volume, including the death of George Flatt, when a coroner's jury's verdict led to the arrest of the mayor and the police force of Caldwell (see chap. 31, n. 20). Folks moved to San Diego, California, sometime prior to 1890 (*History of Kansas Newspapers,* p. 305; Andreas, p. 1498; *Portrait and Biographical Album of Sumner County, Kansas,* p. 271).

challenge to the editor of the press, requesting him to meet him in the Indian Territory and fight a duel to the death of one or both parties concerned.

The editor made mention of the challenge he had received in language something like this: "This was the first time in all our life we had received a challenge to fight a duel, and not being of a chivalrous turn of mind, we refused to accept it." It will be observed by the reader that the press has made no mention of "Yank" being drunk, and why "Yank" had been insulted, it would be difficult to conjecture.[17]

I presume the challenge was not accepted, or at least I am certain the duel was never fought.

---

[17] The issue of the *SCP* in which this event was reported appears not to have survived. Though the newspaper began in May, the first extant issue is 18 September 1873.

CHAPTER 40

Escape of a Horse Thief from the Sheriff of Cowley County,
Kansas—The Arrival of the Thief at the "Last Chance"
Ranch—I Go to Assist the Deputy Sheriff in Making
the Arrest—Our Arrival with the Thief Causes
Great Excitement in Caldwell—An Attempt to
Lynch the Prisoner—a Scheme in Which the
Prisoner Was Taken from the Town—
The Mob Demand the Prisoner from
the Guards—Foiled in Their
Attempt

In the month of July, 1872, the Deputy Sheriff of Cowley county, Kansas, came to Caldwell in search of a horse thief who had escaped from the hands of the sheriff. It seems there was no jail in Winfield in which to keep the prisoner, so it became necessary for the sheriff to guard him. The sheriff shackled one of the prisoners feet and allowed him liberty, to a certain extent, and everything was all right until one evening the prisoner was sent by the sheriff to get his cows and drive them home. The prisoner went to the wood pile, secured an ax, and succeeded in cutting the shackles from his foot; and once loose, he made the best of his liberty, and instead of going for the cows, he went to the Indian Territory, and traveling west, he arrived in a short time at the Ranch called the "Last Chance," which the reader will remember as the place McCarty sought as a refuge after he had killed Fielder and Doc Anderson.

This Ranch has been brought very prominently before the minds of the reader, and what tales of dissipation, night revelry, and bloodshed would be told could its old log foundation reveal to the minds of the inquisitive people of later years.

When the horse thief arrived at the "Last Chance" he remained there over night and on the morrow started for Pond Creek Ranch, which is located twenty-six miles south of Caldwell, and the ranch derives its name from the name of the Creek upon which it is located.

When the sheriff became aware of the prisoners escape, he sent the deputy sheriff, T. H. B. Ross[1] by name, to Caldwell in search of the horse thief. Mr. Ross, or "Bent" as he was familiar called, came to me and asked my assistance in making the arrest. It was then about six o'clock in the evening, and I told "Bent" that I would go to the "Last Chance" and see if the man was there. The Ranch was kept by McLean, and when I arrived there I asked

[1] For data on Ross, see chap. 5, n. 8, and chap. 39, n. 7.

McLean if the man had been there, giving a description of the thief. McLean said there had been no one there answering that description. I imagined I could see a change of countenance in Mr. McLean, and I was satisfied in my own mind that the thief had been at the Ranch and had probably received assistance from McLean.

I turned my horse and started toward Caldwell, and when I had rode about fifty yards, I met a young man who motioned for me to stop. I did so, and he said if I would give him one dollar and not tell any person about it, he would tell me where the man was I wanted. I gave him the money, and he said a man came to the Ranch the night before, arriving there about twelve o'clock. The man was given something to eat, and he left a couple of hours before daylight and had told the proprietor of the ranch that he was going to Pond Creek and remain at the Ranch until he could get into company with some cattlemen and travel with them until he reached Texas.

I went to the town and reported the information I had received to the Deputy Sheriff. "Bent" did not care to arrest the man alone and asked me to accompany him to Pond Creek. I declined doing so unless he would give me half of the reward which had been offered for the arrest of the escaped thief. "Bent" readily agreed to share the reward with me and also said he would furnish the team and buggy to take us to the Pond Creek Ranch.

We made preparations to start for the Ranch; we took along some provisions and a large quantity of beer. "Bent" was a lover of beer; hence he laid in a good supply of that article. When we were ready to start, a man by the name of Colonel Connoble[2] offered to help us make the arrest, so we three "lit out" and reached Pond Creek about noon. We drove up near the door and I jumped out of the buggy and entered the ranch. The Deputy and Colonel Connoble followed me, and as I entered the door, I noticed a man answering the description of the thief as it was given me by "Bent."

I stepped near the man and waited for the other two men to come in the house. When "Bent" came in he gave me an introduction to the man; I held out my hand to shake hands, and I seized his with a good grip and at the same time reached into my pocket with my left hand and produced a pair of hand-cuffs; I put one of them on one of his wrists and requested him to hold his other hand while I made the cuffs secure; thus I acquainted him of my purpose and mission into the Indian Territory. The prisoner was very much frightened and shook as though he was sitting astraddle of an electric wire with the full force of the electricity applied to that particular place in the wire.

We ate dinner at the ranch and had the ranchman feed our horses, and that afternoon we started toward Caldwell. Our prisoner gave us no trouble but became very submissive to our wishes and requests.

[2] Connoble appears earlier. See chap. 24, n. 1, for background.

Upon our arrival in Caldwell, we were met with some difficulty which nearly proved the fate of the prisoner. When we stopped the team, the spring wagon was surrounded with a crowd containing twenty-five or thirty men. I got out of the wagon on the left side of it; the prisoner and the deputy got out on the right side of the wagon, and the men began to crowd around the prisoner, shutting him from our view; then he was seized by several men, and their intentions were, I suppose, to deal with him according to the justice they deemed best.[3] I saw the condition of affairs and realized the perilous situation the prisoner was in, so I ran around the wagon and was followed by three men who came to my assistance, and by immediate action, we succeeded in getting the prisoner from their power, whereupon, we took him to a house and put a strong guard of men around it to protect the prisoner, in case of an attempt to get him by force. The crowd assembled themselves near the house and made a demand for the prisoner. I was very anxious that the prisoner should reach the adjoining county and have his trial, which would undoubtedly prove his guilt or innocence, as the jury might decide; but here the case looked very doubtful whether the prisoner would ever see Cowley county again. I feared the men would take him from us by force and lynch him by hanging him to the nearest tree. I went to the group of men and talked with them concerning the crime for which the prisoner was arrested. I told them the horse had been stolen in Cowley county and I did not think it was of any interest to them as the crime was not committed in our county. I informed them that I would accompany the deputy in taking the prisoner to Cowley county. This seemed to quiet the men, and after much talking and hesitancy on their part they said if I would see that the prisoner reached Winfield as soon as possible, they would not make any more trouble. This satisfied me, and I supposed I would not experience any more trouble. But not so; in less than half an hour a friend came to me and informed me that the party had assembled themselves together in a barn and were making arrangements to take the prisoner from me at about two o'clock that night.

Upon receiving this startling intelligence, I began to ponder and wonder how I could get the prisoner out of town. I thought if I could get him out of town I could rush to Wellington with him and thereby escape falling into the hands of the mob. I was aware that I would be unable to take the prisoner from Caldwell unless it was under concealment, and I began to make the necessary preparations to start immediately with the prisoner and take him to a place of safety. I took four men into my confidence and we laid a scheme,

[3] The willingness of a Sumner County vigilance committee to lynch a Cowley County horse thief must be understood in the context of the time. This was 1872, shortly after "Tom Smith" was lynched for stealing Freeman's horses (see chap. 19) and at a time when a ring of thieves was believed to be operating throughout southern Kansas (see chap. 27, n. 1).

which if properly carried out without exciting the suspicions of the mob, we would be sure of a successful operation and would reach Wellington in safety.

In order to successfully carry out our desired plan, we resorted to a little game of stratagem, in which the prisoner was to get into the buggy, or spring wagon, and lie down, placing himself in a doubled up position; the buffalo robe was thrown over him carelessly, but in such a manner as to conceal him from observation. The harness was also thrown into the wagon and one of my assistants took hold of the wagon tongue while another led the horses, walking behind the wagon, and giving some assistance by pushing the wagon along, thus making the load much easier to pull. I designated a place at which they were to take the wagon, and I would put in an appearance as soon as I possibly could without exciting the suspicions of the mob. As the men, with the horses and wagon, passed a group of men, the man leading the horses asked if any of them knew of a good place to lariat the horses. And likewise in hearing of the crowd, the men who were guarding the house in which the prisoner was supposed to be kept were cautioned to attend strictly to their business and endeavor to keep the prisoner at all hazards, and that they would return as quickly as they could lariat the horses and go home and eat their suppers.

Of course the guards knew the prisoner was into the wagon, but in order to carry out our scheme they were to remain at the house on guard until two o'clock, when we supposed the mob would congregate at the house and demand possession.

I borrowed a horse from a friend and [before I] started home, I went to the barn, where a large crowd of men had assembled, and informed them that I was going home and in all probability would not be back to town until the following morning. I assumed a very indifferent manner concerning the fate of the prisoner, which had the desired effect on the men. I turned and rode toward home and on my way I chuckled with delight at the success I had had so far. When I reached my pasture I turned the horse loose which I was riding, and bridled and saddled my own pony; I knew the speed of my horse was hard to beat, and in the case at hand, I needed a good horse; consequently, I took my horse. I rode up to my house, informed my wife where I was going, and hastened on my way to overtake the parties who had the horses and wagons.

I did not enter the town but started north-east and rode across the prairie and soon found the men, whom were waiting, very anxiously, for my arrival. Quickly we put on the harness and hitched to the spring wagon, and started for Wellington. We did not know how soon the mob would learn of our trick and start in pursuit of us, so we drove as rapidly as we could under the circumstances. I rode the horse, and the deputy drove the team, and about two o'clock [A.M.] we arrived at Wellington with the prisoner. We stopped in

Wellington long enough to feed and rest our horses. Our party went to a hotel and ordered a lunch, and after we had finished eating it, we started for Winfield, Cowley County. About eight o'clock in the morning we arrived in Oxford, where we stopped and fed our horses and went to a restaurant and ordered breakfast.

When we left Oxford I found that "Bent," the deputy, had indulged freely in drinking Oxford "fire water,"[4] and its effects were betrayed by various symptoms; the most prevalent was a desire to run the horses. His rapid driving landed us in Winfield about two o'clock in the afternoon. As we entered the town we met the sheriff, who took charge of the prisoner.

The prisoner was tried, convicted, and sent to serve a term of two years in the state penitentiary. When I arrived in Caldwell, I was informed of the proceedings which occurred on the evening I left there. It seems the mob did not "catch on" to our plans, and about two o'clock in the morning a posse of armed men came to the house in which they supposed the prisoner was guarded, and demanded of the men who were guarding the house that they should give them possession of the prisoner; one of the guards told them that I had taken the prisoner about eleven o'clock and started to Winfield and he presumed we were at Wellington. This caused great excitement, and they said they would settle with me when I returned to Caldwell. But I have never heard from them concerning the "settlement" from that day to this.

[4]Oxford was organized as an officially dry community, even before the state prohibition law was passed in 1881. But, as the *SCP* (21 December 1881) points out, "there never was a time when whiskey could not be obtained in Oxford one way or the other."

CHAPTER 41

Jim Talbot and His Gang of Desperadoes Arrive in Caldwell—They
Remain Several Days—Arrest of One of the Desperadoes—His
Fine Paid by a Comrade—The Bloody Battle Between Talbot's
Men and the Citizens—Jim Talbot Stands Boldly to the
Front—Balls Flying in All Directions—Frightened
Women and Children—Jim Talbot Shoots the
City Mayor—George Spears Is Killed in the
Battle—The Desperadoes Leave Town—
A Posse of Citizens in Hot Pursuit.

The winter has come, and the autumn months have gone. December, the month most cherished by the children because Christmas is coming, has at last arrived. This month is celebrated by much merry making, both by the younger people and the aged ones. The opera house is opened for the theater; "Uncle Tom's Cabin" has been attended by the lovers of the dramatic stage.[1] The month is to be a festival one and filled with all descriptions of mirth and gayety which compose a season of festivities.

Some time during the forepart of December, 1881, a man by the name of Jim Talbot, formerly from Texas, arrived in the town of Caldwell;[2] he

---

[1] *Uncle Tom's Cabin* was indeed playing at the Caldwell opera house. It opened on Friday night, 16 December 1881, the evening before the famous Talbot raid. The *SCP* (22 December 1881), reviewing the traveling company's production in Wellington on the fifteenth, said, "The play is getting so old that people do not appreciate it as they once did."

[2] Jim Talbot—alias James Sherman, alias Jim Daniels—had a long-standing reputation as a Texas desperado, according to a biographical sketch in the *Caldwell Commercial* of 22 December 1881. He had visited Caldwell the previous March, when he was jailed as a result of a drunken spree. Though Freeman places Talbot's next arrival in "the forepart of December, 1881," the *Commercial* indicates it was six weeks to two months prior to the incident of 17 December. Sheriff Joseph M. Thralls's fugitive circular described Talbot as "about 5 feet, 10 inches high; weighs about 170 pounds; light complection; light colored mustache and whiskers; light blue or gray eyes; broad face, high cheek bones; nose turned up a little at the end; low, narrow forehead; his under jaw is the longest; when he shuts his mouth his teeth projects [*sic*] out past upper ones; generally gambles and carouses around saloons. . . . He is wanted in several places for horse stealing and shooting men. Is a bad outlaw" (*Caldwell Post*, 4 January 1883). Talbot was born in Dekalb County, Missouri (*Wellington Monitor-Press*, 18 April 1895). Sam P. Ridings (*The Chisholm Trail*, p. 481) said that Talbot's full name was James Sherman Talbott, Sherman being his mother's family name, and that he adopted the alias of James Sherman after leaving Caldwell. Most sources, however, flatly state that the real name was Sherman (*Commercial, SCP*, 22 December 1881; McNeal, *When Kansas Was Young*, pp. 190-91); corroboration may be found in the name of a brother—Rollan Sherman—who appeared at Talbot's trial (*Monitor-Press*, 11 April 1895). D. D. Leahy reports that Talbot/Sherman was rumored to be the nephew of General W. T. Sherman (*Wichita Eagle*, 4 April 1932).

had in company with him a woman who was represented as his wife. Talbot rented a dwelling house in the eastern part of the town and moved there with his wife.[3] He was joined by six confederates, men who had formerly lived either in Texas or in the southern part of the Indian Territory.[4]

These men were desperadoes and were constantly giving the marshal trouble by their daring feats and the free use they made of their sixshooters. They visited the numerous places of amusement, accompanied by the prostitutes of the "Red Light" dancing hall, and made disturbances by using loud, obscene language in the presence of ladies,[5] or by their braggadocia, which they displayed while they were under the influence of whiskey.

W. N. Hubble was the city mayor,[6] and six or eight men were detailed

[3] In addition to his wife, whom he married in 1876, Talbot had two children with him: a boy named Jimmy, about three or four years old, and a girl of about one or two years (*Post,* 4 January 1883). The house—which he rented from Dan W. Jones (see chap. 31, nn. 5 and 20)—was located to the north of Fifth on Chisholm Street, facing east. A block almost due east of Talbot's back yard was the Red Light dance house, facing south on Fifth (*Commercial, SCP,* 22 December 1881; *Monitor-Press,* 11 April, 18 April 1895. Ridings, p. 473, places Talbot's house more than a block north of Fifth, but the contrary evidence is most convincing).

[4] The six confederates were Bob Bigtree, Dick Eddleman, Doug Hill, Tom Love, Jim Martin, and Bob Munson. Others involved in one way or another were Tom Delaney and two local men, Comanche Bill Mankin and George Spear (*Commercial, SCP,* 22 December 1881). Sheriff Thralls's reward notice describes four of the original six: "*Bob Bigtree,* about 6 feet high; slim build; stoop shoulders, hollow breast; light complection; light blue or gray eyes; coarse features; smooth shaven when last seen; weighs about 150 pounds. *James Martin,* About 5 feet 7 inches high; heavy build; light complection; light blue or gray eyes; round face; no whiskers when last seen; thumb nail on right hand shot off; weighs 165 pounds. *Bob Munson,* About 5 feet 5 inches high, sandy complection, sandy mustache; short hair, blue eyes, slim build, weight 140 pounds. *Dug Hill,* About 5 feet 9 inches high, slim build; hump shoulder; short hair, blue eyes; light complection; light hair and mustache; weight 144 or 150 pounds. They are cow boys and some of them 'Cow Thieves'" (*Post,* 4 January 1883). George Spear will be remembered as the successor to George Woods as proprietor of the Red Light (see chap. 32, n. 8). Commanche Bill Mankin seems to have had no local reputation as a troublemaker up to this time.

[5] The culmination of this offensive behavior occurred on the evening of 16 December: "Last Friday evening the [Talbot] crowd went to hear *Uncle Tom's Cabin,* attended by their prostitutes. Their conversation was so loud and obscene as to disturb the whole house. Mr. Tell W. Walton, editor of the Caldwell *Post,* requested their leader, Jim Talbot, to desist from his obscenity. In return, Talbot cursed him and publicly declared that he would 'fix him the next day'" (*SCP,* 22 December 1881). Walton wryly explained in his own paper that on the next day, "one editor was too sharp for him and was out of his way" (*Post,* 22 December 1881). Yet Walton would be among the most persistent of the citizen pursuers of Talbot before the day was over.

[6] Freeman misremembered. Cass Burrus, not W. N. Hubbell, was mayor of Caldwell at this time. Hubbell was elected in April of 1881 but resigned in September after an intransigent clique of councilmen refused to approve a series of Hubbell nominees for appointment as city marshal. The clique consisted of H. C. Challes (see chap. 31, n. 4,

to act as policemen and to assist the marshal in suppressing riots and in preventing disturbances.[7] Talbot's men were frequent visitors of the "Red Light,"
and several of the men were arrested and fined for creating a disturbance.
His confederates paid his fine, and he was set at liberty. His arrest was
censured by Talbot and his men; they resolved to take the town in true desperado style. The citizens had prepared themselves, and the marshal with his
assistants were on the alert.[8]

Jim Talbot has never been equaled by the bravery and daring which he
portrayed in the city of Caldwell. On the morning of December 17th, 1881,
he, in company with his men, had been drinking and firing off their revolvers promiscuously. The citizens together with the marshals resolved to
rid the town of the blood-thirsty men or make them submit to the rules
and regulations of the city laws. Talbot and his party had made several threats,
prophesying what would be the fate of ex-mayor and city marshals.[9]

---

for biographical details); Levi Thrailkill, a grocer; and L. G. Bailey, a saddler. Burrus, an
attorney, went to Caldwell in 1879. He was elected mayor at a special election on 20 September 1881. A GAR veteran, he served in the Fourteenth Illinois Infantry, from which
service he received a disability pension. A biographical sketch appears in Andreas, p. 1503.
W. N. Hubbell operated Caldwell's largest general-merchandise store. He figures in this
narrative later. (*Commercial,* 31 March, 7 July, 14 July, 21 July, 4 August, 8 September,
23 September 1881, 27 March, 7 February 1884; *Post,* 21 August 1879, 8 January 1880,
13 January 1881). The identity of the mayor of Caldwell at the time of the Talbot raid
is indeed a matter of confusion in the literature. Some modern historians have followed
Freeman in naming Hubbell; McNeal (*When Kansas Was Young,* p. 189) names Mike
Meagher. As early as 1895, however, the *Monitor-Press* (11 April) asserted that H. C.
Challes was acting mayor, and, to compound the confusion, the *Wellington Quid Nunc,*
only six years after the event, identified Mike Meagher as marshal (repr. *Journal,* 16 June
1887).
    [7] Soon after his election Burrus did augment the police force. The *Post* (29 September
1881) reported: "Our Mayor says that if three policemen can't keep law and order and enforce the ordinance[s], sixteen can, and that he proposes to have law and order if he has
to swear in every able-bodied man in town. We understand there were about a few sworn in
Saturday evening." It appears, however, that the force was back to its undermanned state
by December, when the Talbot raid occurred. The city marshal was John Wilson (see chap.
30, n. 5, for background); his assistant was W. D. Fosset, an erstwhile grocer who had
served with the First Minnesota Rangers in the war (*SCP,* 22 December 1881; *Post,* 8
January 1880; *Journal,* 2 June 1887).
    [8] The readiness of the citizens and the marshal's force is questionable, as succeeding
events will show. Though all of the Caldwellites acquitted themselves well, it seems clear
that their responses were ad hoc. Certainly nothing like a contingency plan appears to have
existed.
    [9] The former mayor, as Freeman later states, was Mike Meagher. Meagher, operator
of the Arcade Saloon, which he opened shortly after his arrival in Caldwell in 1879, was
mayor during 1880 and 1881, his term having expired in April (*Post,* 25 December 1879,
8 April 1880). During his tenure as mayor, it will be remembered, he was arrested on
suspicion of complicity in the death of George Flatt (see chap. 31, n. 20). Prior to moving

Talbot acted as the captain of his men, and about nine o'clock in the morning of December 17th, 1881, a disturbance was raised by Talbot, purposely it was presumed, thus affording him the advantage he wanted. He was standing on Main Street, when he began firing his revolver; his voice sounded in the air, "Hide out little ones."[10] A number of citizens armed themselves to assist the marshals. Each man armed with a gun or revolver were in hiding behind the stores, outhouses, and any place that would serve as a fortification or would shield them from the shots fired by the desperate Jim Talbot and his gang.

The bold and fearless form of Jim Talbot was the center of the firing. He stood bravely to the front, with revolver in each hand, firing at the men he had premeditated to kill. Shots fired by the citizens were striking the buildings and tearing up the ground in all directions near the fearless leader who stood undaunted by shot or bullet, watching for the men who were to be his victims.

to Caldwell, Meagher lived in Wichita, where he served as city marshal during the years 1871-74 and 1875-77. He also served as a deputy U.S. marshal. His career in both Wichita and Caldwell is detailed in Miller and Snell, *Why the West Was Wild,* pp. 472-506. D. D. Leahy, writing in the *Wichita Eagle* of 4 April 1932, said Meagher was born in County Cavan, Ireland. The alleged motives behind Talbot's desire to kill Meagher are discussed in chap. 42 and n. 12 of that chapter.

[10]Freeman has compressed a number of details here. According to contemporary newspaper accounts, the disturbance was begun not by Talbot but by George Spear, firing his revolver in the street about daybreak on Saturday, December 17. He was joined in this activity by others of the Talbot retinue. At this point Mike Meagher went to Marshal Wilson's house and reported the situation. At about the time Meagher and Wilson returned to the center of town, Tom Love fired off his weapon in a saloon. Wilson arrested Love and disarmed him, but before the marshal could get Love to jail, Talbot and others rushed to the rescue. Meagher attempted to aid Wilson, but the Talbot crowd turned on him. He was obliged to flee up the stairs of the opera house, Wilson covering his retreat; in the confusion, Love escaped. The gang then repaired to the home of Commanche Bill Mankin (near Fifth and Main streets, perhaps half a block west of Talbot's). Things remained quiet for a few hours, although Wilson was sufficiently apprehensive that he telegraphed Mayor Burrus, who was in Wellington at the time. At about 1:00 *P.M.*, Jim Martin was arrested for carrying a concealed weapon and resisting an officer. He was taken before the police judge and fined. While on his way to obtain money to pay the fine, accompanied by Deputy Fosset, Martin encountered Talbot, Love, Munson, and Eddleman, who attempted to rescue him. They were driven off by Fosset's drawn revolvers, but as Talbot retreated, he fired the shot or shots of which Freeman speaks and which precipitated the ensuing dustup (*Commercial, SCP,* 22 December 1881).

A slightly different version of the foregoing events was reported at the time of Talbot's trial. Since fourteen years intervene, disparity is perhaps not surprising. The chief points of difference are these: Martin and Munson were said to be the sole rescuers of Tom Love, and they were subsequently arrested by the officers, assisted by Meagher and others. The trial version holds that both Munson and Martin were being escorted to secure money and that both Wilson and Fosset were present when Talbot and others attempted the rescue (*Monitor-Press,* 11 April 1895).

The sharp cracks of the deadly revolver rang out in the cool morning air. Women were running to and fro, looking for a loved husband or a son whom they adored. The white, blanched faces of the women foretold the fright, anxiety, and suspense they were laboring under.

Those who were unfortunate enough to be in the city shopping hurried themselves to a place of safety, some taking refuge behind dry goods boxes, while others in their fright, rushed hither and thither looking for a better place to hide and escape the stray bullets, which were crashing through the glass front windows of the stores and tearing through doors and windows of the dwelling houses, damaging pictures, breaking mirrors, and defacing the walls of the buildings.[11]

The bullets flew thick and fast, and still the daring Talbot stood as a target for the guns of many citizens. Was his a charmed life? Had fate decreed that his escape should be a fortunate one? I was standing in the door of the blacksmith shop and had a good view of the battle which was raging,[12] and I expected every moment to see the form of Talbot reel and fall to the ground, shot by the fatal bullet fired at the hands of a law-abiding citizen. But not so. When Talbot had emptied his two sixshooters, he called to his men and said, "Boys, let's get our Winchesters," and started on the run for his house, followed by his gang of outlaws.[13]

The men appeared again, this time armed with Winchester rifles, which fact showed very plainly that the affair was plotted and under the management of the desperate Jim Talbot.

The firing was again resumed by the outlaws, and the firing was returned by the citizens. The marshals were reinforced by a number of citizens who

---

[11] Freeman's vivid description is hardly overstated. The *SCP* correspondent (who may not have witnessed the actual shootout) reported: "Every building in that vicinity is riddled full of bullet holes" (22 December 1881). Ridings reported that as late as 1892 severe bullet damage to the brick Danford Building (the old opera house) was evident (pp. 475-76).

[12] The exact location of Freeman's shop in December, 1881, is uncertain, but it was apparently south of Sixth on Main. The altercation began in the intersection of Fifth and Main streets, so Freeman had a reasonably good view. The reader will notice that Freeman was not one of the citizens returning the gang's fire.

[13] The contemporary newspaper accounts of the sequence of events differ slightly from Freeman's. Moreover, they do not report that Talbot stood and emptied his revolvers before he called to the gang to get their Winchesters. According to the *SCP* (22 December 1881) Talbot, as he retreated from Fosset's drawn guns, fired three (and only three) shots prior to going home to secure his rifle. The *Commercial* (22 December 1881) states that Talbot, as he fired his shots, called out to his companions and that they "began a terrible fusillade . . . , evidently with the intention of frightening everybody off the street so as to carry out their plot." It was, however, the kind of situation where eyewitness accounts would differ greatly. The *Commercial* reporter did not himself witness the affair, explaining that his version "is sifted out of the details as related by at least a hundred different persons." In light of all this, Freeman's account suffers no serious challenge.

were among the unfortunate ones that had had no gun; they borrowed one, however, from the hardware and supply stores.[14] The battle was kept up, and, when the leader saw the form of Mike Meagher sway and fall to the ground, he then told the boys to run for their horses.[15] The citizens were closing in on the desperadoes, but from the fact that their guns were Winchester rifles, the citizens were very cautious about endangering their lives by approaching within full view of the desperadoes.

The citizens were informed of the killing of Mike Meagher (an ex-city mayor) by Jim Talbot, who had manifested the determination to kill Meagher. Meagher had become aware of the intentions of the fearless leader and was all the while shooting at Talbot, but his aim had not been true, or his destiny had been sealed by the arrival of Jim Talbot in the city of Caldwell.

While the desperadoes were running for the livery stables, the bullets fired by the citizens flew thick around them, but the stables were reached and the proprietor was ordered at the point of a Winchester to saddle a sufficient number of horses on which the outlaws could make their escape. While the horses were being saddled, a strict watch was kept by the outlaws, who [were] prepared to shoot the first man that attempted to reach the livery barn, and in this manner the armed citizens were kept at bay by the long range Winchester rifles held in the hands of a desperate gang of desperadoes.

George Spear, a citizen of Caldwell, was shot and instantly killed, while he was in the act of getting a horse which was standing near the "Red

[14]The syntax is obviously garbled here, but the sense is this: The ranks of citizen combatants were joined by those who were able to borrow guns from hardware and supply stores. The *Post* (22 December 1881) reported that A. Witzleben of the York-Parker-Draper Mercantile Co. and C. W. Willet of Hardesty Bros." handed out their stock of arms to the citizens as long as there was a gun left, without receipts and in many instances without knowing who was taking the guns. The two houses had about $800 worth of guns out at one time, and some of them have not been returned yet." A wry comment on crime fighting in the Caldwell of 1881.

[15]The opening shots were fired from just north of the intersection of Fifth and Main Streets. In order to secure their rifles, the gang was obliged to move east between buildings or along Fifth Street to Talbot's house. Meagher and Wilson were apparently on Main Street south of Fifth and paralleled the gang by moving eastward between buildings in that portion of the block. Talbot, once armed with his rifle, returned toward Main. When he had reached the rear of the opera house, he spotted Meagher in the alleyway to the south. "Talbot fired some seven or eight shots," reported the *Commercial* (22 December 1881), "one of which struck Meagher in the breast, killing him almost instantly." The gang then retreated north toward the commercial stable of George Kalbfleisch on Fourth Street, where they intended to secure mounts (*Commercial,* 22 December 1881). At Talbot's trial, Doug Hill would testify that the shootout was such a "Donneybrook fair" that any one of Talbot's gang might have shot Meagher. Indeed, he claimed that they did not know of Meagher's death until freighters at Pond Creek told them of it a day or two later (*Monitor-Press,* 18 April 1895). It should be noted that Hill, having been previously convicted of his part in the affair (see chap. 42, n. 14), was immune from prosecution when he testified.

Light."[16] Whether Spear was a sympathizer with the desperadoes and was getting the horse for them, thus aiding them in making their escape from the excited citizens, is not known, but the presumptions were that Spear was killed by a shot fired by a citizen of the town, who supposed that Spear was helping and encouraging the desperadoes in their murderous attack on the citizens of Caldwell.

When their horses were in readiness, five of the desperadoes started east on the run,[17] and when they had gone but a short distance, one of their horses was shot and killed; as quickly as he could, the rider jumped behind one of his comrades, and the two men rode away on the same horse. The excited citizens ran to their homes, secured a horse, and started in hot pursuit of the desperate men. A telegram was sent to the sheriff at Wellington, and in a short time a special train was run down from Wellington, bringing the sheriff and a posse of citizens from that place.[18]

[16] Ridings (p. 477) states that the gang had horses awaiting them in front of the Red Light dance house. Perceiving this, W. N. Hubbell went from the rear of his store (which fronted Main on the northeast corner of Sixth and Main) across the alley to the back door of A. C. Jones's blacksmith shop and through the shop to the front door (which faced Arrapahoe on the northwest corner of Sixth and Arrapahoe). From there he had a direct view of the Red Light hitching rail to the northeast. According to Ridings, Hubbell took a Winchester and picked off most if not all of the horses. It was the loss of these horses which necessitated the gang's retreating to Kalbfleisch's stable to secure mounts. No contemporary account mentions a systematic slaughter of getaway horses, and indeed the contrary versions are so convincing that I am inclined to doubt Ridings's version, even though Ridings was there as a boy and grew up around people who had participated. The details of Hubbell's action are so compelling, though, that one is moved to wonder whether it was Hubbell who shot George Spear in the act of saddling Talbot's horse near the Red Light (see also n. 17). Ridings makes no mention of the death of Spear.

[17] Freeman has neglected to mention—though he will remember to do so later—that not all of Talbot's crew were able to secure horses. Dick Eddleman and Tom Love were left behind. The accounts differ somewhat as to how many of the party were mounted when they left the Kalbfleisch stable. The *SCP* and the *Commercial* (both 22 December 1881) state that five men left on four horses. The *Post* and the *Wellington Wellingtonian* (both of 22 December 1881) agree with Freeman's version, that all were mounted (except, of course, Eddleman and Love) when they left the stable but that one of the horses was killed soon after. The *Wellingtonian* reports that it was Talbot's horse, shot by one James Matthews of Wellington.

Talbot himself testified that his own horse "was picketed out on the common east of the Red Light" (adjacent to his own back yard) and that when George Spear and Doug Hill went to saddle it for him, Spear was killed and the horse was shot. Talbot mounted behind Hill, who was wounded in the heel, and thus they rode out of town (*Monitor-Press,* 18 April 1895). The escaping outlaws were Talbot, Hill, Munson, Martin, and Bigtree.

[18] The telegram had been sent earlier in the day to Mayor Cass Burrus (see n. 10). Burrus delayed the regular noon train to Caldwell and requested Sheriff Joe Thralls to form a posse and accompany him. A posse of twenty men was collected, and the train made a late departure for Caldwell. It arrived at about 3:00 P.M., or roughly an hour and a half after Talbot and his men had fled the city (*Commercial, SCP,* 22 December 1881).

Upon the arrival of the sheriff, he went immediately to a livery stable and arrested the remaining two outlaws, who had failed to get horses and thus escape with the desperadoes. When they failed to get horses, they threatened the life of the livery man if he informed the citizens of their whereabouts, and they secured themselves from the infuriated citizens by remaining in the barn.[19]

Those who were inclined visited the spot where George Spear met his death. Among those who wished to view the scene of slaughter were the inmates of the "Red Light," who mingled their tears of sympathy with those shed by the grief-stricken relatives of the unfortunate man who had met an untimely death while he was yet in his early manhood.[20]

The body of the murdered ex-mayor was tenderly carried to the home of the wife, who was prostrated with grief when she beheld the dead body of her husband and the protector of her now fatherless children. When she looked upon the face of him who years before had promised to care for and protect her, she could not help but feel a ray of consolation, when she realized he had met death while he was defending his home and town from the desperate works of the desperadoes.[21]

As quickly as possible a posse of men started from the city in pursuit of the Talbot gang. The posse was reinforced all along the route by the arrival of a new man armed with a gun or revolver. The citizens were infuriated at the work done by the gang of desperadoes, and they resolved to follow them and, if possible, arrest and take them either dead or alive, and thus avenge the life of Mike Meagher.

The desperadoes were probably three miles in advance of the posse, but the gang had been followed by a number of citizens on horseback, and a firing was kept up by both parties. The citizens would not get within the range of the desperadoes' Winchesters, hence they waited for more help to arrive.

[19]The newspaper accounts do not confirm that the people at the livery stable were threatened or that a siege of any kind occurred there. Indeed, Eddleman is reported to have put down his gun when he learned that no horse was available for him. No mention is made of Love (*SCP,* 22 December 1881). The *Commercial* (22 December 1881) reports that Love and Commanche Bill Mankin were arrested on Saturday evening and that Tom Delaney and Eddleman were arrested Sunday morning. Mankin and Delaney were released subsequent to the coroner's inquest, where it was shown that neither was involved in the shooting. In fact, W. D. Fosset testified that Mankin had tried to prevent the shooting at some risk to his own life.

[20]The picture of the weeping prostitutes makes sense when one recalls that Spear was the proprietor of the Red Light.

[21]Meagher married his wife, Jenny, in 1875. He was thirty-eight years old at the time of his death; he was buried in Wichita (*SCP,* 29 December 1881). Jenny Meagher was said to be the daughter of Tom Fitzpatrick, the famous Mountain Man (D. D. Leahy in the *Eagle,* 4 April 1932).

When the desperadoes were about a mile from the town, they met a farmer going to Caldwell. He had a horse tied behind the wagon and was leading it to town for his son's use. The desperadoes took this advantage of securing a horse and [replacing] the one that was shot by the citizens, so they halted the team driven by Mr. Mose Swaggart, commonly called "Uncle Mose," and with the muzzle of their guns drawn near his head, bade him to let them have the horse, which they appropriated to their use, and, mounting it, they started south-east, riding their horses on a rapid run. "Uncle Mose" watched them until they were some distance away, then gave a cluck to his horses and drove on toward town, where he informed the people of his escapade with the fleeing men.[22]

Talbot and his men met a boy riding a horse near Bovine Park, the stock ranch and beautiful home of W. E. Campbell, located one mile and a half south-east of Caldwell. The boy's saddle was demanded by the men, which was hastily put on the pony taken from "Uncle Mose."[23] Now the desperadoes were fully equipped with horses and saddles and were making their way as fast as they could travel toward the Indian Territory.

As the different squads were leaving town in pursuit of Talbot, I concluded to go and help round up the gang of outlaws. My son had just driven up to the shop with my team, so I unharnessed one of the horses and went to a livery barn, obtained a saddle and Winchester rifle. I started to the Bluff Creek Ford, intending to arrive there in the advance of the outlaws, and thus I could change their course. I started my horse on the run, but I arrived at the crossing a few seconds too late, for I could see the desperadoes ahead of me, probably two hundred yards, and they were riding as fast as their horses could run.[24] When they were about four hundred yards ahead of me, the girth

[22] Moses H. Swaggart was a farmer from Falls Township, adjacent to Caldwell on the east. He was bringing a load of hay into town when he was accosted by the fugitives (*Commercial,* 22 December 1881). A brief sketch of Swaggart may be found in Ridings, pp. 477-78, 501-503.

[23] No contemporary account mentions the appropriation of a boy's saddle. However, at the Campbell ranch the fugitives did seize a remount or two (the newspaper versions differ) in exchange for a wounded horse or horses (*Commercial, Post, SCP,* 22 December 1881). W. E. ("Shorthorn") Campbell was an active member of the Cherokee Strip Live Stock Association, a longtime resident of Caldwell, and a principal founder of the town of Kiowa, Kansas. Campbell was a veteran who had served in the Iowa Cavalry. He died in Indian Territory at the hand of an assassin (*SCP,* 9 March 1882; *Journal,* 27 March 1884; D. D. Leahy, *Eagle,* 4 April 1932). Campbell figures prominently in the next chapter.

[24] The particular ford of Bluff Creek to which Freeman refers is unclear. One version has it that the outlaws crossed Bluff Creek before they appropriated Campbell's stock. Another states that they crossed Bluff at its junction with the state line after they left Campbell's (*SCP, Post,* 22 December 1881). Since Bluff Creek bisected Campbell's property on a southeasterly diagonal, either version is possible, assuming Campbell would have had horses grazing on either side of the creek. However, to complicate matters, the *Commercial*

of one of the saddles broke, causing the saddle to fall to the ground; the desperadoes were so closely pursued by the people that in order to make their escape, there was no time to be lost, so the saddle was left lying on the ground where it had fallen from the horse. I took the saddle and went back to town, intending to get a fresh horse and a force of men to follow the fleeing fugitives.

I arrived at town about sundown and quickly made the necessary arrangements to leave town in company with others wishing to partake in the pursuit of Talbot. At last we were ready to start, and in a few minutes we were galloping over the prairies, up hill and down, on the supposed trail of the outlaws.

After traveling for some time, we met the county sheriff and several men coming toward the town.[25] They informed us that the desperadoes had been rounded in near a cattle ranch, then owned by Chas. H. Moore of Caldwell. This ranch was located at the head of Deer Creek.[26]

The sheriff said the fugitives were riding on the run, and when they had arrived about half way between a canyon and the ranch, which was located about one-half mile north of the canyon, their horses were so overcome with heat and fatigue that they were unable to carry the outlaws any further, so they left their horses and run to the canyon and took refuge in an old dugout, which had once served as the home of the herders.

The sheriff wanted me to go to Deer Creek and take charge of the horses and see that the desperadoes did not get them. He said a posse of men had

---

states that the fugitives left Campbell's and then crossed both Fall and Bluff creeks. Even this scenario is possible; Campbell owned another spread a mile and a half north of the one just described, and this holding was north of both creeks. However, all descriptions (including Freeman's) considered, the *Commercial* appears to be in error. (Data on Campbell's properties come from Falls Township plats in Edwards, *Historical Atlas of Sumner County, Kansas.*)

[25] Sheriff Thralls and his party may have been traveling in the direction of town, but there is no evidence that he left the general vicinity of the canyon where Talbot and his men were believed to be trapped; indeed, Editor Tell Walton, who was also on the scene all night, reported to the contrary (*Post,* 22 December 1881). Thralls, who did not arrive in Caldwell until after 3:00 *P.M.*, did not catch up with the chase until after dark (*Commercial,* 22 December 1881).

[26] The newspaper accounts identify the ranch at the head of Deer Creek (ten miles southeast of Caldwell, in Indian Territory) as Dutcher's ranch or the "Deutcher Bros's horse ranch" (*Commercial, Post,* 22 December 1881). Yet Ridings (p. 476) with Freeman calls it Moore's. One surmises that the ranch was purchased by Moore subsequent to the Talbot incident and that both Freeman and Ridings, writing years after the event, have inadvertently substituted a more recent identification for the property. Charles H. Moore was a prominent citizen of Caldwell, involved in both banking and cattle raising (see Andreas, p. 1504). It is unlikely that contemporary newspapers would have failed to mention it if he had been leasing the property at that time.

surrounded the canyon and were waiting until daylight, when they would make a charge and get the desperadoes.

We started on our errand; it had now become so dark that we could no longer keep the road, and finally we concluded we were lost. We traveled around on the prairies and found a road which we supposed was the same we had left, but it proved to be a road leading to the L. X. Ranch, where we arrived and found to our surprise that [we] were within five miles of our starting place.[27] We had traveled too far east to find the trail leading to the Deer Creek Ranch.

We watered our horses and ate supper at the L. X. Ranch. We had not had anything to eat since noon; our appetites were keen, and we relished the "good, square meal" set before us by the cook at the ranch.

We concluded, after much reasoning and the adding of many suggestions, that we would go back to the town and get a man that was acquainted with the route we were to travel, and in company with him, we would make another effort to reach the ranch on Deer Creek.

This time we had no adventure, and after traveling until three o'clock in the morning, we arrived at the ranch, whereupon I went immediately to the place where the horses had been left by the fleeing men. I found the horses at the place designated by the sheriff, and a couple of men in company with myself remained near the horses and quietly watched them, wishing for the appearance of the desperadoes.

We were prepared for their approach, and we fully intended to welcome them with a volley of shots. We had an idea that the outlaws had spent all their ammunition, consequently we could easily take them in. We waited in vain for their appearance, so our cherished hopes were blasted, and our wishes were not realized.

[27] The LX Ranch was the Cherokee Strip holding ground for cattle from the Texas LX Company (Debo, *The Cowman's Southwest,* p. 55).

CHAPTER 42

Jim Talbot and Party Reach the Canyons near Deer Creek—The
Citizens of Caldwell Round Them in—W. E. Campbell Shot,
and Is Taken to Caldwell—John H. Hall Receives a Bullet
Hole Through His Hat—At Daylight the Charge is
Made—"The Birds Have Flown"—The Reward
Offered for the Capture of Talbot—The
Desperadoes Take Five Horses from a
Freighter—Talbot's Wife—Rumors
Giving Reason for the Killing of
Mike Meagher—Talbot Said
to Be a Brother of
George Flatt

I will endeavor to give the reader facts concerning the early operations which took place before my arrival at the Deer Creek Ranch. The different squads of men had arrived at the ranch in a very few minutes after the desperadoes had reached that point. The horses were completely exhausted by the constant speed in which they had been compelled to travel since leaving Caldwell. Had the desperadoes had the use of good running horses, they could have evaded the posse, but their horses were large ones, such as are usually found drawing heavy loads or hitched to the plow of a farmer; consequently after they had traveled a certain distance, and being unaccustomed to traveling at such a rapid gait, they were soon overcome with heat and fatigue, and the desperadoes must trust to their agility and active use they have of their legs to carry them to a place of safety. The fleeing men were so closely pursued by those in pursuit that in order to escape from being taken by them, a run must be made to reach the canyon, about one-half mile south of the ranch.

When the desperadoes gained their retreat, the men were deployed and surrounded the canyon. The men were located in close proximity to each other, and they secreted themselves by lying down in the tall grass and quietly awaited and watched the movements of the desperate men whom they had followed and surrounded.

Two of the posse came near losing their lives. W. E. Campbell received a shot fired by one of the Talbot men. Campbell was approaching the old dugout; the roof had long since caved in, leaving the perpendicular sides of earth. This dugout had been dug in the side of the canyon, and the fugitives, when last seen, were entering within its inclosure, which afforded them as a fortification against the shots of the posse.[1] While Campbell was nearing the place of refuge, crack went a shot fired by one of the desperadoes.

[1] The place was an ideal spot to defend, given the waning light and the somewhat dis-

261

When the men nearest him heard the assertion made by Mr. Campbell, "I am shot," they went to him and found he had been shot, the charge taking effect in his arm.[2] Some of the posse started to the city with Mr. Campbell, while the remaining men secreted themselves as best they could from the view of blood-thirsty Jim Talbot and his men.

The desperadoes were on the alert and watched every movement of their enemies. They were ready for any emergency which might call their attention. Their watchfulness and caution was manifested by the shots fired by them when one of the enemy was getting too near their place of retreat.

---

organized state of the pursuers. It was a deep basin containing "the walls of two small stone buildings, built opposite each other, and bearing all the appearance of having been placed there for the purpose of affording a hiding place for horsethieves or outlaws like the Talbot gang. With the exception of a small opening on the north by a stone ridge between it and Deer creek, east south and west, was the high prairie. But at no point except by going up close to its edge, could a view of the interior of the basin be had" (*Caldwell Commercial,* 22 December 1881). Tell Walton, who was with the original band of pursuers, explained that in the waning light, the citizens could do little good: "Being above the outlaws, they were splendid marks for their fire, while the outlaws were in the shadows, so that their position could not be distinguished. . . . Thirty minutes more of daylight would have told the tale for the outlaws" (*Caldwell Post,* 22 December 1881).

The basin opening (which Walton places to the west instead of north as the *Commercial* has it) was the point Campbell was trying to reach when he was shot. Walton explains that one of the gang had taken up a position in this opening in order to defend it. "Had [he] been anywhere else in the gulch the citizens would have taken them in; but this position covered every point that the others were exposed from; in fact, he held the key to the situation. . . . had Campbell escaped the fire of the villain that shot him, he could have killed the other three [*sic*] in as many minutes, as his position commanded the fort in every corner. The two parties were not over seventy-five feet apart at any time during the battle, while Campbell's man was not over twenty-five feet from him when he shot" (*Post,* 22 December 1881). The *Wellington Wellingtonian* (22 December 1881) suggests that this Deer Creek hideout was used by the infamous McCarty back in 1872 (see chap. 12).

[2]The nature and extent of Campbell's wound are inconsistently reported. Walton's version is perhaps the most reliable: "The outlaw's ball took effect in Campbell's wrist, passing between the two bones. Another ball passed through his clothes six or seven times, and made a small flesh wound on the thigh." Later, the distress to Campbell's clothing would be revised: "Twenty-seven holes appeared in his clothing, made by five balls" (*Post,* 22 December 1881). The wrist wound apparently was more serious than it seemed at first. In July of 1882, a correspondent to the *Commercial* stated that Campbell would be crippled for life from the wound. This letter came shortly after the death of Marshal George Brown (see chap. 33) when Editor W. B. Hutchison had been scolding the citizenry for not aiding their police officers. The additional irony pointed out by the correspondent ("A Lady") was that the city had just presented their newly appointed marshal, Bat Carr, with a brace of pistols in appreciation of his scant two weeks of uneventful service (see chap. 34, n. 5). She enclosed $5 toward a subscription to purchase Campbell an appropriate token of community appreciation. Campbell graciously declined, and the subscription was abandoned (*Commercial,* 27 July, 3 August, 17 August 1882).

John H. Hall, a young man living near Caldwell, in company with a friend, had joined the pursuing party of citizens, and, arriving at the scene, they too took a position near the dugout with the intention of remaining as watchers, and they were to allow no man to escape by running through the rank. The young man, Hall, and his companion, when they entered upon the chase, remarked that this is "simply fun;" and indeed it was so long as there was no danger connected with the sport of riding at "tip-top" speed over the broad prairie lands, closely pursuing a squad of fleeing desperadoes. Youth is not presumed to be filled with thoughts of caution, propriety, or consideration. These young men did not consider the probable danger nor give due exercise to their reasoning faculties; but, concluding there would be some sport attended with the attempt at capturing the desperadoes, they resolved to try "their luck" at becoming a "Young America" with the crew of older men.[3]

John Hall was lying in the grass, which was probably three feet high, and after creeping towards the place of retreat held by the desperadoes, he raised his head with the intention of looking over into the canyon, when the sharp crack of a Winchester sounded in the still night air, and Hall felt his hat raise from his head as the bullet passed on without accomplishing its bloody errand. Hall dropped to the ground, and upon examining his hat, he found a bullet passed through it, leaving an awful hole which had a tendency to warn the young man of his dangerous position. Had the ball struck the hat one inch lower in the crown, the top of the young man's head would have been blown off.

When the light of the stars began to wane by the approaching daylight in the east, all men were in readiness to advance upon the hiding place of the desperadoes. When it was sufficiently light the charge was made, and it was soon found that the birds had flown.[4]

---

[3]Freeman is a bit patronizing toward young Hall here. The *Post* (22 December 1881) reported that Hall, among others much older than he, "appeared to be utterly oblivious to danger at times, but kept the major portion of themselves under cover." Freeman, whose own caution may be perfectly understandable, was not engaged in the melee in town and abandoned the pursuit—as Hall did not—when the fleeing gang was still in full view. Hall's friend has not been identified.

[4]The birds had apparently flown soon after Campbell was wounded on the previous evening. As Walton explained it, the original party of pursuers, numbering about fifteen, was reduced to six after Campbell was shot, the others returning to Caldwell then and there. The six men remaining were spread rather thin; they had to attempt to guard the gulch as well as a herd of over thirty horses, this last task alone "requiring the attention of at least four men, for [horses] were what the outlaws needed" (*Post,* 22 December 1881). Some time later, Sheriff Thralls and his party arrived. Apparently two more groups of reinforcements followed thereafter—Freeman's, of which there is no newspaper record, and another led by Mayor Cass Burrus (*Commercial,* 22 December 1881). This brought the group up to a strength of about forty, but all the reinforcements had arrived too late.

A man by the name of Rhoades, in company with myself, entered the hiding place and found a pair of gloves and a coat belonging to one of the desperadoes.[5] We discovered where they got out of the canyon; from the height of its bank, we concluded, one of the party was helped to the top of the canyon, and he lent his aid in pulling up his comrades; and they probably made their escape by creeping out [through] the [ranks of the posse], which easily could have been accomplished, as the night was dark; the twinkling stars gave the only light; and then again, the grass was of a rank growth, and probably two or three feet in height, and would afford a hiding for the creeping men.[6]

They arrived at a freighters' camp, and of them demanded five horses, promising to return them after they had secured horses of their own or when [they] reached their destination, which was Texas.[7] The freighters came to Caldwell and reported their bad luck, for they concluded the desperadoes would never return their horses to them. But in this they were mistaken, for in about three weeks a man came into the city of Caldwell, bringing with him the five horses that had been taken by Talbot and his band of desperadoes.[8]

[5] Caldwell Township Constable Abram Rhoades (see chap. 31, n. 4) was Freeman's companion. The *SCP* (22 December 1881) reported that the gang left "their overcoats and two hats." They had no need of these garments, for they were in no danger of suffering from exposure: the early winter of 1881 was unseasonably mild, rosebushes still setting out leaves through December (*Wellingtonian,* 29 December 1881, 19 January 1882).

[6] When the escape was discovered, most of the posse returned to Caldwell. Those who remained included Sheriff Thralls, Frank Evans (Thralls's deputy), R. W. Harrington (Thralls's future father-in-law, a farmer and implement dealer from Caldwell), John W. Dobson (a Caldwell architect, contractor, and implement dealer), Sam Swayer (see chap. 33, n. 11), Freeman, Rhoades, Tell Walton, and one unidentified man. This party searched the vicinity and put nearby cow camps on the alert to guard against stolen horses. It returned to Caldwell later that day, Sunday, December 18. A second party under the ill-fated George Brown was also reported. It too was unsuccessful. (*Post,* 22 December 1881, 8 January 1880; *SCP,* 22 January 1880, 19 January 1882; *Commercial,* 12 April 1883).

[7] The freighter's camp was on Bullwhacker Creek, some eighteen miles below Caldwell, the outlaws having traveled, by Tell Walton's estimate, six to ten miles after they escaped from Deer Creek (*Post,* 22 December 1881). The freighters included J. K. Harmon, his son Ed, and another man. The outlaws walked into the camp at about 8 o'clock Sunday evening and at gunpoint commandeered five horses, some food, and blankets. They were last seen passing Pond Creek Station at about 9 o'clock (*Commercial,* 22 December 1881).

[8] The horses were returned in less than the three weeks Freeman indicates. On Sunday evening, December 25, a freighter named W. J. "Jake" Keffer or Keiffer, in company with a man named Hostetter of Arkansas City, brought the horses into Caldwell. Keffer, hoping for a reward, claimed to have rescued the horses by stealing them away from the outlaws' camp near Big Turkey Creek north of Cantonment, Indian Territory. Later reports proved his story false. The Talbot gang had turned the horses over to him to return, stating

The Indian Territory was scoured by different posses hoping they might possibly be successful in arresting Talbot or his men and thus secure the large reward that was offered for the arrest of Talbot or his accomplices. But all efforts to capture Talbot proved futile. Several of the county officers went to Texas at the requests of parties, and searched for the outlaws, but no trace of them could be found. Several letters were received by the officers from parties in Texas and Colorado, stating a man was there under arrest who answered to the descriptions of the notorious Jim Talbot. The officer would obey the requests and go to the place where the supposed outlaw was held in bondage, but upon his arrival the prisoner was set at liberty, as the officer failed to identify him as the man who for several days had held the citizens of Caldwell in fear and terror.[9] Reports reached Caldwell that Talbot had been killed in Texas, but whether the report was a true one remains a mystery.[10]

His wife remained in Caldwell a short time. Talbot had left her in destitute circumstances, and the citizens gave her support by furnishing the necessaries of life.[11] She afterwards left town; whether she went to Talbot, I am unable to say, as her whereabouts were never heard of after she left Caldwell.

There were many rumors advanced concerning the murder of Mike Meagher; one of them was that in the early history of Wichita, Mike Meagher was an officer in that city, and it was reported he killed a cousin of Jim Talbot; and to avenge the death of his cousin, Talbot had come to Caldwell for the purpose of killing Meagher.[12] Meagher was keeping a saloon in Cald-

"they were not horse thieves, if they were bad men otherwise" (*Post, Commercial, Wellingtonian*, 29 December 1881).

[9] Sheriff Thralls himself continued the search for over a week before giving it up. Following a new lead, Thralls took a posse into the Territory in September of 1882, this time accompanied by Caldwell's new assistant city marshal, Henry N. Brown (see chaps. 34-36). Leads were followed as late as 1885, when a Sumner County deputy was sent to La Junta, Colorado, to identify a man supposed (wrongly) to be Talbot (*Post*, 29 December 1881; *Commercial*, 12 October 1882; Caldwell *Journal*, 16 July, 30 July 1885).

[10] At the time of writing this, Freeman, of course, had no knowledge that the rumors of Talbot's death were untrue. Talbot's arrest in California and subsequent trial in Wellington came well after both editions of this book were printed. Perhaps the earliest rumor of Talbot's death was heard by W. E. Campbell at Wichita in June following the raid (*Commercial*, 29 June 1882).

[11] The *Commercial* (22 December 1881) reported: "Talbot's family are in a destitute condition, but their immediate wants have been supplied by order of the mayor, and they will be sent to [Mrs. Talbot's] friends." Tell Walton's *Post* complained a month later (19 January 1882): "The city is supporting the wife of Jim Talbot, at least we suppose it is by a bill being allowed by the Council for goods furnished her." When she left Caldwell is unknown.

[12] The *SCP* (22 December 1881) reported that Talbot was "a cousin to one [Sylvester]

well at the time of his death. Another rumor advanced and reported was that Jim Talbot and George Flatt were half brothers, and Talbot came to Caldwell to avenge his death.[13] The reader will remember the manner in which Flatt met his death and that the suspicions had rested upon the police force for this sudden ending.

In order to kill the policemen, Talbot was compelled to have help; so he organized a band of desperadoes of which he was leader. His coming to Caldwell to reside, it was presumed, was for the purpose of learning the facts concerning the death of his half brother, George Flatt. It was presumed by some at the time of the battle that Talbot intended to murder the entire corps of officers, thinking in this manner he would get the assassinator of Flatt.

Jim Talbot had the characteristics of a bold and fearless man and a desperado who recognized cowardice as a crime. He loved to be feared. He had an indomitable will, and, once entering the ring as a contestant in a race, he was sure to come out victorious. He spilled the blood of his fellowmen, freely and without reluctance or care. In the bloody affray he asked no quarter, he would give none. His heart was filled with bitterness and hatred against an offender, and lurking within his bosom was the brooding of revenge. Such was the character of the courageous and fearless Jim Talbot.[14]

Powell, whom Mike Meagher killed in 1876, while marshal of Wichita." Powell, the first (and probably only) man Meagher ever killed, was slain on 1 January 1877 in a shootout which Powell precipitated by trying to murder Meagher: Powell fired several shots into a privy Meagher was using, wounding the marshal in the leg. The full details, taken from the *Wichita Eagle* of 4 January 1877, may be found in Miller and Snell, *Why the West Was Wild,* pp. 493-95. An alternative motive for Talbot's vendetta against Meagher was said to stem from the latter's arrest of Talbot in Caldwell in March of 1881 (*Wellington Monitor-Press,* 11 April 1895). Yet another source claims that the ill-feeling began when Meagher ousted Talbot from his saloon the previous day, Talbot vowing he would "burn powder in Meagher's face for that" (*Wellingtonian,* 3 July 1884).

[13] Talbot denied this rumor in a remarkable letter to the *Kansas City* (Missouri) *Times* over the signatures of himself, Hill, Munson, Martin, and Bigtree (repr. *Commercial,* 26 January 1882): "It has been published that the row grew out of the killing of George Flat, this is . . . false. It never entered our minds." The letter charges, among other things, that the fracas started because Marshal John Wilson, "on a protracted drunk," had given a posse orders to shoot every cowboy that moved. At least one Caldwell citizen would grant that Wilson had been "drunk for some days" (*Wellingtonian,* 3 July 1884).

[14] Freeman's admiration for Talbot's courage is noteworthy. The city of Caldwell was a long time recovering from this affray. Among other things, the city gained the reputation of a town that could be taken, a reputation that probably led to the death of Marshal George Brown some six months later (see chap. 33, n. 3). In the aftermath of the shooting, the town tried to reform. For one thing, it closed its saloons (which were illegal and had been, under state law, for nearly two years). For this Mayor Cass Burrus was advised by the Ku Klux Klan to resign from office or repeal the two prohibition ordinances—or bear the consequences. Burrus ignored the epistle and served out his term (*Post,* 29 December

1881). What the Klan could not do to reopen the bars, however, the pressure of commerce could. By 2 February 1882 the *Commercial* could remark, mocking the words of the saloon interests, "The moral spasm superinduced by the shooting scrape last December, has had a relapse, and everything goes in Caldwell as in the good old days, 'when we was all alike one family, and nobody cared if a fellow did get on a drunk and fire off his revolver.'"

Another "moral spasm" was evidenced by those (chiefly Tell Walton) who felt that it wasn't the whiskey that caused the trouble; it was the cowboys carrying weapons. In its issue of 9 February 1882, the *Post* kicked off a crusade—aimed at the cattleman and not local legislators—"The six-shooter must go!" Surprisingly, the idea was seconded in a number of southwestern papers, including some in Texas, and at their annual meeting in Caldwell on March 1 and 2, 1882, members of the Cherokee Strip Live Stock Association actually passed a resolution deprecating "the carrying of six-shooters [by cowboys] while visiting towns along the border" (*SCP,* 9 March 1882).

The resolution had no more effect on the practice than did the intentions of still another "moral spasm" following on the heels of the Talbot raid—a city resolution to remove "that sink-hole of iniquity, the Red Light dance house . . . from the corporate limits of the city" (*Post,* 16 March 1882).

In 1894, Talbot was arrested in California and brought to Wellington for trial. He was tried twice, the first trial ending in a hung jury and the second in a verdict of acquittal (*Monitor-Press,* 4 April, 11 April, 18 April, 25 April, 19 September 1895). Freeman did not testify at either trial, though Abram Rhoades and Tell Walton, among others, did testify; so did W. D. Fosset, scotching forever, one would suppose, the suggestion that no one was left in Caldwell who could identify Talbot (*State of Kansas* v. *James Talbott, et al.* and Appearance Docket for same, Clerk of the District Court, Sumner County).

The *Wellington Monitor-Press* predicted the acquittal and in so doing provided the probable rationale: "Meagher was killed in an affray which was little short of a pitched battle between the citizens of Caldwell and the cowboys, and the difficulty of fixing the responsibility for the firing of the fatal shot has been greatly increased by the lapse of time. [Talbot] cannot be convicted of the crime unless it can be shown, with a certainty that admits of no possible alternative, that it was his hand and no other's that sent the deadly missile into the body of Meagher, and he is bound to go free if the prosecution can raise nothing more than a strong presumption of his guilt" (4 April 1895).

Talbot returned to Ukiah, California, where he was killed in 1896 by parties unknown (Miller and Snell, p. 505). Sam P. Ridings (*The Chisholm Trail,* pp. 481-82) reports the speculation that John Meagher, Mike's twin brother, did the job, a speculation discounted by D. D. Leahy, who claimed to have interviewed John Meagher after the death of Talbot (*Wichita Eagle,* 4 April 1932). In any case, the killing at Ukiah ended the career of the man whose raid occasioned the famous line in the *Wichita Times* of 17 December 1881: "As we go to press, hell is in session in Caldwell."

Of the other members of the gang, only Doug Hill was tried. In October of 1886, he was arrested in San Antonio, Texas, by Sumner County Deputy William Lee (see chap. 43, n. 7). Hill was convicted of manslaughter and served six months in the Wellington jail (*Journal,* 14 October 1886, 16 June 1887). Both Hill and Tom Love testified at Talbot's trial (*Monitor-Press,* 18 April 1895).

CHAPTER 43

The Citizens Are Struck with Horror with the Information That a
Man was Found Hanging Within the City Limits—The Body
Proves to Be That of Frank Noyes—Enos Blair's House
Burned by an Incendiary—Theories Concerning the
Burning of the Building—Rumors Concerning
the Hanging of Frank Noyes—His Father
Comes to Caldwell.

On the morning of Dec. 8th, 1885, the citizens of Caldwell and vicinity were filled with horror when they received the startling intelligence that a man had been found hanging to a beam over the gate of the shipping pens, located near the A. T. Santa Fe Depot.

Words would be indeed poor vehicles with which to convey to the minds of the readers the amazement and excitement which this news caused in the minds of the citizens. They were astonished with wonder that in this late date of civilization, that such a deed should be committed in the midst of a civilized and christianized community.

The residents of a later date than 1872, '73, and '74 had not been eye witnesses of the thrilling and blood-curdling events that took place during the early part of Caldwell's history. These recent settlers were filled with astonishment at this unexpected event, while those that had had a knowledge of the extent to which the daring deeds of desperadoism and lawlessness were indulged in by the frontier desperado, were struck with awe and surprise when they remembered that the years were advancing toward civilization, and now in the year of 1885, scenes like this were placed before the gaze of the people and deeds of lawlessness was still carried on in the midst of a christianized people.[1]

Early on the morning of Dec. 8th a man went to the stock pens of the "Santa Fe" R. R. for the purpose of loading stock to send on the railroad to an eastern market. It was scarcely daylight, and in visiting the various pens, the stock shipper was suddenly confronted by the body of a man hang-

---

[1] The first three paragraphs of this chapter represent a corn-fattened version of the 10 December 1885 *Caldwell Journal*'s already plump lead to the story, headlined "Have the Days of '71 Returned": "In an earlier day the terrible tragedy that was enacted in this city on Tuesday morning would not have so shocked the people of Caldwell and Kansas, but at this day, with schools and churches, all the moral elements of the best society thrown around our city and our peace officers on every corner, the sight of the body of a man in the prime of life hanging by the neck within the corporate limits of a city of 2,500 inhabitants shock everyone to the utmost." That this crime lurked within the bosom of the "best society" in Caldwell should not have shocked the *Journal;* for, as subsequent notes will show, the *Journal* helped encourage it.

ing in the gateway of one of the pens. The news was quickly circulated through the community, and at an early hour the scene was surrounded by a crowd of excited citizens.[2]

The residents recognized the features of the dead man, and it was at once reported that the victim was none other than Frank Noyes, a gambler who had been residing in the city of Caldwell.[3]

What he was hung for remains a mystery to the many citizens; the only reason for the hanging was founded upon the knowledge given to the public by the finding of a note in the pocket of the dead gambler. This note was written and placed in his pocket and contained the information that Noyes was hung for house burning.

There had been a house burned in Caldwell, some time previous to the hanging of Noyes, belonging to Enos Blair, editor of the Free Press, and evidence showed it had been burned by an incendiary; the walls had been saturated with kerosene, and about one o'clock the fatal match was struck; and in a short time the house was enveloped in flames and was entirely consumed by the fire. Mr. Blair barely escaped with his life, and had it not been for the immediate actions of friends in rescuing him from the building, he would, in all probability, [have] perished by the heat and flames of the fire.[4] There were many theories advanced concerning the reasons for the in-

[2] According to the *Journal* (10 December 1885) a dray driver discovered the body. The crowd, which gathered "immediately," was estimated at one hundred to two hundred.

[3] Noyes, in addition to gambling, was also involved in selling whiskey. By 1885, Caldwell's open saloons had at last been closed. Illicit sales were conducted in "blind tigers"— places where drinks were dispensed through a covered window so that the buyer could not see the seller. Noyes, along with Dave Sharp (see chap. 32, n. 9), was arrested the previous July for selling whiskey and served a thirty-day jail sentence. Following his death, the disappearance of blind tigers (temporarily, as it turned out) was remarked in the Caldwell newspaper (*Journal*, 23 July, 30 July, 17 December 1885). Frank Noyes was forty-two years old at the time of his death. Newspaper accounts described him as "about six feet high and good looking." The offspring of highly respected parents in Mattoon, Illinois, Noyes was said to have abandoned a wife and child in favor of "the company of bad men and vile women" (*Journal, SCP*, 10 December 1885; *Caldwell Free Press*, 12 December 1885).

[4] The fire was discovered about 2:30 A.M. on Monday, August 31. The incendiary device was a bit more complicated than Freeman describes it. A ball of candle wicking saturated with oil was attached by a piece of strap iron to an outer wall of the house. Afterward, the charred ball of wicking was retrieved from the ashes of the house. When kicked away from the rubble, it began to blaze anew. Neighbors spotted the fire and woke Blair. Although the house was consumed, it might have been extinguished had the pump in Blair's well worked more efficiently. As it was, rescuers were able to save all of the household furniture, so Blair's escape was hardly the narrow thing Freeman makes it out to be (*Journal*, 3 September 1885). Enos Blair, the father of John A. Blair (see biographical sketch, chap. 45), was one of Caldwell's original settlers. He was a livestock dealer as well as editor and publisher of the short-lived *Caldwell Free Press*. Blair left Caldwell for Alamosa, Colorado in 1887 (*Portrait and Biographical Album of Sumner County, Kansas*, pp. 375-76).

cendiary's work. One of the floating rumors was, the house had been burned by enemies of Mr. Blair, caused by the active part he took on the side of law and order and the publishing of articles in the Free Press relative to the acts of lawlessness and bloodshed committed within the borders of the city. Mr. Blair was a strong advocate of prohibition and published many articles against the influence of intemperance. This, together with his encouraging the enforcement of the city laws, and against drinking, gambling, and carousing in hours of dissipation until the "wee sma hours" of the morning, caused the rougher element of society to become bitterly opposed to Mr. Blair; consequently by some the burning of Mr. Blair's house was attributed to the roughs of Caldwell.[5]

The evidence given by a woman with whom Frank Noyes was living until the time of his death, covered the whole affair with a mystery. She testified that at a late hour in the night a rap on the door was heard by Noyes; he went to the door and was notified that he was wanted by an officer to go with him to Wellington. Upon looking towards the door, she discovered the forms of three or four men. Noyes hastily dressed himself and went with the men,

[5]As Freeman has stated, a note on Noyes's body declared he was hanged for house burning (*Journal*, 10 December 1885). At the time Blair's house was burned the *Journal* (3 September 1885) pointed an incriminating finger at Noyes and/or Dave Sharp (both of whom had just completed serving their thirty-day jail sentences for liquor sales), though it does not call either by name: "That the fire was the work of an incendiary none will deny for a moment. That the element that is responsible for the fire is that which spends thirty days in jail for transgressing the prohibitory law, no one will deny." What makes the paper's accusation especially interesting, in light of the fate of Noyes, are the following remarks taken from the same article: "That the party, if caught, who will thus vent his spite, will be hanged and tried afterwards, no one in this vicinity will deny. . . . The ropes are being laid to trap these fire-bugs, and if they are taken in their trials will be had by the coroner and not a justice of the peace."

Having printed these provocative statements, the *Journal* (Tell Walton was editor—see chaps. 41 and 42) was the epitome of piety after Noyes was lynched. A single example will illustrate: "Mob law is a poor law and one that should be condemned by all citizens of every class. Let the courts settle the status of men who transgress the laws of either morality or public peace, and not by engaging in crime attempt to punish a man for committing a crime" (10 December 1885).

The ironies abound. Tell Walton, it will be remembered (see chap. 42, n. 14), was not a prohibitionist, having favored disarming the cowboys rather than closing the saloons, so the *Journal*'s lynch talk of September 3 contained at least an element of hypocrisy. What was more embarrassing, having attributed the burning of Blair's house to the liquor element, the *Journal*'s dire prediction of lynching placed that illegal activity squarely in the laps of the prohibitionists. The *Journal* backed out of this gaffe some three weeks later: "The charge that the hanging was done by prohibitionists does not seem to us to have the least bit of sustaining evidence, as the men in this city who are recognized as ultra in that matter are men that no sane person would ever accuse of hanging a fellow man" (24 December 1885). But see n. 7 below.

whom, the woman said, drove rapidly away.[6] Noyes had been gambling and had won several hundred dollars, and some advanced the theory that Noyes had been taken by some of his former associates and robbed, hanged, and, to throw off suspicion, a note was placed in his pocket saying he was hanged for house burning.[7]

[6] The woman, May Feeny, testified that at about 1 A.M., seven or eight men came to the door of her house (which stood behind the old opera house and fronted on Fifth Street—or at about the spot from which Jim Talbot was said to have shot Mike Meagher, as detailed in chap. 41), and told Frank Noyes that they had a warrant to take him to Wellington. She testified that she recognized two of the party (*Journal,* 10 December 1885).

[7] This theory did not appear in print in 1885, but others did: that Frank Noyes was hanged by former associates who feared he was going to turn state's evidence on them (*SCP,* 10 December 1885); that Noyes "was hanged by friends of a young lady he had ruined in another part of the county" (*Journal,* 24 December 1885). Blair's *Free Press* hinted darkly that the lynching was somehow connected with Henry N. Brown and Ben Wheeler (see chaps. 34-36) since Caldwell still contained remnants of "the gang that sent that delegation out last April, one year ago, to replenish their coffers by robbing the Medicine Lodge Bank" (12 December 1885). The note placed on the body, along with the *Journal*'s aspersion (n. 6), gives greatest weight to the theory that Frank Noyes was hanged in retribution for firing Enos Blair's house.

However, the lynching is complicated by a number of elements which make any theory shaky. First is the matter of timing. Blair's house was burned on August 31; Noyes was not lynched until December 8, a fact which seems to speak against Blair's friends acting out of their initial shock and outrage. On the other hand, the note found on Noyes's body is unequivocal about the reason for the hanging. As the *SCP* (17 December 1885) reports, the note contained the "names of Sam Woodson, Ren Moore, Henry LeBritton, Dave Sharp, John Sharp, Dave Speer, Old Speer, Fred Berry and Bruce Younger. The paper was headed, 'To House Burners,' under the names was 'take warning.' The paper was signed 'Vigilance Committee.' Woodson is the landlord of the Lindell hotel, Moore is, or was, a saloon keeper. The others, some are gamblers and others are men whose occupations are unknown to the community. . . . Bruce Younger is a nephew of the celebrated Younger brothers." Most of those named were associated in one way or another with Caldwell's illicit liquor trade (*SCP,* 3 December 1885). On the face of it, it would appear that the prohibition element, with which Enos Blair was identified, had sponsored the lynching. Indeed, Robert Dykstra (*The Cattle Towns,* pp. 285-92) makes the case that the larger issue behind both the burning and the lynching was a simple one of wets versus drys in Caldwell. However, others also received threatening notes advising the recipients to leave town. William Lee, a deputy sheriff, was so warned, as was F. W. Glendenning, foreman in Blair's printing office. Lee's note, signed "Committee," was received the day following the lynching; Glendenning received three such notes, the last on the morning of the lynching (*Journal,* 10 December 1885; *Free Press,* 12 December 1885). Neither Lee nor Glendenning can be linked with the liquor interests. In fact, Lee had been involved a short time before in the wholesale arrest of Caldwell liquor dealers (*SCP,* 3 December 1885). Glendenning's connection with Blair makes his warnings unlikely to have come from a prohibitionist vigilante group. Further, he was personally identified as a prohibitionist (*Journal,* 24 December 1885). Were both factions writing threatening anonymous notes?

In this connection, the incidence of arson—not limited to Enos Blair's house—is worth review, for it suggests that both sides of the controversy might have been engaged in

Whether or not either of the theories advanced was a correct version of the hanging, we are unable to say, but of this we are certain: Frank Noyes met his death in a terrible manner, and the jury gave in a verdict that he was hanged by unknown parties.[8]

---

retributive arson. (If not, a nonpolitical firebug—perhaps Noyes himself—may have been operating and unwittingly causing further enmity between the factions). The Blair fire, seen in context, was one of a series of fires which were attributed to arson or which had mysterious origins. On 7 July 1885, the implement warehouse of Kelpatrick and Yorke was set afire, a nearby tenement owned by Tell Walton also being lost (*Journal,* 9 July 1885). On 16 August 1885, Griffith and Swartzel's stable and granery was destroyed by fire, no cause attributed (*Journal,* 20 August 1885). On 31 August, Enos Blair's home was destroyed by arson. On 27 September, a fire of mysterious origin occurred in a building near the old City Hotel (*Journal,* 1 October 1885). On 3 October, the same building was ablaze, this time destroyed; again the origin was mysterious (*Journal,* 8 October 1885). On 8 October, the City Hotel was destroyed by fire, cause uncertain (*Journal,* 15 October 1885). One blaze occurred after Noyes's death; on 11 December 1885, a fire was discovered on the second floor of the post office in a room customarily occupied by Bruce Younger and Fred Berry. The supposition was that a flue, along with sparks and soot, had fallen on the bed. As the *Journal* (17 December 1885) said, "This is the generally accepted theory." Neither Younger nor Berry had slept in the room for two or three nights. The fire may well have been an accident, but Younger and Berry also were named in the note left on Noyes's body; further, as will be shown, both had damaging testimony to present in connection with the lynching.

Factionalism came to a head with the formation, soon after the lynching, of a Law and Order League, the members of which were principally prohibitionists, though prohibition was not stated as an objective of the group: the League demanded "of the Mayor and all of the city and county officers the enforcement of all state and city laws by which the city may be rid of all gamblers, vagrants, and prostitutes." The league further promised "hearty support and encouragement" (*Journal,* 24 December 1885). What this meant in actuality may be inferred from a *Journal* story in the same issue: "About the most astonished set of fellows ever seen in Caldwell were those fellows who did the shooting on the streets Saturday night, when shotguns in the hands of [local] men popped up from every corner." In the same issue the *Journal* expresses some concern at the readiness of the citizens to use those shotguns. All of this tends to suggest that League members were in some measure capable of vigilante action.

At a town meeting on December 28 at which attempts were made to reconcile factional differences, the "outs" argued that they too favored law and order. The *Journal* (31 December 1885) editorialized on the folly of the citizens, divided into two armed camps, each claiming the other was guilty of crime. Nothing substantive came out of the meeting beyond the airing of feelings.

[8]It is always unwise to second-guess a jury's verdict when one has not heard the testimony or examined the evidence. The coroner's jury did find, as Freeman states, that Noyes was hanged by "person or persons unknown to us, as the testimony in our judgment was not sufficient or definite enough to find otherwise." Of the hanging, the jury added that "we believe the same to have been done feloniously [*sic*]," which is about as tentative as one can be about a lynching (*Journal,* 10 December 1885). The evidence contained one piece of circumstantial matter. George Gentry, one of the first to reach the

The aged father of Noyes came to Caldwell, but left without the necessary evidence to convict any party of the death of his son. Mr. Noyes, Sr., seemed to be greatly affected over the shameful manner in which his son met his death.[9]

Frank Noyes was highly connected with respected and honored relatives. He was formerly from Illinois; his relatives on the paternal side of the family were highly respected officially by the residents of his native state.

As Frank Noyes drifted West with the tide of immigration, he also drifted into the habits of dissipation and ruin. He is said to have been finely educated and an intelligent young man. He was quiet and unassuming, but his evil habit of drinking whiskey,[10] gambling, and passing his hours in idleness and dissipation, were the influences which undoubtedly caused his sorrowful and untimely death at the hands of the men who premeditated his hanging and death.

Thus is added another victim, killed by unknown parties.

---

scene, found a glove near Noyes's body. The glove had a name on it, but none of the contemporary newspapers reveals that name. Beyond that, two witnesses identified people in the party which took Noyes away. One of these witnesses was May Feeny. The other was Fred Berry, whose window on the second floor of the post office overlooked May Feeny's front door. "Bruce Younger corroborated Berry's story," the *Journal* reported. Despite the coroner's verdict, two men were tried on 17 December 1885 before Justice Graham at Wellington in a preliminary hearing. Both May Feeny and Fred Berry testified, but both, the *Journal* (24 December 1885) reported, "were rather badly mixed up by the time they had been thoroughly cross-questioned" and both men charged were acquitted. One of the men was Jesse Lambert and the other was Dan W. Jones, an erstwhile Caldwell lawman, who was one of the suspects in the lynching of George Flatt (see chap. 31, nn. 5 and 20).

[9] Mr. Noyes, in his eighties, came from Mattoon, Illinois, for the funeral and, according to the *Journal,* used "his best efforts to ferret out the parties who participated in the hanging of his son" (17 December 1885).

[10] Noyes was guilty of selling liquor, but drinking it was apparently not his evil habit. Stephen E. Smith recalled: "Frank Noyes was a prof. gambler but was not a dissipated man. I never saw him take a drink" (marginal annotations to *Midnight and Noonday,* p. 385).

CHAPTER 44

Murder of Bob Sharp—Caldwell's development—The "Queen
of the Border"—A friendly game of cards—Douglass Riggs
attacks Robert Sharp—Stabs him eleven times—Effort
to stanch the blood proves futile—"Bob" Sharp
enters the sleep that knows no waking—
Arrest of Dug Riggs—Convicted of murder—
His Sentence—Conclusion of the chapter.

Years roll on. The scene changes. The summer has gone. The bright, sunny days of the autumn are here.

Caldwell's record during the past ten years is simply wonderful. Her population has increased with her years. She is no longer the favorite resort of the desperado and the cowboy, who years ago reigned supreme in her borders.

The medicine tepee of the savage tribes has been a thing of the past, and in its place is the church and school; savagery has given way to civilization. The long-horned Texas cow has disappeared from the grazing lands, and now in their place may be seen large herds of thoroughbred hereford and shorthorn cattle.

Caldwell has assumed the name of the proud "Queen of the Border," and she sits on her throne of peace and prosperity.[1]

The immigrants of later years do not have to suffer the privations they did ten years ago in the new countries, and the early pioneer settler, who commenced the battle of pioneer life without a penny in his pocket, who has endured the many privations and suffering caused by the grasshopper raid and Indian scare of 1874 and entered upon the long, weary chase in pursuit of horse thieves, has by honest labor and toil become the owner of a lovely spot, where men love to go, on this once wild tract of land which he calls home. He has gathered about this little spot his cows, pigs, horses, and chickens. He writes to his eastern relatives and friends: "There is no place like home," especially if it is located in Sumner County, Kansas.

A new Kansas has developed. The youth of 1874 has grown to the full stature on strength of confident and intelligent manhood. The people have forgotten to talk of droughts, which are no more incident to Kansas than to Indiana or Iowa. The newspapers no longer chronicle rains as if they were uncommon visitations. A great many things besides the saloons have gone,

[1] Caldwell's nickname, "Queen of the Border," was apparently coined by the *Cheyenne* (Indian Territory) *Transporter* in June, 1881. By January, 1882, a Caldwell retailer was selling Queen of the Border cigars (*Caldwell Commercial,* 16 June 1881; 5 January 1882). Freeman's implication that the title came to Caldwell in her post-cow-town years is perhaps unintended.

and gone to stay.[2] The bone hunter and the buffalo hunter of the plains, the Indian and his reservations, the jay hawker and the Wild Bills, the Texas steer and the cowboy, the buffalo grass and the dugouts, the loneliness and the immensity of the unpeopled prairies, the infinite stretching of the plains unbroken by tree or shrub, by fence or house—all these have vanished or are rapidly vanishing. In their stead has come, and come to stay, an aggressive, energetic, cultured, sober, law-respecting civilization.

No matter whether in the far east or in the wild, wild west, there are characters of men portrayed to the minds of the people by the courageous and offensive characteristics or the reckless daring and remorseless cruelty which mark their daily transactions in life.

The reader will go with me to the city of Caldwell; it is the year of 1888, and the 29th [28th] day of the month of October.[3] The leaves are clothing themselves in the yellow of autumn and making ready for the appearance of the cold, grim winter.

The afternoon hours have faded into evening dusk and thence into the silver radiance of the moon's warm beams. A small party of men had assembled in the office of Thos. Snow's livery barn.[4] A game of cards was indulged in by several of the party, including a couple of men by name, Robert Sharp and Douglass Riggs.[5]

[2]Much of this flowery section was probably plagiarized or loosely paraphrased from another source. The disappearance of the saloons has been alluded to (see chap. 43, n. 3); the *Caldwell Journal* of 14 April 1887 can declare: "Caldwell has no saloons, gambling dens or bawdy houses. No not one." However, liquor was available from drugstores (by prescription), as well as in the never totally suppressed blind tigers, as other issues of the *Journal* testify.

[3]Freeman says the twenty-ninth.

[4]Tom Snow was a cattleman who established a livery business in Caldwell in November of 1886. He operated with a variety of partners and in a variety of locations. At the time of this incident, he was located in the old Two Orphans livery barn on Main Street south of Sixth, east of Freeman's blacksmith shop (*Journal*, 4 November 1886, 20 January, 10 February 1887; *Oklahoma War Chief*, 27 May 1886).

[5]The card players included Sharp, Riggs, Dan "Duke" Rogers, Dan Burke, George Spicer, and Grant Spiker. Robert E. Sharp was the youngest son of John and Nancy J. Sharp, longtime Caldwell residents noted for their restaurant-boardinghouse and their troublesome progeny. Robert's older brother Dave was, with George Spear, involved in robbing George Woods's grave (see chap. 32, n. 9) and was a partner of Frank Noyes in the blind-tiger business (see chap. 43, n. 3). Dave was regularly in trouble with the law for a variety of minor offenses, the most recent of which had been a disturbance-of-the-peace charge where he had been as much the victim as the perpetrator: one Elmer Davidson smashed Sharp's face with a rock and shot at him for his persistent attention to Davidson's wife. Stephen E. Smith remembered the Sharps as "a bad family, gamblers, saloon keepers, & pimps" (*Journal*, 26 May 1887, 1 November 1888; Smith's marginal notes to *Midnight and Noonday*, p. 392). Douglass "Doc" Riggs, about thirty-two years old, was a veterinary surgeon who had come to Caldwell in 1886. The *Journal* (1 November 1888)

But little attention was given to the game by the proprietor of the barn, and as it progressed, several bystanders were watching the game with much eagerness. It seems a bet was made, and after the game was finished, Bob Sharp and Dug Riggs got into a dispute over the sum of twenty-five cents. This caused a quarrel between the two men, in which Riggs called Sharp a liar. Young Sharp retorted such treatment as he had received from Riggs, and ended by saying: "Who is a liar?" Riggs replied, "You are." Sharp quieted and said he would not have any further trouble over the twenty-five cents, which Riggs claimed was due him from Sharp.

Riggs went down the stairs, but soon returned however. Sharp had not anticipated any more trouble over the money, and when Riggs returned, he was conversing with a friend of his. As Riggs gained the second floor of the barn, one of the party noticed he held an open knife in his hand, but he did not imagine that Riggs had come back with a spirit of malicious resentment and intended to use the knife as his weapon of vengeance. As Riggs approached Sharp, he noticed the glistening blade of the upheld knife. He took in the situation at once, having no way of protecting himself from the murderous fiend, and knowing his means of escape was impossible, for the only way to reach the ground was the rude stairs, up which the enemy had come, and in order to reach them, he must pass the hostile form of Riggs.[6]

As Sharp caught sight of the murderous knife, he said, quickly, "He has got a knife," and started for the stairs, only to be shut off from that means of escape by his dexterous foe. Riggs rushed at Sharp with the knife. His character assumed the remorseless cruelty of a wild tiger; the countenance which a short time before bore a calm and placid expression was now the picture of a fierce and angry human fiend. Sometimes the morning breaks in calm loveliness, the sun shining in splendor, and the heavens are azure blue with nothing to mar its beauty; but before the evening shades draw near, the thunder sounds can be heard in the distance, and the sky is black with the raging storm. And you wonder that a day that had dawned so fair could hold concealed in its shining bosom so fierce a tempest. It would have been hard

---

did not give him high marks for his decorum during his stay in Caldwell and added that he had "a face and head on him that will go a long way towards convicting him of any crime he might be accused of." Further, the paper said, he was too cowardly to attack any man "who was in any way his equal."

[6]The *Journal* of 1 November 1888 reprints the inquest testimony, which differs in some particulars from the version Freeman offers here. The quarrel indeed involved a twenty-five-cent piece, according to the witnesses (chiefly one J. Hunteman, an employee at the stable, and George Spicer; the other card players were, by the next day, when the inquest was held, "out of the city"). However, when Riggs returned to the second floor, the knife, with its blade open, was concealed in his pocket, and Sharp did not see it until after he had been stabbed a few times with it. Spicer described it as a black-handled pocket knife which Riggs called his "baby."

to have prophesied correctly the ferocious disposition which was hidden beneath the bosom of Douglass Riggs.

He plunged the knife into the body of his antagonist, withdrew it reeking with blood, only to plunge it deeper and fatally into the body of the struggling man. Again and again is the knife thrust into the body until the fiendish murderer turns and leaves the scene. Sharp, weak and exhausted, falls from the loss of his life's blood. Messengers are sent hither and thither. Friends and relatives of the injured man arrive at the scene of the bloody conflict.

Riggs becomes conscience stricken or is awakened from his terrible state of mind; when the remembrance of the awfulness of the crime comes to his reason, he rushes to the office of a doctor and sends him immediately to the scene of the slaughter.[7]

Riggs then left Caldwell, going a short distance from the city.[8] Dr. C. H. [Charles R.] Hume[9] arrives at the barn and endeavors to stop the flowing of the blood. Upon examination the Doctor found eleven wounds made by the knife. A deep stab was found under the right arm and another in the small of the back. Dr. Hume did all he could to save the young man, but the flowing of blood could not be stopped by human aid or power, and the end was drawing near.[10]

Kind friends and sorrowing relatives drew near and tenderly cared for the young man until death should claim him.

When he was almost too weak to stand, he mentioned the twenty-five cents and offered it to Riggs, who declined to accept it.[11]

---

[7] The *Journal* (1 November 1888) contradicts this picture of remorse. Riggs is said to have left the stable and "quietly walked down to Hayes' drug store and inquired of Lon Share if there was a doctor there as he 'had just cut Bob Sharp pretty badly and he didn't want him to suffer.'" Riggs apparently did not return to the stable but was standing across the street from the drugstore when Tom Snow came by and told Share that Sharp could not live. Overhearing this, Riggs "ran around the corner and was not seen again" until he was arrested the next morning.

[8] Riggs was arrested without incident "at the residence of Mr. Tuttle, about a mile from town" (*Journal*, 1 November 1888).

[9] Dr. Hume came to Caldwell in 1881 from Ohio. A biographical sketch appears in Andreas, p. 1504.

[10] Hume testified at the coroner's inquest that, of the eleven wounds, the major one was on the anterior part of the right shoulder, but that Sharp "did not bleed scarcely after I got there, as the blood had about run out of him." Stephen E. Smith, a medical student at the time, helped attend Sharp and recalled that the major blow "cut the right brachial artery" (*Journal*, 1 November 1888; Smith, marginal notes to *Midnight and Noonday*, p. 392).

[11] Freeman garbles the chronology here, making it seem that Riggs was present, along with friends and relatives, as Sharp was dying, when Riggs had in fact left the scene. Before he left, however, and just after having stabbed Sharp eleven times, Riggs again demanded the twenty-five cents. Sharp is said to have replied, "Here's your twenty-five

Mournfully and attentively the friends watched the dying man. Shorter and shorter came each breath. Fainter and fainter came the sounds of his breathing. A gasp, a struggle, and all was over. Death had ended his suffering and sorrows of this life.[12]

The scene was a sorrowful one to look upon. Everything near the dead man was crimson with his blood, which had slowly ebbed from his body.[13]

Robert Sharp was about 22 years old. He was an intelligent young man, full of hope and promise of an honorable citizen.[14] He was the youngest boy of his parents and was tenderly nurtured and cherished by his immediate relatives. He had many young friends who mourned the loss of their friend "Bob."

"After life's fitful fever, he is at rest."

Douglass Riggs was arrested the following morning on the charge of murder, found guilty, and sent to the Wellington jail. When the district court convened, he was tried, convicted of murder, and received a sentence of ten years confinement in the state penitentiary.[15]

This chapter closes with the last murder committed in Caldwell. Do I hear the question, "How many murders have been committed within the

---

cents," throwing down a two-dollar bill. Sharp actually preceded Riggs downstairs; he stopped in the livery stable office to await the doctor (*Journal*, 1 November 1888).

[12] Sharp was stabbed before 9 o'clock and expired just before 4:00 A.M. He conversed with family and friends in the interim (*Journal*, 1 November 1888).

[13] The *Journal* reporter, who visited the scene the next morning, said, "In the office a pool of clotted blood on the floor showed very plainly that his life had ebbed out of his wounds, while all the way down the stairs a stream of blood as if spilled from a bucket showed at what rate it was gushing from the gashes. In the room where the cutting occurred, there was blood all over, showing that Riggs had followed his victim from one part of the room to the other" (*Journal*, 1 November 1888).

[14] Sharp became twenty-one the previous August. Despite his family's poor reputation, he himself apparently enjoyed the kind of reputation Freeman describes. The *Journal* (1 November 1888) said he "was a quiet, hard-working boy and the last one a person would think would end his life in [this] manner." Ironically, Robert Sharp may have been the victim of his family's beclouded reputation after all. About two weeks prior to this altercation, Riggs got into an argument with John Sharp, an older brother of Robert. John "gave [Riggs] a severe punishing," according to the *Journal,* and "since then [Riggs] has made the threat that he would 'cut John all to pieces.'" When arrested and informed that Robert was dead, Riggs allegedly replied that "he had stood about as much from that d—d outfit as he could."

[15] Riggs was tried in the district court in late February, 1889. On 1 March a jury found him guilty of murder in the first degree. However, a motion for a new trial was sustained on the grounds that the evidence was insufficient to justify a verdict of first-degree murder. Riggs was tried again in April, and on 7 June 1889, was sentenced to ten years in the penitentiary. The *Journal* observed that sentences such as that cause lynching to be popular (*Journal,* 28 February, 7 March, 28 March, 18 April, 13 June 1889).

borders of the 'Queen of the Border,' or in her immediate vicinity?" I will refrain from answering the question; probably the reader can enumerate the number, count them and give a correct answer.

So ends the bloody tragedies which were enacted within the proud "Queen of the Border" and vicinity.

CHAPTER 45

Sketch of the Lives of the Remaining '71'ers—J. M. Thomas,
Ballard Dixon, W. B. King, J. A. Ryland, A. M.
Colson, M. H. Bennett, and J. A. Blair.

It would perhaps be unfair, and would treat the reader unjustly to conclude this book without giving a brief autobiography of the remaining few original settlers who are still to be found in and about Caldwell. The history of California would be no less complete without a sketch of the 49'ers than would the history of Sumner County, Caldwell, and vicinity without a condensed sketch of the most prominent 71'ers. The number has dwindled to less than a "baker's dozen." Yes, they can almost be numbered on the fingers of one hand. We hope not to weary the reader in this, our last chapter, by a wordy introduction, but will proceed at once to our task of jotting the important events in the lives of those who are still left to tell the tale after almost a score of years on the frontier. The first of these about whom we will write will be:

[James] M. Thomas came to Caldwell in March, 1871. His has, indeed, been a varied and checkered career since he came and settled on the extreme border of civilization. Checkered not in the sense of having his name tarnished by the daring deeds of lawlessness that made so many names of young men on the frontier become so infamous on account of deeds of daring and of crime, but checkered by the different occupations in which he engaged at different times, and his life was varied by the many successes and financial failures in the business in which, for the time being, he seemed willing to engage.

J. M. Thomas was a native of Ohio, but after the war he emigrated to the state of Missouri. While in the latter state, he received a fair education and was thus qualified to be one of the leaders in the settlement of a new country. Soon after his arrival in Caldwell, he hewed the logs and erected a building, in size about 24 by 30 feet, and a story and a half in height. This building he rented to Cox & Epperson of Kansas City, Mo., to be used as a drovers supply store. Mr. Thomas now became the employee of this company, sometimes acting as clerk; and as the firm owned a bunch of cattle, he acted in the capacity of herder.

The firm of Cox & Epperson did a thriving business during the summer of 1871, but after the drive was over, the stock of goods in the store ran low, and Mr. Thomas bought what remained. Now we find him a merchant. In the following spring, as the reader will remember, while negotiating for goods to replenish his stock, Anderson was killed by McCarty. Thomas was an eye witness to this tragedy. While he was never courting a chance to see deeds of desperadoism, being a permanent fixture in Caldwell he beheld many a revolting scene.

In 1876 Thomas was elected justice of the peace and by re-election held the office four years. He was elected trustee in 1880 and served one term. In 1885 he was again elected justice of the peace, and by continued reelections, he still holds that office; he is also a dealer in real estate.

Financially, Mr. Thomas has made several fortunes; but as the old saying is "easy come, easy go" he barely maintains his own. The boom of 1886 in the West left many an enterprising man with less funds than it found him. Probably Mr. Thomas made thousands of dollars at this time, but possibly the relapse had caught him. In conclusion I will say he is the oldest settler still living in Caldwell, having settled in March, 1871.[1]

Ballard Dixon was also quite an early pioneer of this vicinity, having settled on a claim six miles northwest of Caldwell in March, 1871. He came to stay and was willing to endure for the sake of a home in the "Far West." Fortunately or unfortunately, as the reader may be pleased to term it, Mr. Dixon seems to never have found his affinity in a female form and claimed it as his own. All these years he has remained in single blessedness, having no gentle one at his "shanty on the claim" to molest or make him afraid. When coming to Kansas, he looked out for the evil day when hunger might appear, bringing with him about eight hundred dollars in cash.

While Mr. Dixon is unpretentious and unassuming, he commands the respect of all who know him. He was elected to the office of trustee of Caldwell township, and filled the office with great credit to the township and honor to himself. It has been truthfully said that "every man, however perfect, has defections in life." To this rule Mr. Dixon was no exception. The only thing, however, of which he will have to plead guilty is that he never took unto himself a wife and thereby helped to build up society and the future generations. For almost a score of years he had been the cook of his shanty and the farmer of his farm. This, however, is a matter of his own.

It will be remembered by the reader that on several occasions Ballard Dixon has been identified with those who were hastily formed into a band to make a long and weary chase after thieves.[2] It will therefore easily be conjectured that the name of Ballard Dixon, in future history, will stand second to none in upholding the laws of the land. Financially he is now rated some

[1] Thomas's wife, Fannie, died of blood poisoning on 8 February 1883; she was thirty-four years old (*Caldwell Commercial,* 15 February 1883). Stephen E. Smith noted that Thomas " was killed in a drunken row at a fishing party on Bluff Creek." No date is given (marginal notes to *Midnight and Noonday,* p. 393). Thomas served in the Eighty-ninth Illinois Infantry in the Civil War (*Caldwell Journal,* 27 March 1884).

[2] See chaps. 17-19, 26.

ways up in the thousands of dollars. Enough, I have no doubt, to support himself in ease and luxury the balance of his days is at his command.

W. B. King, or as he was usually called, Buffalo King, came to Caldwell, as the reader will remember, in company with me in May, 1871. It is often said, "it takes all kinds of people to make a world." This adage in truth is quite applicable in the case of our friend King. His was one of those peculiar temperaments which can endure pain, hardships, and privations without the least sign of a murmur. Always ready to take the world as it came, if in his efforts it failed to conform to his wishes. He made his settlement seven miles southwest of Caldwell. During the early part of his western life, he, like quite a number of the early settlers, had'nt the least faith in Kansas as a farming country. For this reason he did not open his farm at once, but touched the farming business rather lightly at first, spending much of his time on the plains hunting the buffalo and poisoning wolves, in order to secure the hide and meat of the former and the furs of the latter. It is said that as a buffalo hunter Mr. King had no superior and very few equals. He seemed almost unerring in his marksmanship. While he was not inspired, yet it seemed for him to point his gun toward a buffalo meant sure death to the animal. In this manner he lived and supported his family for the first few years with what little land he saw fit to cultivate, raising a few vegetables and some grain. Time rolled on, however, and farming was no longer an experiment, and the buffalo were fast receding toward the setting sun. Mr. King could now plainly see that there was a good living on his farm for himself and family, and so gradually gave up his hunting and turned his attention to cultivating and improving his farm.

In 1872 he was elected constable but failed to qualify; but, as the reader will remember, on a number of occasions he was found as one of the sheriff's or constable's posse to help chase and capture thieves.

Mr. King came and settled in the vicinity of Caldwell and made it his home until 1886, when he emigrated to Washington Territory. We write his history as one of the 71'ers that is still here, as he left so recently and his name has been so frequently mentioned in these pages.

Financially he came here poor and bare-headed; when leaving he had property to the amount of six thousand dollars, with respectable clothes.

J. A. Ryland, as perhaps the reader may remember, came to Caldwell from Slate Creek with myself and others, on May 25, 1871. Soon after his arrival he formed a partnership with A. M. Colson to engage in the stock business. The company thus formed located on a claim on the Chikaskia River, six miles northeast of Caldwell. Here the boys erected a hewn log house in which to live and call "home" while they followed the business mentioned above. They bought from different herds, at a low price, sore-footed cattle that from the effects of the long drive on the trail had become so disabled that they could not be driven any farther toward the shipping point. Buying these cattle at so low a price, with limited means the boys got together a herd of 125 head. Most of the cattle, after resting awhile, became well; but the uncommonly severe winter of 1871 and 1872 caused a large number of the brutes to succumb to the severity of the wintry storms, and in the spring of 1872 the original number of cattle was found to have decreased by about half. The firm now dissolved, Mr. Ryland retaining the claim, which, by the way, was a very desirable one and susceptible of being made into a fine home and a grand farm. It is still owned by the original settler and by him has been well improved, and is known by the name of "Riverside."

In the fall of 1873 Mr. Ryland—in Indiana, his native state, having received a fair academic education—concluded to engage in his former occupation, that of a teacher. On October 6, he took charge of the public school of Wellington, the county seat of Sumner County. After six months teaching, he again returned to his farm and endeavored to raise a crop, but the drouth of 1874 nipped the crop in the bud, and in July the grass-hoppers closed the deal, leaving the farmer naught for his labor.

In September, 1874, Mr. Ryland was appointed examiner of applicants for teachers' certificates, which position he held for two years, and finally resigned to go east and make a lengthy visit with friends. In the winter of 1874 and 1875, and also in 1875 and 1876, we find the subject of this sketch engaged in teaching the school at Alton, Kan. He has also taught school at other places at different times since then, but his chief occupation has been that of a farmer and stockraiser. He has always seemed to be willing to "labor and to wait," having great faith in the future of Southern Kansas. He has accumulated quite a considerable of this world's goods, so that now, I am told, he owns property to the amount of from fifteen to twenty thousand dollars, having his original farm as a home, and sufficient "filthy lucre" to keep the "wolf from the door."[3]

A. M. Colson came to Kansas, May 19, 1870, and to Caldwell, May 25, 1871. The first year after his coming was spent six miles northeast of Caldwell in partnership with J. A. Ryland, handling cattle. In the spring of 1872, the partnership was dissolved, he continuing in the cattle business ever since that time. Quite a portion of the time he has been engaged in the business alone, but of late years has been running it in partnership with Judge [John L.] McAtee, of Caldwell.[4]

[3]Ryland's wife was a daughter of Enos Blair, who figures in chap. 43 (*Caldwell Messenger,* 8 May 1961).

[4]McAtee, from Hagerstown, Maryland, went into partnership with Colson sometime in 1883. Although he made frequent trips to Caldwell, he remained a resident of Maryland through most of 1884 (*Journal,* 12 July, 26 July 1883, 12 June, 11 September

J. A. Ryland

Mr. Colson is a native of New York State, and in youth received fair educational advantages. When settling in Sumner County, the county being unorganized, he took an active part in its organization and was elected the first county superintendent of schools, but, finding that to fill the office properly would materially interfere with his private business affairs, he failed to qualify, and hence let the office go by default.

Mr. Colson now considered himself of proper age to take unto himself a wife, and in the year 1875 [1874] he was married, Miss Mary Goldy becoming his wife. In 1879 his wife died, leaving an only child—a daughter who was named Fawny and was undoubtedly the first white child born in the land known as the Cherokee Strip.

In 1880 Mr. Colson's widowhood was brought to a sudden close by his contracting a second marriage, with Mrs. Mary J. Garretson, she likewise having an only child, named Katie. He has been engaged in the banking business for several years past, and at present holds the position of president of the Citizens Bank of Caldwell and has also held the office of mayor and president of the council of Caldwell continuously for five years. Upon the opening of Oklahoma he, like thousands of others, became affected by the Oklahoma craze and took an active part in the grand horse race made by President Harrison's proclamation opening that country to settlement. Being one of the first to enter, he, by rapid riding, secured a choice claim adjoining the townsite of Kingfisher, where his home now is.

Financially Mr. Colson has been a success, having brought with him when he came to Caldwell less than $1,000, and now he is estimated to be worth from $30,000 to $40,000.[5]

M. H. Bennett also came to Caldwell in the fall of 1871. He worked for three years for A. Drumm and at the expiration of that time went into the cattle business on his own account and has succeeded remarkably well. Mr. Bennett, however, seems to have been of that disposition that to risk much will gain much. I presume that in different ventures he has probably made several fortunes. But perhaps he, like all others who take great risks, will in

---

1884). By 1892, he was one of the attorneys for the Cherokee Strip Live Stock Association. William W. Savage, Jr., chronicles McAtee's uneasy relationship with the CSLSA in its declining days, when Andrew Drumm (see chap. 16, n. 1) believed McAtee incompetent and McAtee became impatient for his fees (*The Cherokee Strip Live Stock Association,* p. 124ff.).

[5] Colson served as mayor of Caldwell in 1882-84 and 1901-1903 (*Messenger,* 3 September 1953). He was a prominent member of the Cherokee Strip Live Stock Association and a public servant in the early days of Oklahoma settlement. Colson served in the Civil War in the Ninety-first New York Infantry (*Journal,* 27 March 1884). Biographical sketches appear in Andreas, p. 1503, and *Portrait and Biographical Album of Sumner County, Kansas,* pp. 201-202.

time meet reverses. When coming to Kansas he brought no money, but he brought that which always succeeds—perseverance and industry. I should not like to form a guess as to how much he is worth, but one thing I do know, he is in charming circumstances and ranks high as a citizen in Caldwell.

Mr. Bennett, in disposition, has never thirsted for notoriety but has rather courted obscurity, and, I think, has never accepted any official position of any importance.[6] Being a lover of home and family ties, he was slow to accept positions requiring him to be absent from home and to assume responsibilities. He is a native of Ohio, but came to Kansas in an early day and may well be termed a pioneer.

John A. Blair is the last, but by no means the least, of the 71'ers whose biography we will attempt to sketch. It would seem strange that so few are able to "hold the fort" for a score of years, but such is the fact. Some of the original settlers have long since been claimed by that grim monster, Death, while others have gone east and are now safe in the home of "wife's people."

Johnnie Blair, as he was usually called, came to Caldwell in May, 1871. For the first year he clerked in the store of Cox & Epperson; while at this occupation he was gaining an experience in the mercantile business which proved to be the golden stepping stone to success in future life. In 1872, Johnnie became a herder of Texas cattle. Here, likewise, he gained knowledge which proved to be of great benefit. He seems to have had a well balanced temperament which enabled him to engage in any kind of business with equal success; whether a clerk, a merchant, a herder, or a cattle owner his efforts were always crowned with success.

In 1874 we find Mr. Blair clerking in the store belonging to C. H. Stone of Caldwell; but before the year closes we find him the owner, he having bought the store from Mr. Stone. It seems that Johnnie was now in his element and at home in the business. He soon became the popular merchant and, in fact, a very popular man. It is doubtful if any one who ever lived in Caldwell can lay claim to surpassing Johnnie in popularity.

He continued in the mercantile business until 1881, when he sold his store and engaged in the cattle business. His success in his last venture has been almost phenomenal. When coming to Caldwell he was a comparative youth, with very limited means; but having a disposition that will always make friends and a determination to succeed, he now finds himself rated high up in the thousands of dollars. He now lives in Caldwell in a fine home of his own, where he and his family live in luxury and ease, holding the confidence and esteem of all who know him.[7]

[6] Bennett served at least one term on the Caldwell city council (see chap. 36, n. 13).
[7] Blair was Caldwell postmaster from 1874 to 1881; he served as the first secretary of the Cherokee Strip Live Stock Association (Dale, *Cow Country,* p. 201). A biographical resume appears in *Portrait and Biographical Album of Sumner County, Kansas,* pp. 375-76.

BIBLIOGRAPHY

Documents

Census Records, Butler County, Kansas, 1870, 1875. Kansas State Historical Society Archives.

Census Records, Sumner County, Kansas, 1880, 1885. Kansas State Historical Society Archives.

Clippings Files. Kansas State Historical Society Archives.

Governors' Correspondence: T. A. Osborn, James Harvey. Kansas State Historical Society Archives.

Pension Records, George Doud Freeman. National Archives.

Post Returns, Fort Larned, Kansas, November, 1859-July, 1878. National Archives.

Smith, Stephen E. Marginal notes to personal copy of *Midnight and Noonday,* courtesy Kansas State Historical Society.

State of Kansas v. Charles Davis. Clerk of the District Court, Sumner County, Kansas.

State of Kansas v. James Talbott. Clerk of the District Court, Sumner County, Kansas.

Trial Docket, 1873-74, James A. Dillar, Justice of the Peace, Wellington Township. Chisholm Trail Museum Archives. Wellington, Kansas.

W. B. King v. Charles Davis. Clerk of the District Court, Sumner County, Kansas.

Books and Periodicals

Aldridge, Reginald. *Life on a Ranch: Ranch Notes in Kansas, Colorado, the Indian Territory, and Northern Texas.* London: Longmans, Green, and Co., 1884; repr. New York: Argonaut Press, Ltd., 1966.

Andreas, A. T. *History of the State of Kansas.* Chicago: A. T. Andreas, 1883.

Baughman, Robert W. *Kansas in Maps.* Topeka: Kansas State Historical Society, 1961.

Carriker, Robert. *Fort Supply, Indian Territory.* Norman: University of Oklahoma Press, 1970.

Dale, Edward Everett. *Cow Country.* Norman: University of Oklahoma Press, new edition, 1965.

Debo, Angie. *The Cowman's Southwest: Being the Reminiscences of Oliver Nelson . . . .* Glendale, Calif.: Arthur H. Clark Co., 1953.

Dimsdale, Thomas Josiah. *The Vigilantes of Montana; Or Popular Justice in the Rocky Mountains.* Virginia, M.T.: D. W. Tilton & Co., 1866; repr. Readex Microprint Corp., 1966.

Drago, Harry Sinclair. *Wild, Woolly & Wicked: The History of Kansas Cow Towns and the Texas Cattle Trade.* New York: Clarkson N. Potter, 1960.

Dyer, Frederick H. *A Compendium of the War of the Rebellion.* 3 vols. New York: T. Yoseloff, 1959.

Dyer, T. J. *Old Kiowa in History and Romance: A Partial History of the Old Town.* N.p., 1934.

Dykstra, Robert R. *The Cattle Towns.* New York: Alfred A. Knopf, 1968.

Edwards, John P. *Historical Atlas of Sedgwick County, Kansas.* Philadelphia, 1882.

––––––. *Historical Atlas of Sumner County, Kansas.* Philadelphia, 1883.

Emmert, D. B. "History of Sedgwick County, Kansas," in John P. Edwards, *Historical Atlas of Sedgwick County, Kansas.* Philadelphia, 1882. 8-11.

Gard, Wayne. *The Chisholm Trail.* Norman: University of Oklahoma Press, 1954.

––––––. *Frontier Justice.* Norman: University of Oklahoma Press, 1949.

History of Kansas Newspapers. Topeka: Kansas State Historical Society, 1910.

Hunter, J. Marvin, ed. *The Trail Drivers of Texas.* 2 vols. repr. New York: Argosy-Antiquarian Ltd., 1963.

Kansas: A Guide to the Sunflower State. American Guide Series. New York: Hastings House, 1939.

Koop, W. E. "A Rope for One-Armed Charlie," *True West,* February, 1967.

McCoy, Joseph G. *Historic Sketches of the Cattle Trade of the West and Southwest.* Kansas City, Mo.: Ramsey, Millett & Hudson, 1874; repr. Readex Microprint Corp., 1966.

McNeal, T. A. *When Kansas Was Young.* Topeka: Capper Publications, Inc., 1940.

Miller, Benjamin S. *Ranch Life in Southern Kansas and the Indian Territory as Told by a Novice.* New York: Fless & Ridge Printing Co., 1896; repr. New York: Arno Press, 1975.

Miller, Nyle H., and Joseph W. Snell. *Why the West Was Wild.* Topeka: Kansas State Historical Society, 1963.

Mooney, Vol P. *History of Butler County, Kansas.* Lawrence, Kansas: Standard Publishing Co., 1916.

Morris, John W., and Edwin C. McReynolds. *Historical Atlas of Oklahoma.* Norman: University of Oklahoma Press, 1965.

O'Neal, Bill. *Henry Brown: The Outlaw Marshal.* College Station, Tex.: Creative Publishing Co., 1980.

Portrait and Biographical Album of Sumner County, Kansas. Chicago: Chapman Bros., 1890.

Rainey, George D. *The Cherokee Strip.* Guthrie, Oklahoma: Co-operative Publ. Co., 1933.

Richards, Albert A. "History of Sumner County, Kansas," in John P. Edwards, *Historical Atlas of Sumner County, Kansas.* Philadelphia, 1883. pp. 7-10.

Ridings, Sam P. *The Chisholm Trail.* Guthrie, Okla.: Co-operative Publ. Co., 1936; repr. Medford, Okla.: Grant County Historical Society, 1975.

Rister, Carl Coke. *Land Hunger: David L. Payne and the Oklahoma Boomers.* Norman: University of Oklahoma Press, 1942.

Roenigk, Adolph. *Pioneer History of Kansas.* n.p., 1933.

Sanders, Gwendoline, and Paul Sanders. *The Sumner County Story.* North Newton, Kans.: The Mennonite Press, 1966.

Savage, William W., Jr. *The Cherokee Strip Live Stock Association: Federal Regulation and the Cattleman's Last Frontier.* Columbia: University of Missouri Press, 1973.

Seymour, Flora Warren. *Indian Agents of the Old Frontier.* New York: D. Appleton-Century Co., 1941.
Shirley, Glenn. *Law West of Fort Smith.* New York: Henry Holt & Co., 1957.
Stratford, Jesse Perry. *Butler County's Eighty Years, 1855-1935.* [El Dorado, Kans.: Butler County News, n.d.]
Wells, Rolla. *Episodes of My Life.* [St. Louis, 1933.]
Worcester, Don. *The Chisholm Trail.* Lincoln: University of Nebraska Press, 1981.
Yost, Nellie Snyder. *Medicine Lodge.* Chicago: The Swallow Press, 1970.

Newspapers

Belle Plaine (Kansas) *Democrat.* 1873-1874.
Caldwell (Kansas) *Commercial.* 1880-1883.
Caldwell Free Press. 1885.
Caldwell Journal. 1883-1892.
Caldwell Messenger. 3 September 1953; 8 May 1961.
Caldwell News. 21 April 1887; 8 December 1891.
Caldwell Oklahoma War Chief. 1883-1886.
Caldwell Post. 1879-1883.
Caldwell Standard. 8, 15 May 1884.
El Dorado (Kansas) *Walnut Valley Times.* 1870-1879.
Great Bend (Kansas) *Tribune.* 7 October 1956.
Kansas City (Missouri) *Star.* 18 February 1900.
Larned (Kansas) *Tiller & Toiler.* 11 February 1947.
Medicine Lodge (Kansas) *Cresset.* May, 1884.
Oxford (Kansas) *Times.* 1871.
Topeka (Kansas) *Daily Commonwealth.* 1872-1874.
Wellington (Kansas) *Banner.* 25 September, 16 October 1872.
Wellington Daily News. 11 February 1928.
Wellington Democrat. 1877-1881.
Wellington Monitor-Press. April-September, 1895; 24 August 1921.
Wellington Sumner County Press. 1873-1886.
Wellington *Wellingtonian.* 1881-1885.
Wichita (Kansas) *Eagle.* 1872-1874; 3 October 1920; 27 March, 4 April, 28 June, 3 October, 23 October 1932.
Wichita Times. 17 December 1881.

INDEX

Abeel, J. J.: 51n., 54&n.
Abilene, Kans.: 11, 24, 45n., 48, 91, 97, 134, 162n.
Abrell (member of Sheriff Davis's posse): 162n.
Adams, Jake (Jack): 186, 187&n., 190nn., 191n., 197n., 198n.
Alabama: 153n.
Alamosa, Colo.: 269n.
Albuquerque, N.Mex.: 203n.
Alton, Kans.: 283
Anadarko, I.T.: 153n.
Anderson, "Doc" (murdered by McCarty): 76, 77&n., 78, 81, 82, 178&n., 245, 280
Anderson, T. S.: 53
Andersonville Prison (Georgia): 69
Angell, A. J.: 54n.
Anthony, Kans.: 215n.
Arapaho Indians: 155n., 234n.; see also Cheyenne-Arapaho Indian Agency; Indians
Arcade Saloon (Caldwell): 252n.
Arkansas: 140
Arkansas City, Kans.: 6, 229&n., 230, 231&n., 232n., 264n.
Arkansas River: 25, 28, 51nn., 61, 96, 107, 113, 114, 145&n., 165&nn., 166
"Arkansas Traveler, The": 140
Arrapahoe Street (Caldwell): 193n., 256n.
Arson: 81-82, 215n., 269&n., 270&n., 271&n.
Atchison Topeka & Santa Fe R.R.: 35, 165n., 192, 229n., 268; see also railroads
Augusta, Kans.: 4, 5, 24, 37, 60, 67, 70, 150

Babcock & Parmelee (traders): 25n.; see also traders' ranches
Babcock & Wemple (traders): 25n.; see also traders' ranches
Badger, A. E.: 181n., 239n., 240n.; see also "Yank"
Bailey, L. G.: 252n.
Baker's Ranch (I.T.): 153n.; see also Skeleton Creek Ranch; stage stations; traders' ranches
Baldwin, John. T.: 190n.

Barber County, Kans.: 52n., 143n., 163n., 216&n., 227
Barrington, Frank H.: 30&n., 53&n., 161&n., 163; with Sheriff Davis's posse, 161-69
Bates, Mrs. (Caldwell seamstress): 199n.
"Battle Cry of Freedom, The": 179n.
Battle of the Wilderness: 4
Beals, Ephriam H., and family: 234&nn., 235n.
Bean, Edward: 207n., 209n.
Bean, James: 207n., 209n.
Been, Ed: see Edward Bean
Been, Jim: see James Bean
Beeson, O.: 227n.
Belle Plaine, Kans.: 51&n., 52nn., 146, 149&n., 151n., 179n., 180&n., 181, 182n.
Bennett, M. H.: 227n., 285-86, 286n.
"Bent": see Thomas Hart Benton Ross
Beodie, George: 133n.; see also Brodie
Berry, Fred: 271n., 272n., 273n.
Big Casino Creek (Kans.): 35n.
Bigtree, Bob: 251n., 256n., 266n.; member of Talbot gang, 251-59, 261-66
Big Turkey Creek (I.T.): 264n.
Big Walnut River: see Walnut River
Billy the Kid: 86n., 212n., 217n.
Bison, Okla.: 153n.
Black, Dr. (guard of Tom Smith): 120&n.
Black, Dr. Clark: 120n., 229&nn.
Blacks: 123n., 190n., 207n.
Blair, Enos: 86n., 269&n., 270&n., 271n., 272n., 283n.
Blair, John A.: 192&n., 216, 217n., 269n., 286&n.
"Blind tigers" (illicit saloons): 269n., 275nn.
Bloomington Township (Sumner County): 60n.
Blue Springs, Action at (Civil War): 4
Bluff Creek (Kans.): 31n., 32n., 33, 36-38, 39n., 45, 56, 57n., 72, 81, 149n., 160, 258&n., 259n., 281n.
Bluff Township (Sumner County): 51
Boise City, Colo.: 73n.
Boomer movement: 6, 10, 231n.
Booth, George: 77n.
Booth, Louis: 77n.
Boston, Mass.: 152n.

Botkin, John: 162&n., 166; with Sheriff
  Davis's posse, 161-69
Bovine Park Ranch: 258
Boyce, Newt: 223n.
Boyd, Albert Henry: 104n.; *see also* Boyd's
  Ranch
Boyd's Ranch (Kans.): 104&n., 105&n.,
  109, 111, 112, 114, 122, 123, 165n.;
  see also traders' ranches
Bradley, Lee: 222n.
Brande, Charles D.: 51n., 52&n.
Bright, Poley: 205n.
Bristol, Capt. H. B.: 111n.
Brodbent, C. S.: 51&n., 52n., 149n., 152n.
Brodie (Augusta, Kans., businessman): 5,
  133n., 151&n.
Brodie (Freeman's partner): 5, 133n., 151n.
Brooks, William L. ("Bully"): 149n.,
  156&n., 168&n., 171&nn., 172&nn.,
  173&n., 174&n., 176
Brown (horse thief): 5
Brown, Alice Maude Levagood (Mrs.
  Henry Newton Brown): 215&n., 222,
  225&n., 226n.
Brown, Fannie: *see* Fannie Brown Swayer
Brown, George S.: 5n., 9, 194n., 205n.,
  206&nn., 207nn., 208nn., 209, 210&n.,
  211n., 212n., 262n., 264n., 266n.
Brown, Hendry: *see* Henry Newton Brown
Brown, Henry (early Kansas settler): 51
Brown, Henry Newton: 12, 212&n., 213,
  214&n., 215&nn., 216ff., 216nn.,
  219n., 223ff., 223n., 225nn., 226n.,
  234-35&n., 271n.
Buffalo: 62ff., 101, 140ff., 143ff., 162;
  wallows of, explained, 107; best mode of
  killing, 136; habits of, 141, 144
Buffalo chips, cooking with: 106, 163
Buffalo Springs Ranch (I.T.): 152, 153nn.,
  156&n., 160n.; *see also* stage stations;
  traders' ranches
Bull Foot Ranch (I.T.): 153&n.; *see also*
  stage stations; traders' ranches
Bullwhacker Creek (I.T.): 264n.
Burke, Dan: 275n.
Burkett, Dr. P. J. M.: 160&nn., 171&n.,
  172nn.
Burrus, Cass: 251n., 252nn., 253n., 256n.,
  263n.
Burton, Ben F.: 215n.; *see also* Ben F.
  Wheeler
Butler County, Kans.: 4, 5, 35, 60&n.,
  67n., 73n., 77&n., 78, 79n., 82&n.,

99n., 123n., 129&n., 133, 150, 151n.,
  177n., 211n.

Cain: 210
Calaway, Thomas: 152n., 156n.
Caldwell, Alexander: 44
Caldwell, Kans.: 3ff., 21, 23-24&n., 25n.,
  26, 28nn., 29-31, 35-37, 39n., 42,
  47&n., 48&n., 51n., 57&n., 58, 59, 73,
  76, 86ff., 88n., 90, 91, 93, 94, 96n., 97,
  101n., 104, 115, 118ff., 119n., 120nn.,
  121n., 123n., 125&n., 129&n., 133&n.,
  134&nn., 140, 143n., 144, 145, 147ff.,
  147n., 148nn., 149nn., 151&n., 152,
  153&n., 155&nn., 156n., 157, 158ff.,
  158n., 160nn., 161n., 163n., 167,
  168n., 169, 170&n., 171nn., 173,
  176&nn., 178, 179ff., 183nn., 185,
  187n., 189n., 190&n., 191n., 192ff.,
  193nn., 194n., 199n., 200n., 201ff.,
  202n., 203nn., 205n., 206ff., 206nn.,
  208n., 210ff., 211nn., 212n., 214n.,
  215nn., 216&n., 217&n., 220, 223&n.,
  225nn., 226&n., 227&n., 229&nn., 231,
  234ff., 234nn., 236n., 238n., 240nn.,
  243n., 245ff., 250ff., 250nn., 251nn.,
  252nn., 253n., 256n., 258nn., 259nn.,
  261, 262n., 263&n., 264&nn.,
  265&nn., 266&nn., 267n., 268ff.,
  268n., 269nn., 271n., 272n., 273n.,
  274ff., 274n., 275nn., 277n., 280ff.,
  283n., 286n.; tough-town notoriety of,
  21, 185&n., 191n., 192ff., 197n.,
  201n., 207n., 210&n., 213, 237,
  266n., 275; settlement of, 31n., 32nn.,
  34n., 44, 45, 58n., 96, 192ff., 237, 274,
  280ff.; organization of, 44&n., 181n.,
  192, 197n.; early elections in, 179&nn.,
  180ff., 238n.
Caldwell Free Press: 269, 270&n.
Caldwell Journal: 6, 13
Caldwell News: 7n.
Caldwell Post: 13, 251n.
Caldwell Publishing Company: 216n.
Caldwell Standard: 12
Caldwell Township (Sumner County): 4,
  51, 264n., 281
California: 265n., 267n., 280
Calkins, Judson H.: 158n., 168&n.,
  171&n., 172&nn., 173n.
Campbell, W. E. ("Shorthorn"): 258&nn.,
  261-62, 262nn., 263n., 265

Cantonment, I.T.: 264n.
Carr, B. O.: 211n.
Carr, B. P. ("Bat"): 10, 120n., 211-14, 211nn., 212n., 214&n., 215n., 262n.
Carter, Dan: 120
Catamounts: 11, 43n.
Cattle drives: 23-24, 28, 91, 93-95, 97-98, 118-19, 134, 148n., 190, 193n., 399; *see also* cattle outfits; cowboys
Cattle outfits: 91, 190n., 264n., 274; T5 outfit, 209n., 217n., 218n.; Eagle Chief Pool, 218n.; W. E. Campbell, 258&nn.; LX outfit, 260&n.; *see also* cattle drives; cowboys
Cavan County, Ireland: 253n.
Cedar Mountains (Kans.): 138
Challes, H. C.: 192&n., 251n.
Charlotte, Mich.: 3
Chautauqua County, Kans.: 30n.
Cherokee County, Kans.: 48n.
Cherokee Strip: 57n., 85n., 209n., 217n., 218n., 260n., 285
Cherokee Strip Live Stock Association: 10, 43n., 101n., 134, 155n., 217nn., 258n., 267n., 285nn., 286n.
Cheyenne, Wyo.: 194n.
Cheyenne-Arapaho Indian Agency: 147n., 148n., 153n., 155n., 233n., 234n.; *see also* Darlington Agency
Cheyenne Indians: 136&n., 146&n., 147, 150, 155n., 234n., 236n.; *see also* Cheyenne-Arapaho Indian Agency; Indians
Cheyenne Street (Caldwell): 35n., 193n.
Chicago, Ill.: 6
Chickasaw Nation (I.T.): 190n.
Chikaskia River: 30&n., 51n., 53n., 58, 117, 120&n., 122, 149n., 158n., 160, 161n., 162, 174, 282
Chikaskia Township (Sumner County): 51, 53n.
Chisholm, Jesse: 23n.
Chisholm Street (Caldwell): 194n., 251n.
Chisholm Trail: 23ff., 23n., 25n., 44, 79, 90, 91, 97, 120n., 125, 162&n., 192, 193n.
Chisum, John: 23n.
Christian County, Ill.: 152n.
Citizens Bank of Caldwell: 285
City Hotel (Caldwell): 171&n., 183&nn., 272n.
Civil War: 3-4, 25, 32n., 47n., 52n., 69, 79&n., 104, 105n., 150, 153n., 162n.,

193n., 252nn., 281n., 285n.
Claim jumping: 33
Claim staking: 33
Clark, Roll: 222n.
Cleveland, Grover: 6
Coffeyville, Kans.: 45n., 105n.
Collins, R. H.: 200n.
Colorado: 133, 265
Colorado City, Texas: 211n.
Colson, A. M.: 5n., 7n., 29&n., 30&n., 35, 51&n., 53&n., 120, 160&n., 161n., 163, 165, 166&n., 179n., 225n., 236n., 282, 283n., 285n.; with Sheriff Davis's posse, 160-69; biographical sketch of, 283-85
Colson, Fawny: 285
Colson, Mary Goldy (Mrs. A. M. Colson): 285
Colson, Mary J. Garretson (Mrs. A. M. Colson): 285
Comanche Indians: 234n.; *see also* Kiowa-Comanche Indian Agency; Indians
Concho, Okla.: 153n.
Confederates: 57nn., 81n., 121n.
Connoble, Col. (Caldwell grocer): 143-44, 143n., 246&n.
Constables: 4, 5, 53, 75, 134&n., 180, 186&nn., 187n., 189, 193n., 200n., 207n., 229-31, 238n., 241, 264n., 282
Cooper, I. N.: 43n., 119&n., 122, 214n.
Cooper, Jonathan K.: 125n.
Corbin, Jack: 77n.
Coronado: 57n.
Coroner's inquests: 96, 122, 190-91, 191n., 200n., 202n., 243n., 257n., 270n., 272&n., 276n., 277n., 278
Covert, Emmaline: *see* Emmaline Covert Freeman
Covert, James: 133n.
Covington, J. A. ("Amick"): 155&n., 233n., 235n.
Covington, Sarah (or Sally) Darlington (Mrs. J. A. Covington): 155n.
Cowboys: 39n., 44, 45&n., 48, 91, 93-95, 95n., 97-98, 118, 121n., 134, 155n., 185, 187n., 188n., 209, 212, 213, 217nn., 231, 237, 266n., 270, 274, 286; characterized, 25, 26, 40, 196, 197; at work, 26, 40; activities of, in town, 93-94, 101n., 133-34, 179-80, 185-91, 194-97, 207-209, 213, 267n.; and "Texas whoop," 187; "taking the town," 191n., 194-97&n., 266n.

Cowley County, Kans.: 47n., 229, 245,
    247&n., 249
Cowskin Creek (Kans.): 25&n.
Cox, Morgan: 32n.
Cox & Epperson Supply Store: 32&nn., 37,
    43, 45n., 47, 76, 280, 286; *see also*
    traders' ranches
Crats, "Dutch" Fred: 11, 37-39, 37n.,
    39nn., 43n., 129&n., 151
Cross, Bob: 189n.
Cude, W. F.: 39n.

Dagnar, J. H.: 31n., 44&n.
Daguerreo car: 133
Dakota Territory: 226n.
Dallas, Texas: 211n., 214n.
Dalton (horse thief): 105&n., 109, 113,
    115, 118, 122-23
Dancing: 194n.
Danford, J. S.: 10
Danford Building (Caldwell): 254n.
Daniels, Jim: 250n.; *see also* James Talbot
Darlington, Brinton: 155n.
Darlington, Sarah (or Sally): *see* Sarah
    Covington
Darlington Agency: 235n.; *see also*
    Cheyenne-Arapaho Indian Agency
Davidson, Elmer: 275n.
Davidson, H. H.: 46&n., 57
Davis, C. Wood: 68ff., 67n., 68n., 70n.
Davis, Charlie: 203&nn.
Davis, John: 161&nn., 162, 165, 166n.,
    171n., 173n., 175n.; leads posse after
    horse thieves, 161-69; leads posse in
    arrests at Caldwell, 170-72
Davis, Mrs. C. Wood: 68ff., 68n.
Dean, John: 198n.
Decatur, Texas: 209n.
Deer Creek (I.T.): 83, 171, 259&n., 260,
    261ff., 261n., 264n.
Deer Creek Ranch: *see* Deer Creek
Dekalb County, Mo.: 250n.
Delaney, Tom: 251n., 257n.
Denn, Sam: 220n.
Deputy federal marshals: 47n., 75&n., 89,
    118, 163n., 189n., 253n.
Deputy sheriffs: 47&n., 57ff., 121n.,
    173n., 208n., 212n., 245-47, 249,
    264n., 265&n., 267n., 271n.
Deputy town marshals: 189n., 199&n.,
    200&n., 201&n., 202, 212ff., 212n.,
    215nn., 216ff., 216n., 220n., 252&n.,

    254, 265n., 273n.
Deutcher Brothers Horse Ranch (I.T.):
    259n.; *see also* Deer Creek
Devil's Lake, D.T.: 226n.
Devore, Fannie: *see* Fannie Devore Thomas
Devore, H. J.: 7n., 32n., 43n., 160&n.,
    161, 162
Dickie, John: 32&n.
Dillar, James A.: 160n., 171n., 172n.
Dillon, Matt: 10
Dimsdale, Thomas Josiah: 9
Dixon (early Caldwell resident): 58
Dixon, B. H.: 58n.
Dixon, Ballard: *see* C. B. Dixon
Dixon, C. B. ("Ballard"): 7n., 106&n.,
    117, 161; with Freeman's posse, 102-19;
    biographical sketch of, 281-82
Dixon, Noah J.: 58n., 189nn., 191n.,
    192&n., 193n.
Dobbs (early Caldwell resident): 106&n.;
    with Freeman's posse, 102-19
Dobson, John W.: 227n., 264n.
Dodge City, Kans.: 156n.
Dogberry (constable): 200n.
Dogs, mad: 214n.
Donohue, Thomas: 149n.
Doran, Tom: 222n.
Douglass, Kans.: 77n., 82, 151n.
Dover, Okla.: 153n.
Downs Township (Sumner County): 29n.,
    51
Dray, Mike: 77n.
Drought of 1874: 130-31, 131n., 147,
    150, 283
Drumm, Andrew: 101&n., 161, 285&n.
Drummond, Bob: 158&n., 161&n.,
    167&n., 174
Dugouts, construction and furnishing of:
    39-40
Dull Knife: 136n., 138n.
Dutcher's Ranch (I.T.): 259n.; *see also*
    Deer Creek
Duval, Claude: 26
Dye, Seymour: 168n.

Eaton County, Mich.: 3, 36n.
Eddleman, Dick: 251n., 253n., 256n.,
    257n.; as member of Talbot gang,
    251-57
Edwards, W. T.: 186n.
Eighty-ninth Illinois Infantry: 47n., 281n.
Eldred, Charles H.: 217&n.

Eleventh Indiana Cavalry: 153n.
Ellington, Mo.: 28n.
Ellsworth, Kans.: 162&n.
Ellsworth Cattle Trail: 160n., 162&n., 164
Ellsworth County, Kans.: 79n.
Elm Creek (Kans.): 165
Emporia, Kans.: 44, 45&n.
Enid, Okla.: 89n., 153n.
Epps (killer of William Manning): 56ff., 57n., 72
Epps, C. P.: 53&n.
Eureka Springs, Ark.: 214n.
Evans, Frank: 264n.

Fall Creek (Kans.): 31, 33, 41n., 161, 171, 259n.
Falls Township (Sumner County): 51, 258n.
Fant, George: 152n., 156n.
Fargo, Henry N.: 77n.
Feeny, May: 271n., 273n.
Ferguson, J. J.: 52&n.
Fielder (brother of Dan Fielder): 85
Fielder, Dan: 72-74, 73n., 74n., 75n., 76, 78, 178&n., 245
Fielder, Eugene: 72n.; *see also* Dan Fielder
Fifth Infantry (frontier): 111n.
Fifth Street (Caldwell): 193n., 235n., 251n., 253n., 254n., 255n., 271n.
Firearms: 8, 29, 37, 38, 39n., 41, 42, 45-47, 48n., 63ff., 68, 69, 73, 74, 80, 83ff., 85n., 90, 91, 94-95, 100, 108-109, 112, 115, 120-21, 123, 126-28, 134, 135, 137, 139, 141, 143-44, 149n., 167&n., 170n., 171, 173&n., 176-77, 180, 186ff., 188nn., 189n., 190n., 191n., 194n., 196ff., 197n., 198nn., 199n, 200n., 201ff., 203n., 206ff., 208n., 209n., 211nn., 213, 219ff., 219nn., 225&n., 229ff., 234ff., 234n., 235nn., 238, 249, 251ff., 253n., 254nn., 255nn., 256n., 257n., 262n., 263, 267n., 272n., 282
First Chance Saloon: *see* Last Chance Ranch
First Independent Sharpshooters, Twenty-seventh Michigan Infantry: 3-4
First Iowa Battery: 43n.
First Minnesota Rangers: 252n.
Fitzgerald, Milam: 32n.
Fitzpatrick, Tom: 257n.
Flatt, Fannie Lamb (Mrs. George W. Flatt): 199n.
Flatt, George W.: 9-11, 186&nn.,

187&nn., 188&nn., 189&nn., 191&n., 193n., 198&nn., 199&nn., 200&nn., 202&n., 210n., 243n., 266&nn., 273n.
Flatt, Georgie: 199n.
Fleming, John: 222n.
Fletcher, George: 8n.
Folks, John H.: 51n., 148n., 149n., 200n., 241n., 243-44, 243n.
Force (early Sumner County resident): 161, 163, 166; with Sheriff Davis's posse, 161-69
Ford, Charles: 125n.; *see also* Charlie Smith
Ford, George S.: 105n., 125n.; *see also* Charlie Smith
Ford, Sewell: 125n.; *see also* Charlie Smith
Ford, Thomas (governor of Illinois): 105n., 125n., 174n.
Ford, Thomas Gord: 105n.; *see also* Tom Smith
Fort Dodge, Kans.: 160
Fort Harker, Kans.: 79nn.
Fort Larned, Kans.: 104&n., 110ff., 111n., 135, 136, 165n.
Fort Leavenworth, Kans.: 148n.
Fort Reno, I.T.: 136&n., 147&n., 148, 152, 153n., 155
Fort Riley, Kans.: 32n.
Fort Sill, I.T.: 136n., 152, 153n., 158, 182n., 193n.
Forty-niners: 280
Fosset, W. D.: 252n., 253n., 254n., 257n., 267n.
Foster, Robert R.: 226n.
Fourteenth Illinois Infantry: 252n.
Fourth Street (Caldwell): 183n., 194n., 255n.
Fox, Dr. B. W.: 39n., 86n., 181n., 238&n., 240&n., 243
Franklin (early Caldwell resident): 106&n., 114; with Freeman's posse, 102-19
Freeman (brother of G. D. Freeman): 60n., 99n.; on buffalo hunt, 60, 63; meets hunting party, 67; prepares G. D.'s horse, 84; waylaid by horse thieves, 99&n., 100-102, 119, 123; farms with G. D., 130
Freeman (father of G. D. Freeman): 60&n., 99n., 130
Freeman (sister of G. D. Freeman): 131, 133
Freeman (son of G. D. Freeman): 258; *see also* Elihu Freeman; Oscar Freeman

Freeman, Elihu (son of G. D. Freeman): 4, 37n., 131n.
Freeman, Emmaline Covert (Mrs. G. D. Freeman): 4, 6n., 133&n.
Freeman, George Doud: and *Midnight and Noonday,* 3, 6-13, 8n., 12n.; biographical sketch of, 3-8; military service of, 3-4, 7; as law officer, 4, 5, 75&n., 134&n., 187n.; arrests horse thief at Kingfisher, 5; as photographer, 5&n., 133-34, 133n.; and Boomer movement, 6; as settler, 31-43; confronts mountain lion, 42-43; in posse after Mannings, 57-58; hunts buffalo, 60-67, 102, 135-36, 141-44; hunts McCarty, 82-84; arrests Nicholson, 89-90; serves papers on Oliver, 97-98; leads posse after Tom Smith, 102-19; as blacksmith, 102, 133n., 183&n., 254&n.; loses Smith to vigilantes, 120-21; confronts Charlie Smith, 125-27; at Kiowa, Kans., 136-40; pursues mule thieves, 144-45; witnesses Flatt shootout, 186-89; mode of making arrests, 197, 231; arrests shotgun thief, 229-31; as bailiff, 238-41; sued by McLean, 241-43; assists "Bent" Ross in arrest, 245-49; saves horse thief from vigilantes, 247-49; witnesses Talbot raid, 254; with posses after Talbot, 258-60, 264&n., 265
Freeman, James M.: 60n., 99n.
Freeman, John: 60n., 99n.
Freeman, John W.: 60n., 99n.
Freeman, John W. (son of G. D. Freeman): 4
Freeman, Laura Pool (Mrs. G. D. Freeman): 3, 4, 36-37, 36n., 40, 42, 84, 102, 128-29, 129n., 131&n., 248
Freeman, Milton (brother of G. D. Freeman): 99n.
Freeman, Oscar (son of G. D. Freeman): 4, 37n., 131n.
Freeman, R.: 52&n.
Freeman, Rhoda (daughter of G. D. Freeman): 4, 37n., 131n.
Freeman, Susan (daughter of G. D. Freeman): 4, 131n.
Freeman, William: 60n.
Freighting (wagon): 24n., 34&n., 149n., 152-53, 153nn., 232&n., 264&n.; and Indians as freighters, 155n., 232-33, 232n., 233n., 234&nn.
French-Canadians: 207n.

Friedley, George: 222n.
Frontier House (Wellington): 53n., 122n.

García, Gen. Calixto: 208n.
Garfield, Kans.: 165nn.
Garfield County, Okla.: 163n.
Garretson, Katie: 285
Garretson, Mary J.: *see* Mary J. Garretson Colson
Gatliff, Neal: *see* Thomas C. Gatliff
Gatliff, Thomas C.: 162, 163&nn., 172n.; with Sheriff Davis's posse, 161-69
Gentry, George: 272n.
Geppert, George: 218nn., 219&nn., 227
Gilbert,Charles: 44n.
Gilpin, Jim: 77n.
Glendenning, F. W.: 271n.
Godfrey, George N.: 53&n.
Goldy, Mary: *see* Mary Goldy Colson
Graham (Wellington Township justice): 273n.
Grand Lake, Colo.: 171n.
Grasshopper invasion of 1874: 130-31, 131n., 147&n., 150, 192, 274, 283
"Great American Desert": 25, 49
Green, Ed: *see* Edward Bean
Green, J. D. ("Jess"): *see* Edward Bean
Green, Jim: *see* James Bean
Green, Steven: *see* James Bean
Greene Township (Sumner County): 51
Griffith and Swartzel (stable and granery, Caldwell): 272n.
Guelph Township (Sumner County): 149
Gypsum Hills (Kans.): 220n.

Hackney, W. P.: 77n, 149n.
Hagerstown, Md.: 283n.
Hahn, Dr. T. D.: 30&n.
Haines, Perry: 120
Haines House (Caldwell): 193n.
Haines Ranch (I.T.): *see* Bull Foot Ranch
Hall, John H.: 263&n.
Hamilton, George A.: 57n., 121n., 161n.
Hardesty Bros. hardware store (Caldwell): 255n.
Harmon, Ed: 264n.
Harmon, J. K.: 264n.
Harper, Kans.: 219
Harper County, Kans.: 32n., 160n.
Harrington, R. W.: 264n.
Harris, Grant: 234n.

Harris, James: 95n.
Harrison, William Henry: 285
Harvey, James M.: 49n., 51, 53&n., 54n., 96n., 121n.
Hasbrouck, L. B.: 168&n., 171&n., 172&nn., 174, 176
Hayden, Clate: 190n.
Hayes drug store (Caldwell): 277n.
Heitrich (saloonkeeper): 32n.
Henderson, Frank: 208n.
Hennessey, Okla.: 153n., 155n., 157
Hennessey, Pat: 147n., 152ff., 152n., 156n., 157n., 158&n., 168n., 174
Hill, Doug: 251n., 255n., 256n., 266n., 267n.; member of Talbot gang, 251-59, 261-66
Holcroft, Frank: 28n.
Hollister, Cassius M. ("Clay"): 189&n., 193n.
Homer, Harvey: *see* S. Harvey Horner
Hopkins, J. C.: 149n.
Hopkins, Lou: 149n.
Horner, S. Harvey: 13, 216&n., 217n., 226n.
Horse stealing: *see* theft of livestock
Horseman, William: 198n., 200n.
Hostetter (freighter): 264n.
Howe, S. F.: 145n.
Hubbell, W. N.: 193n., 251&n., 256n.
Hume, Dr. Charles R.: 277&n.
Hunnewell, Kans.: 189n., 204n., 205n.
Hunt, Frank: 189n., 200n., 201-202, 201nn., 202nn., 204n., 210n.
Hunteman, J.: 276n.
"Hurricane Bill" (horse thief): 167&n.
Husson, F. G.: 192&n.
Hutchison, W. B.: 200n., 201n., 202n., 205n., 206n., 209n., 212n., 239n., 262n.

Illinois: 3'4, 52n., 99, 105n., 123n., 125n., 174&n., 273
Indiana: 4, 274, 283
Indianola, Nebr.: 215n.
Indian raids: 11, 39n., 234n.; on Fred Crats, 11, 37-39, 37n., 39nn., 129, 151; alleged, 111, 148ff., 148n., 149n., 150n., 151n., 152n.; on Kiowa, Kans., 135n., 136ff., 136nn., 137n., 146&n.; "Outbreak of 1874," 136n., 147ff., 147nn., 158n., 192, 274
Indians: 61n., 62, 65, 67, 71, 78, 79, 109, 123n., 137-38, 138n., 139, 140, 149n.,

152&nn., 164, 207n., 213, 232ff., 232n., 233n., 234nn., 236nn., 274, 275; *see also* Indian raids
Indian Territory: 6, 8n., 9, 23, 33, 34n., 43n., 44, 51, 76, 77, 79, 83, 87, 89&n., 125, 134&n., 136, 147, 148n., 150, 153&n., 160, 162, 168, 170n., 171n., 182, 190, 192, 193n., 203, 208, 209n., 210, 216n., 229n., 232&n., 233n., 236n., 244-46, 251, 258&n., 259n., 265&n.
Iowa: 52, 81, 274
Iowa Cavalry: 258n.
I. X. L. Saloon (Caldwell): 193n.

Jackson Township (Sumner County): 51
James, Jesse: 137n.
James boys: 242n.
Jayhawker: 275
Jeffries, Ed C.: 149n.
Jewitt, Noble: 53
Johnson, James: 200n.
Johnson, W. C. ("I Bar"): 218&n., 226, 227n.
Jone, "Red Bill": 198n.
Jones (horse-race judge): 127
Jones (saloonkeeper): 32n.
Jones, A. C. ("Lengthy"): 6n., 192, 193n., 256n.
Jones, Dan W.: 134n., 193n., 199n., 200n., 251n., 273n.
Jones, J. L. ("Deacon"): 32n., 171&n.
Jones, Mrs. A. C.: 6n.
Jordan, A. A.: 96n., 121n., 161n.

Kalbfleisch, George: 255n., 256nn.
Kansas: 4, 23, 24, 34, 49n., 52n., 56, 57n., 60, 90, 101n., 138, 147, 148n., 150n., 155nn., 162n., 175, 185&n., 213, 216n., 227, 247n., 268n., 274, 281, 282, 283, 286
Kansas City, Mo.: 32n., 280
Kansas Immigration Society of Leavenworth: 54n.
Kansas Pacific R.R.: 162
Kansas State Historical Society: 225n.
Kansas State Militia: 96n., 137&n., 142, 145-46; *see also* militia
Kechi Township (Sedgwick County): 53n.
Keffer, W. J. ("Jake"): 264n.
Keiffer, W. J.: *see* W. J. Keffer

Kelly, James D., Jr.: 192n., 194n.
Kelly, James D., Sr.: 192&n.
Kelly, W. C. B. ("Wash"): 186nn., 187n.
Kelpatrick and Yorke implement store
    (Caldwell): 272n.
Kentucky: 13
Keystone Kops: 10, 167
King, I. N.: 200n.
King, Wilder B. ("Buffalo"): 5n., 13, 24ff.,
    24n., 26nn., 31ff., 36ff., 37n., 47,
    101n., 135, 137, 140-42, 161, 163,
    165, 166n., 240-41, 241n.; with Free-
    man at Kiowa, Kans., 135-44; with
    Sheriff Davis's posse, 161-69; biographi-
    cal sketch of, 282
Kingfisher, Okla.: 153n., 285
Kingfisher Ranch (I.T.): 5, 153n., see also
    stage stations; traders' ranches
Kingman, Kans.: 163&n., 165n.
Kingman County, Kans.: 163n.
Kiowa, Kans.: old Kiowa, 135n., 136ff.,
    136n., 139ff., 140n., 146&n.; modern
    Kiowa, 258n.
Kiowa-Comanche Indian Agency: 155n.,
    234n.
Kiowa Indians: 137nn., 234n.; see also
    Kiowa-Comanche Indian Agency; Indians
Kirk, J. A.: 149n.
Kiser, W. H.: 188n., 191n.
Knoxville Campaign (Civil War): 4
Kuhlman, Fred: 204n.
Ku Klux Klan: 266n.

La Junta, Colo.: 265n.
Lamb, Fannie: see Fannie Lamb Flatt
Lambert, Jesse: 273n.
Lariat: 103
Larned, Kans.: 104n., 160, 162
Last Chance Ranch-Saloon: 28n., 79&nn.,
    80, 81ff., 86n., 88nn., 94n., 125-27,
    160n., 171&n., 241, 245-46; described,
    79-81&n., 125; outbuilding of, burned,
    81-82&n.; see also traders' ranches
Law and Order League (Caldwell): 272n.
Leavenworth, Kans.: 44, 54n., 148n.
LeBritton, Henry: 271n.
Lee, William: 267n., 271n.
Leonard and family (Kiowa, Kans., settlers):
    136n., 137, 140, 141, 143-44, 146
Lester, M. H.: 53, 238n.
Levagood, Alice Maude: see Alice Maude
    Levagood Brown

Lincoln County War: 213n.
Lindell Hotel (Caldwell): 271n.
Lingenfelter, W. J.: 7n.
Little Arkansas River: 61
Little Casino Creek: 41n.
Little Turkey Ranch (I.T.): 153n.; see also
    stage stations; traders' ranches
Little Walnut River: 77n.
Livingstone, A.: 161
Lockwood and family (Kiowa, Kans.,
    settlers): 136n., 139-41, 144-46
Long Branch Saloon (Caldwell): 235n.
Longhorn cattle, origin of: 24
Lookout Point Mountain (near Caldwell):
    57n.
Loomis (Red Light night watchman): 202n.
Love, Tom: 251n., 253n., 256n., 257n.,
    267n.; as member of Talbot gang, 251-57
Lumis: see Loomis
LX Ranch: 260&n.
Lynch, John D.: 96n.
Lynchings: 9, 49, 77&n., 83-86, 96&n.,
    120-23&nn., 125, 160, 169n., 170,
    173nn., 174&n., 177-78, 185, 199-200,
    225-26, 225n., 227, 268-72, 268n.,
    271n., 272n.; threats of or allusions to,
    89-90, 113, 119, 170n., 175, 177,
    247-49, 270n., 278n.; see also vigilantes
Lytle, Vernon: 222n.

McAtee, John L.: 283&n.
McCarty, Michael J.: 72ff., 72n., 73nn.,
    74nn., 75n., 76ff., 77n., 81ff., 82n.,
    85nn., 86n., 89, 90, 96n., 245, 262n.,
    280; described, 72-74, 73n.
McCoy, Joseph G.: 11
McDonald, J. Wade: 241-43, 241n.
McFarland, George W.: 200n.
McGuire, Jim: 106&n., 117; with Free-
    man's posse, 102-19
Mack, George: 46&n., 53&n., 238n.
McKinney, Alec: 222n.
McKinney, Wayne: 222n.
McLean, A. C.: 28n., 160nn., 167n.,
    168n., 171n., 172nn., 241-43, 241n.,
    245-46
McLean and Russell (traders' ranch): 28n.;
    see also traders' ranches
McMahon, J. S.: 54&n.
Mail service to I.T.: 152n., 153n.,
    158&nn., 168, 182&n.; see also South-
    west Missouri Stage Co.; Vail & Co.

Main Street (Caldwell): 183n., 201, 214n., 253&n., 254n., 255n., 256n., 275n.

Malaley, William E.: 153-56, 153n., 156n., 157n.

Mammoth Drug Store (Caldwell): 43n.

Manhattan, Kans.: 157

Mankin, "Comanche Bill": 251n., 253n., 257n.

Manning, William: 53n., 56, 57nn., 72

Manning brothers: 56-59, 57nn.

Manning's Peak: 57&n.

Marion, Jasper ("Granger"): 158n., 167n., 168n.

Marion County, Kans.: 51n., 187n.

Market Street (Caldwell): 183n., 235n.

Marshall, John E. ("Curly"): 79-80, 79nn., 83, 86-88, 86n., 87n., 88n., 122

Marshals, federal: 75&n., 137, 146&n., 155n.

Marshals, town: 120n., 156n., 163n., 185, 189n., 192&n., 193n., 197-98, 197n., 198nn., 199n., 200&n., 202, 203n., 204n., 206ff., 206nn., 207n., 210ff., 210n., 211nn., 212n., 214n., 215nn., 216ff., 216n., 220n., 223&n., 225n., 234-36, 251&n., 252&nn., 253nn., 254, 262n., 266nn., 268n.

Martin, Howard: 222n.

Martin, "Hurricane Bill": 167n.

Martin, Jim: 251n., 253n., 256n., 266n.; as member of Talbot gang, 251-59, 261-66

Maryland: 283n.

Matteson, William: 152n., 153n., 156nn.

Matthews, James: 256n.

Mattoon, Ill.: 269n., 273n.

Meagher, Jenny (Mrs. Mike Meagher): 257&n.

Meagher, John: 146n., 267n.

Meagher, Mike: 146n., 200n., 252nn., 253nn., 255&n., 257&n., 265, 266n., 267n., 271n.

Medicine Lodge, Kans.: 12, 164, 165&n., 216ff., 216nn., 217nn., 223n., 225nn., 226-27, 226n., 235n., 271n.

Medicine Lodge River: 136n., 137, 143, 144, 218

Medicine Valley Bank (Medicine Lodge): 218, 227, 271n.; attempted robbery of, 218-20, 218n., 219nn., 223

Meridian, Kans.: 53-54, 53n., 54n.

Metcalf, Willis: 207n., 208nn.

Mexicans: 207n.

Mexico: 179

Meyers, L. K.: 149n.

Michigan Volunteer Infantry: 3-4

Miles, John D.: 147n., 148&n., 149, 152n., 155n., 156nn., 168n.

Militia, informal: 149&nn.; *see also* Kansas State Militia

Miller, Benjamin S.: 216&n.

Miller, G. M.: 51n., 52

Missouri: 34, 52n., 96, 133, 202n., 280

Moore, Charles H.: 259&n.

Moore, Dr. W. H.: 217&n.

Moore, Frank: 95n.

Moore, Ren: 271n.

Moore, Thomas C. (E.?): 105n., 125n.

Moore, Thomas Gord: 105n., 123n.; *see also* Tom Smith

Moreland, James M.: 186n., 187n., 189, 190n.

Moreland, Mrs. Patton ("Mother"): 187n.

Moreland, Patton ("Pap"): 187n.

Moreland House (Caldwell): 187n.

Morris, Dr., and son (lynched in Butler County): 77n.

Morris, William: 155n., 216n., 235&nn.

Morris Township (Sumner County): 51

Mosier, Ed ("Burr"): 152&n., 156&n., 160n., 172n.

Mosley, Ed S. (E. H.?): 136-37, 136n.

Mosley, John: 136n.

Mountain Lion: 43&n.

Munson, Bob: 251n., 253n., 256n., 266n.; as member of Talbot gang, 251-59, 261-66

Muntzing (married to George Flatt's widow): 199n.

Muntzing, Fannie: 199n.; *see also* Fannie Lamb Flatt

Nebraska: 52n.

Negroes: *see* blacks

Nelson, Oliver: 24n., 209n., 217n.

Nennescah, Kans.: 52n., 53n.

New Mexico: 187n.

New York: 216n., 285

New York City: 179

Newport, R.I.: 208n.

Newton, Kans.: 44, 123, 156n., 217n.

Nicholson, Busey: 83&n., 84, 89-92, 129n.

Nicholson, John: 190n.

Ninety-first New York Infantry: 285n.

Ninnescah, Kans.: *see* Nennescah, Kans.

Ninnescah River: 28&nn., 68, 79n., 88, 125n., 164
Ninnescah Township (Sedgwick County): 28n.
Nixon, William: 52n.
Noyes (father of Frank Noyes): 273&n.
Noyes, Frank: 9, 10, 269-73, 269n., 270n., 271nn., 272n., 273nn., 275n.
Nyce, Clara: *see* Clara Nyce Overall

Oakes, Col. James: 32n.
O Bannon (slayer of George Peay): 45-47, 45n., 53n.
Occidental Saloon (Caldwell): 10, 11, 186nn., 187n.
O'Connor, Barney: 222n.
Ohio: 280, 286
Oklahoma: 7n., 101n., 156, 285&n.; *see also* Indian Territory
Oklahoma Boomers: *see* Boomer Movement
Oklahoma City, Okla.: 217n.
Oklahoma War Chief: 6
Oldham County, Texas: 212n.
Oliver (cattleman): 97-98
Oliver, L. L.: 176-78, 176n.
Oliver, T. T.: *see* L. L. Oliver
139th Illinois Infantry: 105n.
Oregon: 121n.
Osage Indian Fund: 39
Osage Indians: 137nn.; *see also* Indians
Osage Mission, Texas: 211n.
Osborn, Thomas A.: 52n.
"Outbreak of 1874": *see* Indian raids
Overall, Asa B.: 101n., 102, 106, 109, 110, 117; with Freeman's posse, 102-19
Overall, Clara Nyce (Mrs. Asa B. Overall): 101n.
Oxford, Kans.: 39n., 52n., 53nn., 54nn., 149, 179n., 180n., 243n., 249&n.
Oxford Times: 52n., 243n.
Oyster Bay Cafe (Caldwell): 206n.

Page (Freeman's partner): 5
Pan Handle Stage Route (I.T.): 193n.
Pawnee County, Kans.: 165n.
Pawnee Creek (Kans.): 105n.
Pawnee Indians: 234n., 236nn.; *see also* Indians
Payne, Wylie E.: 218nn., 219&nn., 227
Peas, George: *see* George Peay
Peay, George: 45-48, 45n., 48n., 53n.

Peoria, Ill.: 125n.
Perringer, George: 161&n.
Persimmon Creek (I.T.): 193n.
Peters, G. W.: 53
Pierce, Chris: 44n.
"Pilgrim Bard," The: *see* Orange Scott Cummins
Place (U.S. marshal): 75&n.
Polecat Creek (I.T.): 5
Pole Cat Ranch (I.T.): 125, 126, 153n., 160n.; *see also* stage stations
Pond Creek (I.T.): 162&n., 193n., 245
Pond Creek, Okla.: 153n.
Pond Creek Ranch (I.T.): 90, 143n., 149n., 153n., 246, 255n., 264; *see also* stage stations; traders' ranches
Pool, Laura A.: *see* Laura Pool Freeman
Pope, Gen. John: 148n., 152n.
Posses: 57ff., 81-83, 101&n., 104n., 105&n., 135, 158n., 160-61, 161nn., 162n., 164n., 168n., 169n., 170-71, 171nn., 173n., 175n., 186&n., 187n., 209&n., 220, 222n., 256&n., 257, 259, 263n., 264n., 265n., 266n., 281, 282; pursuit of Tom Smith by, 107-19; of Jasper Marion et al., 160-69; of Talbot gang, 256-64
Post Office (Caldwell): 272n., 273n.
Pottawatomie County, Kans.: 72, 99
Powell, Sylvester: 265n.
Prairie Creek (Kans.): 29&n., 30n.
Prickly pear, used to clarify water: 116
Priest, Nate: 222n.
Prohibition: 10, 249n., 266n., 270&n., 271n., 275n.
Prostitution: 9, 79-80, 86, 87, 193ff., 194nn., 196n., 202n., 205n., 251n., 272n., 275nn.; *see also* Red Light Dance House

"Queen of the Border": 11, 21, 27&n., 279; *see also* Caldwell, Kans.
Quimby, William: 77n.

Rachal, E. R.: 31n., 32n.
Railroads: 45&n., 134&n., 135, 182, 192n., 213, 217&n., 232&n.; reaches Caldwell, 192, 232n.
Ramsey, W. A.: 53
"Red" (horse thief): 167-68, 169n.
Red Fork Ranch (I.T.): 153&n., 155; *see*

also stage stations; traders' ranches
Red Light Dance House (Caldwell): 193ff., 193n., 194n., 196nn., 197n., 198, 201ff., 201n., 203n., 204n., 207-208, 215&n., 251&n., 252, 255-56, 256nn., 257&n., 267n.; location of, 193n., 251n.; demise of, 204&nn., 215n.
Reed (alleged companion of Pat Hennessey): 152n.
Reed, Aggie: *see* Aggie Reed Wilson
Reid, John E.: 34-36, 34n., 38, 74
Reitz, J. M.: 149n.
Renfrow, Okla.: 153n.
Revolutionary War: 138
Rhoades, Abraham: 192, 193n., 264&nn., 267n.
Rice County, Kans.: 190n.
Ricer, Frederick: 176n., 178n.
Richards, A. A.: 243n.
Richards, David: 51&n.
Richland, Ohio: 3
Richmond, J. T.: 7n.
Riggs, Douglass ('Doc"): 275-78, 275n., 276n., 277nn., 278nn.
Riggs, Reuben: 13, 51&nn., 143n.
Riley, T. J.: 149n.
Riswell (Freeman's partner): 5
"Riverside" (J. A. Ryland's farm): 283
Roberts, Lizzie: 203n.
Robertson, Ben: 215n.; *see also* Ben F. Wheeler
Robinson (buried McCarty): 86n.
Robson, G. W.: 125n.
Rockdale, Texas: 215n.
Rock Island R.R.: 35
Rocky Mountains: 130
Rogers, Dan ("Duke"): 275n.
Rogers, Samuel H.: 193n., 199nn., 200n.
Rohrabacher, Dr. C. A.: 81n.
Rolla, Mo.: 213n.
Romine, J.: 52&n.
Rosencrans, A. D.: 51
Ross, T. B.: 47n.
Ross, Thomas Hart Benton ("Bent"): 47&n., 143n., 186n., 239&n., 245-46, 249; as lawyer in mock trial, 238-40; pursues fugitive to Pond Creek, 245-49
Rowan, John: 203n.
Rue, Richard: 215n., 226n.
Russell, Charles: 28n.
Ryland, J. A.: 7n., 12n., 29&n., 35, 51&n., 120&n., 161n., 179n.; biographical sketch of, 282-83, 283n.

Ryland, John F.: 8n., 12n.
Ryland's Ford (Chikaskia River): 120n., 174
Ryland's Grove: 120n.

St. Clair, H. C.: 32n., 52n., 149n.
St. John, John P.: 203n.
St. Nicholas Hotel (Caldwell): 186n., 199n.
San Antonio, Texas: 52n., 267n.
Sand Creek (Kans.): 163&n., 164n.
San Diego, Calif.: 243n.
Santa Fe Trail: 105n.
Scouts: 79&n., 88&n., 111-12
Second Missouri Cavalry: 79n.
Sedgwick County, Kans.: 25n., 28n., 52n., 53n., 69n., 125n., 146n., 150&n., 160n., 204n.
Seventh Iowa Cavalry: 162n.
Seventh Ohio Cavalry: 32n.
Sewell Branch Supply Station: *see* Sewell's Ranch
Sewell's Ranch (I.T.): 31n.; *see also* Pond Creek Ranch; traders' ranches
Share, Lon: 277n.
Sharp, David: 204n., 269n., 270n., 271n., 275n.
Sharp, John: 271n., 275n.
Sharp, John, Jr.: 271n., 278n.
Sharp, Nancy J. (Mrs. John Sharp): 275n.
Sharp, Robert: 275-78, 275n., 276n., 277nn., 278nn.
Sheriffs: 52, 57n., 121&n., 146n., 152n., 161&nn., 162, 163n., 165, 166n., 171&n., 173n., 208n., 225, 245, 249, 250n., 251n., 256ff., 256n., 259n., 263n., 264n., 265n., 282
Sherman, A. W.: 149n.
Sherman, Gen. W. T.: 250n.
Sherman, James: 250n.; *see also* Jim Talbot
Sherman, Rollan: 250n.
Sherman, Texas: 242n.
Short, James: 127
Showalter, John T.: 242&n., 243
Silver Lake, Ind.: 172n.
Simons, R. T.: 7n.
Sixth Street (Caldwell): 193n., 254n., 256n., 274n.
Skeleton Creek (I.T.): 89n.
Skeleton Creek Ranch (I.T.): 43n., 153n., 158n.; *see also* stage stations
Slate Creek (Kans.): 28&n., 29n., 52n., 54n., 57n., 149, 169, 173&nn., 174, 185, 282

Slaughter, William B.: 31n.
Smith, Charlie: 8, 28n., 120, 123, 125ff.,
  125n., 149n., 168&n., 171ff., 171n.,
  172n., 173n., 174n., 175, 176; threatens
  Freeman's life, 125-29, 125n.; background of, 25n., 174&n.; hanged as a
  horse thief, 174-75
Smith, G. A.: 44&n.
Smith, Jim: 77n.
Smith, Stephen E.: 277n.
Smith, Tom: 6, 105&n., 109&n., 110ff.,
  119ff., 122n., 123nn., 125&n., 126,
  174&n., 247n.; helps steal Freeman's
  team, 100; background of, 105n., 174n.;
  flight and capture of, 109, 112-13;
  hanged as a horse thief, 120-22, 123n.
Smith, William ("Billy"): 217ff., 217n.,
  218n., 222n., 225nn., 226&n.
Smith's ranch: 58&n.
Snow, Thomas: 275&n., 277n.
South America: 208n.
Southern Stage Co.: 158n.
South Haven, Kans.: 149, 151&n.
South Haven Township (Sumner County):
  51
Southwest Missouri Stage Co.: 158n.,
  168&n.
Spaniards: 208n.
Spear, Charles L.: 199&nn., 200n.
Spear, David: 202nn., 204n., 271n.
Spear, George: 204n., 251n., 253n.,
  255-56, 255nn., 256nn., 257&n., 275n.
Spear, "Old" (father of David Spear): 271n.
Spicer, George: 275n., 276n.
Spiker, Grant: 275n.
Spotted Horse: 223n., 234-36, 234n.,
  235nn., 236nn.
Spring Creek (Kans.): 178n.
Stage routes: 120n., 153nn., 182&n.,
  193n.
Stage stations: 43n., 152, 153&nn., 155,
  156, 158-59, 158n., 160n., 264n.; *see
  also* traders' ranches
Stevenson (member of Sheriff Davis's
  posse): 162n.
Stipp, James: 149n.
Stone, C. H.: 31&n., 37, 44&n., 45n., 58,
  101, 181&n., 241&n., 286
Stone's store: 9, 31&n., 32nn., 241&n.,
  286; *see also* C. H. Stone; traders' ranches
Sullivan (member of Freeman's posse):
  106&n.
Sullivan, C. E.: 53&n.

Sumner, Charles: 49
Sumner City, Kans.: 53&n., 54n., 57&n.
Sumner County, Kans.: 28n., 29n., 46n.,
  48n., 52nn., 53nn., 57, 79n., 96n.,
  105n., 121n., 129n., 147, 151&n.,
  161n., 163n., 168n., 169n., 170, 171n.,
  173n., 174, 175&n., 176, 180, 185,
  192&n., 200n., 203n., 212n., 239,
  241n., 242n., 247n., 265n., 267n., 274,
  280, 283, 285; description of, 23, 33&n.,
  49, 51&n.; organization of, 49-51, 49n.,
  51nn., 53n., 54n., 56, 285; commissioners of, 49n., 51&nn., 54&nn.;
  county-seat contest in, 53-54, 53nn.,
  54n., 179n., 180&n.
Sumner County Herald: 52n.
Sumner County Historical Society: 7
Sumner County Press: 241n., 243&n.
Sumner Township (Sumner County): 28
Swaggart, Moses H. ("Uncle Mose"):
  258&n.
Swayer, Fannie Brown (Mrs. Samuel
  Swayer): 208&n., 209&n.
Swayer, Samuel: 209n., 264n.

Talbot, James ("Jim"): 191n., 193n.,
  207n., 250ff., 250n., 251nn., 253n.,
  254n., 255n., 256nn., 261ff., 264n.,
  265nn., 266nn.; and Caldwell raid, 9,
  10, 186n., 193n., 197n., 207n., 252-56,
  252nn., 253n., 254nn., 255nn., 259n.;
  background of, 250&n., 251&n., 265-66,
  265n., 266n.; described, 250n., 251,
  266; flight and escape of, 256-65, 256n.,
  258nn., 259n., 261n., 264nn., 265n.
Talbot, Jimmy: 251n.
Talbot, Mrs. James: 251&n., 265&n.
Taliaferro, Charley: 222n.
Tascosa, Texas: 212n.
Taylorville, Ill.: 238n.
Temperance movement: *see* Prohibition
Tennessee: 52n.
Tenth Indiana Infantry: 193n.
Terrill, B. N.: 168n.
Terrill, Dave P.: 32n., 86n., 88&n., 125,
  126, 168&n., 171&n., 172&n., 173n.
Texas: 10, 23-24, 23n., 52nn., 57n., 73,
  79, 81, 90, 91, 93, 94, 97, 121, 126,
  134, 135, 140, 146&n., 176, 187&n.,
  192, 198, 204n., 207&n., 208, 210,
  211n., 214, 217, 237, 246, 250&n.,
  251, 260n., 264, 265, 267n., 274,

275, 286
Texas Rangers: 207n., 209n.
"Texas whoop," described: 187
Theft of livestock: 5, 8n., 9, 26-30&n., 44,
    45, 56, 78, 80, 87, 89, 96, 99, 100ff.,
    113, 119, 122-23&n., 135, 142, 143n.,
    144-46, 158ff., 158n., 160n., 161n.,
    167nn., 170, 172n., 185, 200n., 213,
    216, 217n., 218, 245, 247n., 255,
    257n., 258&nn., 262n., 264&nn., 274;
    by organized bands, 77&n., 79n., 105n.,
    122, 123&n., 152n., 156n., 158nn.,
    160n., 167-68&n., 170n., 171n.,
    174-75&n., 247n.
Thomas, Fannie Devore (Mrs. James M.
    Thomas): 32n., 101n., 281n.
Thomas, James M.: 7n., 32&nn., 37, 39,
    43, 76, 101n., 119, 202n., 281n.;
    biographical sketch of, 280-81
Thompson, W. A.: 51n., 53&n.
Thompson, William: 202n.
Thrailkill, Levi: 252n.
Thralls, Joseph M.: 149n., 162, 163n.,
    174n., 250n., 251n., 256n., 259n.,
    263n., 264n., 265n.; with Sheriff
    Davis's posse, 161-69; leads Talbot
    pursuit, 256ff., 263&n., 264n., 265n.
Thralls, W. E. ("Elzie"): 149n., 163n.
Topeka, Kans.: 55&n., 150&n., 225n.
Traders' ranches: 25&n., 28&nn., 30,
    31n., 32nn., 45, 58, 79&nn., 88&n.,
    90, 104&n., 112, 125&n., 136&n.,
    165n., 245-46, 280; *see also* stage
    stations
Turkey Creek (I.T.): 160&n.
Turner, John: 240, 241n.
Tuttle (harbors Douglass Riggs): 277n.
Twenty-seventh Michigan Infantry: 3-4&n.
Two Orphans Livery Stable (Caldwell):
    275n.

Ughler, W. J.: 54&n.
Ukiah, Calif.: 267n.
Uncle Tom's Cabin: 250&n., 251n.
Union City, Kans.: 53n.
Union Pacific R.R.: 73n., 162n.

Vail & Co. (U.S. mail contractor): 153n.,
    158&nn., 167n., 168&n., 172n.
Vantilberg, George: 44n.
Vermont: 204n.

Vigilantes: 49&n., 77n., 79, 81-82, 81n.,
    83ff., 85n., 96&n., 105n., 122, 123n.,
    125, 160, 170&n., 173-75, 173nn.,
    247n., 272n.; *see also* lynchings
Viola Township (Sedgwick County): 69n.
Voss, Fred: 176n.; *see also* Frederick Ricer

Waco Township (Sedgwick County): 25n.
Walnut City, Kans.: 133n.
Walnut River: 67, 77&n., 230
Walnut Township (Butler County): 60n.
Walnut Valley (Kans.): 77n.
Walton, Tell W.: 6, 251n., 259n., 262nn.,
    264nn., 265n., 267n., 270n., 272n.
Washington Territory: 36, 282
Webb (McCarty's companion): 76&n., 86n.
Weller, Lee S.: 216, 217n.
Wellington, Kans.: 28n., 46, 51, 52nn.,
    53-55&n., 57&n., 58, 76, 96n., 119,
    120n., 121&n., 122n., 123n., 148n.,
    149&nn., 151, 160-63&nn., 169, 171n.,
    172&nn., 173-75, 182n., 185, 186n.,
    193n., 200n., 205n., 214n., 223n.,
    241&n., 243&n., 248, 249, 250n.,
    253n., 256&nn., 267n., 270, 271n.,
    272n., 278, 283; becomes county seat,
    53&n., 54&nn., 180&n., 181; railroad
    reaches, 134n., 232n.
Wellington Township (Sumner County):
    160n.
Wells, Mrs. Orman G.: 43n.
Wells, Orman G.: 43&n.
Wesley, John: 217ff., 217n., 219n.,
    225nn., 226&n.
West Wichita, Kans.: 145&n.
Wheeler, Ben F.: 189n., 214, 215nn.,
    216&nn., 219&n., 220, 222, 223&n.,
    225&nn., 226&nn., 271n.
White, William: 145n.
Wichita, Kans.: 24, 25n., 44&n., 45nn.,
    54n., 55n., 67-69, 73n., 79&nn., 83,
    87&n., 88&n., 104, 120, 123, 125, 126,
    134&n., 135, 136n., 145&n., 150n.,
    152, 153, 162n., 164, 165n., 167n.,
    172n., 181, 182&n., 193&nn., 196,
    203, 204n., 205n., 207n., 232&n., 241,
    253n., 257n., 265&n., 266n.
Wichita Indian Agency: 153n., 215n.
Wiedeman, Joe: 214n., 215nn.
"Wild Bills" (desperadoes): 275
Wild Horse: 234n.; *see also* Spotted Horse
Wild Horse Creek (I.T.): 89&n.

Willet, C. W.: 255n.
Williams, Jerry: 167n.
Williams, John: 161, 163n., 167n.; with Sheriff Davis's posse, 161-69
Williams, Newt: 85n., 86-88, 138, 145; with Freeman at Kiowa, Kans.: 135-44
Williamson (horse thief): 167&n.
Williamson, Alex: 161, 163, 166; with Sheriff Davis's posse, 161-69
Williamson, John: 158&n.; *see also* L. T. Williamson
Williamson, L. T.: 158&n., 175
Willsie, Charles E.: 200n.
Wilson, Aggie Reed (Mrs. John Wilson): 186n.
Wilson, John: 186&n., 187n., 188nn., 189n., 191n., 252n., 253n., 255n., 266n.
Winfield, Kans.: 47&n., 245, 247, 249
Wise (shelters refugees at Douglass, Kans.): 151n.
Witzelben, A.: 255n.
Wood, B. B.: 212n.

Wood, George: 186, 187&n., 190n., 197n., 198n.
Woods, George: 193&n., 203&n., 204&nn., 251n., 275n.
Woods, Mag (Mrs. George Woods): 193&n., 203&n., 204&n., 205n., 207, 215n.
Woodson, Sam: 271n.

"Yank" (lawyer and township justice): 181n., 239&n., 243-44; as lawyer in mock trial, 241-43; *see also* A. E. Badger
York-Parker-Draper Mercantile Co. (Caldwell): 255n.
Youell, John J.: 53
Young America: 263
Younger, Bruce: 271n., 272n., 273n.
Younger brothers: 13, 271n.

Zuber, Hank: 32n.